LABOR AND THE WARTIME STATE

Labor and the Wartime State

LABOR RELATIONS
AND LAW
DURING
WORLD WAR II

James B. Atleson

UNIVERSITY OF ILLINOIS PRESS

URBANA AND CHICAGO

Library of Congress Cataloging-in-Publication Data
Atleson, James B.
Labor and the wartime state : labor relations and law during World War II /
James B. Atleson.
p.   cm.
Includes bibliographical references and index.
ISBN 0-252-02370-6 (acid-free paper). — ISBN 0-252-06674-x (pbk. : acid-free paper)
1. Industrial relations—United States—History—20th century.
2. Labor laws and legislation—United States—History—20th century.
3. Industrial mobilization—United States—History—20th century.
4. World War, 1939–1945—Economic aspects—United States.
5. Trade-unions—United States—History—20th century.
6. Working class—United States—History—20th century.
I. Title.
HD8072.A82 1998
331'.0973'09044—dc21 97-21069
CIP

To Carol, Michael, and Jonathan

CONTENTS

PREFACE

The need to reform the federal law of labor relations has been a staple of discussion for many years, but the current debate on the wisdom and possible types of change is more thorough and sustained than at any time in recent memory. A good deal of discussion has centered on the types of substantive or procedural changes that would make the promises of the National Labor Relations Act more of a reality. At the same time, serious consideration has been given to the state of labor relations, and the traditional orthodoxy is now open for discussion and challenge.

The reason for this rethinking is not difficult to discover, and I will avoid the dreary listing of labors' troubles. As we look to an uncertain future, it is necessary to also look back to the formative stages of labor law and labor relations in the United States. Many periods, of course, are worthy of study and have legitimate claims to importance. This book looks to the 1940s and, specifically, to the wartime period as a critical time in the formation of legal ideas and labor relations policies and institutions. The analysis attempts to demonstrate that legal regulation, policies, and pressures during the war had a profound effect upon labor union structure, labor law, and collective bargaining in the postwar period.

I began this project with the notion that legal regulation during the war profoundly affected the contours of postwar law, but I soon realized that the exigencies of the war itself were as important as wartime legal rules. For instance, the need for continued production and selfless patriotism profoundly affected and limited the power labor could assert during the emergency. Thus, much of the discussion will focus upon the impact of the war itself and how the context, and not legal decisions alone, affected labor relations both during and after the war. Indeed, wartime ideas, policies, and even language were smoothly carried over into peacetime.

The rapid expansion of production and supportive legal regulation helped unions grow dramatically during the war, and such growth and stability were critical for many of the fledgling unions born in the 1930s. The dominant postwar labor relations paradigm, propounded in large part by scholars who worked for the government during the war, was composed of many of the ideas which seemed obvious during wartime. Moreover, the centralization and bureaucratization of unions, encouraged by legal decisions as well as by governmental pressures, survived the war and seemingly limited the options open to union officials when they faced renewed rank-and-file militancy in the late 1960s and 1970s.

So many colleagues have offered helpful suggestions and advice over the book's long gestation period that it is difficult to name individuals. My Buffalo colleagues have been a stimulating source of ideas and assistance. Jack Schlegel provided insightful comments, and Fred Konefsky, as always, provided clarity, stimulation, and encouragement. Karl Klare and Clyde Summers, of Northeastern and Pennsylvania Law Schools respectively, read the manuscript with great care and provided perceptive comments and helpful critiques. I am indebted to them for their comments and, just as important, their vital contributions to the fields of labor law and labor relations. Nelson Lichtenstein and Dennis Nolan also read and commented upon parts of the book. Chapters 4 and 5 were published in a revised and abbreviated form in *Industrial Democracy in America: The Ambiguous Promise*, edited by Nelson Lichtenstein and Howell John Harris (Woodrow Wilson Center Press and Cambridge University Press, 1993). An earlier version of Chapter 10 was presented at the Hagley Museum and Library's conference on "The Language of Law and Labor in the Transition from War to Peace," in October 1995, and a version of Chapter 12 was presented at the Law and Society meeting in Philadelphia in May 1992. Over the long march to publication, other portions were presented at the 1992 annual meeting of the North American Labor History Conference in Detroit, the Southwestern Labor Association annual meeting in May 1991, and the annual Law and Society meetings in Amsterdam in 1991 and in Vail, Colorado, in 1988. Research assistants Richard Woods and Flo Ann Harris provided early assistance. Joyce Farrell provided her always careful and perceptive secretarial work.

LABOR AND THE WARTIME STATE

I

The Context of Wartime Labor Relations

American labor histories have often ignored wartime as a period in which the future trajectory and pattern of labor relations and law are determined. Chapters discussing the tumultuous 1930s, for instance, are often followed by a chapter titled "The Post-War Period."[1] The wartime period is often viewed as a holding pattern, one in which wartime developments do not affect the shape of postwar labor relations or law. Although the World War II period involved substantial governmental intervention and regulation, the dawn of the postwar period is often perceived as unaffected by the war yet somehow quite different from the prewar era. Indeed, a good deal of labor history generally treats *both* world wars as having little effect on subsequent labor-management relations and governmental regulation.[2]

There is considerable evidence supporting a quite different view of the World War II period, as a time in which many of the important aspects of contemporary labor law as well as labor relations were developed. Following the important work of Nelson Lichtenstein and Joel Seidman,[3] I wish to analyze labor regulation during World War II and its subsequent effect on postwar labor relations and, especially, labor law.

Between 1941 and 1945 governmental regulation of labor was obviously intended to deal with the exigencies of war and the critical need for uninterrupted production, and the context obviously affected the substance of legal regulation. More broadly, even aside from legal rules, the war itself affected the way Americans viewed labor, and the images created tended to carry over *after* the war. Wartime policies were focused upon the need to insure increased and continuous production, to encourage the stability of labor relations as well as unions, and to control rank-and-file militancy. The policies and doctrines designed to respond to these concerns would live on after the war ended.[4] Moreover, war-aided or -generated notions of the appropriate procedures and practices of labor relations would be transferred to the peacetime era without any serious questioning of the wisdom of the application of policies originally designed for a quite different time.

Periods of war require unprecedented efforts to stimulate production and to protect its hopefully smooth operation from any interference. In order to accomplish these goals, it is common to create governmental agencies to supervise production and manpower concerns and also to establish and encourage private means of resolving labor-management conflict. These private structures, labor arbitration for instance, backed by federal regulation should they fail, require stable unions to effectuate such procedures and also to contain rank-and-file militance. These policies served as the foundation for the National War Labor Board and, I wish to stress, they underlie much of the current body of labor law as well.

Contemporary law was not created in wartime, for many of the underlying values in American labor law long predate the National Labor Relations Act and the federal regulation of the wartime era.[5] I wish only to argue that the perceived requirements of war helped to create, to encourage, or to cement visions of the most viable labor-management system and the appropriate role of the state. Wartime legal regulation was important but was only a part of a context which offered unions great promise and also serious dangers.

Before turning to the impact of the war and its regulatory system, it is worthwhile to consider four developments which help us to understand the state of unions in 1941 and to highlight the legal context as it then existed. First, early in the depression, workers expressed a surprisingly strong and militant desire to form and join labor unions. Such an expression distinguishes the period, I believe, from any of the other American economic calamities, and the initial wave of organization in the 1930s took place *prior* to the passage of the Wagner Act in 1935. The only supportive legislation could arguably be said to be the practically unenforceable and generally ignored section 7(a) of the National Industrial Recovery Act (NIRA).

Section 7(a) of the NIRA provided that every approved code of fair competition, agreement, or license must recognize that employees have the right to organize and bargain collectively free of "interference, restraint or coercion" both in making the choice of a representative or "in other concerted activities for the purpose of collective bargaining."[6] Despite the infamous lack of enforcement of section 7(a), many believe that the statute may nevertheless have had important symbolic effect.[7] Bruce Nelson and others, for instance, have argued that the act indeed had positive, symbolic value to workers. Nelson has described how section 7(a)'s recognition of the right to "organize and bargain collectively through representatives of their own choosing" led quickly to the reestablishment of and rapid membership increase in an ILA local in San Francisco.[8] Similarly, Gary Gerstle has noted that the NIRA "saved the ITU [Independent Textile Union] from oblivion," leading to a series of successful organizing efforts by Rhode Island textile workers. So successful was the belief in a sympathetic federal administration that the failures of the NIRA were seen to be primarily the result of employer violation of, and resistance to, efforts of the federal government.[9] Thus, many workers may have seen the NIRA's passage as a sign "that social change was possible" and that the state would no longer automatically support employers in labor disputes.[10]

The statute's recognition of collective worker rights seemingly indicated governmental support for workers, a message skillfully exploited by labor leaders.[11] Gerstle argues that the statute helped overcome the stigma of un-Americanism that had dogged the ITU's efforts since the end of World War I, and that such concerns help explain the appropriation of "the symbols, values, and traditions of American political culture for their own causes."[12] The desire of unions to demonstrate their patriotism would help explain their behavior during World War II.

Thus, it is possible that the passage of the National Industrial Recovery Act had a stimulating effect on the desires of workers to organize, but that eagerness for organization came primarily from the rank and file. The AFL, however, seemed unable to respond effectively to the interests of unskilled workers, and the initial support for industrial unionism was quickly thwarted by the AFL's unwillingness to countenance industrial unions or to take militant action.[13] Six hundred "federal" locals, the AFL's response to this wave of organization by industrial workers, were discontinued or suspended in 1935 and 1936 as many thousands of workers in basic industries left newly formed unions. Without the aid of national structures and leaders, and given the indifference of NRA labor boards, the new organizations proved unable to direct widespread unrest.[14]

Militant actions such as the sit-downs of the mid-1930s stemmed from worker dissatisfaction and not simply from tactical decisions of union leaders.[15] Indeed, unorganized workers caused the greatest incidence of strikes since World War I. Most of these actions took place after the passage of the Wagner Act (National Labor Relations Act) but prior to the Supreme Court's 1937 decision holding the statute constitutional.[16] A good deal of scholarly argument has focused upon the effect of strikes on the statute's passage, although it seems that something more than a high incidence of strikes led to the enactment of the Wagner Act. Strikes were increasing in 1934, but the result was Public Resolution 44, a decidedly mild response seemingly motivated by the administration's desire to deflect Senator Wagner's efforts for an effective regulatory scheme.

The first National Labor Relations Board, created by Public Resolution 44, had no greater power than its predecessor, the National Labor Board. Nevertheless, strikes fell off in mid-1934 and were declining when the Wagner (NLRA) Act was passed in 1935.[17] The dramatic incidence of sit-down strikes in 1936 and 1937 parallels the period between the passage of the NLRA and the Supreme Court's declaration of the NLRA's constitutionality. It is possible to argue that the expressions of worker militance during this entire period were caused by impressions or false impressions of even inadequate law, but such cause and effect arguments are very problematical.

Whatever the reason, the militancy of unorganized workers in the early 1930s and the later CIO organizational drives occurred during a period of high unemployment, a situation which existed throughout the decade. The worst years, 1932 and 1933, saw almost one out of every four workers unemployed. Over twelve million workers were unemployed in 1933 and the number fell under ten million only in 1936, only to exceed that figure in the renewed recession of 1938. With so many unemployed, with a downward pressure on wages, the actual degree of militancy and unionizing activity is historically unique.

Widespread strikes, often containing a political dimension, occurred in 1934.[18] Strike activity persisted at a high level in 1935, although the number of strikes declined from the previous year. The failure of the NIRA and the sweeping Democratic victories of the 1934 midterm elections "expanded congressional reform forces and widened their field of maneuver. There was polarization between the national administration and business."[19] David Plotke argues that the Wagner Act was passed by "progressive liberals inside and outside the government, in alliance with the mass labor movement."[20] The AFL lobbied hard for the Wagner Act in 1935, despite its long-held tradition of voluntarism.[21] As Plotke notes, the Democratic Party provided little overt support to labor, and labor issues were not critical in the 1934 campaign.[22] Nevertheless, forces opposing the NLRA's passage, primarily business interests and the Republican Party, were considerably weakened in the mid-1930s. A key element was popular pressure from workers, and "it is unlikely the NLRA would have been passed without the labor upsurge of 1934 and 1935."[23] Strikes increased slightly in 1936, although the number of workers involved declined. In 1937, however, strikes more than doubled to 4,740, the highest figure to that point in the twentieth century.[24] This massive strike wave, involving many sit-down strikes, was critical in implementing the statute and, perhaps, in leading the Supreme Court to uphold its constitutionality.

Significantly, the incidence of strikes over the issue of union recognition rose in the 1935–37 period. In 1937 itself, almost twice as many strikes were over recognition as over wages or hours.[25] Strong unions, of course, would seek and protect wage gains, although it is quite likely that workers were primarily concerned about other working conditions such as the pace of work, arbitrary supervisory action, and the lack of seniority protection.[26]

The tumultuous year of 1937 involved significant use of economic and political force—workers sat down and occupied factories. Politicians and police made critical choices about their role in these disturbing times. The New Deal state, "reshaped through progressive liberal initiatives, reestablished control over legitimate violence on a terrain in which violence had often been deployed by employers against workers. The centralization of violence and the refusal to use it indiscriminately or as a matter of first resort against workers was a radical shift. It is entirely missed by analysts who berate Roosevelt's occasional castigation of labor, or by cheerful arguments that the eventual outcomes once again demonstrate the flexibility and openness of American politics."[27]

The NLRA, the sit-down strikes, and the Supreme Court's support for the statute in 1937 forced employers to negotiate, however grudgingly, leading to increases in unionization.[28] The result, as Gary Gerstle has noted, was that "a large segment of the American working class was able to lift itself out of poverty, insecurity and powerlessness. Millions, in other words, experienced a profound transformation in the conditions of their lives and labor."[29] The gain did not consist simply of wage increases, for throughout history workers have been concerned with arbitrary discharge and supervisory behavior. This explains the efforts to seek seniority clauses and provisions barring discharge except for "just cause." Almost immediately thereafter, starting in 1938 and especially after the war, however, employers began to seek ways to chip away at the rights of workers protected by the NLRA. After many failures, the forces of restriction would eventually amend the NLRA in 1947.

Second, even after passage of the NLRA, it is difficult to credit the Wagner Act with more than a symbolic effect between 1935 and 1937 because its constitutional status was in serious doubt. Symbols, of course, often have considerable power, and workers did not wait for the legal questions to be decided. They resumed the militant struggle against unorganized employers begun in 1933 and 1934, and they continued to rely on direct action.[30] This is not to say that the NLRA had no effect during this period, just that the legal apparatus could only function effectively after the statute's constitutionality was upheld in *Jones & Laughlin Steel* in April 1937. After the decision, the in-flow of business to the NLRB increased dramatically, and a substantial majority of the board's activity involved charges of employer unfair labor practices. Thus, while the board's average workload had been about 130 cases a month, it jumped in May 1937 to 1,064 cases, went to 1,283 in June, and peaked at 1,325 in July. For the year ending June 30, 1938, the total was 10,430. Interestingly, it did decline for the next two fiscal years, running from 6,000 to 7,000 cases annually.[31]

The surprise decision of U.S. Steel to recognize the Steelworkers Organizing Committee (SWOC) in 1937 and the United Auto Workers breakthrough at General Motors occurred some weeks *before* the Supreme Court upheld the constitutionality of the act.[32] In neither case could the unions involved have effectively availed themselves of the procedures of the act. As Lee Pressman, counsel for SWOC, admitted: "We could not have won an election for collective bargaining on the basis of our own membership or the results of the organizing campaign to date."[33] Similarly, at the time of the Flint sit-down the United Auto Workers had only organized a minority of workers at General Motors. Indeed, neither company granted exclusive representation, the form of recognition specified in the act. The first collective agreements were sketchy—the first UAW-GM agreement could be printed on one page. Nevertheless, the CIO grew dramatically after the victories at GM and Chrysler, both instigated by sit-downs.

The assumption is often made that, assured of their safety by the National Labor Relations Act, "workers flocked into the unions."[34] This may be valid after *Jones & Laughlin*, although it is possible that the very existence of the NLRA, apart from actual decision making, spurred organization. Yet, we must be cautious in accepting the common assumption that the growth of the CIO, for instance, was strongly influenced by the National Labor Relations Act. Staughton Lynd has argued that "it is doubtful whether the national unions required the assistance of the Wagner Act to establish themselves. . . . [T]he CIO rubber workers, the UAW, the SWOC, and other CIO unions achieved at least initial union recognition before April, 1937, and, thus, before there existed a Federal administrative agency with enforcement powers."[35]

By mid-1941 the NLRB had supervised nearly six thousand representation elections. Given a free choice, employees overwhelmingly preferred a union to no union. But as David Brody notes, the value of the Wagner Act should not mask the importance of the attitudes and behavior of employees themselves.[36] Their "accommodation" to the industrial system had been weakened by the depression, which had also led employers to abandon the expensive welfare capitalism schemes of the prior decades, shaking the workers' faith in their company's strength and generosity. And to some extent, the depression also tended to undermine the will of employers to fight unionization.[37] Anti-union measures may not have been costly, but strikes and workplace conflict were, and employers became reluctant to jeopardize the anticipated return of profitable operations. Finally, management could no longer assume government support or even neutrality.

Union recognition, however, did not necessarily mean that collective bargaining would occur or that a collective bargaining agreement would result. The act, after all, encouraged collective bargaining, a contractual model which assumes that ultimate results would turn on economic power and not legal rules. Moreover, adopting the parallel to commercial transactions, no contract need be reached so long as employers bargained in "good faith," a legal standard whose absence is devilishly difficult to establish. Workers learned that they needed more than the Wagner Act to gain both representative status and collective agreements.

As Lisabeth Cohen has noted, the NLRA "necessitated shopfloor activism not only because of weaknesses in its bureaucratic procedures but also because of its supposed strengths." That is, the requirement that workers seek majority support "pushed militants to develop shopfloor strategies to broaden their base of support among the rank and file." Once a contract was signed, however, a centralized organization like SWOC "found itself anxious to suppress the rank-and-file participation it had encouraged."[38] The gaps left by the first collective agreements were, in many places, filled in by shop floor actions led by militant stewards. This was a period, especially in automobile plants, in which production issues were often handled at the workplace, a practice to be repeated during the war.[39] This budding shop-steward, workplace-oriented form of bargaining could foreseeably have been ended by the pressure of employer resistance and, to some extent, the bureaucratic needs of the unions. In any case, two other significant events radically altered the potential for shop floor control: the serious economic downturn of 1937–38 and the war would have drastic effects upon the potential of workplace control. These events must affect our view of both the potential empowerment of the NLRA as well as its co-opting possibilities.[40]

Thus, the third development that affected the response of labor to the opportunities and challenges of the defense and wartime period was the drastic economic downturn that began in late 1937. The labor movement had grown from fewer than four million union members in 1935 to over eight million by 1938, and the AFL, in response to the CIO challenge, had begun to organize aggressively. This period of hope and potential, however, is followed by the first of a series of unanticipated and damaging events. On the heels of *Jones & Laughlin*, the severe economic downturn of 1937–38 threatened to undo all the initial gains. The new recession came as a surprise to many and a catastrophe to the new CIO unions. Indeed, Howell John Harris concludes that the possibilities for change closed for the CIO by 1939.[41]

In early 1937 many had believed, as did Senator James Byrnes, that "the emergency has passed." Unemployment was still double-digit (nine million or 14 percent) but production was above 1929 levels and stock prices and profits had also increased. Some began to talk about, and fear, inflation, that dreaded affliction said to be caused by increased levels of employment and worker demands for higher wages. Fiscal conservatism took hold of the White House, some recovery programs were cut back, and the Federal Reserve Bank tightened credit. In August 1937, the stock market again collapsed and sales and employment fell. The rate of decline over the next ten months was sharper even than in 1929. Industrial production fell by 33 percent, industrial stock prices by 50 percent, and national income dropped by 12 percent. Nearly four million people lost their jobs, boosting total unemployment to 11.5 million. By March 1938, unemployment had claimed four million more persons, raising the unemployment rate to 20 percent.[42] This slump is believed to have occurred largely because the administration had cut expenditures sharply in attempting to balance the budget.[43]

Roosevelt was uncertain as to how to respond, and the downturn seemingly damaged any hope for reform legislation.[44] Fiscal conservatives and businessmen, unsurprisingly, urged further retrenchment, while New Dealers urged a return to government spending. FDR vacillated, even promising new budget cuts and a balanced budget for a time, but eventually, as earlier in the decade, turned to a $3 billion spending program. Within a few months, "economic indicators," as they are now called, were again heading upward.[45] Nevertheless, the CIO was seriously threatened by the faltering economy, declining membership in some unions, and internal dissension.[46] When the number of jobless surged in 1937 union organizers faced the debilitating effects of a full-scale depression. Unlike the early years of the depression, the effect upon unions mirrored that of earlier economic downturns. The UAW lost 90,000 members, largely as a result of layoffs,[47] and the CIO's prestige suffered while a resurgent AFL gained a larger membership.[48] Within nine months of August 1937, production fell 30 percent and employment declined by 23 percent.[49] In 1938 industrial unions had to fight to stave off wage cuts; less visible concessions were granted in other cases.[50]

As employment fell sharply, the UAW estimated that by the end of January 1938, 320,000 auto production workers were totally unemployed and most of the remainder of the normal complement of 517,000 were on short time. The union's membership was soon down to 90,000. The same story was repeated elsewhere. In SWOC's Chicago district, for instance, dues payments fell by two-thirds in the twelve months after July 1937. SWOC dismissed 250 field representatives, placing the remainder on a nineteen-day-a-month salary, effectively ending serious organizing efforts and forcing the union to concentrate instead on those mills where the union already held representative status. Similarly, the UAW abandoned organization of Ford, cutting back fifty staff members. Nelson Lichtenstein notes that the CIO membership may have dropped as low as 1.35 million in this period.[51]

Declining membership and internal dissension in some unions led to doubts about the viability of a number of unions. As David Brody notes, unions faced a fearful choice: "If they became quiescent, they would sacrifice the support of the membership. If they pressed for further concessions, they would unavoidably become involved in strikes. By so doing, they would expose their weakened ranks in the one area in which labor legislation permitted the full expression of employer hostility—and in this period few even of the law-abiding employers were fully reconciled to trade unionism."[52] Ten years after the crash of 1929, 17.2 percent of the workforce, or 9.4 million workers, were unemployed. Deficit spending was back in vogue, but FDR's attention was turned to the needs of mobilization and, slowly, prosperity was restored "by spending on military needs at levels they had rejected for social needs."[53] "Dr. New Deal" was exhausted, and FDR's "Dr. Win the War" pose had not yet been assumed. Despite deficit spending, now used for military purposes, 14.6 percent of the workforce was unemployed in 1940 and the mean rate even in 1941 was 9.9 percent.

A casualty of mobilization was reform. In such an atmosphere, it is not surprising that labor regulation begins to reflect the new mood. Moreover, the options for self-help seemed closed off, and the new unions would necessarily have to rely on NLRB machinery. In this atmosphere, Harris argued that "even those unions which had started life as rank and file organizations, rooted in activist militancy, were becoming bureaucratized and responsible. It was the only way they could survive in an essentially hostile environment and meet the demands of the mass of their members for services, improved contracts, and protection against managerial arbitrariness."[54]

The political atmosphere for reform had actually begun to sour as early as the beginning of FDR's second term in 1936. There was mounting hostility in Congress toward the New Deal, reflected in the defeat, weakening, or repeal of key measures.[55] Public support for unions declined as measured by the success of conservative Democrats and Republicans in the 1938 elections. There was also a growing tendency of the president and members of the administration to move away from domestic reform and to devote more of their energies to national defense or foreign policy.[56] As Richard Polenberg notes, while congressmen in 1935 had sometimes stood to Roosevelt's left, after 1937 they invariably stood to his right. Where once Congress had merely diluted New Deal measures, now it could and did defeat them.[57] Congressional resistance, of course, also stemmed from FDR's substantive proposals. The plan to pack the Supreme Court divided liberals, and proposals to construct low-cost public housing, to regulate wages and hours, and to deal with civil rights split the southern and northern wings of the Democratic Party.

The new recession and concurrent nativist fears resulted in considerable Republican successes in 1938, as the party gained eighty-one seats in the House and eight in the Senate. Thirteen new Republican governors were elected. FDR's attempt to unseat unfriendly Democrats had failed.[58] In addition, congressional resistance and declining public acceptance led FDR to turn to the right, and he could no longer form majorities without southern or Republican support.[59] The House passed the Hatch Act and began investigations of the WPA and NLRB. The LaFollette Committee came to an end, and the new Dies Committee reflected antilabor and antiradical animus. In addition, prolabor administrations were ejected in Michigan, Wisconsin, and Pennsylvania, and antilabor legislation was enacted.[60] Long before the late 1940s and 1950s, Republicans found that political hay could be made by connecting liberal Democrats to the CIO, communism, and industrial unrest.[61]

The legislative backlash to the NLRA, thus, began only two years after its passage. Indeed, immediately after the statute was upheld by the Supreme Court in 1937, bills were filed to drastically amend the act, and the Chamber of Commerce and the National Association of Manufacturers (NAM) proposed sweeping amendments. A number of bills contained prohibitions of certain types of union activity, early precursors of the 1947 Taft-Hartley Act.[62]

Thus, it seems clear that by 1938 the tide of public sympathy was swinging away from labor. The sit-down strikes of 1937–38 may have been non-revolutionary in their goals, but the *act* of sitting in itself was significant and was viewed by many with alarm. Two of every three persons polled favored outlawing sit-down strikes and using force, if necessary, against them.[63] The reaction against the sit-downs could be linked to the rise of nativist and anti-Communist sentiment,[64] but there were other causes as well.

> The emergence of powerful unionism and the warfare between the AFL and the CIO, combined with the inconvenience caused by strikes, led to a grow-ing public impatience and irritation with the labor movement, an attitude that was heightened by violations of democracy and other abuses in a num-ber of unions, and the disregard of public opinion by some labor leaders. Efforts by business organizations and by Congressmen friendly to them to amend the Wagner Act, to restrict sharply labor's legal rights, were to benefit from this mounting public criticism of organized labor.[65]

Yet, public opinion does not exist in a vacuum, and, indeed, the press and other avenues of communication mold public opinion.

Thus, the honeymoon with which the government treated the National Labor Relations Board (and, of course, unions too) ended fairly quickly.[66] Moreover, by 1938 the AFL and employer forces joined together in a strange alliance, generally using Representative Howard Smith's Committee of the House of Representatives to limit the freedom and militance of the Nation-al Labor Relations Board.[67] In 1940 a restrictive bill advanced by Smith ac-tually passed the House with a 259-129 vote.[68] The AFL was especially con-cerned with the NLRB's unit determinations which, it argued, favored plantwide industrial units which often excluded craft unions from basic indus-tries.[69] In addition, the AFL practice of signing agreements with employers without, or at least prior to obtaining, majority support of employees was rejected by the NLRB.[70] Although Roosevelt was reelected and Howard Smith's bill eventually died, the committee's investigation, as James Gross concludes, "triggered drastic and long-lasting changes in American labor policy and in the administration of that policy by the National Labor Rela-tions Board. Many of these organizational, procedural, and doctrinal changes were firmly in place years before they were formally confirmed by the Taft-Hartley Act. Other fundamental changes came with the enactment of the Taft-Hartley Act which itself was a legacy of the Smith Committee."[71]

Moreover, Roosevelt's appointment of Harry Millis to the NLRB, and his refusal to reappoint Warren Madden, reflected the president's and Sec-retary of Labor Perkins's displeasure with the board's independence. The threat of war may have played a role for, as Gross states, "Millis' appoint-ment resulted from the president's need to begin to prepare for a non-controversial bi-partisan conduct of the war."[72]

Especially important is the turn to the right on the board which begins in 1939 when William Leiserson was appointed to replace Donald Wakefield Smith. The appointment lessened some of the adverse political pressure on FDR. Even without the mobilization and war, Roosevelt and Perkins wanted a new style at the board.[73] Christopher Tomlins assumes that Roosevelt sought to appease the AFL by denying retiring board member Donald Smith reappointment and appointing William Leiserson in his place. Leiserson was already known as a critic of the board and was under instruction from Roosevelt to change the board's administration of the act.[74] Indeed, Leiserson's appointment precipitated bitter conflicts within the board, for he arrived determined to rebuild labor law around "the private processes of accommodation engaged in by the organized parties." He thought the board should learn from the institutions already established in the field and seek harmony with their environment rather than imposing new rules based on "its own notions of reasonableness."[75]

Thus, pressures on FDR and the Smith investigations in the House succeeded without a legislative change in bringing into existence a different board. Yet, we cannot evaluate the Smith investigation separate from the period of mobilization and fear of war, increasing employer resistance, and the fact that the CIO was reeling from the recession.[76] The New Deal, at least as a significant reform movement, may have survived only five years,[77] but the "Golden Age" of the NLRA was considerably shorter.

In such an atmosphere, it is not surprising that the security of unions was still precarious five years after the formation of the CIO and the passage of the Wagner Act. Despite the passage of the NLRA, and the Supreme Court's ruling that it was constitutional, collective bargaining, as David Brody has stated, could have little meaning in such a period.[78] Despite the act, bargaining is ultimately a power relationship, and little can perhaps be expected in a period of legal backlash and economic difficulty.

This is not to argue that the NLRA had no impact. For instance, Nelson Lichtenstein has written of one example of the power of the NLRA. A Supreme Court decision in 1940 upheld an order of the NLRB reinstating several unionists at Ford's River Rouge plant. The workers' return, he argues, "made a powerful impression throughout the Rouge." A "steward system sprang up in virtually every department" and an ongoing organizational campaign was significantly energized.[79]

Nevertheless, in such a period the more expansive goals of the CIO had to be put on hold. The Wagner Act did help to institutionalize labor conflict in this period, although the confining effects would be more clearly apparent in the future. The situation led CIO leaders to concentrate on the routinization of labor-management relations and gaining security for the new unions, helping to explain the importance of the union security issue during the war.

Finally, the CIO was eventually solidified, not by the Wagner Act but by defense mobilization and, ultimately, by World War II, which dramatically raised employment, weakened the resistance of employers to engage in collective bargaining, and caused a substantial expansion of the federal role in labor-management relations.[80] As in all economic upswings, increasing job opportunities led to an upsurge in militancy just as management's willingness to accept strikes or other labor disruption declined.[81]

Notes

1. See, e.g., Henry Pelling, *American Labor* (Chicago: University of Chicago, 1960), 181.

2. Notable exceptions are Foster Rhea Dulles and Melvyn Dubofsky, *Labor in America: A History* (Arlington Heights, Ill.: Harlan Davidson, 1984), 319–42, and Robert Zieger, *The CIO: 1935–1955* (Chapel Hill: University of North Carolina Press, 1995), 141–90. See also George Lipsitz, *Rainbow at Midnight: Labor and Culture in the 1940s* (Urbana: University of Illinois Press, 1994), 19–20.

3. Nelson Lichtenstein, *Labor's War at Home: The CIO in World War II* (New York: Cambridge University Press, 1982); Joel Seidman, *American Labor from Defense to Reconversion* (Chicago: University of Chicago Press, 1953).

4. The tendency to ignore wartime periods extends beyond our borders. Japan's system of "welfare corporatism," for instance, has been explained either as a product of unique cultural characteristics or as a response by private employers to the scarcity of skilled labor. Recent scholarship, however, suggests that many of the pillars of the Japanese labor system were the result of state action. In turn, these pressures were primarily the result of military efforts to encourage stability, productivity, and morale.

As Linda Weiss notes, declining morale, low productivity, and labor scarcity during World War II led to a "military and bureaucratic campaign to reform wages and social welfare" ("War, the State, and the Origins of the Japanese Employment System," *Politics and Society* 21 [Sept. 1993]: 325).

In addition to imposing a system of guaranteed seniority-based wages, in 1942 government regulation barred workers from changing employers. The state then mandated a training structure. Since employers were required to train their workers, it was rational to retain them despite short-run interests.

5. See, generally, James Atleson, *Values and Assumptions in American Labor Law* (Amherst: University of Massachusetts Press, 1983).

6. National Industrial Recovery Act, 48 Stat. 195 (1933).

7. There has been a long debate concerning the actual impact of NIRA section

7(a). See, e.g., Stanley Vittoz, *New Deal Labor Policy and the American Industrial Economy* (Chapel Hill: University of North Carolina Press, 1987); Sidney Fine, review of ibid., *Labor History* 29 (Winter 1988): 101–3; Michael Goldfield, "Worker Insurgency, Radical Organization, and New Deal Labor Legislation," *American Political Science Review* 83 (Dec. 1989): 1257. Fine argues that section 7(a) was in part responsible for the increase in membership of the UMW, ILGWU, and ACW and the principles established by the National Labor Board and the first NLRA.

8. Bruce Nelson, *Workers on the Waterfront: Seamen, Longshoremen, and Unionism in the 1930s* (Urbana: University of Illinois Press, 1989).

9. Gary Gerstle, *Working-Class Americanism* (New York: Cambridge University Press, 1989), 105–7, 128.

10. Joshua B. Freeman, *In Transit: The Transportation Workers Union in New York City, 1933–36* (New York: Oxford University Press, 1989), 40.

11. See Gary Gerstle, "The Politics of Patriotism: Americanization and the Formation of the CIO," *Dissent* 33 (1986): 84.

12. Ibid., 92.

13. See Irving Bernstein, *The Turbulent Years* (Boston: Houghton, Mifflin, 1970); Atleson, *Values and Assumptions*, 46.

14. Lichtenstein, *Labor's War at Home*, 10–11.

15. See Bernstein, *Turbulent Years*; Sidney Fine, *Sit-Down* (Ann Arbor: University of Michigan Press, 1969); Henry Krauss, *The Many and the Few* (Urbana: University of Illinois Press, 1985); Edward Levinson, *Labor on the March* (New York: Harper, 1938; Ithaca, N.Y.: ILR Press, 1995), 169–86.

16. See NLRB v. Jones & Laughlin Steel Corp., 301 U.S. 1 (1937).

17. See Atleson, *Values and Assumptions*, 46.

18. See Bernstein, *Turbulent Years*; Melvin Dubofsky, ed., *American Labor since the New Deal* (Chicago: Quadrangle Books, 1971).

19. David Plotke, "The Wagner Act, Again; Politics and Labor, 1935–37," *Studies in American Political Development* 3 (1989): 112.

20. Ibid., 105. An interesting revision of existing explanations for the passage of the act is provided in Colin Gordon, *New Deals: Business, Labor and Politics in America 1920–1935* (New York: Cambridge University Press, 1994).

21. See Melvyn Dubofsky, *The State and Labor in Modern America* (Chapel Hill: University of North Carolina Press, 1994); William Forbath, *Law and the Shaping of the American Labor Movement* (Cambridge, Mass.: Harvard University Press, 1991); Victoria Hattam, *Labor Visions and State Power* (Princeton, N.J.: Princeton University Press, 1993).

22. Plotke, "Wagner Act," 114.

23. Ibid., 116; Atleson, *Values and Assumptions*; Goldfield, "Worker Insurgency," 1257.

24. Plotke, "Wagner Act," 128–29, citing Bureau of the Census, Historical Statistics, D970–985, *Work Stoppages, Workers Involved, Man-Days Idle, Major Issues, and Average Duration: 1881–1970*.

25. Plotke, "Wagner Act," 129.

26. See David Montgomery, *Workers' Control in America* (New York: Cambridge University Press, 1980), 140–49.

27. Plotke, "Wagner Act," 129.

28. Plotke does not believe there was a significant labor radical presence which was somehow thwarted through collective bargaining. He argues that "The objectives of the labor movement's upsurge focused not only on gaining the securely increased wages but on establishing the factory regime in which workers had greatly increased protection against managerial guises, both in hiring and firing and in the day-to-day organization of work. Unions were recognized as an instrument through which such goals might be won. That this would imply an institutionalization of seniority, grievance procedures, and wage determination was for most of the labor movement not an unfortunate stopping point in the dynamic whose essential nature would have led toward more and more radical initiatives. Instead, the institutionalized rejection of conventional practices was precisely the point. The real aims of the mass labor upsurge were understood to entail drastic changes in the prior industrial regime; that some of them were actually won testifies to the political skill as well as the courage of the labor movement" (ibid., 151).

29. Gary Gerstle, "The Politics of Labor in 1930s America," in *IRRA Proceedings of the 46th Annual Meeting* ([Madison, Wis.]: Industrial Relations Research Association, 1994), 108.

30. See James R. Green, *The World of the Worker: Labor in Twentieth Century America* (New York: Hill & Wang, 1980), 150–65.

31. See Bernstein, *Turbulent Years*, 647.

32. Various explanations have been offered for U.S. Steel's action. Colin Gordon argues that the corporation's primary goal was to reassert its price leadership while seeking to protect itself against competition based upon wage levels. U.S. Steel also wished to avoid disruption at a time when steel demand was rising (*New Deals*, 226–30).

33. See Atleson, *Values and Assumptions*, 195 n. 43.

34. David Brody, "The Emergence of Mass-Production Unionism," in *Workers in Industrial America* (New York: Oxford University Press, 1980), 101.

35. Staughton Lynd, "Beyond 'Labor Relations': Thesis on the History of the NLRA and the Future of the Labor Movement," paper presented to Workshop on Critical Perspectives on the History of American Labor Law, Georgetown Law Center, June 10, 1987.

36. Brody, "Emergence of Mass-Production Unionism," 103.

37. Atleson, *Values and Assumptions*, 42–43.

38. Lisabeth Cohen, "Race, Ethnicity, and the Culture of Industrial Unionism," in *Contemporary Collective Bargaining in the Private Sector*, ed. Paula Voos ([Madison, Wis.]: Industrial Relations Research Association, 1994), 118–19.

39. Lichtenstein, *Labor's War at Home*, 12–13.

40. Although business interests vociferously opposed the Wagner Act, Colin

Gordon, in his interesting and controversial book, argues that "many employers saw federal labor law as a partial and necessary solution to market instability, the persistence of the Depression, and the failure of earlier organizational experiments." Given the failure of the NRA, in other words, many viewed "union-enforced regulation of hours and wages as the key to economic stability and industrial unions as the only effective (and constitutional) means of establishing or maintaining that stability" (*New Deals*, 204). See also ibid., 194–203. Gordon argues that despite the vocal business opponents of the Wagner Act, it would not have passed if the opposition was as deep and serious as claimed by detractors.

41. Howell John Harris, *The Right to Manage: Industrial Relations Policies of American Business in the 1940s* (Madison: University of Wisconsin Press, 1982), 4. See also Stephen Amberg, *The Union Inspiration in American Politics* (Philadelphia: Temple University Press, 1994), 94–95.

42. See Robert S. McElvaine, *The Great Depression* (New York: Times Books, 1984), 296–300.

43. Richard Polenberg, "The Decline of the New Deal, 1937–1940," in *The New Deal: The National Level*, ed. John Braeman, Robert H. Bremner, and David Brody (Columbus: Ohio State University Press, 1975), 255.

44. Ibid., 256.

45. Ibid., 299.

46. Brody, "Emergence of Mass Production Unionism," 267.

47. Harris concludes that the UAW was almost displaced at General Motors in 1939 (*Right to Manage*, 38).

48. The Teamsters, for instance, were making substantial gains (Green, *World of the Worker*, 165).

49. See David Milton, *The Politics of U.S. Labor: From the Great Depression to the New Deal* (New York: Monthly Review Press, 1982), 117.

50. For example, Brody notes that SWOC and UAW granted changes which weakened the grievance procedure at U.S. Steel and General Motors ("Emergence of Mass Production Unionism," 111). See also Lichtenstein, *Labor's War at Home*, 13–19.

51. Lichtenstein, *Labor's War at Home*, 18–19.

52. Brody, "Emergence of Mass Production Unionism," 111–12.

53. McElvaine, *Great Depression*, 307.

54. Harris, *Right to Manage*, 38.

55. Polenberg, "Decline of the New Deal."

56. See Harris, *Right to Manage*, 41.

57. Congressional resistance may have partially reflected resentment at the enlargement of executive authority and the desire to reclaim lost legislative prerogatives. In part, the very size of the Democratic majorities encouraged factionalism and discord. In 1937 the House contained 331 Democrats and 89 Republicans, the Senate 76 Democrats and 16 Republicans. Moreover, congressmen elected by large majorities tended to be less dependent upon party leaders, and less likely to follow

them, than those chosen in close contests. In 1936, outside the South, 140 Democrats were elected from safe districts, compared to 110 in 1934; by contrast, only 77 Democrats came from marginal districts, compared to 95 two years before (Polenberg, "Decline of the New Deal," 247).

58. McElvaine, *Great Depression*, 304–5; Polenberg, "Decline of the New Deal," 260. In the new House the combination of 169 Republicans and 73 southern Democrats could overpower the 169 Democrats from outside the South.

59. McElvaine, *Great Depression*, 308–11; Polenberg, "Decline of the New Deal," 260.

60. Harris, *Right to Manage*, 37.

61. Polenberg, "Decline of the New Deal," 159–60.

62. At the same time, Wisconsin, Pennsylvania, Michigan, and Minnesota enacted legislation which imposed restrictions on labor as well as on employers. Two of these states (among others) had passed legislation modeled after the Wagner Act only two years earlier. The new state laws created union unfair labor practices, limited the right to strike and the scope of union security clauses, and eased restrictions on the use of injunctions (Seidman, *American Labor*, 14).

63. Polenberg, "Decline of the New Deal," 258.

64. Ibid., 256–58.

65. Seidman, *American Labor*, 18–19.

66. See Aaron Levenstein, *Labor, Today and Tomorrow* (New York: A. A. Knopf, 1946), 20–23.

67. James Gross, *The Reshaping of the National Labor Relations Board* (Albany: State University of New York Press, 1981), 73–108.

68. See J. Hutmacher, *Senator Robert F. Wagner and the Rise of Urban Liberalism* (New York: Atheneum, 1968), 235–36.

69. Seidman, *American Labor*, 14–16.

70. The AFL's practice, based upon its notion of property rights in certain work, is sympathetically discussed in Christopher Tomlins, *The State and the Unions* (New York: Cambridge University Press, 1985), 161–84.

71. Gross, *Reshaping of the NLRB*, 225.

72. Ibid., 227.

73. See Bernstein, *Turbulent Years*, 664–71; see also Gross, *Reshaping of the NLRB*, 89–91, and Tomlins, *State and the Unions*, 23.

74. Tomlins, *State and the Unions*, 204; Gross, *Reshaping of the NLRB*, 89.

75. Tomlins, *State and the Unions*, 207–13. See also Bernstein, *Turbulent Years*, 665. Millis's appointment led to the resignations of several NLRB officials, including Secretary Nathan Witt and review division chief Thomas Emerson.

76. By 1937 the CIO learned that it was neither as united nor as determined as many believed. See Bruce Nelson, "The CIO at Bay: Labor Militancy and Politics in Akron, 1936–1938," *Journal of American History* 71 (Dec. 1984): 565.

77. Polenberg, "Decline of the New Deal," 263.

78. See Brody, "Emergence of Mass Production Unionism," 111–12.

79. Nelson Lichtenstein, "Life at the Rouge: A Cycle of Workers' Control," in *Life and Labor: Dimensions of American Working-Class History*, ed. Charles Stephenson and Robert Asher (Albany: State University of New York Press, 1986), 241.

80. Atleson, *Values and Assumptions*, 195 n. 43. Brody states that the eighteen-month period between June 1940 and December 1941 "marked the turning point for the CIO" ("Emergence of Mass Production Unionism," 258). Average hourly earnings rose over 10 percent for manufacturing generally, and collective bargaining agreements contained a variety of improvements.

81. Excluding CIO unions in coal mining and needle trades, which were almost fully organized when they joined the federation, the CIO's gains had been quite modest up to 1940. See Christopher Tomlins, "AFL Unions in the 1930s: Their Performance in Historical Perspective," *Journal of American History* 65 (1979): 1023. The CIO, however, doubled in size between 1940 and 1941. Brody states the growth as being between 1,350,000 and 2,850,000 members in one year. Most of the figures deal with the decade of the thirties rather than any particular year ("Emergence of Mass-Production Unionism," 258). For instance, Green stresses that the number of unionized employees tripled from 2,805,000 in 1933 to 8,410,000 in 1941. The proportion of workers enjoying union rights and protection jumped from 9 percent to 34 percent in manufacturing, 21 percent to 72 percent in mining, 23 percent to 48 percent in transportation, and 54 percent to 65 percent in construction (*World of the Worker*, 173). Bernstein's figures on union membership also compare 1930 and 1940, thereby leaving open the question about the actual role of the National Labor Relations Act. See Bernstein, *Turbulent Years*, 769–71, 774–75, 784–86. The membership of the ten largest CIO affiliates between 1939 and 1962 is charted in Lichtenstein, *Labor's War at Home*, 80.

The importance of the war can be graphically demonstrated. Milton Derber estimates that there were 5.5 million jobless, constituting 9.9 percent of the civilian labor force in 1941. Derber's chart notes that there were 1.5 million unemployed in 1929, a number which jumped to 8 million or 16 percent of the workforce in 1931. This number jumped to 12.8 million or 25 percent of the civilian labor force in 1933, declining only somewhat to 10.6 or 20 percent in 1935. The number "fell" to 7.7 million or 14 percent of the workforce in 1937 but then jumped again to 9.4 million or 17 percent in 1939. This reflects the secondary recession which occurred in 1938 and 1939. Derber believes the number declined to 5.5 million or 9.9 percent in 1941 and then, due to the war, declined to 1 million or 4.7 percent in 1943. See Milton Derber, "The New Deal and Labor," in *The New Deal: The National Level*, ed. John Braeman, Robert H. Bremner, and David Brody (Columbus: Ohio State University Press, 1975), 123.

The UAW, which stood at 165,000 members in 1939, jumped to 461,000 by 1941 but more than doubled by 1944 to 1,650,000. The steelworkers' union stood at 225,000 in 1939, moved to 373,000 in 1941, but jumped again to 780,000 by 1944. The membership of electrical workers moved from 48,000 in 1939 to 133,000 in 1941 but rose enormously to 432,000 by 1944. Statistics vary, however. Joshua

Freeman, for instance, cites the U.E.'s gain from September 1940 of 154,000 members to a wartime high of over 600,000 ("Delivering the Goods: Industrial Unionism during World War II," *Labor History* 19 [1978]: 574). After the war, the labor movement would number 15 million union members, compared with fewer than 9 million during the defense crisis of 1940 (Seidman, *American Labor,* 248). Union contracts covered 14,800,000 workers in 1946, compared to 10,300,000 at the start of the war.

The Mobilizing Period:
Dress Rehearsal for Wartime

The defense-related production boom which began in 1940 brought relative prosperity after the prolonged depression, but the period also created strains in American labor. Eight years of the Roosevelt administration had contained but not overcome unemployment. Between April of 1940 and Pearl Harbor, however, nonfarm employment grew from thirty-five million to more than forty-one million and wage rates increased nearly 20 percent. A rejuvenated union movement used the opportunity to attempt to organize Ford, Little Steel, and the unorganized coal companies.[1] Yet, labor officials recognized that employers might use the situation to their own advantage. Although benefiting from the New Deal labor legislation, some unionists had become convinced by the late 1930s that courts and even the NLRB "were using the Wagner Act not only to advance, but also to limit, labor's goals."[2] Indeed, the defense buildup gave business the opportunity to use patriotism as an excuse for anti-union activity, to argue that labor peace was essential to production, and to attack mandatory union membership as undemocratic and un-American. The result was a high incidence of strikes in 1941, involving 8.4 percent of the industrial workforce. There were 4,288 disputes involving more than two million persons, double the number of disputes that occurred in 1940 and involving four times as many workers.[3]

Anticipating further labor troubles, in March 1941 Roosevelt replaced the National Defense Advisory Committee with the tripartite National Defense Mediation Board (NDMB), consisting of four representatives each from labor, management, and the public, a structure that would subsequently be employed for the National War Labor Board. The National Defense Mediation Board could use either mediation or voluntary arbitration to try to resolve disputes in defense industries. Many unions were skeptical but they were also were aware of bills then pending in Congress which would have restricted labor's right to strike.

The prewar defense mobilization period is important because the general contours of wartime labor relations would be established. First, although unions did not formally surrender the right to strike before the United States entered the war, unions uniformly declared their support for the mobilization effort. William Green, president of the AFL, for instance, stated that the "fate of our free labor movement is bound up with the fate of democracy."[4] Like Green, John L. Lewis had initially been opposed to any involvement in the European war. Trade unionists commonly believed that war economies initially benefited labor but ultimately strengthened the enemies of labor and weakened labor's power, an assessment based upon labor's experience after World War I. The state had "allowed control of economic mobilization to flow into the hands of corporate figures and had offered workers only transitory benefits—almost all of them stripped away, sometimes violently, in the immediate aftermath of the conflict." There was fear that a second world war could also "reinvigorate capital and derail the labor movement's most ambitious and controversial aims." The "war bureaucracy could accelerate the process the NLRB had already begun, the process of defining labor management relations narrowly and entrenching labor mediators at the center of those relations."[5] Alan Brinkley argues that Lewis, perhaps more than other leaders, feared the war could destroy whatever chances remained for progressive change, and that is why he opposed FDR's interventionist policies in 1940 and 1941 and supported Wendell Willkie.[6]

Once committed to involvement, Green, like other labor leaders, pledged the AFL's "active and cooperative support with industry and with every appropriate government agency."[7] At the same time, conservative union leaders like Teamster president Dan Tobin linked labor policies to patriotism, stating that strikes which "retard production" or "embarrass our Government" would be "considered as a menace to our Government."[8] These views mirrored, and were no doubt influenced by, public pressure on unions, and the threat of antilabor legislation was also constant during the war. Similar sentiments would also be repeatedly expressed by government and military figures as well as by employers and anti-union legislators.

Another parallel to the wartime period is that although organized labor received some representation on governmental policy-making boards, labor's influence never came close to equaling that of management.[9] Corporate leaders effectively dominated the mobilization agencies, which were largely staffed by businessmen.[10] By mid-1942 over ten thousand business executives had moved into war agencies, and liberals had warned about the influence of the new "dollar-a-year" men even before the mobilization had begun. The *Nation* and the *New Republic* complained that these executives, mostly Republican, were "more worried about their competitive position after the war than about winning the war" and their main interest was "protection of their competitive positions."[11] The absence of significant union influence could be due to the administration's political calculations at the time, but it also reflected the unions' relative lack of political power. As Joel Seidman stated, "labor's influence [in defense agencies] was vastly inferior to that of management spokesmen."[12] For Green and other union officials, labor's lack of representation and power on government boards was an act of betrayal. Some representation was no doubt an improvement over none, and the defense-stimulated economic boom perhaps muffled labor's criticisms.[13]

After many labor demands, the Office of Production Management (OPM) created labor advisory committees which labor hoped would serve as tripartite planning agencies. Yet, the industry advisory committees refused to meet with union representatives because, they believed, unions had no right to intrude upon management functions.[14] Many critical posts, moreover, over eight hundred by 1943, were held by "dollar-a-year" men loaned from their employers, providing an extreme example of the postwar notion of administrative "capture." Industry branches of the War Production Board (WPB), for instance, were often staffed and led by men from the industries involved.[15] The "whole thrust of the Franklin D. Roosevelt administration's massive intervention in the depression-ridden economy was designed to preserve, not change, American corporate capitalism. When a planned wartime economy became essential, the administration turned to the business community which owned the nation's productive plant and had the personnel and knowledge necessary to run it."[16] In addition, the growth and influence of the military was a significant development in the operation of the economy. The armed services became the nation's largest consumer and investor, and the ally of the industrial community.[17]

Labor's lack of political power was constantly demonstrated during this period, and the need for defense production served as a convenient excuse to circumvent other policy concerns. For instance, labor argued strongly that the National Defense Advisory Commission (NDAC), of which Sidney Hillman was a member, should withhold defense contracts from companies that were in violation of federal labor laws.[18] As early as 1939 Lewis pressed Roosevelt to deny military contracts to labor law violators, but the president responded cautiously. FDR had suggested new legislation as a more expedient means of addressing the problem, but in 1938 Lewis and CIO counsel Lee Pressman had sought amendments to the Walsh-Healey Act requiring the government to consider adherence to the law in granting contracts, and their failure had convinced them that the legislative route would not be useful.[19]

In September 1940, the National Defense Advisory Committee enunciated its labor policy, and labor pressure seemed to have achieved a signal victory. The NDAC required companies seeking defense contracts to comply with federal and state laws and to avoid discrimination in both race and sex. Released to the press on August 31, 1940, the document declared that "all work carried on as part of the defense program should comply with Federal statutory provisions affecting labor." On October 1 Hillman told the press that "Army and Navy contracts will no longer be given companies violating the Federal labor laws." Attorney General Robert H. Jackson ruled that firms which violated the NLRA could be denied defense contracts after the NLRB's decision.

Nevertheless, Lewis responded critically because the statement said nothing about how the policy would be enforced and the policy itself did not penalize violators or affect existing contracts. "Moreover, all of the government's statements were so studded with qualifications so that [in Lewis's opinion], they amounted to little more than pious hopes that military procurement agencies would suddenly turn into aggressive watchdogs."[20] Qualifications, ultimately, were less important than perceived economic and political realities. "As the need for defense production mounted, however, government procurement agencies dropped their requirement for compliance with the National Labor Relations Act as a condition for receiving defense contracts."[21] According to Matthew Josephson, the White House ordered Jackson to ease the issue of labor law compliance until the elections of 1940.[22]

Pressures from congressional and military sources soon forced Hillman to retreat as well. The NDAC's policies were questioned before Congressman Howard Smith's special House committee, and Hillman, the service secretaries, and Attorney General Robert Jackson all "backed off from any but the most innocuous interpretation of the Hillman-developed program."[23]

A fascinating part of the CIO's hopes for the mobilization was that a corporatist, tripartite program of planning and reform could be forged. Philip Murray's Industrial Council Program, proposed in 1941, envisioned centralized planning for each basic defense industry involving the "direct and active participation within each industry on the part of management and labor." Each council would allocate available raw materials within the industry, allocate contracts among available plant facilities, adjust the labor supply to the plant facilities, and arrange for necessary and appropriate facilities for housing and training. The president would also establish a national defense board consisting of an equal number of representatives from industry and labor with the president or his designee as chair. The board would establish rules and regulations for the operation of the councils, and the "basic planning in order to determine the domestic and armament requirements for each industry will have to be determined by this national defense board."[24] John L. Lewis also proposed the creation of industry councils composed equally of union and employer representatives to coordinate the processes of specific industries in light of wartime demands.[25]

Obviously, urging industrial cooperation and union involvement in politics is not the same as seeking union co-option by the state, but there seemed to be an awareness that this could occur. In any event, Murray's plan went nowhere, but it reflects his willingness to think about industrial coordination at the highest levels and in industry-wide terms.[26] Labor's membership on many boards might give the impression that labor had secured some success in its industrial planning efforts,[27] but, as already noted, labor influence was small throughout the mobilization and the war. Nelson Lichtenstein argues that, indeed, such hopes were dashed by the time of Pearl Harbor or at least soon after.[28]

In the winter of 1940–41, Walter Reuther, then the head of UAW's General Motors Department, presented a startling proposal dealing with the conversion of automobile plants for defense purposes. The plan was premised on the assumption that the automotive industry was using only half of its potential production capacity and that almost all of the idle tools and space could be adapted for the construction of military aircraft. Reuther proposed a presidentially appointed nine-member industrial counsel, with representatives of labor, business, and government, to supervise the production process. Unlike the plans for advisory agencies proposed by Hillman, Reuther's, like Murray's, involved administrative agencies which would make critical decisions about production, labor requirements, and contracting. In addition, Reuther's plan stressed productive advantages rather than the restructuring of economic relations and would involve labor in critical decision making in the auto industry, thus shaping industrial relations after the war ended.[29] Reuther declared that within six months the automobile factories could turn out 500 planes per day, 150,000 planes per year.[30] As Nelson Lichtenstein notes, the plan reflected the approach of labor liberalism in the 1940s, that is, "an assault on management's traditional power made in the name of economic efficiency and the public interest, and an effort to shift power relations within the structure of an industry and politics, usually by means of a tripartite governmental entity empowered to plan for whole sections of the economy."[31]

There was a flurry of interest in the Reuther plan after Pearl Harbor, but it quietly died. David Brody has stated that it was a "genuine proposal for basic change, and its rejection demonstrates not only the uncertainty attending the nation's slow advance towards full mobilization, but the unwillingness of the major interest groups to embrace any scheme that threatened to alter fundamental economic relationships, even in the name of national defense."[32] Such a reluctance would eventually be reflected in decisions of the War Labor Board.

Until the very eve of the war, the auto industry successfully protected its factories from conversion. Alan Clive has noted that from mid-1941 onward, if not before, "thousands of tons of critical materials and countless man hours were wasted in the production of passenger cars. The auto makers allowed concern for the preservation of their industry and for profit to obscure their very vision upon which the government was depending for the creation of production 'materials.'"[33] As a result of the delay, the industry was only partly ready for the quick conversion to war production needed in December 1941.

The early stages of conversion resulted in massive unemployment, especially in automobile states such as Michigan.[34] Indeed, unemployment rose in Michigan to 225,000 in January 1942. Automotive conversion was substantially complete by October 1942, however, and American war production as a whole reached its peak in the fall of 1943. The auto industry vastly expanded its facilities in order to fulfill the wartime demands, and GM, for example, built nearly $900,000,000 worth of new plants between 1940 and 1944, almost all of which were paid for by the government.[35]

Unionists could hardly fail to note the unusually attractive government inducements granted to industries as incentives to produce for the war effort, including generous depreciation allowances, a relaxation of antitrust laws, and an excess profit tax written so as to return to industry much of the revenue collected from it during the war. These benefits had been demanded by the auto industry as the price of its abandonment of profitable civilian production. The secretary of war, Henry Stimson, observed in a blunt 1940 diary entry, "If you are going to try to go to war, prepare for war in a capitalist country, you have got to let business make money out of the process, or business won't work."[36] This recognition of profit patriotism was not, as we shall see, carried over to labor.

Moreover, the left wing of the New Deal, whose support was critical to the ambitions of radicals and progressive labor, had begun to lose the initiative within the administration. "Even before the War, Roosevelt had began to turn away from social-Keynesian proposals calling for extensive government intervention into the economy's capital, labor, and resource markets and to favor advisors who argued that the government should maintain healthy macro-economic environment without interfering in the management or regulation of particular capitalist enterprises."[37] Thus, during the mobilization period, which is critical for understanding the wartime period, the "government would seek to stimulate such production by offering capitalists hefty contracts with guaranteed profits, but would otherwise sharply limit its economic role. It would not build its own production facilities, nationalize existing ones, or even seek for itself a partial managerial role."[38]

The antireform slant of the administration, which had begun in 1938, now had a new explanation. FDR rejected proposals for social reform on the ground that war planning was a more critical objective: "I am not convinced that we can be realists about the war and planners for the future at this critical time."[39] It should also be noted that Republicans continued to undermine Democratic majorities in both houses. In November 1942, Republicans gained forty-four new seats in the House and nine in the Senate. Indeed, Brody concludes that the conservative coalition, southern Democrats and conservative Republicans, reached its most effective point in 1943–44.[40]

The shifting power in Congress, and FDR's need to gain support for his military program and foreign policy, led to the surrender of domestic initiatives and raised labor's fears of hostile legislation.[41] In this atmosphere it would have been difficult for unions to coerce industry to share decision-making functions. As Koistinen notes, "strong-arming industry in a nation devoted to business values would probably have lacked popular appeal. While there was much discontent with how the American business system worked and widespread desire for it to function more equitably, there was no consensus over how to reform the system and little sentiment in favor of changing capitalism. The split emotions of American liberalism over marketplace economics, which the New Deal accurately reflected, created enormous obstacles to modifying significantly industry's power."[42]

Thus, Koistinen stresses that some unions during the war fought in vain to escape business unionism, but they could not afford endlessly to neglect their immediate self-interest. "Realism dictated that labor accommodate to, instead of resist, an environment which it had neither created nor could do much to change."[43]

Another parallel between the mobilization and war periods is the pressure upon unions to avoid strikes. After the serious economic downturn in

1938 and 1939, the defense mobilization period was a boon to American industry and workers. The huge military construction program in the prewar mobilization period of 1940–41 substantially increased employment, with the number of employed rising three million within a year of the initiation of the defense program. Although wages rose, especially in defense industries, employees were caught as prices rose due to both increasing demand and shortages.[44] Noting the huge increase in business profits as well as increased productivity, labor demanded that wages should rise with living costs, a precursor of postwar cost of living (COLA) arrangements. Despite the substantial profits gained from defense contracts, employers vigorously resisted union demands even though the government was willing to accept moderate pay raises for defense workers. Managerial behavior, according to Joel Seidman, seems to have been related to its long-range views:

> The outcome of defense strikes, in the eyes of many employers, would have an important bearing on the competitive position of their enterprise when it returned to its regular peace time products. Wages, easily raised so long as the government paid the bill for defense materials, might not easily come down to meet post-war competition. Similarly, union power, consolidated under the cover of the defense emergency, would remain after the fighting ended to increase wages, reduce profits and limit management's power to direct the enterprise. Current industrial disputes, said the editors of *Business Week*, were not "a series of isolated battles for isolated gains. Rather they are part of a long-term, irrepressible struggle for power."[45]

Despite these tensions, the incidence of strikes in 1940 declined significantly from 1939, and few had any real impact upon defense production. Nevertheless, despite the low level of strikes in 1940, there were strong political pressures to avoid strikes.[46] This pressure would be greatly intensified after the United States would officially become a belligerent.

The reaction to a brief strike by the CIO's Industrial Union of Marine and Shipbuilding Workers against a New Jersey shipbuilding and dry dock company highlights the prewar atmosphere. The strike was called off after two days to avoid charges of obstructing the defense program. Nevertheless, Representative Cox of Georgia deemed the strike "treason," and Representative Clare E. Hoffman of Michigan, another long-standing critic of labor, proposed legislation to outlaw strikes in defense plants.[47]

The language of treason would be employed by labor's opponents even in a period when the United States was not at war. Thus, even before Pearl Harbor some congressional representatives referred to John L. Lewis as a "miserable traitor" for calling a strike in the captive coal mines. One of the most extreme suggestions came from Chairman Hatton W. Sumners of the House Judiciary Committee: "When the time comes that it is necessary to deal with the enemies of the nation and the factory or elsewhere, I believe I can speak for each member of the committee. If it is necessary to preserve this country, they would not hesitate one split second to enact legislation to send them to the electric chair."[48]

Many of these voices were prone to criticize labor, but a wider concern existed. For instance, a congressional committee which investigated the naval defense program concluded in January 1942 that "the greatest single cause for delay in the defense program has been the strike situation."[49] Four days after the coal strike began, a bill was introduced to consider defense-related strikes treasonous, providing for twenty-five years in prison as a minimum penalty and execution as the maximum sentence. Although the bill was an extreme example of anti-union hostility, unions would fear such legislation throughout the wartime period, and such apprehension would explain a good deal of their behavior.

Indeed, concerns were raised within the labor movement as well. A number of conservative union leaders also opposed strikes during this period, no doubt fearing that adverse legislation could result. Daniel Tobin warned that strikes "are doing more to help place on the statute books adverse legislation against labor than all the enemies of labor combined."[50] As Tobin was no doubt aware, however, the "enemies of labor" were capitalizing on pro-defense public sympathy, despite the absence of any real evidence that strikes were adversely affecting defense production.

A strike at the Los Angeles Vultee plant in the fall of 1940 led to another charge that would haunt unions through the 1940s and 1950s. Attorney General Robert Jackson and others claimed that Communists were directing the strike, leading to further congressional demands that strikes in defense plants be outlawed.[51] In a speech at the Philadelphia Rotary Club, William Green, president of the AFL, also pointed to Communists (and the CIO) as responsible for current labor troubles. As Green must have been aware, however, the presence of Communists was often used as a cover for criticism that, surely in part, was directed at unions themselves.[52] Although William Knudsen, director of the Office of Production Management, and Secretary of Labor Perkins both agreed that "Communism has meant little in strikes,"[53] these attacks on militant unions seemed to affect the public's perception of unions. A Gallup poll in April 1941, for instance, revealed a popular perception that Communists were indeed responsible for defense strikes. In May 1940, 74 percent had expressed support for labor unions, but the number fell to 67 percent by June 1941.[54] The drumbeat of criticism directed at labor had an effect, demonstrating that public opinion does not simply exist but is always in the process of being formed.

In the spring of 1941, the autoworkers and the steelworkers made break-throughs, forcing Ford, Bethlehem Steel, and other Little Steel companies to recognize their unions.[55] For the first eight months of 1941, strike totals leaped upward. Organized workers now at last saw the possibility of gaining tangible advantages from their union membership, and union membership surged. Between June 1940 and December 1941, organized labor gained approximately a million and a half new recruits, increasing the membership of unions by over a quarter.[56]

The AFL's strategy of trying to hold its enemies at bay by displaying its patriotism and its willingness to cooperate proved even more difficult in 1941, when strikes occurred in almost every major industry. Strikes doubled in 1941 over the 1940 rate, and the number of strikers quadrupled.[57] As Craig Phelan caustically states, William Green's "propaganda war of 1941 had as much effect as his campaigns of the 1920s and 1930s—none. Employers ignored him, conservatives pressed forward with their anti-labor agenda, and the public's perception of unions began to erode."[58]

Throughout this period and, indeed, the war, antilabor and "patriotic" forces successfully equated patriotism with full production and unions with strikes. Despite these pressures, the strike wave of 1941, surpassed only by the historic levels of 1919, caused great consternation in the government and generated renewed vigor in the antilabor forces which had already practiced the use of patriotism to stifle unionism. Interesting, the AFL, although generally considered the least radical wing of labor, had been responsible for more strike calls (54 percent) in 1941 than the CIO (37 percent). The remainder involved independent unions. The CIO strikes, however, received more attention because its unions were largely represented in the mass production industries, and, therefore, CIO members tended to be more involved with defense production. Moreover, CIO strike calls brought out the greatest number of workers, as the CIO accounted for nearly 70 percent of the 1941 strikers.[59]

Sidney Hillman, a member of the NDAC, eventually recommended a tripartite mediation board to the president, believing it might be acceptable to union leaders in order to forestall passage of antistrike legislation. The AFL quickly endorsed the proposal, although the CIO's Philip Murray clearly expressed reluctance. Murray supported the defense effort, but he also realized that the CIO was in position to strengthen itself after the severe blows of the late 1930s. As the wartime period would also reveal, however, pressures against strikes would be highest when union power would appear to be at its zenith. In a private memorandum to Hillman, Murray perceptively recognized that a "mediation" board would primarily be charged with the responsibility of preventing or ending strikes, and, thus, it would "find its attention directed against labor in order to maintain the status quo as much as possible." Moreover, Murray correctly predicted that the new board would soon "bring terrific pressure on labor to agree to arbitration in practically all situations."[60] Nevertheless, despite these doubts, Murray did not oppose the creation of such a board.[61]

On March 19, 1941, the president's Executive Order 8716 established the National Defense Mediation Board to "exert every possible effort to assure that all work necessary for national defense shall proceed without interruption and with all possible speed."[62] The board was empowered to aid in the settlement of any controversy or dispute between management and labor which threatened "to burden or obstruct the production or transportation of equipment or material essential to national defense."[63] When the secretary of labor certified that the U.S. Conciliation Service was unable to settle a labor dispute affecting a defense industry, the controversy would be referred to the NDMB.[64] The board was to make every effort to adjust and settle a dispute and, for this purpose, the board was directed to offer the parties mediation services and to afford them the necessary means for collective bargaining or for voluntary arbitration. The board was also empowered to investigate controversies, conduct hearings, make findings of fact, and formulate and publicize recommendations. Publicity was deemed important since the board's decisions were not formally binding on the participants to a dispute.[65]

Wartime emergencies tend to highlight the need for both public and private processes of dispute resolution. Thus, the functions of the World War I National War Labor Board were expressed in similar terms: "to settle by mediation and conciliation controversies arising between employers and workers in fields of production necessary for the conduct of the war." The World War I board had no express authority to enforce its recommendations, and Wilson in practice compelled compliance through the exercise of presidential war powers.[66]

Prior to creating the World War I board, President Wilson asked representatives of labor and management to convene in order to establish a labor dispute adjustment process. Representatives pledged to abstain from strikes and lockouts and guaranteed the freedom of workers to organize and bargain collectively. This procedure was followed after Pearl Harbor. Unlike the situation in World War II, however, the closed shop controversy was deleted from the scope of the World War I board's authority. That board could not order the abandonment of an existing open shop, although plants that had the closed shop could keep them for the duration of the war.[67]

One principle established by the labor-management conference of World War I is strikingly similar to the language of the subsequent NLRA: "The right of workers to organize in trade unions and to bargain collectively through chosen representatives is recognized and affirmed. This right shall not be denied, abridged, or interfered with by the employers in any manner whatsoever. . . . Employers should not discharge workers for membership in trade unions, nor for legitimate trade union activities."[68] With respect to organizational problems, the World War I War Labor Board anticipated later NLRB rulings when it recommended the reinstatement of workers with back pay who were discharged because of union activities, generally required employers to bargain collectively with representatives of workers' organizations, and ordered the polling of workers in secret elections to determine their choices of bargaining agents.[69]

Like its World War I predecessor, the National Defense Mediation Board of 1940 seemingly was a powerless governmental agency. Under the presidential order, the board could take jurisdiction only on certification from the secretary of labor that there was a dispute threatening defense production which the federal conciliation service could not resolve. "Thus the board was handicapped from the start by cumbersome machinery and overlapping jurisdiction with other federal agencies."[70]

Partly because of its limitations, the NDMB emphasized collective bargaining rather than federal determination of disputed issues, and it sought first to have the disputants settle their differences privately. The NDMB engaged in formal findings and recommendations only after mediation efforts failed and the parties had refused voluntary arbitration. Such efforts had a degree of success, for formal recommendations were necessary in only a small percentage of cases.[71]

The public members of the new board were generally thought to be prolabor: Frank P. Graham, president of the University of North Carolina; William H. Davis, a New York patent attorney who became chairman, replacing Clarence A. Dykstra after several months; and Charles Wyzanski.[72] The public members, as might be expected in a tripartite board, wrote most of the opinions. Although the board had little power and its recommendations were not binding, leading to conservative criticisms of its seeming lack of effectiveness, it was empowered by widespread public pressure and the real threat of governmental seizure. Indeed, in the two cases in which companies refused the board's recommendations, the government seized the plants.[73] There is also some evidence that the board was willing to use the threat of congressional action to gain union acquiescence. Most importantly, the public members saw themselves as needing the support of the disputants, a perception which made "acceptability" a preeminent value.

A mediation model is difficult to apply unless some middle ground exists between the disputants or can be conceptually created. The union security cases, for instance, were more difficult than the wage controversies because they could not easily be compromised. Yet, in the very first case in which the union security issue was involved, the board persuaded the parties to accept a "maintenance of membership clause," which required employees who were already union members to remain members during the life of an agreement, and this form of union security would later become the War Labor Board's customarily granted compromise between employer desires for the open shop and union requests for the closed shop. The maintenance of membership clause protected the union against membership losses and relieved the union's need to constantly seek dues each month while at the same time not forcing any worker to join.[74] The rationale for the grant of maintenance of membership was also similar to that which the successor War Labor Board would use: the security afforded by the clause would lead to union stability, intra-union discipline, and responsible conduct.[75]

The NDMB's life ended when the CIO members quit in protest over a decision involving the United Mine Workers and the "captive" mines, mines owned and operated by the steel companies and overwhelmingly organized by the UMW. John L. Lewis closed the mines briefly in September and again in October 1941, in a shutdown that threatened steel production in the country. The strike led to a storm of abuse and criticism, and FDR, in language strikingly similar to that President Truman would subsequently use in 1946, said that "that small minority is a menace to the true cause of labor itself, as well as for the nation as a whole." Similarly, a leading AFL publicist, Philip Pearl, called the captive mine strike "not only a betrayal of America, . . . not only a betrayal of the workers involved, but . . . a dastardly and indefensible betrayal of the best interest of all labor in America."[76]

The board decided against the UMW's demand for a closed shop clause (requiring *all* employees to pay union dues) on the ground that 95 percent of the employees were already union members, and the union was capable of organizing the remainder. The vote against the UMW was 9 to 2, with AFL members Green and Meany voting *with* management and the public members. Joseph Goulden states that Meany strongly favored the closed shop and abhorred voting against a fellow unionist, but "what Lewis was demanding ran counter to a principle Meany considered basic to trade unionism: The closed shop was something to be won by collective bargaining, not by edict of a governmental agency."[77] The decision killed the board. The two CIO representatives, Philip Murray and Thomas Kennedy, both officers of the UMW, resigned and the board never met again.[78]

In its short life, the NDMB created labor policies which foreshadowed those of the post–Pearl Harbor National War Labor Board. Specifically, bargaining and private arbitration would be encouraged as a substitute for strikes and, if they were unsuccessful, federal determination of labor disputes would occur.

The period of mobilization reflects many of the themes present throughout the war period. First, the period reflects the great paradox of wartime. Increased employment and the need for increased production provided great opportunities for union growth and worker advancement. At the same time, however, the very same situation created patriotic pressures *against* the use of union power. Indeed, the defense emergency gave greater legitimacy to calls for legislative restraints on union collective power, pressure which itself forced unions to operate with considerable caution. In addition, the operation and staffing of government defense agencies reveals labor's lack of clout in an administration which, for a number of reasons, had eschewed social reform.

Another parallel between the two periods is the constant pressure for legislative restrictions against unions and, especially, limits on the strike weapon. Despite the creation of the National Defense Mediation Board, legislative proposals for restricting labor's right to strike continued to be presented. For instance, in March 1940 the special House committee appointed to investigate the administration of the NLRA , chaired by Representative Howard W. Smith of Virginia, issued an intermediate report charging the NLRB and its staff with bias and inefficiency.[79] The Smith Committee soon proposed broad amendments to the NLRA, including proposals to separate the board's judicial function from its investigatory and prosecutorial functions, to subject its findings of fact to judicial review, to permit employers to petition for elections, to protect employer free speech, and to bar the reinstatement of sit-down strikers.

Reflecting tensions between the AFL and CIO, and AFL criticism of the perceived CIO-bias of the NLRB, AFL president Green initially approved the committee proposals as long as certain changes were made, including an amendment to protect craft bargaining rights. These changes were subsequently incorporated into the bill and it was adopted by the House on June 7, 1941, by a vote of 258 to 129. Green's action did not have the support of the entire AFL executive council, however, and Green soon backtracked, informing the Senate Committee on Education and Labor that the AFL would prefer to have the Wagner Act unchanged rather than distorted by the Smith amendments. Ultimately, the Smith Committee proposals failed to pass the Senate.[80]

In November 1941, Harry Millis succeeded J. Warren Madden as chairman of the National Labor Relations Board, to join William Leiserson who had been appointed the previous year. The changes they made in board policy and organization may have reassured some critics and may have helped to avoid the Smith proposals.[81] The change in membership and direction of the board, however, had little effect upon congressional interest in regulating strikes.

The most discussed type of antistrike legislation during the prewar period involved a mandatory cooling-off period before a strike at a defense plant could legally be called. The need to "cool off" workers seems to be based on the assumption that collective actions are often irrational, obviously not functional, and that unless restrained, workers will act in irrational ways.[82] The CIO criticized such proposals as steps toward "involuntary servitude." A CIO pamphlet issued in April 1941 noted that "the basic idea back of 'cooling off' is to put the blame for strikes entirely on the workers. It is designed to make the strike look like the work of hot-headed union leaders who need some kind of cold shower to bring them back to their senses. It completely ignores the fact that strikes were caused by real grievances standing over a long period of time. It ignores the fact that CIO unions spend weeks and months in negotiations before they even take a strike vote."[83]

Philip Murray strongly criticized various statutory measures at the CIO convention in 1941: "These legislative proposals . . . would have clamped upon labor workers a system of forced labor. They would have imposed compulsory mediation or compulsory arbitration."[84] In addition, some proposals would permit employers to dismiss employees on the ground that they possessed a "subversive character." The proposed legislation, he believed, would also sanction the use of troops to break strikes and permit injunctions, thus suspending the protections of the Norris-LaGuardia Act.

In December 1941, on the Wednesday before Pearl Harbor, the House of Representatives passed another bill sponsored by Representative Howard Smith of Virginia by a 252 to 136 vote with little serious consideration of its provisions. Unlike the prior bill, this statute dealt primarily with strikes in defense industries rather than "reforms" of the NLRA. The statute, according to Joel Seidman, was the most extreme antistrike bill presented to Congress, and it was the first piece of anti-union legislation to get this far since the Wagner Act of 1935. The statute, foreshadowing the Taft-Hartley Act of 1947, provided for a thirty-day cooling-off period before a strike or lockout could occur at a plant with defense contracts and then only after a majority of employees had approved the strike by secret ballot. Unions could not strike in any defense industry at any time for a closed shop, and unions guilty of illegal strikes would lose all statutory rights. In addition, jurisdictional strikes and boycotts affecting defense contracts were outlawed. The bill was shunted aside because of the attack on Pearl Harbor.[85] A similar bill, however, would be adopted in 1943 over FDR's veto.

Thus, another parallel between the defense mobilization period and wartime was the proliferation of bills designed to weaken the Wagner Act and discipline workers, especially in defense plants. Although only one of these many proposals was actually enacted, and that in 1943, the very real threat of hostile legislation would affect union policy throughout the war.

Government regulation of labor comes in a variety of forms, and legislation is not necessarily the most important or most effective means of control. For its purposes, the administration preferred more informal methods. In one case, Sidney Hillman, associate director of the Office of Production Management in 1940, worked with SWOC leaders to persuade Regional Director Van Bittner to "call off massive and enthusiastic organizational strikes at Bethlehem Steel before the union had secured a collective bargaining agreement."[86] Leaders of other unions and the AFL executive council declared their opposition to strikes at defense installations to avoid charges that they were thwarting the defense effort. Nevertheless, strikes occurred as local union leaders saw a golden opportunity to organize or to settle outstanding grievances, and the sit-downs of the late 1930s were replaced by massive and militant picket lines.[87]

Persuasion was only one of the methods employed by the government to control unions. Thus, the government prosecuted left wing militants like Farrell Dobbs and other Minneapolis Teamsters[88] and used troops without legislative sanction to end strikes at defense installations at Allis-Chalmers and North American Aviation.[89] The Minneapolis Teamsters were eventually defeated through a combination of Justice Department raids, prosecution of leaders for criminal syndicalism under the recently passed Smith Act, and private suppression of rank-and-file militance by Teamster organizers, like the young Jimmy Hoffa.

During the war, as will be subsequently more fully discussed, FDR seriously considered compulsory national service for defense workers, a proposal constantly advocated by the armed services and others, and the threat of the draft and other types of governmental regulation always loomed. Indeed, there is a considerable amount of anecdotal evidence that organizers were drafted to still their efforts.[90] The armed services also launched a publicity campaign against the defense strikes, and the military repeatedly lobbied for national service as well as antistrike legislation.[91] Moreover, during the mobilization period the military repeatedly urged the direct use of troops to end strikes at defense installations, a tactic ultimately used successfully at North American Aviation.[92] Though FDR resisted most of the military's demands, Paul Koistinen found that Roosevelt did agree to increase the FBI's surveillance of labor unions.[93]

The June 1941 strike at North American Aviation in Inglewood, California, was perhaps the most notorious of the period. Steven Fraser has noted that the great demand for military planes "upset the labor market, generating acute shortages, the pirating of skilled cadre by rival manufacturers, black market wages, and a chaotic shattering of customary job hierarchies."[94] The plant, which made 20 percent of the nation's military airplanes, was obviously vital to the defense effort.[95] Short-term strikes along the West Coast had preceded the "explosion at Inglewood . . . as old-timers and new recruits protested pay rates, exhausting overtime, and punishing shift schedules."[96]

The union local at North American had refused a request of the National Defense Mobilization Board to continue working while attempts were made to resolve the dispute, and the local faced a solid front of opposition from the government and the press. This was not unusual, but for the first time opposition existed within the UAW itself.[97] Backed by CIO and UAW officials, FDR broke the strike, and union officials were forced to disown the strike to maintain their relationship with the administration. The strike ended when the president ordered the army to reopen and operate the plant; over twenty-five hundred troops with fixed bayonets marched in to disperse the picket lines.[98] This was the first case in which property was seized by the U.S. Army during the mobilization period, and, apparently, the only case in which the union was seen as the guilty party.[99]

Despite some of the public criticism of the strike, there is little evidence that the strike at North American was Communist-inspired. Employees had real grievances, as they had in other strikes in defense industries, for example, at Vultee and Allis-Chalmers. North American's visibility, however, was heightened by administration officials and congressional leaders who expressed the need for restrictive measures against strikes in defense industries. Assistant Attorney General Thurman Arnold, for instance, suggested outlawing strikes. Draft regulations were changed so that workers who had been deferred because of essential defense jobs might be drafted if they went on strike, and many labor leaders became reluctant to support aggressive action for fear of encouraging repressive measures.

Even before the entrance of the United States to the war, therefore, labor was often forced to surrender the power of well-timed economic pressure to placate the administration, to demonstrate their patriotism, and to finesse an increasingly hostile Congress.[100] As the war years also made clear, labor's great strength and potential disruptive power ironically existed during a time of great danger.

Notes

1. Andrew Workman, "Creating the Center: Liberal Intellectuals, the National War Labor Board, and the Stabilization of American Industrial Relations, 1941–1945" (Ph.D. diss., University of North Carolina, 1993), 14.

2. Alan Brinkley, *The End of Reform: New Deal Liberalism in Recession and War* (New York: Alfred A. Knopf, 1995), 202.

3. Joel Seidman, *American Labor from Defense to Reconversion* (Chicago: University of Chicago Press, 1953), 52–53.

4. Seidman, *American Labor,* 24.

5. Craig Phelan, *William Green: Biography of a Labor Leader* (Albany: State University of New York Press, 1989), 159.

6. Brinkley, *End of Reform,* 202–3.

7. Phelan, *William Green,* 160.

8. Seidman, *American Labor,* 24.

9. Ibid., 29.

10. Howell John Harris, *The Right to Manage: Industrial Relations Policies of American Business in 1940s* (Madison: University of Wisconsin Press, 1982), 41–42. Harris notes that the government provided business with a congenial environment involving investment grants, the cessation of prosecutions under antitrust laws, and generous tax treatment of profits and investments (42). In addition, the auto industry successfully demanded an escalator clause permitting it to add to the final price any materials or costs not estimated in the original contract. See also Art Preis, *Labor's Giant Step: Twenty Years of the CIO* (New York: Pathfinder Press, 1972), 148–49.

11. Brinkley, *End of Reform,* 190.

12. Seidman, *American Labor,* 28–29.

13. Job opportunities were increasing as were wages; in the twenty months between June 1940 and Pearl Harbor, 4 of the 8.5 million unemployed found jobs (Phelan, *William Green,* 160).

14. Paul A. C. Koistinen, "Mobilizing the World War II Economy: Labor and the Industrial-Military Alliance," *Pacific Historical Review* 42 (1973): 450.

15. David Brody, *In Labor's Cause* (New York: Oxford University Press, 1993), 289.

16. Koistinen, "Mobilizing the World War II Economy," 444.

17. Koistinen indicates that out of total wartime expenditures approximating $315.8 billion, the war department spent about $179.9 billion and the navy department $83.9 billion. Through 1944, the armed services contracted with some 18,539 firms. Consistently, however, one hundred corporations received at least two-thirds of the contracts; thirty corporations almost one-half. Expenditures for research and plants and equipment followed a similar pattern (ibid., 446).

18. Although Sidney Hillman served as associate director of the Office of Production Management, labor soon perceived him to be FDR's man, not theirs. Hillman was photographed at FDR's side as he telephoned orders for troops to break the strike at North American, which was seized by the president on June 9, 1941 (Thomas Brooks, *Toil and Trouble: A History of American Labor* [New York: Delacorte Press, 1964], 195–96). In addition, although he was not chosen by the CIO, the AFL deemed him to be a CIO man (David Brody, "The New Deal and World War II," in *The New Deal: The National Level*, ed. John Braeman, Robert H. Bremner, and David Brody [Columbus: Ohio State University Press, 1975], 290). Hillman, in any event, was soon shunted aside and, after he resigned from the War Production Board, no union representative took his place.

19. Robert H. Zieger, *The CIO, 1935–1955* (Chapel Hill: University of North Carolina Press, 1995), 106–7.

20. Ibid., 107.

21. Seidman, *American Labor*, 28. See also Koistinen, "Mobilizing the World War II Economy," 461; Paul A. C. Koistinen, *The Hammer and the Sword* (New York: Arno Press, 1979), 134–44.

22. Matthew Josephson, *Sidney Hillman: Statesman of American Labor* (Garden City: Doubleday, 1952), 522. Josephson argues, however, that Jackson and Hillman's objections may have played a role in Ford's, and perhaps Bethlehem Steel's, decision to recognize the CIO (527–28).

23. Zieger, *CIO, 1935–1955*, 106–7.

24. See Clinton Golden and Harold Ruttenberg, *The Dynamics of Industrial Democracy* (New York: Harper, 1942), 343–47.

25. See Melvyn Dubofsky and Warren Van Tine, *John L. Lewis: A Biography* (Urbana: University of Illinois Press, 1986), 303; Ronald Schatz, "Battling over Government's Role," in *Forging a Union of Steel*, ed. Paul Clark, Peter Gottlieb, and Donald Kennedy (Ithaca, N.Y.: ILR Press, 1981), 92–93.

26. Many believe that Murray was influenced by Leo XIII's 1891 encyclical Rerum Novarum as well as ideas of national planning in the New Deal period (David Brody, "The Origins of Modern Steel Unionism: The SWOC Era," in *Forging a Union of Steel*, ed. Paul Clark, Peter Gottlieb, and Donald Kennedy [Ithaca, N.Y.: ILR Press, 1987], 28); Brooks, *Toil and Trouble*, 200–201. David McDonald takes

credit for Murray's concept. See David McDonald, *Union Man* (New York: Dutton, 1969).

27. Donald Nelson, chairman of the War Production Board, however, argued that labor played a significant role in war production planning. See Donald Nelson, *Arsenal of Democracy: A Story of American War Production* (New York: Harcourt, Brace and Company, 1946).

28. Nelson Lichtenstein, *Labor's War at Home: The CIO in World War II* (New York: Cambridge University Press, 1982), 6.

29. Brinkley, *End of Reform*, 203–9.

30. Alan Clive, *State of War: Michigan in World War II* (Ann Arbor: University of Michigan Press, 1979), 22.

31. See Nelson Lichtenstein, "From Corporations to Collective Bargaining: Organized Labor and the Eclipse of Social Democracy in the Postwar Era," in *The Rise and Fall of the New Deal Order, 1930–1980*, ed. Steve Fraser and Gary Gerstle (Princeton, N.J.: Princeton University Press, 1989), 126. Nelson Lichtenstein, *Walter Reuther: The Most Dangerous Man in Detroit* (Urbana: University of Illinois Press, 1997; originally published as *The Most Dangerous Man in Detroit: Walter Reuther and the Fate of American Labor* [New York: Basic Books, 1995]), 154–74.

32. Brody, "New Deal and World War II," 287.

33. Clive, *State of War*, 25.

34. Ibid., 28.

35. Ibid., 29.

36. Quoted in ibid., 33.

37. Gary Gerstle, *Working-Class Americanism: The Politics of Labor in a Textile City* (New York: Cambridge University Press, 1989), 267.

38. Ibid.

39. Quoted in Richard M. Dalfiume, "The 'Forgotten Years' of the Negro Revolution," *Journal of American History* 55 (1968–69); Brody, "New Deal and World War II," 105–6.

40. Brody, "New Deal and World War II," 272.

41. A confidential survey of public opinion, requested by Roosevelt in June, 1943, found that a substantial portion of people surveyed felt that the administration was "too soft" on strikers (Brody, "New Deal and World War II," 280).

42. Koistinen, "Mobilizing the World War II Economy," 473.

43. Ibid., 477.

44. Seidman, *American Labor*, 31. Weekly earnings may have risen faster than the cost of living, but this may have been due as much to longer hours and overtime as to wage increases.

45. Ibid., 46, citing *Business Week*, Mar. 29, 1941, 64.

46. Ibid., 42.

47. Seidman, *American Labor,* 42–43.

48. *New York Times,* Mar. 29, 1940; Aaron Levenstein, *Labor, Today and Tomorrow* (New York: A. A. Knopf, 1946), 45; Seidman, *American Labor,* 44.

49. Seidman, *American Labor,* 44.

50. Ibid., 48. Tobin's comments must also be seen in light of challenges to the conservative Teamsters Union from within, especially from left-wing militants. As Irving Bernstein has noted, Tobin bided his time until he could destroy the Trotskyite-led Minneapolis local: "The War provided that opportunity." Thus, in 1941 Tobin revoked the local's charter, applying the anti-Communist clause in the IBT constitution to membership in the Socialist Workers' Party. The Trotskyites subsequently joined the CIO, and "violent warfare now broke out between the rival unions and Tobin sent to Minneapolis some of his toughest men, including a young warehouseman, Jimmy Hoffa." In the same year Tobin asked the federal government to intervene against "those disturbers who believe in the policies of foreign, radical governments" during a period when the United States "is in a dangerous position." The federal government indicted twenty-nine members of the Socialist Workers' Party under the Smith Act, including Farrell Dobbs and the Dunne brothers, leading organizers in Minneapolis, and they were subsequently convicted. Attorney General Francis Biddle would later write of his regret over this prosecution, which used federal law in the service of rival unionism (Irving Bernstein, *The Turbulent Years* [Boston: Houghton, Mifflin, 1970], 780–81; Farrell Dobbs, *Teamster Bureaucracy* [New York: Monad Press, 1977]).

51. Seidman, *American Labor,* 43.

52. Phelan, *William Green,* 161–62.

53. Levenstein, *Labor, Today and Tomorrow,* 46.

54. *New York Times,* June 13, 1941, 12:3; cited in Phelan, *William Green,* 162.

55. Zieger, *CIO, 1935–1955,* 121–22, 123–25, 127–30.

56. Ibid., 122.

57. Phelan, *William Green,* 161.

58. Ibid., 162.

59. Levenstein, *Labor, Today and Tomorrow,* 47.

60. Lichtenstein, *Labor's War at Home,* 50–51.

61. The CIO remained skeptical, however, and published a pamphlet in April, "The Right to Strike—Keystone of Liberty," which denounced congressional compulsory arbitration proposals as a step toward "involuntary servitude" (ibid., 51).

62. See National War Labor Board, *The Termination Report of the National War Labor Board. Industrial Disputes and Wage Stabilization in Wartime. January 12, 1942–December 31, 1945,* 3 vols. (Washington, D.C.: Government Printing Office, 1947–48), 2:48.

63. Executive Order 8716, para. 2, 6 Fed. Reg. 1532 (Mar. 19, 1941).

64. The role of the Department of Labor revealed the constant attempts by Secretary Frances Perkins to protect and enlarge the role of her department. See Workman, "Creating the Center," 36–37.

65. The continued creation of agencies without effective enforcement powers needs further study. The argument that state administrative institutions and practices were insufficiently developed does not explain this phenomenon, given the creation of the NLRB and, indeed, the Interstate Commerce Commission.

66. As during the mobilization period, some companies during World War I were seized when they either refused to bargain collectively or would not cease discharging employees who joined unions. See Fred Witney, *Wartime Experiences of the National Labor Relations Board, 1941–1945* (Urbana: University of Illinois Press, 1949), 116.

67. Ibid., 116 n. 4; Edward Shils, Walter J. Gershenfeld, Bernard Ingster, William W. Weinberg, *Industrial Peacemaker: George Taylor's Contribution to Collective Bargaining* (Philadelphia: University of Pennsylvania Press, 1979), 133.

68. Witney, *Wartime Experiences*, 116 n. 5. It was understood that the NWLB would not render decisions which were not in conformity with the policies of the NLRA, although the WLB could request that the NLRB expedite matters within its jurisdictional area. See Executive Order 8716, section 2(e); Witney, *Wartime Experiences*, 117 n. 7.

69. See Witney, *Wartime Experiences*, 117.

70. Seidman, *American Labor*, 56.

71. Ibid., 56. In its first ten months, the board had 118 cases certified to it by the secretary of labor. Wages were an issue in 75 percent of the cases, and 50 percent involved union security. The board settled 96 of its 118 cases. In four troublesome cases, the board sought action by the president (ibid., 59–60).

72. For a summary of Williams Davis's career, see Workman, "Creating the Center," 29–33. See also Ibid., 39–44.

73. This occurred at North American Aviation and Federal Shipbuilding and Dry Dock Company, and in the captive mines dispute where the president's recommendation of arbitration was accepted. In this case, the CIO members of the board had previously resigned because of dissatisfaction with an award of the board involving union security (Witney, *Wartime Experiences*, 104).

74. Nevertheless, Seidman notes that the Defense Mediation Board recommended the clause in relatively few cases (*American Labor*, 62). Only in seven cases out of some fifty-six in which union security was an issue did the board propose membership maintenance and in four cases it explicitly refused to recommend it.

75. The Federal Shipbuilding and Dry Dock Company refused the clause.

Roosevelt met the challenge by seizing the company's plant and the disputed clause was put into effect. The facility was operated by the government for over four months (ibid., 63; Workman, "Creating the Center," 79).

76. Seidman, *American Labor,* 64.

77. Joseph Goulden, *Meany* (New York: Atheneum, 1972), 85–86.

78. The UMW, however, resumed its strike after the board decision. FDR retreated and submitted the proposal to a special arbitration board which, perhaps predictably, granted the union shop in the captive mines on the grounds that it could help build unity and increase production, and, thus, help the nation meet the emergency.

79. Seidman, *American Labor,* 68.

80. Ibid.

81. See Christopher Tomlins, *The State and the Unions* (New York: Cambridge University Press, 1985), 224–30.

82. This assumption seems to undergird many judicial decisions under the NLRA (James Atleson, *Values and Assumptions in American Labor Law* [Amherst: University of Massachusetts Press, 1983], chap. 1). See also James Atleson, "Work Group Behavior and Wildcat Strikes: The Causes and Functions of Industrial Civil Disobedience," *Ohio State Law Review* 34 (1973): 750, 770–72.

83. Congress of Industrial Organizations, "The Right to Strike—Keystone of Liberty" (pamphlet), 1941, 11–12, quoted in Seidman, *American Labor,* 70 n. 17. See also Lichtenstein, *Labor's War at Home,* 51.

84. See Seidman, *American Labor,* 72.

85. Lichtenstein, *Labor's War at Home,* 47–48. Interestingly, the Committee on Manufacture of the United States Chamber of Commerce issued an analysis which suggested that antistrike laws would be ineffective and would deny fundamental rights to citizens. It was not convinced that there was any present need for additional federal legislation and, in particular, any need for antistrike legislation (Levenstein, *Labor, Today and Tomorrow,* 44).

86. Lichtenstein, *Labor's War at Home,* 48.

87. Ibid., 49.

88. See Dobbs, *Teamster Bureaucracy.* See also Bernstein, *Turbulent Years.*

89. Harris, *Right to Manage,* 45. See also Lichtenstein, *Walter Reuther,* 178–83.

90. See Marc Scott Miller, *The Irony of Victory: World War II and Lowell, Massachusetts* (Urbana: University of Illinois Press, 1988), 29–30.

91. Koistinen, "Mobilizing the World War II Economy," 467; Koistinen, *Hammer,* 106.

92. Koistinen, *Hammer,* 110–13. The author notes that the War Department conferred with the national leadership of the UAW, the secretary of labor, Sidney Hillman, and other administration officials.

93. Ibid., 108–9.

94. Steven Fraser, *Labor Will Rule: Sidney Hillman and the Rise of American Labor* (New York: Free Press, 1991), 465; Zieger, *CIO, 1935–1955*, 127–30.

95. Josephson, *Sidney Hillman*, 544.

96. Fraser, *Labor Will Rule*, 465.

97. Roger Keeran, *The Communist Party and the Auto Workers Unions* (Bloomington: Indiana University Press, 1980), 212–18.

98. Lichtenstein, *Labor's War at Home*, 60–62.

99. Josephson, *Sidney Hillman*, 544–46. See also Lichtenstein, *Walter Reuther*, 182–83.

100. During this period, however, significant union gains occurred. Perhaps a million and a half members were added to trade union roles. Ford and the Little Steel companies, among others, were organized.

3

The Response to War

Six days after Pearl Harbor, President Roosevelt, like Woodrow Wilson before him, issued a call for a conference of representatives of labor and management. In issuing the proclamation convening the conference, the president declared that he desired speed, a complete agreement that all wartime disputes would be settled peacefully, and a no-strike pledge.[1] The subsequent conference, which consisted of twelve labor representatives and an equal number from management, recommended the creation of a wartime labor board having jurisdiction over all issues, but no agreement was reached on the critical and contentious issue of union security. The president accepted the conference's agreement and short-circuited the politically sticky union security issue by interpreting the conference report as meaning that "all disputes," including the union security controversy, were within the jurisdiction of the new war labor board.[2]

Union leaders had independently acted to grant no-strike promises even prior to the conference. A week after Congress's declaration that a state of war existed, William Green called a special session of the AFL's executive council, which ordered "that a 'no-strike' policy shall be applied in all war and defense material production industries." A meeting of representatives from all the AFL unions endorsed the statement, urging that no repressive legislation should be passed and, oddly, that the right to strike as a last resort weapon be safeguarded.[3] "Labor will produce, and produce without interruption," promised William Green.[4] Similarly, the CIO pledged its assistance in achieving "all-out production for the national defense," but cautioned that it would defend the "material interests of the working people and their democratic rights."[5] Murray stated soon after Pearl Harbor that

"Labor is determined to place itself in the forefront in the battle of achieving maximum production."[6]

Since American involvement in World War II was caused by an attack on an American military base, union leaders apparently assumed membership support and a need for quick action. Apparently, no union consulted its membership in advance or afterward.[7] The no-strike pledge was theoretically a voluntary surrender of labor's most important right, yet the government deemed it compulsory.[8] The pledge reflected labor's desire to demonstrate support for the war effort, but also the fear of legislative restrictions, a fear demonstrated during the mobilization period. By late 1941, Congress was considering legislation to outlaw strikes and to conscript, and thereby pacify, industrial workers.[9] There were virtually no strikes for several weeks after Pearl Harbor, and, as noted earlier, the Senate shelved the Smith bill, which the House had passed just prior to Pearl Harbor.[10]

The war necessitated a major expansion of the federal role in labor-management relations. A number of wartime agencies were quickly created to manage the nation's response to war. One of the most important, the National War Labor Board, was formally created on January 12, 1942, by the tersely worded Executive Order 9017.[11] Following the New Deal structure of pre-NLRB labor relations agencies and the NDMB, the new War Labor Board was to be tripartite, composed of twelve members, of which four each would represent labor, management, and the public. William Davis, the former chair of the NDMB, was named chair. The other public members were George W. Taylor, Frank P. Graham, and Wayne L. Morse. Should a dispute threaten to interrupt work related to war production, the parties were initially required to attempt to settle the dispute by direct negotiation.[12] If this failed, the executive order required that the parties seek the aid of the Federal Conciliation Service of the Department of Labor. Should the Conciliation Service be unsuccessful in effecting a settlement, the secretary of labor was required to certify the dispute to the board.

Once the board assumed jurisdiction, its power to resolve the dispute was all-encompassing. The board was authorized to reach a final settlement of labor disputes which might interrupt any work "which contributes to the effective prosecution of the war." Unlike the National Labor Relations Board, the War Labor Board's responsibility extended to the actual settlement of disputes by "mediation, voluntary arbitration, or arbitration." Indeed, the president ordered the board "to finally determine the dispute, and for this purpose [to] use mediation, voluntary arbitration, or arbitration."[13] The War Labor Board, therefore, had more complete authority than either the National Defense Mediation Board which preceded it or the World War I National

Labor Board. As subsequently elucidated by the 1943 War Labor Disputes Act, the War Labor Board had the power "to decide the dispute and provide by order the wages and hours and all other terms and conditions (customarily included in collective bargaining agreements) governing the relations between the parties" and to "provide for terms and conditions to govern relations between the parties which are to be fair and equitable between an employer and an employee under all the circumstances of the case."[14]

Congress was not initially requested to provide legislative sanctions, but the fact that the United States was at war, in addition to the enormous increase in presidential power, made the War Labor Board far stronger and more prestigious than its predecessor during the mobilization period. Ultimately, however, its powers were supported by public opinion and the threat of seizure.[15]

The National War Labor Board largely determined the wartime terms of employment in American industry, and wartime regulation had permanent consequences for mass production unionism. As Nelson Lichtenstein has noted in his impressive study of wartime labor, "It was the specific social and political context of World War II that created the institutional framework for the kind of collective bargaining that evolved in the decade or so after the war."[16] The National War Labor Board, for instance, helped to set industry-wide wage patterns, legitimized fringe benefits bargaining, strongly encouraged arbitration as a method of resolving contractual disputes, and influenced the internal structure and role of the new unions, primarily through the grant of union security clauses. On the other hand, the problem of delay necessarily weakened the impact of many War Labor Board decisions.[17] In one noteworthy case, for example, the board received a dispute in 1942 involving the West Coast longshore industry and employer attempts to regain some control over hiring halls and discipline. The board's decision was not reached until October 1944.[18]

In its first three years, the WLB decided fourteen thousand dispute cases, affecting a majority of the organized workers in the country.[19] There were twenty-five occasions when government seizure was invoked to enforce compliance. In thirty-one cases in which the board called on the president for enforcement action, seventeen involved union defiance and fourteen employer refusal. In four cases the workers backed down, and in one the employer retreated before the president acted.[20] Not only was a firm foundation created for the CIO but wartime regulation had permanent consequences for mass production unionism.

Until recently, the WLB has been universally praised for its wisdom and prudence.[21] Thomas Brooks, to choose only one example, believed that "maintenance of membership," the WLB's response to union claims for institutional security, "helped dovetail the 'New Unionism' into the new corporatism."[22] That is, what unions deemed "industrial democracy" was viewed by sophisticated management as a practical means for handling the personnel problems that could no longer be resolved in a face-to-face manner. The crucial issues were not seen as substantive but, instead, were the means by which disputes could be resolved. Collective bargaining became a system for drawing up the rules for employment, and the job of unions was to see that those rules were followed.[23] The usefulness of unions in this new role was made clear during the war because of the influx of new and what were believed to have been undisciplined workers.

The generally salutary view of wartime labor regulation taken by some historians is generally based on trade union growth during the war: "Union memberships swelled from about 10.5 million when the Japanese bombed Pearl Harbor to about 14.75 million when the war ended in August 1945. The new industrial unions of the CIO were firmly established in auto, rubber, steel, and other mass production industries. The craft unions of the AFL were even more firmly entrenched and were organizing on an industrial basis as well. Union officials, as members of wartime advisory boards, gained a prestige they had not had before the war."[24]

In addition, Brooks noted that "the WLB had corrected wage inequities, set equal pay for equal work for women workers, allowed a pattern of fringe benefits to emerge, and made increases to prevent substandard living."[25] Because of the enormous increase of war-related production, the war itself clearly helped to strengthen organized labor. For instance, the war basically ended unemployment, which had not fallen below 10 percent throughout the entire decade of the 1930s. Moreover, tens of thousands of workers in the mass production industries were unionized for the first time along industrial lines. Indeed, by the end of the war over 80 percent of the workers in basic manufacturing were unionized.[26]

Many policies of the War Labor Board aided unions and eventually became the staples of postwar bargaining. For instance, the WLB granted union demands for automatic wage progression, which restricted some customary management techniques to control labor costs, and it also granted and stabilized various kinds of fringe benefits such as shift differentials, sick leaves, holidays, and vacations. Creativity in fringe benefits was encouraged by the WLB's severe restrictions on wartime wage increases.[27]

World War II had a powerful impact on industrial workers and the CIO. For workers it brought four years of relatively full employment and heftier pay packets. It eroded traditional ethnic identities and encouraged the development of broad notions of racial and religious toleration. It brought workers forcefully into a mobile, consumerist, syncretic culture and into far more regular and intimate contact with the national government than ever before. Conflict and disruption accompanied these changes, but the industrial working class that emerged from the global conflict was less provincial, more tolerant and more expectant of material gain than it had been in 1940. It was at once more regimented, better organized, and less willing to put up with scarcity, unemployment and hard times.[28]

The wartime period is more complex, however, as there were losses as well as gains. The Wagner Act survived the war, only to be significantly altered by Taft-Hartley in 1947. But by this time some of its critical aims had already been ignored, and values which arguably conflicted with the statute's goals had been read in by the judiciary.[29] But the war period is critical to an understanding of the terms and ideas which ultimately shaped the law under both the Wagner Act and its later amendment in 1947.[30]

Four aspects of wartime governmental regulation will be especially stressed for their effect and long-range significance: the National War Labor Board's encouragement of arbitration, its position on managerial prerogatives, and its policies on strikes and union security. In addition, the discussion will deal with scope of wartime strikes, their causes, and the government's responses. Concededly, focusing on these matters ignores wage stabilization issues which seem to have accounted for the bulk of its work. The War Labor Board's *Termination Report* devotes a little over one hundred pages to the settlement of disputes and nonwage issues, while wage matters take up two hundred pages. Many cases involved both wage and nonwage issues, yet only 17 percent of the WLB's caseload involved solely nonwage issues and 40 percent of the cases involved only wage issues.[31] Even as to nonwage issues, the matters which will be discussed, except for union security, constitute only a small portion of the board's work.[32]

Focusing on the WLB admittedly slights other agencies, for instance those dealing with production and manpower, which significantly affected labor and labor relations during the war and, perhaps, afterwards as well. The War Manpower Commission, for instance, struggled with the problem of labor scarcity and issued rulings establishing the standard workday and limiting labor mobility. The War Production Board, established in January 1942, dealt with the conversion of production facilities from civilian to military use. The WPB pressured unions to forgo established premium pay practices and to avoid production-based or incentive wage payment plans.

The War Production Board was also a supporter of labor-management cooperation. By early 1942 the WPB urged the formation of labor-management production committees in order to increase production. Chairman Nelson of the War Production Board felt compelled to say that the proposal was solely designed to increase production and that it did not "put labor into management or . . . management into labor."[33] Like the WLB, governmental agencies exhibited a highly cautious attitude toward areas deemed by employers to be within their prerogatives. In both labor and management the reaction "ranged from enthusiasm to skepticism or even hostility. To some labor groups the proposal sounded simply like a speed-up device, or one that would degenerate into company unionism. Many employers, on the other hand, feared the entry of labor into an area of decision-making that in their view belonged to management alone, or hesitated to establish machinery that might increase union prestige."[34]

There were almost three thousand labor-management committees covering four million workers in existence by the end of 1942. These committees dealt with production scheduling and absenteeism, turnover and health, but they generally avoided overlap with collective bargaining questions paralleling the modern Quality of Work Life Programs.[35] The Conciliation Service tried to end difficulties by insisting on factory-level joint committees for discussions and grievances and was "credited with keeping many steel-mill production schedules on course." Mark Reutter has stated that the service received twenty calls a day from management and labor in the Pittsburgh district alone.[36] Few of the joint committees were continued after the war's end, and workplace participation was not to return as a serious labor relations issue until the 1980s.

The Office of War Mobilization, created in May 1943, was a kind of superagency, serving as an arbiter of last resort in disputes among government officials, military procurement chiefs, and civilian producers. The Office of Price Administration initiated price, rent, and wage controls and implemented a system of rationing.[37] In addition, other agencies may have been more critical than the War Labor Board in particular industries.[38] For example, an important legal battle fought by the United Mine Workers throughout the 1940s involved the definition of work and of the workday under the Fair Labor Standards Act. Much of this dispute was phrased in "portal to portal" terms, that is, whether worktime should include travel time from plant or mine entrances to work stations.[39]

One example dramatically highlights the effect of the pressures of the wartime era and the union response. In 1942 the War Production Board put pressure on unions to eliminate premium pay provisions in existing contracts. These contractual clauses, usually mandating time and a half for work done on Saturday and double time on Sunday, represented successful attempts by industrial unions to discourage weekend operation, or at least to reward workers for it, and also to encourage the spreading of existing work. Employers, however, now argued that premium pay retarded seven-days-a-week operation in defense plants, an argument which seemingly overlooked the generous cost-plus agreements made by the government. Legislation was introduced to suspend such pay as well as time and a half for work in excess of forty hours.[40] Under intense pressure, the CIO, heavily involved in military production, agreed on March 24, 1943, to capitulate.[41] The UAW and other unions, however, were soon embarrassed by craft unions, such as the International Association of Machinists (IAM), which were more reluctant to trade off economic interests during the war. Many IAM lodges refused to relinquish premium pay despite the government's request, and the issue often surfaced as an issue in representation elections where the IAM and UAW were rivals.[42]

In a classic example of the union's growing reliance upon government, the UAW sought government aid against this form of embarrassment and interunion rivalry. The UAW's Buffalo local, for instance, petitioned the NLRB to void an election in which the IAM was successful, arguing that the IAM had "deliberately spread confusion and disruption with subversive propaganda against the government's war policies on overtime pay."[43] Belatedly, the UAW voted at its August 1942 convention to rescind its abandonment of premium pay unless all other unions complied, a pointed reference to the IAM. Subsequently, CIO leaders pressured FDR to order an end to all contractual provisions providing for premium pay.[44] Roosevelt eventually responded with Executive Order 9240, which restricted premium pay for work on Saturdays and Sundays, thus taking the heat off the UAW and other CIO unions which had voluntarily surrendered premium pay.[45] The executive order noted that "many labor organizations have already adopted the patriotic policy of waiving double time compensation or other premium pay for work on Saturday, Sunday and holidays . . . for the duration of the War," and that it was necessary to insure "uniformity and fair treatment" by stipulating uniform policies.

A number of unions were willing to give away important benefits for the duration of the war. The United Electrical Workers (UE), for instance, proposed a 15 percent increase in output and cooperation with employers. Vacations were surrendered, and the international called for only cost-of-living wage increases.[46] Despite this, Fillipelli and McCulloch argue that "wartime contracts in the UE and other left-wing unions did not cede increased prerogatives to management, nor did they weaken workers' protection in the grievance process."[47]

Despite the lid placed upon wages and the pressure to end premium pay, managerial salaries were apparently another matter. The president initially limited managerial salaries so that they could not exceed the highest level between January 1 and September 15, 1942, unless companies obtained the approval of the Treasury's Salaries Stabilization Unit.[48] Businessmen violently and unsurprisingly denounced the president's action. By a vote of 268 to 129, the House of Representatives set aside the limitation; in the Senate there were only three dissenting votes. As WLB chairman Davis dryly stated in a letter to Vice President Henry Wallace, "We have become increasingly conscious of the fact that we are asking one segment of our society to do its part to protect all Americans from the ravages of inflation, while, at the same time, our similar obligation has not been placed as heavily upon the shoulders of some of the other segments of this society."[49]

Such incidents led union leaders to be increasingly wary of governmental economic regulation, despite union gains. The most objectionable policy of the WLB to labor was the restriction on wages and, especially, the formula developed to implement the government's anti-inflation policy. The "Little Steel" formula, implemented in July 1942, provided that wages could not be increased more than 15 percent, the increase in the cost of living between January 1, 1941, and May 1, 1942.[50] No other government policy so seriously invaded deeply held union prerogatives. Green, for instance, wrote FDR a letter highly critical of the "invasion of labor's basic rights. It is not necessary to freeze wages and suspend collective bargaining in order to prevent inflation."[51] The sense of betrayal, of falling behind while employer profits skyrocketed, was to become a significant cause of labor unrest during the war. On top of the no-strike pledge, the formula meant that labor was not going to be able to use its clout during the war to increase its share of wealth, and, second, that wages were to be tied to the cost of living. The major role of the WLB, therefore, was to limit strikes and fight inflation. Limited by the pledge, and with wage increases severely limited by the state, "unions had to depend on the goodwill of the war agencies for whatever gains or protections they hoped to secure."[52]

Notes

1. Fred Witney, *Wartime Experiences of the National Labor Relations Board, 1941–1945* (Urbana: University of Illinois Press, 1949), 118.

2. Ibid., 118–19; Joel Seidman, *American Labor from Defense to Reconversion* (Chicago: University of Chicago Press, 1953), 80–81.

3. Seidman, *American Labor*, 78.

4. *New York Times*, Dec. 17, 1941, 1:1; cited in Craig Phelan, *William Green: Biography of a Labor Leader* (Albany: State University of New York Press, 1989), 163. Green also called for a quid pro quo—as during World War I, the government should provide labor with representation on all defense agencies. The AFL never gave a no-strike pledge in World War I, although Samuel Gompers strove to secure the AFL's support for the war effort (David Montgomery, *The Fall of the House of Labor* [New York: Cambridge University Press, 1987], 375).

5. *CIO News*, Dec. 15, 1941; Seidman, *American Labor*, 78–79.

6. Robert H. Zieger, *The CIO, 1935–1955* (Chapel Hill: University of North Carolina Press, 1995), 143. Victor Reuther stated that the war "was just another phase of the long historical struggle of people to free themselves from authoritarian rule and win a measure of individual freedom."

7. Martin Glaberman, *Wartime Strikes: The Struggle against the No-Strike Pledge in the UAW during World War II* (Detroit: Bewick Editions, 1980), 4–5.

8. Howell John Harris, *The Right to Manage: Industrial Relations Policies of American Business in the 1940s* (Madison: University of Wisconsin Press, 1982), 47.

9. Alan Brinkley, *The End of Reform: New Deal Liberalism in Recession and War* (New York: Alfred A. Knopf, 1995), 210.

10. Seidman, *American Labor*, 80–81.

11. National War Labor Board, *The Termination Report of the National War Labor Board. Industrial Disputes and Wage Stabilization in Wartime. January 12, 1942–December 31, 1945*, 3 vols. (Washington, D.C.: Government Printing Office, 1947–48), 2:49.

12. Executive Order 9017, para. 3, 7 Fed. Reg. 237 (1942).

13. Executive Order 9017, section 3, 3 C.F.R. 1075 (1938–43 compilation).

14. Public Law No. 89, 59 Stat. 163 (1943). The statute was commonly referred to as the Smith-Connally Act.

15. See Witney, *Wartime Experiences of the NLRB*, 119 n. 25.

16. Nelson Lichtenstein, "Industrial Democracy, Contract Unionism and the National War Labor Board," *Labor Law Journal* 33 (Aug. 1982), 524.

17. By December 1942, the pressure of the WLB's caseload led to a reconstitution of the ten regional advisory boards into regional war labor boards with authority to make decisions on labor disputes and wage issues. The WLB would primarily serve as an appellate body, although it often assumed original jurisdiction over cases which would have national importance (National War Labor Board, *Termination Report*, 1:12–13).

18. Charles P. Larrowe, *Harry Bridges: The Rise and Fall of Radical Labor in the United States* (New York: Lawrence Hill & Co., 1972), 251–57. See also Marc Scott Miller, *The Irony of Victory* (Urbana: University of Illinois Press, 1988), 32–34.

19. Aaron Levenstein, *Labor, Today and Tomorrow* (New York: A. A. Knopf, 1946),

53. The relationship of the NWLB and the NLRB is discussed in Witney, *Wartime Experiences of the NLRB*. Witney notes that the WLB "broadly construed its powers and took action over some matters normally subject to N.L.R.B. authority," including directing the reinstatement of employees discriminatorily discharged and ordering employers to bargain with certified unions. The power to designate bargaining units, conduct representation elections, and certify successful unions, however, was left in NLRB hands (149–50).

20. See Levenstein, *Labor, Today and Tomorrow*, 53.

21. The public members, according to George Taylor, had the responsibility of not favoring "the extreme position of either side; that would have broken it up in no time. Our job was to come up with a proposal, one side would vote with you for, and the other wouldn't withdraw. Those are the parameters in which we worked." Taylor said that "our threat always was, 'you had better go along with us, or else Congress will move in on you.' If Congress moved in, especially in the early days of the war, ye gads!" (quoted in Joseph Goulden, *Meany* [New York: Atheneum, 1972], 95).

22. Thomas Brooks, *Toil and Trouble: A History of American Labor* (New York: Delacorte, 1965), 204. "Maintenance of membership" was the board's favored form of union security, following the policy of the NDMB, and it meant that union members had to "maintain" their union membership for the duration of the agreement (Marshall Field & Co., 1 War Labor Rep. 47 [1942]). Although the weakest possible form of union security, maintenance of membership was perceived as better than nothing, and the board made clear it was not going to grant closed shop clauses. The clause was often tied to the mandatory checkoff of dues, thus strengthening unions financially and relieving them of confrontations with individual members for dues. With the split of the CIO from the AFL, the significance of union security increased because it now also protected unions from raids by rival unions. See Seidman, *American Labor*, 91–108.

23. See David Feller, "A General Theory of the Collective Bargaining Agreement," *California Law Review* 61 (1973): 663.

24. Brooks, *Toil and Trouble*, 207.

25. Ibid.

26. Patrick Renshaw, "Organized Labour and the United States War Economy," *Journal of Contemporary History* 21 (1986): 3.

27. Harris, *Right to Manage*, 57. Harris notes WLB support for multiplant and even multifirm bargaining units.

28. Zieger, *CIO, 1935–1955*, 141.

29. James Atleson, *Values and Assumptions in American Labor Law* (Amherst: University of Massachusetts Press, 1983).

30. See James Atleson, "Wartime Labor Regulation, the Industrial Pluralists, and the Law of Collective Bargaining," in *Industrial Democracy*, ed. Nelson Lichtenstein and Howell John Harris (New York: Cambridge University Press, 1993).

31. National War Labor Board, *Termination Report*, 1:489.

32. Ibid., 1:492.

33. Seidman, *American Labor,* 177.

34. Ibid.

35. Ibid., 178.

36. Mark Reutter, *Sparrows Point* (New York: Summit Books, 1988), 305–6.

37. Zieger, *CIO, 1935–1955,* 164.

38. See Larrowe, *Harry Bridges,* 251–57.

39. For a thorough and fascinating analysis of these disputes see Mark Lindner, "Class Origins at the Door: The Origins of the Portal-to-Portal Act of 1947," *Buffalo Law Review* 39 (1991): 53.

40. Nelson Lichtenstein, *Labor's War at Home: The CIO in World War II* (New York: Cambridge University Press, 1982), 96–97.

41. Ibid., 98.

42. Ibid., 103; Zieger, *CIO, 1935–1955,* 167.

43. Lichtenstein, *Labor's War at Home,* 103–4.

44. Zieger, *CIO, 1935–1955,* 107; Nelson Lichtenstein, *Walter Reuther: The Most Dangerous Man in Detroit* (Urbana: University of Illinois Press, 1997; originally published as *The Most Dangerous Man in Detroit: Walter Reuther and the Fate of American Labor* [New York: Basic Books, 1995]), 197–98.

45. National War Labor Board, *Termination Report,* 2:656. The order was amended by Executive Order 9248, 7 Fed. Reg. 7419 (1942), and Executive Order 9340, 8 Fed. Reg. 5695 (1943).

46. Ronald L. Fillipelli and Mark D. McCulloch, *Cold War in the Working Class: The Rise and Decline of the United Electrical Workers* (Albany: State University of New York Press, 1995), 78.

47. Ibid., 79.

48. Levenstein, *Labor, Today and Tomorrow,* 90.

49. Quoted in ibid., 92; see Lichtenstein, *Labor's War at Home,* 106.

50. Lichtenstein, *Labor's War at Home,* 70. For some, like the miners, it meant no wage increases at all because they had won a 16 percent increase in 1941 (Brinkley, *End of Reform,* 210–11).

51. Cited in Phelan, *William Green,* 165.

52. Brinkley, *End of Reform,* 212.

4

The War Labor Board and the
Law of Collective Bargaining

[T]he Board has turned out relatively little that is new. On the contrary it has relied upon industrial experience as the primary source of its rulings, and has turned to the best practices of employers and unions, developed through years of collective bargaining and of trial and error, as guides for the solution of present-day controversies.
—Lloyd K. Garrison, public member, statement before the American Management Association, New York City, May 24, 1944; quoted in National War Labor Board, *Termination Report*, 1:65

The basis for the national war labor policy in America today is still the voluntary agreement between the responsible leaders of labor and industry that there be no strikes or lockouts for the duration of the war. All labor disputes, including grievances, therefore, must be settled by peaceful means.
—Statement of the War Labor Board, July 1, 1943, quoted in ibid.

Since the end of World War II, labor relations theory and the law of collective bargaining have been closely intertwined. Both systems are premised upon the stabilizing influence of unions, collective bargaining, and arbitration. Yet, the industrial and economic convolutions of the 1980s and 1990s have created a crisis in the once unchallenged orthodoxy that has until recently constituted industrial relations thought.

A loose-knit group of postwar scholars and practitioners, often characterized as "industrial pluralists," are largely responsible for the body of rules regulating collective bargaining, as well as the supportive vision of industrial relations.[1] This group developed a set of assumptions about the necessary legal structure of collective bargaining, its regulation, and the appropriate forms of dispute resolution, which has been clearly reflected in the Supreme Court decisions of the late 1950s and 1960s. Although strongly supporting the right to strike for collective agreements, the group believed that disputes over the meaning and application of contractual provisions should be exclusively resolved by grievance and arbitration procedures. The pluralist vision would affect the federal judiciary, which defined in this period the legal structure of collective bargaining, creating a system dominated by the promotion of arbitral settlement of contract disputes and the discouragement of collective action for the resolution of such disputes.[2]

Industrial pluralist thought had much in common with consensus theories in other disciplines in the 1940s and 1950s, combining a search for peaceful dispute resolution mechanisms with a reluctance to discuss existing imbalances in power or issues of class. The industrial pluralists focused upon the creation of legal rules and administrative processes to resolve workplace conflicts. Pluralists believed, as did Robert Wagner, that bargaining would only occur if unions possessed the right to strike. The predominant device to resolve disputes once a contract was in place, however, was to be arbitration, a private mechanism that could supplant self-help, judicial intervention, or administrative regulation. The pluralists desired to humanize and regularize the workplace, transforming "the anarchy of the marketplace, which exploited workers, into the harmony of a 'modern' cooperative capitalism, which protected workers."[3] The views of the pluralists themselves can perhaps be traced to the Wisconsin School and John Commons and also to prewar theories of efficient, administrative resolution of industrial relations.[4]

Many of the pluralists were in government positions during World War II, a period in which it was critical to find efficient systems for the resolution of labor disputes which would serve as alternatives to strikes. Labor lawyers and economists, often very young and sometimes just out of college, supplied the demand for wartime specialists. The first public members of agencies such as the National War Labor Board were men who were or became skilled in mediation and arbitration. As characterized by Howell Harris: "They were liberal pluralists, committed to the development of a labor relation system in which the triple objectives of efficiency, order, and representative democracy could be reconciled. They believed in the Wagner Act's legislative philosophy, and in strong, responsible unions as agents for its implementation. They preferred to see industrial disputes settled in decentralized, voluntarist negotiations between the parties rather than on terms imposed by the state from the center, or unilaterally determined by employers."[5]

One of the War Labor Board's most important and enduring contributions was the development of a group of experienced arbitrators who profoundly affected postwar labor law and practice. As Edwin Witte noted in 1952, the "great majority of the labor arbitrators of the present day gained their first direct experience in service on the staff of the War Labor Board or on its disputes panels."[6] With much justification, a speaker at an early meeting of the National Academy of Arbitrators greeted his audience as "The War Labor Board Alumni Association."[7]

The academy's first president, Ralph T. Seward, for instance, had been executive secretary of the National Defense Mediation Board and a public member of its successor, the War Labor Board. In 1944 he became the impartial umpire for General Motors and the UAW. William Simkin, one of the academy's first vice presidents and later president, had been chairman of the Shipbuilding Commission and associate member of the War Labor Board. The academy's original board of governors was also filled with veterans of wartime Washington. Although not active in the formation of the National Academy of Arbitrators, George W. Taylor often spoke at early meetings and helped draft the code of ethics eventually accepted by the academy as well as by the American Arbitration Association and the Federal Mediation and Conciliation Service.

Influential scholars and writers gained experience in the wartime agency, including Benjamin Aaron, David L. Cole, G. Allan Dash, Alex Elson, Nathan E. Finesinger, Jesse Freiden, Alexander H. Frey, Sylvester S. Garrett, Jr., Lloyd Garrison, Lewis M. Gill, James J. Healy, Theodore W. Kheel, Thomas E. Larkin, Eli Rock, Peter Seitz, Harry Shulman, and W. Willard Wirtz. In addition, WLB staff positions were filled by individuals who would become influential in labor history, economics, and labor relations, such as E. Wright Bakke, Douglas V. Brown, John T. Dunlop, George H. Hildebrand, Louis Jaffe, Vernon H. Jenson, Clark Kerr, Richard Lester, E. Robert Livernash, Lester B. Orfield, Sumner H. Slichter, Edwin H. Witte, and Dale Yoder.[8]

This group of scholars and writers created an impressive body of private law, including fair and humane restrictions upon employer disciplinary power. In addition, the pluralists and the War Labor Board deferred to the power of owners and managers to direct their enterprises, but qualified the arbitrary exercise of such power by insisting that responsible unions have a voice in the determination of those conditions of employment which did not invade the protective zone of managerial prerogative.[9] Management's role was to organize and direct the production process, but this power was to be circumscribed by the rules and past practices established through collective bargaining. The union's role, therefore, was to police the employer's compliance with the rules which had been negotiated.[10]

Consistent with these views, the War Labor Board helped to institutionalize the critical assumption of contract administration—management acts and the union can only grieve, one of the central premises of postwar pluralist thought. Management, therefore, has the critical right of initiation; the union can seek redress, but not through self-help. The strike, or the threat to strike, would make bargaining work, but it was not to be a part of contract administration.

The exigencies of wartime stressed productivity and the critical need for labor peace, profoundly shaping pluralists' views on arbitration and collective bargaining. This group would become the most influential postwar writers and practitioners of labor law and labor relations as well as arbitrators. Indeed, the writings and decisions of these arbitrators and scholars form the basic structure of arbitration law today. Younger arbitrators follow their teachings, which are codified in various treatises or handbooks used by the parties as well as arbitrators. Indeed, by virtue of long acceptance as well as persuasive reasoning, these ideas and decisions become part of the context in which collective agreements are created and applied. Most importantly, this group is the crucial link which explains why the current law dealing with the enforcement and application of collective agreements mirrors the web of rules created by the War Labor Board.

This chapter and the following focus upon two areas of War Labor Board jurisprudence and their current parallels. The first area concerns the administration and enforcement of collective agreements, and the second deals with the range of subjects falling within the scope of mandatory bargaining under the National Labor Relations Act. Prior to the Taft-Hartley Act of 1947, there was little federal law defining the scope of collective bargaining or the means by which agreements could be enforced.[11] The Wagner Act of 1935 required employers to bargain in good faith, and the Supreme Court had made collective agreements predominant over individual contracts of employment.[12] The act, however, did not focus upon dispute resolution, and certainly not upon arbitration, except for its general encouragement of collective bargaining. The administration and enforcement of collective agreements was necessarily left to the vagaries of state law.[13]

State courts, however, had initially encountered difficulty envisioning collective bargaining agreements as enforceable contracts, or unions as proper vindicators of employment rights. Although some courts began to enforce agreements against employers in the 1920s and 1930s, belatedly paralleling the traditional willingness to enjoin breaches of contract by unions or to enjoin strikes, promises to arbitrate were not enforceable in most states.[14] Since the enactment of the Taft-Hartley Act, however, one of the most creative and vital areas of federal labor policy has concerned the contractual relationship of employers and unions, and the views of the judiciary have been profoundly affected by the writings of the pluralists. The source of judicial power is section 301, enacted as part of the Taft-Hartley amendments of 1947, which permits unions and employers, and employees as well, to bring actions in federal court to enforce collective agreements. To find the statute constitutional, the Supreme Court was moved to hold that federal courts were empowered to create substantive law, that is, judicially created policies that would define the nature of "mature" collective bargaining agreements, their methods of enforcement, and the remedies for breach.[15]

The War Labor Board would vitally affect the incidence and structure of arbitration during, as well as after, the war. In addition, as the following chapter will reveal, the War Labor Board would adopt a restrictive view of the scope of mandatory bargaining, that is, the WLB limited the subjects upon which employers were legally compelled to bargain. Although the postwar NLRB would adopt a less limited view of such bargaining, the notion that a vague zone of managerial exclusivity existed stems from several key War Labor Board decisions.

World War II required unprecedented efforts to maintain and stimulate production. The War Labor Board believed that "Maximum production during the war is a duty; the duty is not discharged when production is impaired by lowered morale or strikes caused by the failure to settle grievances. The duty to achieve and maintain production implies, therefore, the establishment of grievance procedures and the prompt settlement of grievances according to that procedure."[16] Labor arbitration, backed by federal support, required stable unions, both to effectuate such procedures and also to contain rank-and-file militance. The war, therefore, provided a rational basis for stressing bureaucratic dispute resolution, the restriction of midterm strikes, and union control over rank-and-file action. More broadly, the war itself affected the way Americans viewed labor, and the images created extended *after* the war. After the emergency ended, the "needs of the peacetime economy" replaced the requirements of war, and federal policy continued to be based upon increased and continuous production and the stability of labor relations as well as unions.

The underlying themes of contemporary law were not, of course, exclusively created in wartime, for many of the underlying values in American labor law long predate federal statutes.[17] The war, however, helped to create, encourage, or cement visions of the proper labor-management system and the appropriate role of the state. The War Labor Board helped advance a definition of industrial democracy exclusively in process terms—outcomes or fairness were to be irrelevant. Postwar labor law has proceeded in a similar fashion.[18] In addition, the Supreme Court in the postwar period has, like the War Labor Board, repeatedly demonstrated its opposition to collective action or self-help in the resolution of labor disputes which could be settled via contractual grievance procedures.[19] Self-help is opposed in industrial disputes when "private" and "peaceful" avenues of resolution, such as arbitration, exist. The result is a set of rules which protect the "integrity" of arbitration, permitting this institution to carry out federal policy.

ARBITRATION: THE INDISPENSABLE TOOL

Although grievance procedures and arbitration clauses were included in some prewar collective bargaining agreements,[20] and may well have flourished even without the strong encouragement of the War Labor Board, "it was left to the War Labor Board to convince American industry and labor that here was an indispensable tool to 'make collective bargaining work.'"[21] As a WLB statement noted in July 1943: "The basis for the national war labor policy in America today is still the voluntary agreement between the responsible leaders of labor and industry that there be no strikes or lockouts for the duration of the war. All labor disputes, including grievances, therefore, must be settled by peaceful means."[22] The War Labor Board stressed the indispensable value of grievance and arbitration procedures for resolving contractual disputes, refined the structure and scope of such procedures, forced the system on unwilling employers, and provided rules for legal enforcement that would eventually be adopted by the Supreme Court almost twenty years later.

"Arbitration" has had various meanings, extending from mediation to any dispute resolution system involving binding determination by a neutral third party. Labor arbitration as used here, and as it is commonly understood, refers to the resolution of disputes over the meaning or application of collective agreements. This is often referred to as "rights" arbitration to distinguish it from third-party determination of new contract terms, referred to as "interest" arbitration. Although the WLB was empowered to resolve disputes which had reached impasse over new and proposed contract terms, it was involved in "rights" arbitration in two ways. First, it often appointed arbitrators to hear and decide contract disputes, that is, disputes over the meaning of existing agreements. In addition, it encouraged or forced parties to set up private grievance and arbitral systems to resolve "rights" disputes.

Even without government encouragement, grievance procedures provided advantages for unions and employers. Although employers generally resisted arbitration both prior to and during the war, arbitral systems provided an orderly means to resolve contractual disputes in place of strikes or other job actions, and they also served to enforce a system of rules for both employees and managerial personnel. A private system of rules was important for unions as well in order to protect employees from arbitrary supervisory behavior. Unions also found it valuable to have a means which avoided the constant need to consider strikes over every dispute. As Sidney Lens persuasively argued forty years ago, arbitration procedures were not necessarily reflective of a loss of union power. Unions cannot strike over every dispute, and a grievance procedure "offers an opportunity for realignment of forces, for fencing minor skirmishing, for strengthening of positions." A well-operating and effective grievance procedure, therefore, continues membership support during the life of a contract: "The grievance procedure in actual practice is used as a weapon . . . as a way to muster strength for class warfare."[23] In short, the existence of arbitration procedures helps shield union leadership from the constant pressure to take or support workplace action, a consideration which helps explain the support for arbitration by some unions even before the war.

In 1937, the autoworkers and General Motors agreed to establish a multistep grievance procedure ending in arbitration. The agreement provided for the exhaustion of the grievance procedure before a strike could occur, but disputes were referred to arbitration only by mutual agreement. The result proved unsatisfactory and only two cases were arbitrated between 1937 and 1940. In the latter year the parties agreed on the establishment of an umpire to whom complaints of alleged violations of the contract would be referred, coupled with the prohibitions of strikes over those questions.[24] The agreement expressly limited the arbitrator to disputes over the interpretation of the agreement, a notion which was to become standard by war's end.[25]

Grievance procedures tend to centralize dispute resolution in the union hierarchy, not in the affected work group, and the union generally controls the extent to which grievances will be pursued.[26] Indeed, the normal multitiered grievance process exactly mirrors the hierarchies of both employer and union. Unions, however, defended institutional control as democratic because the representative of the employees controlled the dispute, and arbitration would serve as a judicial-like restraint upon managerial excess. This argument nicely meshes with the view of industrial democracy held by the War Labor Board and the postwar Supreme Court, focusing less on worker participation and influence than on routine and peaceful processing of grievances.[27] Notions of hierarchy and control were embedded in this view of industrial democracy, since, given the policies of international officials, independent rank-and-file action or wildcat strikes could be seen as undemocratic.[28]

It is difficult to plot precisely the development of the War Labor Board's views on arbitration, and perhaps it is misleading to try to rationalize its actions based upon the random flow of cases. From the beginning the board set up arbitration panels to decide specific cases, with the board generally appointing the arbitrator itself.[29] Early decisions merely encouraged the parties to voluntarily accept arbitration clauses for future disputes.[30] Unions that had voluntarily surrendered the right to strike had an especially critical need to find a means to hold employers to their promises and, after 1943, the board often imposed arbitration clauses.[31] The board's public members noted that "grievance procedures without eventual arbitration is [*sic*] a one-sided affair." The absence of arbitration systems, said the board, "does not assure the employees of any settlement except on the company's terms and in that respect it invites labor trouble."[32]

The board held that unions were entitled to clauses which provided for a "mutually satisfactory form of arbitration for adjustment of all grievances as a final step in the grievance procedure." Indeed, such a dispute resolution procedure was a "necessary alternative to giving up the right to strike for the war's duration."[33] The arbitration clause, therefore, was not a quid pro quo for the promise not to strike. Instead, arbitration was necessary *because* unions had surrendered the right to strike for the duration of the war.[34]

Although there often was little bargaining relationship between the arbitration and the no-strike clause, there was thought to be a clear relationship between strikes and arbitration. The WLB, for instance, often explained its grant of arbitration, in part, on the union waiver of the right to strike during the war.[35] Unions seeking arbitration clauses continuously claimed that they were willing to sacrifice their right to strike, although that right may not have actually existed in wartime, and unions sometimes blamed strikes on the absence of arbitration clauses.[36]

The structure of arbitration advocated by the War Labor Board strongly resembled arbitral systems established in the hosiery and clothing industry by the Amalgamated Clothing Workers Union in the 1920s. George W. Taylor, the vice-chair of the War Labor Board, had been heavily influenced by the experience of the needle trades.[37] In a chronically unstable industry, the union and larger manufacturers strove to control the anarchy caused by both the market and the mass of small entrepreneurs by instituting procedures that would permit advanced planning.

The system which evolved out of the clothing industry looks very familiar. There was a multistep grievance process which had the effect of transferring authority from shop floor leaders to the union hierarchy. Rights were no longer to be based upon tradition or customs but upon the contract and the volume of arbitral case law. The parallel was the "rule of law" in society. "Just cause" would restrict the right to fire, but orders had to be obeyed, that is, the grievance system would substitute for self-help.[38] Such a process requires patience over militancy, a substitution of third-party resolution in place of the exercise of shop floor power. That such a system could be imposed, not easily to be sure, upon often militant craft workers helps explain its imposition upon less-skilled industrial workers during World War II.[39]

Part of this general drive for rationalization seems to have also involved the rationalization of labor disputes. This may have resulted from an acceptance of the methods and goals of scientific management by the ACWU, or at least a reluctant embrace, "so long as greater efficiency was accompanied and accomplished by mechanisms of democratic (i.e., union) control and substantial economic concessions to the rank and file."[40] It could be, though, that a real merger occurred in that the union believed in "modern" notions of rationalization and efficiency and simply carried these notions over to labor matters.

The hosiery experience was influential in a variety of ways. For instance, a General Motors representative observed hosiery arbitrations prior to the creation of the General Motors–UAW arbitral arrangement. General Motors, however, insisted upon a more restrictive umpireship, in which decisions were to be based upon evidence submitted in a formal hearing and on the basis of contractual language. Its first umpire in 1941 was George Taylor. Thus, Taylor had experience with both the more fluid hosiery system and the more legalistic process in the auto industry.

The War Labor Board's own experience served to confirm the value of arbitration, and the situation at Chrysler, where arbitration was imposed upon a vigorous shop steward system, is instructive. At Chrysler's Dodge Main plant in Detroit, the very first collective agreement provided that both the elected plantwide bargaining committee and the chief stewards could confer with foremen or other management representatives during working hours. As historian Steve Jeffreys notes, the agreement provided for "two parallel systems of plant bargaining."[41] After a crucial forty-five-day strike in 1939, Local 3 altered its constitution, establishing the "primacy of the steward over the plant committee on departmental issues" and rank-and-file control over the chief shop steward. Deputy stewards were to be provided for every twenty employees. What is most fascinating about this development is that it occurred solely within the union's own internal legal system and not via collective bargaining.

By 1943 many activists at Dodge Main, as at many other industrial plants, had been dispersed to other locations or to the armed services, but a core remained, one sufficient to instruct the newly hired war workers on issues of job control. Like other companies in 1943, Chrysler attempted to tighten workplace discipline, refusing to deal with stewards and referring issues to the seriously backlogged War Labor Board. A walkout followed by firings led to a widespread sympathy strike in all of Chrysler's Detroit plants, at the very moment when the War Labor Board was holding hearings on the fail-ure of the UAW and Chrysler to reach a new agreement. The board viewed its duty as resolving "the problems of which the industrial unrest is a symp-tom," noting that there had been sixty-six strikes at Chrysler between De-cember 23, 1941, and January 8, 1943. To that end, the board insisted on an arbitration procedure similar to the system created at General Motors in 1940 and at Ford in 1941. At both firms, the UAW had advocated a griev-ance procedure which terminated in final arbitration by a permanent arbi-trator or umpire. The existing grievance procedure involved a board con-sisting of two representatives of labor and management. The grievance would remain unresolved should the parties fail to agree, a system the board viewed as "obsolete." Instead, the board appointed an "impartial chairman."[42] This action in *Chrysler*, therefore, meshed with national UAW policy.

Within a year of the board's creation, the basic contours and the basic rules of arbitration were established. Decisions in 1943 reflected the board's support for a formalized, multistep grievance process which would ultimately end in adjudication by a neutral arbitrator, a pattern which has long since become commonplace.[43] The War Labor Board's structure of rules, although explainable by wartime exigencies, would also be consistent with the themes of industrial pluralism in the postwar period. More broadly, these themes were congruent with contractualist notions long present in American legal thought. Thus, the jurisdiction of the arbitrator would be restricted to the settlement of questions concerning the interpretation or application of the terms of collective bargaining agreements.[44] Arbitration fit a voluntarist, contractual model of industrial relations in which disputes could be settled without apparent government involvement.[45]

The contractualist vision extended to other aspects of the arbitration process as well. If the parties had an arbitration agreement, for instance, the War Labor Board would order arbitration despite an employer's objection that the grievance lacked merit.[46] Moreover, once an award was rendered, the board held that "every reasonable presumption is made in favor of such an award," and awards would be upheld if there was no proof "of fraud, misconduct or other equally valid objection."[47] Thus the refusal to comply with an award was treated as a refusal to comply with an order of the War Labor Board.[48] Moreover, the WLB affirmed arbitration awards despite an employer's contention that compliance would not be "in the interests of full production." As the board noted in one decision, "labor and industry generally throughout the country have come to regard arbitration as the wisest, fairest, and speediest method of settling industrial disputes, especially during wartime."[49] This broad protection of arbitration awards would also be reflected in the Supreme Court's postwar jurisprudence.

The state courts had generally been hostile to arbitral arrangements, perhaps because they viewed the arbitration process generally as a threat to supplant the courts.[50] Many, therefore, refused to enforce such promises. Breaking from the common law view, the War Labor Board held that parties to an arbitration agreement must live up to their promises to arbitrate, and the board would enforce such awards.[51] In addition, the determinations of the War Labor Board would not be affected by any arbitration laws which might exist in various states.[52] Subsequently, the Supreme Court would also determine that collective bargaining law was exclusively federal, thus preempting contrary state statutes and rules.

Despite the board's general protection of arbitral systems, some revealing limitations in the scope of arbitration were recognized, perhaps because of managerial concern that arbitrators would have "the final decision on all matters which the union may want to treat as grievances."[53] The board made clear that arbitration would involve only disputes "about the interpretation and application of particular clauses of the agreement," reversing regional boards which had directed that the grievance procedure was to include any difference "with respect to any of the terms . . . or conditions of employment."[54] The approach meant that arbitration would not deal with matters of "managerial prerogative."[55] In the highly publicized *Montgomery Ward* decision in which management prerogatives was an issue, for instance, the board ordered a contractual definition of a "grievance" which would exclude "changes in business practice, the opening and closing of new units, the choice of personnel (subject, however, to the seniority provision), the choice of merchandise to be sold, or other business questions of a like nature not having to do directly and primarily with the day-to-day life of the employees and their relations with supervisors."[56]

Managerial authority was also recognized in areas clearly within arbitral jurisdiction. The board had no difficulty in holding that disciplinary matters were subject to arbitration, especially given the high incidence of clauses in collective bargaining agreements preventing discipline or discharge without "just cause,"[57] but it nevertheless strongly supported management's authority to take prompt action, including suspending or removing an employee from a job pending investigation or a hearing, subject to the right of the employee or the union to grieve. As War Labor Board public member Jessie Freiden and Francis Ulman confidently stated in 1945, "Arrangements have never been directed whereby the union's approval must be secured before discipline can be meted out." Indeed the authors note that a contractual requirement of union approval had existed at Brewster Aeronautical Corp., but it was "changed by the parties in conferences in which a Board representative participated, so as to restore to management its initial power to discipline. The Board approved the changes."[58]

Thus, the now commonly accepted principle that the employer acts and the employee or union can only grieve is not primarily based on the fear that employees will otherwise engage in self-help. Moreover, the "obey now, grieve later" doctrine was not created because it was perceived to be a necessary requirement of the grievance process, as would be argued after the war. Instead, it is based upon the board's assumption that such a concept was an incident of managerial prerogative, protecting hierarchy and aiding continued production.[59]

Yale Law School's Harry Shulman helped propose these views in a most forceful manner.[60] Shulman, who became umpire for the Ford Motor Company/UAW in 1943, recognized the role of law in protecting unions, but he stressed that the law left the conditions of work to the "autonomous determination" of employers and unions.[61] Like all the pluralists, Shulman recognized that employment was a conflictual relationship, a contention which must have been repeatedly highlighted by the contentious labor relations at Ford, but he believed conflict should be restricted due to the imperatives of production, and disputes "will be adjusted by the application of reason guided by the light of the contract, rather than by force or power."[62] Strikes, an "integral part of the system of collective bargaining," were referred to as a "cessation of production" rather than as a refusal to work. Although Shulman believed that litigation was unsuited to the enforcement of agreements, he stressed that it did not "follow that the alternative is jungle warfare" because arbitration "is an integral part of the system of self government. And the system is designed to aid management in its quest for efficiency, to assist union leadership in its participation in the enterprise, and to secure justice for the employees. It is a means of making collective bargaining work and thus preserving private enterprise in a free government."[63]

Grievance procedures to Shulman were not merely an "orderly, effective and democratic way of adjusting contractual disputes," because the procedure also represented the substitution of "civilized collective bargaining for jungle warfare."[64] Shulman's repeated reference to "jungle warfare"[65] is instructive, for the term apparently included the concerted withdrawal of labor, the basic right underlying the NLRA. To Shulman, walkouts and sit-downs were improper not only because the 1943 Ford/UAW agreement barred work stoppages but also because of "the moral and patriotic duty arising from organized labor's pledge to the government and to the country."[66] Yet, Shulman's argument is not premised upon an explicit union promise to avoid strikes, an argument that would be significant after the war. Instead, the very existence of an arbitration procedure foreclosed strikes over matters which fell within the ambit of such clauses.

Shulman was the most influential arbitrator during the war and in the immediate postwar period, but many of his most cited decisions were reached in wartime. Thus, his statement that "while management and labor are in adverse bargaining positions, they are joint participants in the productive effort" flows smoothly from wartime needs,[67] as does his comment that "maintenance of efficient production is of vital importance . . . to the community as a whole."

In perhaps his best-known award, issued in 1944, Shulman stressed the requirement that employees must follow the grievance procedure instead of resorting to self-help or simply refusing what are thought to be improper supervisory orders. Employees must obey and subsequently grieve, but they may not refuse an order even though it may contradict the employee's view of the collective agreement. Such behavior was "essential in order to avoid disruption of relations between the parties and anarchy in the operation of the plant." In one of his most famous phrases, he argued that an "industrial plant is not a debating society."[68] This sentiment, reflected in thousands of postwar arbitration awards, makes clear that contract rights of unions will be treated differently than the assertion of such rights by employers because "to refuse obedience because of a claimed contract violation would be to substitute individual action for collective bargaining and to replace the grievance procedure with extra-contractual methods." Self-help or worker self-definition of contractual rights, therefore, was "extra-contractual" where a grievance procedure was in existence. "When a controversy arises, production cannot wait for exhaustion of the grievance procedure. While that procedure is pursued, production must go on." A challenge to a managerial order interferes with the "authority to direct work," which, Shulman believed, is vested in supervision "because the responsibility for production is also vested there; and responsibility must be accompanied by authority." Shulman's concerns were not limited to enterprises run for profit; instead, "any enterprise in a capitalist or socialist economy requires persons of authority and responsibility to keep the enterprise going."[69]

An alternative approach, however, would not necessarily create a "debating society" or be "extra-contractual." Thus, the propriety of the employee's refusal to comply with a supervisory order could itself be tested via the grievance process, with the employee bearing the risk of an incorrect interpretation of the agreement. The arbitrator's determination whether just cause for discipline exists, therefore, would turn on the *propriety* of the supervisory order rather than simply concluding with the finding that the employee refused an order. Such an approach, only one of a number of possible rules, would not be inconsistent with the grievance and arbitration process nor would it legitimize employer power and delegitimate the ability of workers or the union to assert its own interpretation of the agreement. Finally, such a concept would recognize a rough equality of contracting parties and hardly be deemed "self-help" or "jungle warfare."

The argument that arbitration tames the often unruly rank and file has been used both by some scholars to criticize the institution and by the postwar judiciary to strengthen it. Few authorized strikes occurred during the war, due to labor's no-strike pledge, but workers demonstrated their power through the large number of wildcat strikes which did occur. The existence of arbitration procedures may well have served as a substitute or alternative to wildcat strikes, but, obviously, these procedures did not eliminate the use of the weapon. Indeed, frustration with War Labor Board delays and policies, and employer obstruction, was the cause of some wartime stoppages. Regulators, however, might have believed that arbitration reduced the incidence of wildcats, and experience in the apparel industry earlier in the century suggested that rank-and-file militance could be moderated, at least with time, and replaced by a more bureaucratized system of dispute resolution.

There was a long and heated postwar debate among arbitrators and labor scholars on the role of the arbitrator. To most of the pluralists, and perhaps with George Taylor and Harry Shulman in mind, arbitrators were superior to judges because they could be less rigid, less rule-oriented, as well as more informed of the "practices, assumptions, understandings, and aspirations of the going industrial concern," factors certainly relevant to contractual interpretation.[70] Indeed, this confident view of the arbitrator's role and ability was used by the Supreme Court in 1960 to explain its broad deference given to arbitration awards: "Even the ablest judge cannot be expected to bring the same experience and competence to bear upon the determination of a grievance, because he cannot be similarly informed."[71] Professor Lon Fuller, however, cautioned that the arbitrator had no "roving commission to straighten things out." The assumptions that arbitrators could "loosely" interpret the agreement, Fuller argued, serving as a "labor-relations physician," could not be based upon any generally assumed intent of the parties.[72]

Yet, the job of the arbitrator, many believed, was to do more than simply search for, or create, the "intentions of the parties." As Katherine Stone has effectively demonstrated, the pluralist approach also was based upon the assumption that arbitration could be used as part of a therapeutic effort to lessen underlying tensions and discontent at the workplace.[73] It is true, however, that arbitration awards can lessen tensions and, indeed, this effect may be exactly what the parties desire. Moreover, it is doubtful whether most arbitrators actually decide cases on the basis of alleviating workplace tensions, but the assumption nevertheless reveals the role arbitrators are to theoretically play in easing tensions, rather than simply interpreting the agreement. The War Labor Board, however, had more immediate concerns, and its arbitration and union security policies were basically in place before the wildcat strike wave of 1943 and 1944. Moreover, the board's common grant of arbitration clauses was not simply based upon the need to find a peaceful and effective means to resolve workplace conflicts but also to find a *fair* method to settle contractual conflicts in a situation in which unions had surrendered the right to strike.[74]

The wartime need for continued production meant that not only could employees not interfere with production to deal with workplace disputes, contractual or not, but that the issues would be resolved elsewhere and at a later time, and eventually, based only upon the language of the contract.[75] Self-help was inconsistent with such a process, and the War Labor Board would refuse to hear a dispute if a strike was in process.

In 1943, Constance Williams noted the spread of arbitration clauses as well as their increasing complexity:

> In view of labor's no-strike pledge, the existence of an orderly procedure for handling grievances between unions and employers and the opportunity to appeal unsettled disputes to the decision of an impartial arbitrator have become of increasing importance. In early 1943 a large majority of union agreements already provided that either party not satisfied by negotiations between labor and management concerning grievances, might submit the dispute to arbitration. The proportion of agreements providing for arbitration to take place automatically when requested by either party has increased in recent years, largely due to orders by the National War Labor Board.[76]

Williams's review of developments in 1943 noted that many of the WLB's changes tightened up existing procedure, such as setting time limits for each arbitration step, requiring grievances to be written at specific stages, allowing time and/or pay for grievance work, or requiring a shop committeeman of the union to be responsible for discussing grievances with the foremen and the employee when the grievance is first raised.[77]

By war's end, therefore, the basic structure of today's common arbitral system was in place. Typically, contracts called for a multistep grievance process which had the effect of transferring authority from shop floor leaders to the union hierarchy. Rights were no longer to be based upon tradition or custom but, instead, upon the contract and arbitral case law, a process paralleling the "rule of law" in society. Discharge or discipline could only be for "just cause," but supervisory orders had to be obeyed, that is, the grievance system would substitute for self-help.[78]

In the *Chrysler* decision, the board required that the existing arbitration procedure should provide for the appointment of a permanent arbitrator rather than ad hoc arbitration because of the possibility that arbitrators might give different interpretations of the agreement and also might lack basic understanding of the relationship of the parties.[79] The *Chrysler* case reflects the WLB's growing belief that there was a connection between arbitration and strikes. It would later seem clear to a generation of labor practitioners that the presence of arbitration meant that unions could not contractually strike over those matters. It was as clear during the war as now, however, that the wartime no-strike pledge or an explicit no-strike clause is broader than the arbitration clause.

Wayne Morse was one of the four public members of the WLB. Previously dean of the Oregon Law School, Morse had extensive arbitral experience on the West Coast prior to joining the War Labor Board. Experience in the "bare-knuckle environment" of longshoring, said former WLB member Lewis Gill, "had doubtless convinced him that only a firm grip by the arbitrator, in a strictly judicial proceeding, could insure reasonably orderly and workable *modus operandi*."[80] Morse strongly believed the board should not resolve contractual disputes while a strike was in progress. "The effective prosecution of the war cannot wait until the leisure of the party litigants," he stated in a 1944 law review article.[81] More importantly, the board would insist that strikes were improper even while disputes were being processed through the contractual grievance system. Even without the ideology of grievance administration, strikes would obviously not be tolerated in wartime. These notions would find favor long after, in both Supreme Court and arbitral decisions barring self-help where grievance systems existed.

Postwar decisions of the Supreme Court also encouraged the resolution of disputes via arbitration rather than self-help. In addition, postwar legal decisions made clear that the unions had an important role in fostering in-

dustrial peace, which had by then become the exclusive goal of federal policy as far as the courts were concerned.[82] It is commonplace in judicial as
well as scholarly writing to refer to arbitration as a substitute for strikes rather
than for litigation. This perception is used to heighten the notion that arbitration needs legal recognition and support, but the critical point is the
included assumption that midterm strikes must be avoided.

Collective bargaining and the arbitration process were also thought to
require a different kind of union leader. Golden and Ruttenberg noted in 1942
that "most militant local union leaders, who rise to the surface in the organizing stage of unions, fall by the side when the union moves into the state of
constructive relations with management."[83] "Constructive" labor relations,
therefore, require responsible unions led by "cooperative" leaders.[84]

In addition to the supposed need to substitute "constructive" for "militant" leaders, bargaining and arbitration tend to change the issues to be
decided. A grievance process transforms disputes, which could be based upon
concerns for personal integrity or moral and political issues, into narrower,
more legalistic questions.[85] Indeed, over time, disputes become contractual
or else they are improper. For as rights become more clearly based solely
upon the contract, disputes over other matters are treated as irrelevant,
unimportant, or, at least, unjustifiable.

The move from a system of workplace confrontation to higher-level
bargaining may alter the *substance* of bargaining, that is, the nature of the
issues. Workplace conflict tended to deal with speed of production, discipline, or the actions of foremen.[86] "Mature" collective bargaining, on the
other hand, often deals with other issues. Thus, a change in the focus of
concern, in the definition of what is important, occurred, rather than simply a change in the location of, and participants in, dispute resolution. Although unions of the 1940s often declared their intention to invade hitherto sacred management preserves, and employers clearly believed that such
threats were real,[87] the labor movement primarily sought involvement in
major capital decisions, not the types of workplace issues which often seem
of greater immediacy to workers. Nevertheless, the combination of legal
restrictions on the scope of bargaining and the asserted role and status of
arbitration tended to deprive workers of influence on both capital decisions
and workplace conflicts.

The public members and staff of the WLB gave full deference to the
rights of owners and managers to direct their enterprises, to managerial
prerogatives, but qualified the arbitrary exercise of such power by insisting
that responsible unions have a voice in the determination of those conditions of employment which did not invade the protective, but never defined,

zone of managerial prerogative. In line with these views, the War Labor Board established the critical assumption of contract administration—management acts and the union can only grieve. Management has the right of initiation as well as broad discretion in asserting its view of the contract, and the union can seek redress, although not through self-help. Strikes, or the threat of them, would make bargaining work, but the strike was not to be a part of contract administration.

There is reason to believe, therefore, that wartime regulation not only strengthened a growing governmental-union relationship but also encouraged a reliance upon collective bargaining and state assistance rather than employee self-help activities. Robert McElvaine has noted that:

> For all the horror the CIO induced among business leaders, in the end they, too, benefited from it. The organization directed the workers' essentially egalitarian discontent into streams that became in time acceptable, if unpalatable, to American capitalism. The economic royalists found that they could survive as economic parliamentarians. When the decade's class struggle subsided, new (and some old) union leaders rose on the backs of their members and made the CIO an industrial version of the AFL. The union administrators were generally happy to work with reformed captains of industry. Capitalism's problems led to worker unrest, worker unrest produced the CIO, the CIO helped resuscitate capitalism, and a revived capitalism devitalized the CIO. Working-class discontent ebbs and flows with prosperity and depression. With the return of prosperity, unions gradually resumed their parochial concerns. Ultimately, the CIO wed the AFL and begat George Meany."[88]

Julius Emspak sorrowfully noted that the militancy of the CIO dimmed as the wartime situation encouraged a "nice, cushy, administrative apparatus form of organization, and [unionists] got accustomed to bureaucracies and paperwork and looking for things through magic formulae."[89] It is likely, moreover, that wartime regulation encouraged the growth of bureaucratic control within unions, although beginnings of such trends could be seen in CIO unions even prior to the war.

THE POSTWAR LAW OF COLLECTIVE BARGAINING

Arbitration's postwar legal structure was erected upon the Supreme Court's decision in *Textile Workers v. Lincoln Mills*,[90] which held that section 301 of the Taft-Hartley Act implicitly granted courts the power to fashion the substantive law of collective agreements. The Court argued that arbitration clauses could be specifically enforced because they were the quid pro quo for no-strike clauses.[91] This bootstrap approach permitted the use of injunctions to enforce arbitration clauses despite the anti-injunction provisions of the Norris-LaGuardia Act. Given later developments it is interesting to note that Justice Frankfurter dissented in *Lincoln Mills* and criticized the union for seeking an injunction in light of the traditional union opposition to this form of judicial power.

Under current law, the Court has repeatedly referred to the notion that the no-strike clause, now found in over 90 percent of collective agreements, is the "quid-pro-quo" for an arbitration clause. The Textile Worker's Union brief submitted to the Supreme Court in the pathbreaking *Lincoln Mills* decision assumed and, indeed, urged the Court to accept the interrelationship of the no-strike and arbitration clauses. The union argued that "whatever the formula in the individual labor agreement, the same pattern appears. The agreement to arbitrate grievances is the concomitant of the agreement not to strike; the arbitration process is the substitute for the strike and the picket line for settling questions of application of the agreement."[92] As one of the unions' counsel, David Feller, would later state: "Except in the rare cases in which the union reserves the right to strike over claims of violation by the employer without any prior use of the grievance procedure, the establishment of that procedure impliedly, and usually expressly, prohibits the use of economic force, at least until the procedure has been exhausted. If the terminal point of the procedure is arbitration as it is in the great majority of modern agreements, the commitment to arbitrate is the exclusive alternative to the strike."[93]

Feller has noted that the quid pro quo notion "is accurate insofar as it reflects the historical development of arbitration from a method of avoiding strikes over what the terms of an agreement shall be to a substitute for the strike as a means of resolving claims of employer non-compliance during the period of an agreement, in only a few agreements does it describe an equivalence."[94] Thus, he notes that there are various kinds of no-strike clauses, although most prohibit a strike to protest any employer conduct during the life of the agreement. Approximately half of the no-strike provisions analyzed by the Bureau of Labor Statistics in 1966 were of this type.[95]

Feller is aware that the "no-strike provisions of most collective agreements constitute a *quo* considerably in excess of the *quid* of the agreement to arbitrate."[96] Wartime statistics, however, reveal the weakness of the quid pro quo argument. A Bureau of Labor Statistics study in 1943 studied thirty-six agreements in the agricultural-machinery industry which covered nearly 90 percent of the employees in the industry working under agreements. It found that all but four agreements placed some restrictions on strikes. Almost half prohibited work stoppages altogether and an additional thirteen prohibited stoppages pending operation of all stages of the grievance machinery. Arbitration was provided in fourteen of the sixteen agreements which prohibited stoppages during the life of the agreement, again suggesting that there was no necessary trade-off between no-strike clauses and arbitration provisions. Importantly, only two of the thirteen agreements which forbade stoppages pending resort to the grievance machinery included provisions for arbitration. Thus, the no-strike clauses, even though they might relate to the grievance procedure, were not necessarily related to the existence of arbitration provisions.[97]

Despite the urging of the Textile Workers' Union, the Supreme Court's inexplicable equation of the no-strike clause and the arbitration clause may well have its origin in the wartime experience. To some extent, however, as the garment worker experience and the writings of Golden and Ruttenberg reveal, these ideas were already in existence. There is a difference, of course, in the use of arbitration to reduce the likelihood of strikes and the use of law to bar strikes when arbitration is available.[98]

The quid pro quo notion assumes a bargaining relationship which generally did not exist. In the postwar period, employers often demanded a no-strike clause as a counterpart to union security clauses. As during the war, therefore, no-strike promises were often the quid pro quo for union security arrangements, not for arbitration clauses.[99] Moreover, despite the language of equal treatment, the no-strike clause is considerably broader than the arbitration clause.[100] Although arbitration generally deals with disputes over the meaning and interpretation of the collective bargaining agreement, no-strike clauses may literally bar any strike during the term of a collective agreement.

Even more critical is the fact that the terms of the collective agreement itself are affected by the scope of bargaining as defined by federal law. In the famous arbitration Trilogy of 1960, the Supreme Court held, first, that courts should apply broad presumptions of coverage when questions arise about the scope of arbitration clauses and, second, that arbitration awards should be presumed valid unless their "words manifest an infidelity to the agreement."[101] These conclusions not only mirrored the decisions of the War Labor Board but also flowed directly from the concern of pluralists that courts would unduly enmesh themselves in the private dispute-resolution process unless they deferred to arbitration procedures.[102]

Repeated here is the story of courts regulating labor relations without clear legislative guidelines. As in the pre-1935 period, the judiciary's own view of proper labor relations was the primary motivator of legal rules. In the name of protecting the private, consensual system of dispute resolution, issues are to be sent to arbitration without any thoroughgoing inquiry into the parties' intention, and awards will be similarly upheld so long as the "arbitrator's words manifest no infidelity to the agreement."[103] These rules are justified because the contracting parties voluntarily opted for arbitral resolution, but the existing body of rules is not at all based upon the actual intentions of the parties. Just as in private contract law, the law is not primarily concerned with the results of bargaining or substantive fairness—they are of no or limited importance to federal policy. What is important is maintaining the "integrity" of this system and maintaining the fiction that the range of legal intervention has been kept to a minimum. The alleged emphasis upon enforcing the intentions of the parties masks the attempt to "civilize" industrial relations and restrain "jungle warfare."

Despite both contractual and legal restrictions on the right to strike, however, wildcats or strikes violating no-strike clauses have not disappeared.[104] This suggests that such activity cannot be fully suppressed by contract, institutional pressure, or law. As David Brody has perceptively noted, the contractual regime cannot totally supplant the "core of informal shop-floor activity," but it does "narrow the scope of such activity" and increasingly designates noncontractual activity and prerogatives as "extralegal in character."[105] The current state of the law makes this connection explicit. Indeed, it goes much further, for it makes the contractual grievance process the exclusive method of resolving contract disputes even where NLRB jurisdiction might exist. Thus, a double narrowing occurs, for the collective agreement reflects the relative balance (or imbalance) of economic power, a situation itself affected by law.

These Supreme Court decisions were initially perceived as a victory for unions, partly because arbitrators were seen as more sympathetic to unions than courts and also because most unions had supported arbitration since the late 1930s or 1940s. The judicial support for arbitration, however, would result in a string of important cases which could hardly be deemed union victories. Perhaps the most revealing decision, *Local 174, Teamsters v. Lucas Flour Co.*,[106] held in 1962 that a union could be properly held liable in damages for striking over a matter which fell within the contractual arbitration clause despite the *absence* of a contractual no-strike clause. To hold otherwise, stated the majority, "would be completely at odds with the basic policy of national labor legislation to promote the arbitral process as a substitute for economic warfare."

The Court, in effect, assumed that the *presence* of an arbitration clause meant that the union had waived its otherwise statutorily protected right to strike over arbitrable grievances. The quid pro quo notion now had substantive effects. The decision meant that the earlier judicial victories for unions, permitting, for instance, the broad interpretation of arbitration clauses, now came with additional baggage. The fact that the strike was the crucial union right granted by the NLRA, and the basic lever to make collective bargaining function, was less important than the Court's view of civilized dispute resolution, a conclusion which followed from the ideas of pluralists like Harry Shulman who were frequently cited by the Court.

In hindsight it seems almost inevitable that these views, accepted by many on the Supreme Court, would eventually involve the return of the labor injunction, a far more effective weapon against strikes than monetary awards. Thus, the Court's *Boys Market* decision in 1970 permitted federal courts to enjoin strikes in breach of no-strike clauses, despite the seemingly clear anti-injunction language of the Norris-LaGuardia Act,[107] but only if the union could have resolved the matter via the contractual arbitration procedure. The Court deemed the Norris-LaGuardia Act a relic of a different era, one in which "federal courts were regarded as allies of management." When "congressional emphasis shifted from protection of the nascent labor movement to the encouragement of collective bargaining and to administrative techniques for the peaceful resolution of industrial disputes," said the Supreme Court, it became the task of the courts to "accommodate the older statute to the new reality." The unavailability of the injunction in breach of contract cases would be a "serious impediment" to the (judicially created) policy favoring arbitration. *Boys Market* flowed from the Court's express desire to protect arbitration, resulting in a decision which does violence to traditional standards of legal reasoning and the appropriate uses of legislative history.[108]

The stress on industrial peace, and the substitution of arbitration for strikes, would even extend to cases where the union had not contractually waived its right to strike, for the Court would permit the enjoining of strikes in violation of the "implied no-strike agreement" recognized by *Lucas Flour*.[109] The absence of an explicit no-strike clause was irrelevant if the strike was caused by an arbitrable matter, and the assumptions of the Trilogy would be used to make arbitrable basically all matters which had not been expressly excluded from arbitration.[110] To refuse an injunction and permit the strike might force the employer to concede an issue which it could perhaps win at arbitration or, it was alleged, create a situation which might affect the arbitrator's view of the merits. These are the risks which the Court apparently desired to avoid. By so holding, however, the Court *permitted* another set of risks. Should a court enjoin the strike that an arbitrator would subsequently find was actually over a *nonarbitrable* issue, federal courts would have improperly enjoined conduct of great significance, not to mention of great statutory import. The perceived harm to the arbitral process, and perhaps the employer's economic interests, outweighed the risk of judicial error concerning the right to withhold labor. The arbitration process is, therefore, a stand-in for the interest in continued production.

These decisions made clear that arbitration was to be the primary vehicle for the resolution of industrial disputes involving the interpretation or application of collective bargaining agreements. In line with pluralist precepts, the courts would *support* the grievance and arbitration process while concurrently trying not to *interfere* with it, since the collective bargaining system was viewed as a form of private self-government. These policies precisely mirror those of the industrial pluralists. It should be stressed, however, that whatever the model the Supreme Court envisioned, the decisions reflected, rather than created, a system of labor relations. By 1960, the date of the trilogy, arbitration clauses were found in over 90 percent of collective agreements.[111] The Supreme Court may have wished to support the arbitration process, but the War Labor Board had already accomplished that result over fifteen years earlier.

Notes

1. See Katherine Von Wezel Stone, "The Post-War Paradigm in American Labor Law," *Yale Law Journal* 90 (1981): 1509–80; Staughton Lynd, "Government without Rights: The Labor Law Vision of Archibald Cox," *Industrial Relations Law Journal* 4 (1981): 483; Howell John Harris, "The Snares of Liberalism? Politicians, Bureaucrats, and the Shaping of Federal Labour Relations Policy in the United States, ca. 1915–1947," in *Shop Floor Bargaining and the State*, ed. Steven Tolliday and Jonathan Zeitlin (New York: Cambridge University Press, 1987), 148.

2. The Supreme Court in *Textile Workers v. Lincoln Mills*, for instance, cites Archibald Cox, "Grievance Arbitration in the Federal Courts" (*Harvard Law Review* 67 [1954]: 602–4), to support its conclusion that the Norris-LaGuardia Act does not bar specific enforcement of the arbitration clause. In the famous trilogy of arbitration decisions in 1960, Cox was cited in two cases and Harry Shulman is cited in United Steelworkers v. Warrior & Gulf Navigation, 363 U.S. 574, 578–79, 579 n. 6, 581, 583 n. 7 (1960). See also United Steelworkers v. American Mfg., 363 U.S. 564, 568 n. 6 (1960).

3. Melvyn Dubofsky, "Legal Theory and Workers' Rights: A Historian's Critique," *Industrial Relations Law Journal* 4 (1981): 497. The pluralists' relationship to the government-liberal tradition embodied by Senator Robert Wagner has not been studied. Both groups believed in a government framework for private action, although the Wagner Act focused upon bargaining, not contract administration. See Daniel

Sipe, "A Moment of the State: The Enactment of the National Labor Relations Act, 1935" (Ph.D. diss., University of Pennsylvania, 1981); Stanley Vittoz, *New Deal Labor Policy and the American Industrial Economy* (Chapel Hill: North Carolina University Press, 1987); Theda Skocpol, "Political Response to Capitalist Crises: Neo-Marxist Theories of the State and the Case of the New Deal," *Politics and Society* 10 (1980): 155–201; and Peter Irons, *The New Deal Lawyers* (Princeton, N.J.: Princeton University Press, 1982).

4. The current arbitral system looks very much like that created by Sidney Hillman's garment workers union in the 1920s, except for the present supportive legal apparatus (Steve Fraser, "Dress Rehearsal for the New Deal: Shop-Floor Insurgents, Political Elites, and Industrial Democracy in the Amalgamated Clothing Workers," in *Working-Class America: Essays on Labor, Community, and American Society*, ed. Michael H. Frisch and Daniel J. Walkowitz [Urbana: University of Illinois Press, 1983], 212).

5. Howell John Harris, *The Right to Manage: Industrial Relations Policies of American Business in the 1940s* (Madison: University of Wisconsin Press, 1982), 49.

6. Edwin Witte, *Historical Survey of Labor Arbitration* (Philadelphia: University of Pennsylvania Press, 1952), 58, quoted in Roger Abrams and Dennis Nolan, "American Labor Arbitration: The Maturing Years," *University of Florida Law Review* 35 (1983): 577.

7. Charles Killingsworth, "The Chronicle," *Journal of the National Academy of Arbitrators* (Feb. 1988): 5.

8. These individuals are listed in National War Labor Board, *The Termination Report of the National War Labor Board. Industrial Disputes and Wage Stabilization in Wartime. January 12, 1942–December 31, 1945*, 3 vols. (Washington, D.C.: Government Printing Office, 1947–48), 1:2–46. This listing omits those who served with other wartime agencies such as the Office of Price Control and the War Production Board.

9. Michael Piore and Charles Sabel, *The Second Industrial Divide* (New York: Basic Books, 1984), 100. Where unions exercised a great deal of shop floor control, however, the "distinction between management's right to act and the union's right to challenge actions was irrelevant" (ibid., 101).

10. David Brody, *Workers in Industrial America* (New York: Oxford University Press, 1980), 200; Nelson Lichtenstein, "Industrial Democracy, Contract Unionism, and the National War Labor Board," *Labor Law Journal* 33 (Aug. 1982): 524.

11. The 1937–41 period was too brief for a significant body of NLRA law to develop. In one significant case, however, the Supreme Court had held that strikes in breach of contract would be unprotected by NLRA section 7, but the Court assumed it had the power to interpret the agreement. See NLRB v. Sands Mfg. Co., 306 U.S. 332 (1939); Karl Klare, "Judicial Deradicalization of the Wagner Act and the Origins of Modern Legal Consciousness, 1937–1941," *Minnesota Law Review* 62 (1978): 303. The union had sought to enforce its interpretation of the agreement, announcing that employees would not work unless this view was upheld. The Court interpreted the agreement to favor the employer's contractual position; thus, the

workers "were irrevocably committed not to work in accordance with their contract" (NLRB v. Sands Mfg, 306 U.S. 332 at 344 [1939]). Such a "repudiation" by employees of the agreement was deemed a severance of their employment, meaning that, since the workers' action was unprotected by the NLRA, they could be discharged. The decision suggests that the Court would be no less hostile to self-help when an arbitration procedure was present.

12. J. I. Case Co. v. NLRB, 321 U.S. 332 (1944).

13. See, generally, Stone, "Post-War Paradigm," 1509.

14. See, generally, James Atleson, "The Circle of *Boys Market:* A Comment on Judicial Inventiveness," *Industrial Relations Law Journal* 7 (1985): 88; Stone, "Post-War Paradigm," 1518–21.

15. The federal courts under article 3, section 2, of the Constitution generally have authority only to decide cases arising under federal statutes and the Constitution. Generally, federal courts cannot be given jurisdiction to enforce rights which do not arise from these sources. Some argued that federal jurisdiction existed because collective agreements were encouraged by the NLRA. The Supreme Court, however, found that Congress had empowered the Court to create federal law.

16. "Instructions to Regional War Labor Boards: Importance of Grievance Machinery," War Labor Report 9 (1944): 24–25 (National War Labor Board Memorandum Release, issued July 24, 1943).

17. See generally, James Atleson, *Values and Assumptions in American Labor Law* (Amherst: University of Massachusetts, 1983).

18. Karl Klare, "Labor Law and Liberal Political Imagination," in *The Politics of Law*, ed. David Kairys (New York: Pantheon, 1982), 60–61.

19. Ibid., 51; Atleson, *Values and Assumptions*, chap. 3.

20. Sylvester Garrett, "Resolving the Tension: Arbitration Confronts the External Legal System," *Case Western Reserve Law Review* 39 (1988–89): 557; Dennis Nolan and Roger Abrams, "American Labor Arbitration: The Maturing Years," *University of Florida Law Review* 35 (1983): 575–77.

21. Paul Fisher, "The National War Labor Board and Post-War Industrial Relations," *Quarterly Journal of Economics* 59 (Aug. 1945): 505. See also Benjamin Aaron, "Catalyst: The National War Labor Board of World War II," *Case Western Reserve Law Review* 39 (1988–89): 519.

Dennis Nolan and Roger Abrams state that "the contributions of the Board to labor arbitration were chiefly of three types: increases in the number and percentage of labor agreements containing arbitration clauses; refinement of certain arbitration concepts and rules; and creation of a larger pool of experienced arbitrators" (Nolan and Abrams, "American Labor Arbitration, " 575–76). The authors conclude that the War Labor Board can be found responsible for some increase in the extent of arbitration clauses in collective bargaining agreements although the impact was "not overwhelming" (ibid., 576). The number of arbitration clauses in collective agreements may mask the fact that the board was responsible for increasing the number of collective agreements.

22. Quoted in National War Labor Board, *Termination Report*, 1:65.

23. Sidney Lens, "Meaning of the Grievance Procedure," *Harvard Business Review* 26 (1948): 713.

24. David Feller, "A General Theory of the Collective Bargaining Agreement," *California Law Review* 61 (1973): 663, 746 n. 364. See also Nelson Lichtenstein, *Walter Reuther: The Most Dangerous Man in Detroit* (Urbana: University of Illinois Press, 1997; originally published as *The Most Dangerous Man in Detroit: Walter Reuther and the Fate of American Labor* [New York: Basic Books, 1995]), 144–53.

25. The board also defined a grievance as a question involving the application or interpretation of an agreement. See Mills Novelty Co., Case No. 111-1548-D (1944); National War Labor Board, *Termination Report*, 1:105. Nolan and Abrams believe that by the 1930s arbitration was generally understood in its current sense, that is, the resolution of disputes over the interpretation and meaning of existing agreements (Nolan and Abrams, "American Labor Arbitration," 412).

26. The board permitted individuals to file grievances at the first step, but after that the union was to participate in the settlement (National War Labor Board, *Termination Report*, 1:113–45). Current law, paralleling the language in most collective agreements, grants the union control over the grievance process and the initiation of arbitral settlement. See James Atleson, "Disciplinary Discharges, Arbitration and NLRB Deference," *Buffalo Law Review* 20 (1971): 355, 384–89.

27. Thus, as Nelson Lichtenstein notes, the USWA would be called "democratic" by the War Labor Board, despite its top-down form of organization, primarily because it was cooperative with the policies of the administration (Nelson Lichtenstein, *Labor's War at Home* [New York: Cambridge University Press, 1982], 181).

28. The board sometimes instructed international officials to investigate local officials and impose fines on wildcatters (Chrysler Corp., 10 WLR 553 [1943]). See also Lichtenstein, *Labor's War at Home*, 180–82.

29. See, e.g., New York Telephone Co. 1 WLR 259 (1942); Willamette Valley Lumber Operators, 1 WLR 151 (1942); Steel Drop Forge Group, 1 WLR 22 (1942).

30. Acmeline Mfg. Co., 9 WLR 524 (1943).

31. Chrysler Corp., 10 WLB 551 (1943); Champlin Refining Co., 3 WLR 155 (1942); Nolan and Abrams, "American Labor Arbitration," 571–73; Lichtenstein, "Industrial Democracy," 524.

32. Niles-Bement-Pond Co., 5 WLR 489 (1943).

33. Caterpillar Tractor Co., 2 WLR 75 (1942).

34. Thirteen Jobbing Machine Shops, 2 WLB 423 (1942). The board in one case granted an arbitration clause because the 1941–42 collective agreement contained a no-strike clause but no provision for arbitration. Although the prior no-strike promise was employed as one of the justifications for arbitration, the situation reflects the lack of a trade-off between the two provisions.

35. Borg-Warner Corp., 6 WLR 233 (1943).

36. See, e.g., East Alton Mfg. Co., 5 WLR 47 (1942).

37. From 1931 to 1941, Taylor served as the second impartial chairman of the Full Fashioned Hosiery Manufacturers and the American Federation of Hosiery

Workers and in 1934 became the chairman of the Philadelphia Men's Clothing Arbitration Board.

38. Fraser, "Dress Rehearsal for the New Deal," 222–23.

39. Note, though, that both groups seem to have rebelled, at least for a time. Fraser notes that skilled workers in the ACW struck more than less skilled workers, and the strikes of the latter group seemed more spontaneous.

40. Fraser, "Dress Rehearsal for the New Deal," 221. As Nelson Lichtenstein has noted, even the prewar UAW/GM umpire arrangement was based upon the needle trades experience and the umpires, George Taylor and Harry Millis, both had arbitration experience in that industry (Nelson Lichtenstein, "Great Expectations: The Promise of Industrial Jurisprudence and Its Demise, 1930–1960," in *Industrial Democracy in America: The Ambiguous Promise*, ed. Nelson Lichtenstein and Howell John Harris [New York: Cambridge University Press, 1993], 116–20).

41. Steve Jeffreys, *Management and Managed: Fifty Years of Crisis at Chrysler* (New York: Cambridge University Press, 1986), 74–75.

42. Chrysler Corp., 10 WLR 551 (1943). In 1942 the board had refused to order arbitration of new wage rates although it did approve arbitration of differential rates paid to men and women performing comparable work (Chrysler Corp. 3 WLR 447 [1942]).

43. See, e.g., Eclipse Fuel Engineering Co., 6 WLR 279 (1943).

44. Chrysler Corp., 3 WLR 447 (1942); 10 WLR 551 (1943).

45. See, e.g., National War Labor Board, *Termination Report*, 1:131; Realty Advisory Board, 2 WLR 183 (1942).

46. Texoma Natural Gas Co., 10 WLR 438 (1943).

47. See Sullivan Drydock & Repair Co., 6 WLR 467 (1943); Smith & Wesson, 10 WLR 148, 153 (1943); National War Labor Board, *Termination Report*, 1:404–5. The board would refuse to review an award even though the arbitration agreement stipulated that either party could appeal to the War Labor Board (Sullivan Drydock & Repair Co., 6 WLR 467 [1943]). See also "Statement of Policy concerning Review of Arbitration Awards," National War Labor Board, *Termination Report*, 2:694.

48. National War Labor Board, *Termination Report*, 1:411–12, 2:694–95.

49. Alexander Milburn Co., 5 WLR 529 (1942).

50. See, e.g., Gatliff Coal Co. v. Cox, 142 F.2d 876 (6th Cir. 1944); Charles Gregory and Richard Orlikoff, "The Enforcement of Labor Arbitration Agreements," *University of Chicago Law Review* 17 (1950): 233.

51. See, e.g., Smith & Wesson, 10 WLR 148 (1943). See generally, Jessie Freiden and Francis J. Ulman, "Arbitration and the War Labor Board," *Harvard Law Review* 58 (1945): 315.

52. Ibid.

53. Montgomery Ward & Co., 10 WLR 415, 420 (1943).

54. Lewittes and Sons Co., Case No. 3970-D (Apr. 13, 1994); U.S. Gypsum Co., Case No. 111-2354-D (May 25, 1944). See National War Labor Board, *Termination Report*, 1:104–6.

55. See, e.g., Atlas Power Co., 5 WLR 371 (1942) (Denial of extension of arbi-

tration to cover transfer and promotion disputes where hazardous nature of operations necessitates complete control by company). See also Harris, *Right to Manage*, 55–56.

56. Montgomery Ward & Co., 4 WLR 277, 280 (1942).

57. The board's decisions, however, show a marked unevenness on the subject of discipline. In Mead Corporation, 8 WLR 471 (1943), for instance, the prior agreement had a broad managerial prerogative clause which included the right to "hire, promote, suspend or devote, discipline or discharge." The union sought the addition of "for cause" after "discharge," but the WLB refused to grant this request on the inexplicable ground that "just cause" was "too broad." Instead, the WLB made the entire management functions clause subject to the grievance process. The result was to broaden the scope of arbitration, encouraging management fears that its own prerogatives were threatened without clearly granting the protection of "just cause." See also Hospital Supply Co., 7 WLB 526 (1943).

58. Freiden and Ulman, "Arbitration and the War Labor Board," 355–56.

59. See, for instance, Brewster Aeronautical Corp., 12 WLR 40 (1943); Norge Machine Products Division of Borg-Warner Corp., 15 WLR 651 (1944); Briggs Mfg. Co., 5 WLR 340 (1942).

60. Harry Shulman's 1955 Holmes Lecture, "Reason, Contract and Law in Labor Relations," was printed in both the *Harvard Law Review* and the *Proceedings of the Ninth Annual Meeting of the National Academy of Arbitrators*. It is probably the most widely quoted article in the area of arbitration and contract dispute settlement (Harry Shulman, "Reason, Contract and Law in Labor Relations," *Harvard Law Review* 68 [1955]: 999; Harry Shulman, "Reason, Contract and Law in Labor Relations," *Management Rights and the Arbitration Process, Proceedings of the Ninth Annual Meeting of the National Academy of Arbitrators*, ed. Jean McKelvey [Washington, D.C.: BNA, Inc., 1956], 169).

61. Shulman, "Reason," *Harvard Law Review* 68 [1955]: 1000.

62. Ibid., 1007.

63. Ibid., 1024.

64. *Opinions of the Umpire, Ford Motor Co. and UAW-CIO, 1943–1946*, Case No. A-116.

65. Many of cases handled by Shulman involved altercations, often involving violence. See ibid., Case No. A-1, June 3, 1943, the first case under the 1943 agreement.

66. Ibid., Case No. A-70, Mar. 1, 1944; see also ibid., Case No. A-197, Aug. 14, 1945.

67. *Opinions of the Umpire, Ford Motor Co. and UAW-CIO, 1943–1946*, Case No. A-561.

68. Ibid., Case No. A-116, also published as Matter of Ford Motor Co., 3 LA 779 (1944). See also Case No. A-29.

69. *Opinions of the Umpire*, Case No. A-116.

70. Archibald Cox, "Reflections upon Labor Arbitration," *Harvard Law Review* 72 (1959): 1500.

71. United Steelworkers v. Warrior & Gulf Navigation Co., 363 U.S. 574 (1960).

72. Lon Fuller, "Collective Bargaining and the Arbitrator," *Collective Bargaining and the Arbitrator's Role*, ed. M. Kahn, *Proceedings of the Fifteenth Annual Meeting of the National Academy of Arbitrators* (Washington, D.C.: Bureau of National Affairs Inc., 1962), 8. See also, J. Noble Braden, "Problems in Labor Arbitration," *Missouri Law Review* 13 (1948): 143.

73. Stone, "Post-War Paradigm," 1559–73.

74. Caterpillar Tractor Co., 2 WLR 75 (1942); Borg-Warner Corp., 6 WLR 233 (1943). An arbitration clause was imposed in one case where the prewar agreement contained a no-strike clause (Thirteen Jobbing Machine Shops, 2 WLR 423 [1942]).

75. Brody, *Workers in Industrial America*, chap. 5; Lichtenstein, *Labor's War at Home*, 179–80.

76. Constance Williams, "Developments in Union Agreements," in *Yearbook of American Labor*, vol. 1, *War Labor Policies*, ed. Colston E. Warne (New York: Philosophical Library, 1945), 128.

77. Ibid., 129.

78. By late 1943 the board's policies fostering the routinization of workplace disputes existed alongside a managerial counterattack on union power in the workplace. For a description of the centralization and bureaucratization of disciplinary power at Ford's Rouge plant, see Nelson Lichtenstein, "Life at the Rouge: A Cycle of Workers' Control," in *Life and Labor: Dimensions of American Working-Class History*, ed. Charles Stephenson and Robert Asher (Albany: State University of New York Press, 1986), 248–51.

79. Chrysler Corp., 10 WLR 551 (1943).

80. Lewis Gill, "The Nature of Arbitration: The Blurred Line between Mediatory and Judicial Arbitration Proceedings," *Case Western Reserve Law Review* 39 (1988–89): 546.

81. Wayne Morse, "The National War Labor Board Puts Labor Law Theory into Action," *Iowa Law Review* 29 (1944): 175, 181. See Lee Wilkins, *Wayne Morse: A Bio-Bibliography* (Westport: Greenwood Press, 1985), 14–18.

82. See, for instance, Emporium Capwell v. Western Addition Community Organization, 420 U.S. 50, 62 (1975).

83. Clinton Golden and Harold Ruttenberg, *The Dynamics of Industrial Democracy* (New York: Harper and Brothers, 1942), 58. In Richard Lester's words, the successors of the founding leaders of a union tend to be not "crusading agitator[s]," but the "skillful political operator and level-headed administrator" " (Richard Lester, *As Unions Mature* [Princeton, N.J.: Princeton University Press, 1958], 26).

84. Although the nonmilitant, "constructive" union official was not the exclusive type of leader, the pattern described does seem to parallel that of some revolutions in which militant leaders are often forced out, killed, or shipped abroad to be replaced by more managerial, bureaucratic types.

85. Lynn Mather and Barbara Yngvesson, "Language, Audience, and the Transformation of Disputes," *Law and Society Review* 15 (1981): 775.

86. "Reported Work Stoppages in Automobile Plants in December 1944, Jan-

uary, February 1945," in Martin Glaberman, *Wartime Strikes: The Struggle against the No-Strike Pledge in the UAW during World War II* (Detroit: Bewick Editions, 1980).

87. Harris, *Right to Manage*. Although unions seemed to have deemphasized such attempted incursions during the 1945–49 period, there were legitimate economic reasons for such behavior. The primary concern of unions during this period was job security and protection against raging inflation, concurrent with a vigorous counterattack in defense of managerial prerogatives. See Brody, *Workers in Industrial America*, 173–214.

88. Robert S. McElvaine, *The Great Depression* (New York: Times Books, 1984), 296–97.

89. Quoted in David Brody, "The New Deal and World War II," in *The New Deal: The National Level*, ed. John Braeman, Robert H. Bremner, and David Brody (Columbus: Ohio State University Press, 1975), 298. Such views would be strengthened after the losses suffered by unions during the postwar strike wave.

90. Textile Workers v. Lincoln Mills, 353 U.S. 448 (1957).

91. After the *Lincoln Mills* decision, arbitrators split on the wisdom of judicial intervention, but even those favoring *Lincoln Mills* counseled the Supreme Court to stress the protection of the arbitration process itself (Charles Gregory, "The Law of the Collective Agreement," *Michigan Law Review* 57 [1959]: 635; Cox, "Reflections on Labor Arbitration," 1482).

92. Lincoln Mills, Brief for Petitioners, 34. The argument was not a new one. George Taylor, for example, had long claimed that grievance arbitration was complimentary to the no-strike agreement, and arbitration was a substitute for the strike, not for negotiation (George W. Taylor, "Effectuating the Labor Contract through Arbitration," in *The Profession of Labor Arbitration* [Cumulative selection of addresses at first seven annual meetings, 1948–1954] (Washington, D.C.: Bureau of National Affairs, 1954).

93. Feller, "General Theory," 657.

94. Ibid., 757.

95. U.S. Dept. of Labor, Bureau of Labor Statistics, Bulletin No. 1425-6, Major Collective Bargaining Agreements: Arbitration Provisions (1966).

96. Feller, "General Theory," 760.

97. *Monthly Labor Review* 58 (Jan. 1944): 91. But see David Brody, *Workers in Industrial America* (New York: Oxford University Press, 1980), 203.

98. Harris, *Right to Manage*, 54. It is important to note that employers often strongly resisted arbitration on a variety of grounds, especially objecting to the binding determination of grievances by arbitrators.

99. Brody, *Workers in Industrial America*, 200; Lichtenstein, "Industrial Democracy," 524.

100. Staughton Lynd, "Investment Decisions and the Quid-Pro-Quo Myth," *Case Western Reserve Law Review* 29 (1979): 396.

101. The arbitration "trilogy" involves three Supreme Court decisions made on the same day in which the United Steelworkers successfully achieved broad projec-

tions for arbitration: United Steelworkers of America v. American Mfg. Co., 363 U.S. 564 (1960); United Steelworkers of America v. Warrior & Gulf Navigation Co., 363 U.S. 574 (1960); United Steelworkers of America v. Enterprise Wheel & Car Corp., 363 U.S. 593 (1960).

102. The Supreme Court has reaffirmed the broad deference to arbitral discretion, even where a court finds the arbitration award inconsistent with some public policy (Union Paperworkers Int'l. Union v. Misco, 484 U.S. 29 [1987]). More recently, however, the Court has hinted that it may be ready to rethink the entire thrust of the Trilogy (Litton Financial Printing Div. v. NLRB, 501 U.S. 190 [1991]).

103. USWA v. Enterprise Wheel and Car Corp., 363 U.S. 593 (1960).

104. James Atleson, "Work Group Behavior and Wildcat Strikes: The Causes and Functions of Industrial Civil Disobedience," *Ohio State Law Journal* 34 (1973): 750; Alvin Gouldner, *Wildcat Strike* (New York: Harper & Row, 1954); George Sayles, "Wildcat Strikes," *Harvard Business Review* 43 (1954): 42; James Kuhn, *Bargaining in Grievance Settlement: The Power of Industrial Work Groups* (New York: Columbia University Press, 1961).

105. Brody, *Workers in Industrial America*, 202.

106. Teamsters, Local 174 v. Lucas Flour, 369 U.S. 95 (1962).

107. Boys Market Inc. v. Retail Clerks Union, Local 770, 398 U.S. 235 (1970).

108. See Atleson, "Circle of *Boys Market*," 88.

109. Gateway Coal Co. v. United Mine Workers, 414 U.S. 368 (1974). This decision drastically limited the right of mine workers to quit work when faced with safety hazards, despite the seemingly applicable section 502 of the NLRA and UMW bargaining history. See James Atleson, "Threats to Health and Safety: Employee Self-Help under the NLRA," *Minnesota Law Review* 59 (1975): 681–86.

110. The Court has made clear that the presumptions of arbitrability of the Trilogy will be applied in injunction cases (Gateway Coal Co. v. UMW, 414 U.S. 368 [1974]). When the Court in its 1972 *Buffalo Forge* decision declined an opportunity to broaden the range of permissible injunctions, in a case involving a sympathy strike which did not involve an arbitrable matter, it was the liberal members of the Court, including Justice William Brennan, who dissented. The dissenters believed it was irrelevant whether the strike was over an arbitrable matter. Since the union had promised not to strike, and the strike might have breached the no-strike clause, the strike itself should be enjoined and *its* contractual validity tested in arbitration. The dissenters, consistent with industrial pluralist premises, expressed undying support for arbitration and extreme hostility to midterm strikes (Buffalo Forge Co. v. Steelworkers, 428 U.S. 397 [1976]). See also Atleson, "Circle of *Boys Market*," 88; Florian Bartosic and Gary Minda, "Labor Law Myth in the Supreme Court, 1981 Term," *University of California at Los Angeles Law Review* 30 (1982): 271. The predominant scholarly view, based upon pluralist views, is to praise *Boys Market* and to criticize *Buffalo Forge*.

111. Bureau of Labor Standards, Bulletin No. 1425-1, "Grievance Procedures," 1 (1964).

5

Managerial Prerogatives: Collective Bargaining's Forbidden Zone

The Board's policies will be significant as a starting point for peacetime developments in those bargaining units where they will have exerted a direct influence during the war; and they will serve as a precedent in those units where the Board's actions will not have left any lasting impact during the war.
—Joseph Shister, "The National War Labor Board: Its Significance," *Journal of Political Economics* 53 (1945): 37

Management has no divine rights. Management has only functions, which it performs well or poorly. The only prerogatives which management has lost turned out to be usurpations of power and privilege to which no group of men have exclusive right in a democratic nation.
—"Management's Future in Labor Relations," UAW Research Dept. Collection Box 23, file "Walter Reuther—Unused Articles," 1948, ALHWSU, cited in Nelson Lichtenstein, "Great Expectations: The Promise of Industrial Jurisprudence and Its Demise, 1930–1960," in *Industrial Democracy in America: The Ambiguous Promise*, ed. Nelson Lichtenstein and Howell John Harris (New York: Cambridge University Press, 1993), 25

At the end of the war the primary fear of American employers was the union challenge to managerial control of the workplace. Executives focused this concern less upon strikes than upon "the serious and lasting limitations on their freedom of action resulting from the orderly collective bargaining achievements of bureaucratic unionism, assisted by the orders of arbitrators and the NWLB."[1] Managerial fears, however, must have been based primarily upon union bargaining power and workplace pressures because the wartime "law" was certainly generous in regard to managerial prerogatives.[2]

The first National Labor Relations Board, created by executive order in 1934, had endorsed a broad reading of the duty to bargain, expanding interpretations from its predecessor, the National Labor Board. Employers had been ordered to bargain over a wide range of matters that had an impact on terms and conditions of employment, including changes in terms occasioned by plant relocation or the introduction of a new line of products.[3] Despite this history, the War Labor Board at an early date recognized an area of decision making it designated as "managerial prerogatives." The determination that a matter was solely a management function meant, first, that the employer need not bargain over the subject despite the union's request that it do so, nor would the War Labor Board be receptive to a union demand to restrict managerial authority in these areas. Second, and often most important, an employer could initiate action in these areas without first bargaining with the union and, as noted in the previous chapter, without having to face subsequent arbitral challenge. Although the scope of bargaining would be a vital question under the NLRA, little litigation under that statute had occurred on these questions up to the outbreak of war.[4] The War Labor Board's assumptions, however, would become deeply embedded in NLRA jurisprudence after the war.[5]

In 1946, Ludwig Teller, prolific writer of labor law articles and treatises, was pleased to report that "the decisions of the War Labor Board in labor dispute cases did much to reinstate management confidence in business continuity, in the right to initiate business decisions."[6] Teller argued that when the war and the War Labor Board ended, there was "increasing reliance" on the decisions of the War Labor Board "because of the belief that its decisions are a source of guidance for desirable practices in the field of labor relations." As Teller perceptively noted in 1946, the War Labor Board's "decisions . . . [were] the beginnings of a labor jurisprudence." Indeed, it was the War Labor Board, not the National Labor Relations Board, which institutionalized the notion that the scope of mandatory bargaining is restricted by certain inherent managerial rights.

When faced with a dispute over the terms of the collective bargaining agreement, the War Labor Board might be required to write much or all of the agreement for the parties. A dispute might concern a right asserted by the employer or a practice that either the employer or the union wanted established or terminated. In either case, employers often contended that the exercise of a particular right should be or remain part of the employer's "reserved rights." These asserted "managerial prerogatives" often involved production matters as well as union proposals for health insurance, company-financed unemployment funds, sick leave, and medical, hospital, maternity, and pregnancy benefits.

The War Labor Board tended to be keenly protective of managerial rights and it routinely denied union welfare proposals. Despite the progress made in fringe benefit bargaining, the War Labor Board was "hesitant about breaking new ground."[7] Walter Gellhorn, who served as vice-chair and then chair of the WLB's region two, recently noted that novel proposals, for instance, for paid sick leave, had to be considered "in terms of whether it was or was not destabilizing. It would be destabilizing if it were innovative." The war, he noted, was not the occasion for creating or raising fringe benefits, except that the WLB might raise a benefit to the norm in a particular industry.[8] The War Labor Board, however, did grant unions a measure of participation in many matters previously thought to be exclusively managerial. For instance, the board supported automatic wage progression plans which affected employers' control of labor costs and the workforce.[9] In addition, board-ordered job classification plans and other work arrangements gave unions the right to be consulted in both the creation and administration of such schemes.[10] Nevertheless, what is noteworthy about the board's rulings is the lack of any felt need to explain the nature or scope, or to even justify the existence, of managerial prerogatives.[11]

The board's clearest statement of its approach is probably to be found in its *Montgomery Ward* decision. Management functions, said the WLB, were excluded from arbitration to the extent that they related to "changes in the general business practice, the opening or closing of new units, the choice of personnel, the choice of merchandise to be sold, or other business questions of a like nature not having to do directly and primarily with the day-to-day life of the employees and their relations with their supervisors."[12] The scope of bargaining, therefore, was to be narrowed to the "day-to-day" concerns of employees. As would be subsequently true under the National Labor Relations Act, it is the challenge to the employer's control of production, and the state's unwillingness to sanction such challenges, which seem to underlie these cases.

A good deal of labor's creativity in this period arose from the fact that possible wage gains were strictly controlled by the board's "Little Steel" formula. Even matters clearly involving working conditions, however, were often avoided. The board would not always explicitly rule that particular issues were improper subjects for bargaining; instead, it often sent such issues back to the parties for further negotiation, a resolution with foreseeable results given the no-strike pledge. As Aaron Levenstein, a strong critic of WLB, noted: "[The Board's] refusal to decide made it impossible for the unions to bargain on those matters altogether. Since the strike weapon had been put in cold storage, the issues remained an economic no man's land which the Board would not enter and which labor could not invade because it had no persuasive power. In this region of disputed issues, the employers' only obligation was to negotiate before saying no."[13] The unions argued that the no-strike pledge obliged the board to rule on all issues. The "no-strike, no lockout agreement," they argued in vain, was conditioned on the submission of "all disputes" to the board. The board's position, however, was essentially that its jurisdiction was narrower than the no-strike promise. Effectively, then, the no-strike obligation was unlimited, but the right to bargain was not.[14]

The United Auto Workers, for instance, demanded that General Motors create an employee security fund equal to the one it had already put aside for postwar business contingencies. The fund would purchase war bonds and, after the war, it would supplement unemployment insurance for workers who could not be provided with a forty-hour workweek. The board agreed with General Motors that the union's demand was essentially a "profit-sharing plan and is beyond the powers of the War Labor Board to adjudicate."[15] The public members of the board believed they should prevent the introduction of "sociological innovations" during the war. The powerful wartime interest in labor peace could have led to a broad, inclusive reading of the scope of bargaining, especially given the unions' no-strike pledge. Yet, the interest in co-option, or in the institutionalization of dispute resolution, was apparently weaker than the War Labor Board's preference for unrestricted managerial freedom over certain matters.

In the first decision in which the issue was raised, *Arcade Malleable Iron Co.*, the board denied the employer's request for a clause which specifically listed various management functions. The board's denial was accompanied by the statement that "adequate protection is afforded the company by law and by the many decisions of the courts and of other tribunals concerned with the question."[16] Given the paucity of NLRA decisions dealing with the scope of bargaining, it is difficult to know what body of law the board had in mind. Even in this case, however, the board, without dissent from its labor representatives, agreed to insert a clause to the effect that "the functions of management are vested exclusively in the Company except as modified by the specific provisions of this agreement." The union was enjoined from interfering "in the rights of the management in the matter of hiring, transfer, or promotion of any employees and in the general management of the plant." The board's only objection was to the employer's proposed "long list" of exclusive management functions.

The basis for the decision became clear in the later *Banner Iron Works* case: "the rights are inherent in management anyhow."[17] Nevertheless, in 1942 the board, often without comment, began to approve management requests to insert express clauses into collective bargaining agreements which would protect specific management rights. Inherent rights, apparently, were sometimes deemed worthy of clear expression. These clauses generally gave management, among other things, the exclusive power to hire, promote, fire for just cause, and maintain and schedule production. Moreover, the clauses often explicitly acknowledged the employer's exclusive control over the products to be manufactured as well as the locations of plants.[18]

Under the rubric of "plant operations," the WLB deferred to many aspects of management decision making. For instance, the board denied a union request to reestablish a six-day workweek instead of a five-day swing-shift week, stating that "this matter is a technical administrative problem, which should be left to management to decide, involving as it does the rearrangement of working schedule by large scale transfers of personnel and changes in the entire system of the company's operations."[19] The War Labor Board also generally believed that limitations and arbitration of employee transfers would interfere with efficiency.[20]

Indeed, the board's decisions on the scope of managerial prerogatives were far broader than the position of the postwar NLRB. For instance, the War Labor Board held that even the distribution of overtime work was within the exclusive prerogative of management. Thus, the board denied a union's request for an equal division of overtime work on the grounds that the "ultimate decision as to who is qualified to perform specific overtime work should rest with management."[21] Other matters swept into the broad management prerogatives category were the initiation of technological changes, even if layoffs should occur, determination of the size of the workforce, and determination of supervisory members.[22] Subcontracting work was also generally regarded a managerial prerogative despite a union's claim that the company had used subcontracting in the past to evade contractual provisions and wage rates.[23]

Although the board generally protected what it felt were critical managerial prerogatives, there were some exceptions. In one case the union was held entitled to its requested contract clause providing for the transfer of the employees at the prevailing rate for a new job without loss of seniority when a department or operation was eliminated, despite the employer's objection on managerial prerogative grounds.[24] On the other hand, an employer could be granted a clause providing that it could expand or reduce facilities despite the union's objection that the clause would be used to discharge union members.[25]

A company's request that it be permitted to require employees on piecework to punch a time clock at the beginning and end of each operation was denied on the ground that it would cause unnecessary delays in production, a position presumably inconsistent with the board's view that management was the best judge of efficiency.[26] Despite its view on managerial prerogatives, the board was not immune from lecturing management on its obligations: "Management may indeed have evidence on which to base its conviction that the union enforces what it considers a fair tempo of production. But the way to prevent such regulation is not by mechanical devices such as time clocks, for these cannot reach the inner springs of motive and incentive which really guide the muscle power of the worker. The way to reach the inner consent is by creating confidence in the men that their welfare and progress is as precious to the company as is the welfare of the stockholders."[27]

A more typical case is one where the board approved the deletion of a contract clause which required that intraplant transfers be made only with employee consent. In place of that clause, the board approved a provision which gave the company unrestricted right to make such transfers, although seniority was to be the ground for such decisions.[28] The board felt that "no blanket rule as it effects seniority in relation to transfers can be laid down in view of the fact that different problems arise in each . . . type of transfer." This apparently meant that no blanket rule should be adopted protecting the employees' right not to be transferred without their consent, for the board approved a clause which granted the company the blanket, *unrestricted* right to make such transfers.[29]

The board's decisions may not be altogether consistent, but the desire to protect managerial power against what it felt were efficiency-robbing inroads by unions was never too far below the surface. The board's willingness to grant a detailed management prerogative clause, after its initial refusal to do so, however, arguably reflects a more liberal approach to collective bargaining. The board initially seemed to have believed that no explication of management rights was required because they were "inherent" in the relationship. This is a reflection of what could be referred to as the "Genesis" theory of collective bargaining, one often found in judicial decisions and especially in hundreds of postwar arbitration awards. "In the beginning," the theory goes, there was light, and then there were inherent managerial powers over the direction of the enterprise. Such power obviously included unfettered discretion to direct production and the workforce and to make all decisions involving these matters. Later, there came statutes and collective bargaining, but employers nevertheless still possessed all powers which had not been expressly restricted by statute or agreement. The inclusion of express managerial rights in collective agreements, however, weakens the argument that certain prerogatives are "inherent" in the relationship.

A more sophisticated argument, and one made by the conservative legal scholar Ludwig Teller, is that collective bargaining was a replacement rather than a supplement to common law theories of labor relations. Thus, collective bargaining was created to supplant "common law individualism" with "new conceptions suitable to problems and situations which did not exist when the common law molded its intensely individualistic structure." Teller was aware that having replaced the old order with the new, "organized labor is properly suspicious of efforts to give continued life to the old order through the medium of emphasis upon 'the common law rights of management.'" Moreover, as many observers of industrial relations recognized, there is no objective or rational way to determine what is or what is not a managerial prerogative.[30] A decision concerning which matters should be exclusively in the managerial domain is basically a determination of the area from which labor should be excluded. In addition, as David Montgomery's work has shown, the context of this issue involves those areas in which management/ownership has taken power from employees as well as those areas in which collective employee action and statutes have restricted managerial control.

An explicit managerial prerogatives clause offers a number of other values, both real and symbolic.[31] First, according to Teller, it "has certain value in teaching the contracting union to think in terms of the problems and rights of management."[32] More importantly, such a clause limits the scope of proper union concern, a serious matter in a period in which many unions were both developing and experiencing economic power. Thus, the board upheld the grant of a management functions clause by a regional board because "the present union is a new union and the inclusion of the clause will serve to educate the union more definitely as to management functions, thus serving to reduce the areas of conflict between union and management without loss of protection of the union under the other terms of the contract and especially of the grievance machinery."[33] In addition, the managerial functions clause creates a source of legitimation when management takes a particular action, a further reflection of the contractualization of labor-management relations.

In this area, at least, the existence of the National Labor Relations Act had seemingly little effect on the War Labor Board and its subsidiary boards.[34] This was no doubt due in large part to the paucity of cases dealing with the scope of mandatory bargaining under the NLRA in the 1940s. In addition, labor had made few forays into critical managerial decisions. Unskilled workers have not traditionally attempted, at least via negotiation, to assert control over production. As David Montgomery noted of the unskilled workers of the later half of the nineteenth century, "There is no evidence that local assemblies of unskilled workers or of semi-skilled operatives ever attempted to regulate production processes themselves in the way assemblies of glass blowers and other craftsmen did."[35] Unions, however, constantly argued that employer actions could not be taken in regard to "wages, hours or other conditions of employment" without prior bargaining. Some War Labor Board panels actually affirmed such arguments in relation to changes in the scheduled hours of employment, although these recommendations were not accepted by the War Labor Board.[36]

Gary Gerstle has clearly demonstrated the effect of the wartime years and the rulings of the War Labor Board on the Independent Textile Union's (ITU) collective bargaining agreements in Woonsocket, Rhode Island. Noteworthy in Gerstle's account is the fact that the Woonsocket workers had secured a substantial amount of participation rights in local plants before the war. Although an arbitration board, whose decisions were binding, existed under a number of prewar contracts, the final step in some of the grievance procedures was a strike rather than binding arbitration. Even those that provided for neutral arbitration as the final step, however, involved a substantial degree of influence for unions. "Woonsocket employers had to submit virtually all unresolved disputes with workers to an arbitration board that they did not control." None of these contracts had a management rights clause nor did any try to exempt from the scope of the contract or bargaining the right to make major capital decisions or to institute new machines or technologies.[37]

Most startling, two ITU contracts provided that discharges had to be "mutually agreed upon by the employer and the union." Not only could employers not fire an employee without the union's agreement, but if a discharge occurred, the union had a right to strike without having to wait for the resolution of a grievance. In other mills, managers could not change workloads or speeds of production, alter technology, or affect piece rates, for instance, without the union's approval.[38] Democratization of the workplace thus meant that changes in working conditions could not be made without the mutual agreement of both the employer and the union. Under such conditions, arbitration could not be viewed as a surrender of union power, even though some employees objected, one referring to this method of dispute resolution as "arbetraytion."[39]

The ITU had, therefore, secured a remarkable degree of workplace influence over working conditions. Gerstle stresses that the Woonsocket employees were organized in strong unions earlier than in auto and steel, and they benefited "enormously from the open-ended bargaining, encouraged in the late 1930s by the pro-labor NLRB." Since the NLRB had not recognized a zone of managerial prerogatives, "a strongly organized group of workers was able, therefore, to force employer concessions on virtually every managerial function. This open-ended period of bargaining came to a close during World War II, just as most industrial unions were first gaining the institutional security they desperately needed to carry on aggressive bargaining; many of these unions, therefore, never enjoyed the same opportunities as the ITU in the late 1930s and thus never gained the same kind of shop floor power."[40]

The postwar agreements of 1945 and 1946 studied by Gerstle solidified many of the successes of the union in the prewar period, and also included many of the fringe benefits which had been promoted during the wartime period, yet contracts "revealed a serious erosion of the control that ITU unionists had enjoyed in 1941."[41] For instance, nine of the twelve agreements now contained a management rights clause whereas none of the 1941 contracts had included any statement that the "plant and direction of the personnel, subject to the provisions of the agreement, shall be vested exclusively in the employer."

The new arrangements dramatically altered the social aspects of employment. Thus the 1946 French Spinning Mill contract no longer provided a management obligation to secure union consent before an employee could be discharged or before creating a change in workload or any other aspect of working conditions.[42] The employer still had an obligation to notify the union of an intent to discharge an employee, but the union's consent was no longer required. The union's only alternative was to grieve. A grievance, of course, only asserts that the agreement has been broken, and the success of that claim turns on the language and scope of the agreement.

Similarly, although the prewar contracts had stated that employees could strike if management did not redress their grievances, the 1946 Woolen Mill contract substituted arbitration for the right to strike as the final step of the grievance procedure. These changes signaled "the decisive defeat of the union's quest for complete mutuality, or joint sovereignty, in the operation of Woonsocket industry. Moreover, the fact that this defeat coincided with the augmentation of workers monetary rights (in the form of insurance and vacation benefits) set in motion a bargaining pattern of unions trading collective shop floor power in return for increases in their members' individual purchasing power that would continue, even intensify, in the postwar years."[43]

MANAGERIAL PREROGATIVES IN THE POSTWAR PERIOD

The War Labor Board's role included the actual creation of contractual terms, a role which might explain its reluctance to invade "managerial prerogatives." Despite the quite different function of the National Labor Relations Act, the War Labor Board's recognition of a zone of managerial exclusivity would eventually be employed by the Supreme Court to narrow the scope of bargaining under the NLRA. The Supreme Court held in 1964, for instance, that subcontracting, at least in certain situations, was within the ambit of mandatory bargaining in *Fibreboard Paper Products v. NLRB*.[44] The opinion, typical of many Warren Court opinions, began with broad statements of policy only to finish by narrowing the ruling to the precise and very particular facts of the case before it.[45] A concurring opinion by Justice Potter Stewart noted that not "every management decision which necessarily terminates an individual's employment is subject to the duty to bargain." Echoing the War Labor Board's *Montgomery Ward* decision, Stewart noted that even decisions clearly affecting "conditions of employment" are excluded because of the nature of the managerial action, listing, among others, decisions to invest in labor-saving machinery or decisions to liquidate assets and go out of business. These decisions, Stewart argued, "lie at the core of entrepreneurial control." Stewart's explanation was that "decisions concerning the commitment of investment capital and the basic scope of the enterprise are not in themselves primarily about conditions of employment, though the effect of the decision may be necessary to terminate employment." Thus, excluded from the zone of mandatory bargaining are matters of capital investment and decisions "fundamental to the basic direction of a corporate enterprise."[46] Despite the union's victory in *Fibreboard*, Stewart's cautionary phrases were not significantly at variance with the majority's conclusion that mandatory bargaining in this instance would not "significantly abridge . . . [the employer's] freedom to manage the business."

The Court's concern for the freedom to manage would subsequently become the basis for restrictive rulings of the Burger Court. In 1981, for instance, the Supreme Court held that partial closing of an enterprise was not subject to mandatory bargaining.[47] The issue, said Justice Blackmun, is whether a decision to terminate "should be considered part of petitioner's retained freedom to manage its affairs unrelated to employment." Like the War Labor Board, Blackmun thus assumed that an inherent body of exclusive management functions existed, and "management must be free from the constraints of the bargaining process to the extent essential for the running of a profitable business." Congress, said Blackmun, "had no expectation that the elected union representative would become an equal partner in the running of the business enterprise in which the union's members are employed."[48]

CONCLUSION

Although there are negative aspects of contractualism and legalization, there are also clear advantages for unions. Institutionally, grievance procedures, like collective bargaining, centralize power in the hands of union officials, but there are gains for employees as well. Guarantees written into collective agreements cannot easily be taken away, and this becomes the basis for one of the unions' most powerful arguments for representative status. In light of labor's relative weakness during the war, the constant and very real threat of hostile legislation, and the erosion of public support due to wartime strikes, these gains were highly significant.

The WLB strongly criticized strikes as early as mid-1942, and public member Wayne L. Morse, especially upset over union jurisdictional conflicts, warned that the laws against treason would be applied to strikers in such disputes. In the Seventy-seventh Congress alone, twenty-one bills were introduced dealing with wartime strikes, three of which sought to make strikes in defense plants treasonous and punishable by death. Employer groups, notably the NAM, charged that strikes were damaging war production even though workdays lost due to strikes were very low. It was the successive miners' strikes of 1943 that made that year so exceptional, strikes which led to the War Labor Disputes Act of 1943 and helped inflame public opinion against strikes.[49]

Nevertheless, despite the gains, the practices and law of arbitration also have negative effects on industrial democracy. First, arbitration focuses upon the written agreement as the exclusive source of employee rights. The agreement is the result of economic struggle and, thus, represents the existing balance, or imbalance, of economic power, a situation generally favoring employers. The reliance upon contractualism, therefore, means that rights are based upon the relative economic strength of the parties, although the goal of the Wagner Act was to achieve a measure of equality. Moreover, the relative power of the parties is itself affected by the interpretations of the NLRA, and these were often not favorable to union interests. Just as important, centralized bargaining often alters the kinds of issues that are thought to be important. Second, arbitration removes the conflict, and its resolution, from the workplace and the immediately affected workers.

Finally, arbitration procedures reflect the hierarchical system of the plant, and the substantive rules indicate, despite the rhetoric, that only a limited participatory democracy is to be created. The basic rule of arbitration, that employees must obey work orders and grieve, makes it clear that management may act upon its interpretation of the agreement but the union may not. Arbitration becomes the device to maintain production and the only avenue to test the union's view of its contractual rights. Inherent in the rule itself is a choice of managerial hegemony and continued production over more participatory forms of industrial self-government.

This is not to argue that legal rules necessarily reflect reality or substantially affect behavior. Indeed, the effect of a broader scope of bargaining is problematic, for only unions strong enough to secure clauses limiting "managerial prerogatives" could take advantage of such a liberalization.[50] The argument is only that the very assumptions of, and tensions within, pluralist thought would affect the shape of postwar law and aid in creating restrictive rulings, especially when labor's power is perceived to wane. Pluralist thought, after all, was immeasurably aided by the appearance of relative equality in the postwar period. Alan Fox's perceptive analysis of labor relations in the United Kingdom in the early 1970s is also applicable to the experience of the United States to the 1970s. With few exceptions, labor accepted

> as given those major structural features which are crucial for the power, status and rewards of the owners and controllers. It is because this condition is usually fulfilled that owners and controllers are rarely driven to call upon their reserves of power in any overt and public exercise. Only the margins of power are needed to cope with marginal adjustments. This, then, is what accounts for the illusion of a power balance. Labour often has to marshal all its resources to fight on these marginal adjustments; capital can, as it were, fight with one hand behind its back and still achieve in most situations a verdict that it finds tolerable.[51]

The generally superior power of capital has been unleashed in a period when reduced profit margins and international competition induced management to contest labor and working conditions, the one aspect of production over which it has historically had most control.

Arbitration is but a part, albeit perhaps a necessary part, of collective bargaining, and it is no more confining than bargaining itself. Bargaining, after all, is affected by relative economic power, and imbalances will be reflected in the resulting contracts that arbitrators are called upon to interpret. Perhaps the most important legacy of the War Labor Board is its view that the scope of bargaining is itself limited so as to exclude matters deemed critical to managerial efficiency, including capital mobility. These views after the war became part of the assumptions underlying the NLRA, helping to render unions impotent when faced with the torrent of plant removals and closures in the 1970s and 1980s.

Pluralist premises rest upon substantially equal power because only then can collective bargaining be considered "industrial self-government." The current sharp decline in the labor movement reveals that equal power does not exist and that the bargaining system, defined by legal decisions often restricting union economic power, will not likely result in substantial equality. The problem stems in part from the War Labor Board's recognition and protection of inherent managerial (or property) rights, a concern which even the needs of wartime production could not weaken. Such recognition of managerial rights would ultimately lead to the Supreme Court's assertion that the Wagner Act Congress could not have conceived that the union "would become an equal partner in the running of the business enterprise in which the union's members are employed."

The pluralists as well as the War Labor Board deferred to the rights of owners and managers to direct their enterprises, although they qualified the arbitrary exercise of such power by insisting that responsible unions have a voice in the determination of those conditions of employment which did not invade the protective zone of managerial prerogative. The tensions between the protection of managerial power and the encouragement of a broad scope of collective bargaining have never been resolved, either by the pluralists or the courts.[52] The problem, like many legal problems, is more than definitional, for the location of a boundary turns on the often-unexpressed reasons one feels compelled to draw one in the first place. Yet, the language of pluralism reflected in the writings of scholars and arbitrators is proudly antitheoretical and ahistorical. The pluralist vision is seen as pragmatic, an emphasis on what works. Thus, William P. Murphy, president of the National Academy of Arbitrators during its fortieth year, discussed the accomplishments and continued problems of arbitration in 1987. Some problems such as "reserved management rights, implied obligations, past practice," he noted, still remained unresolved. Murphy suggested "that the subject has no final definitive answer, that we are now burdened by over-analysis, and that the best a conscientious arbitrator can do is to be aware of and understand the various points of view and then do what seems right in the particular case."[53] Noteworthy are both the absence of any discussion of the profound changes in industrial structure and labor relations and the implicit assumption that the unresolved issues in arbitration do not involve choices in policy and theory. Another reaction in industrial relations circles, until recently, has been the simple denial that a radical shift in bargaining power has occurred in America, creating substantially weaker unions and great instability for workers.[54]

Collective bargaining in its decentralized American form left the labor movement particularly dependent upon the success and viability of certain mass production industries. Their decline weakens the institutional strength of unions, but the unions' history provides no way to question current institutional arrangements or to propose transformative ideas. Union structure has tended to match that of the employers with whom they bargain, but locally based bargaining would appear to make little sense in relation to large, multiplant firms with typically centralized labor policymaking. Moreover, the modern growth of conglomerates and multinational corporations drastically affects the power relationships of labor and capital. Unions find themselves increasingly dealing with firms that can easily weather economic struggles, conceal information, and transfer, or more credibly threaten to transfer, work to other locales or, indeed, other countries. This drastic change in corporate and capital structure mandates a rethinking of our labor laws.

Notes

1. Howell John Harris, *The Right to Manage: Industrial Relations Policies of American Business in the 1940s* (Madison: University of Wisconsin Press, 1982), 67. For an argument that managers had lost considerable power during the war years, see Robert M. C. Littler, "Managers Must Manage," *Harvard Business Review* 24 (1946): 366.

2. Despite the wartime statements by some union officials expressing their interest in further influence in management, statements by unionists supporting the concept of managerial rights could also be found. Thus, Philip Murray and Morris J. Cooke stated in 1940: "To relieve the boss or the management of proper responsibility for making a success of the enterprise is about the last thing any group of employees—organized or unorganized—would consider workable or even desirable. The Unions are on record in numerous instances as recognizing that in the last analysis management has to manage, if any concern is to be a success financially or in any other way" (Philip Murray and Morris Cooke, *Organized Labor and Production* [New York: Harper, 1940], 84).

3. James Atleson, *Values and Assumptions in American Labor Law* (Amherst: University of Massachusetts Press, 1983), 118.

4. Ibid., 115–22.

5. See, generally, ibid.

6. Ludwig Teller, "The War Labor Board and Management Functions," *New York University Law Quarterly Review* 21 (1946): 365.

7. Constance Williams, "Note on Management Prerogatives," in National War Labor Board, *The Termination Report of the National War Labor Board. Industrial Disputes and Wage Stabilization in Wartime. January 12, 1942–December 31, 1945*, 3 vols. (Washington, D.C.: Government Printing Office, 1947–48), 2:623.

8. Walter Gellhorn, "Development of Arbitration," in *Between Management and Labor! Oral Histories of Arbitration*, ed. Clara H. Friedman (New York: Twayne, 1995), 23.

9. At the same time, Japan's military was imposing automatic seniority-based wage increases. See Linda Weiss, "War, the State, and the Origins of the Japanese Employment System," *Politics and Society* 21 (Sept. 1993).

10. Timothy Willard, "Labor and the National War Labor Board 1942–1945: An Experiment in Corporatist Wage Stabilization" (Ph.D. diss., University of Toledo, 1984), 40.

11. "One of the most remarkable features of the War Labor Board cases dealing with management functions is the failure to define at length the meaning of management function in a union relationship, or even to discuss its essential qualities as a guide to future policies" (Teller, "War Labor Board," 365).

12. Montgomery Ward, 10 WLR 415 (1943).

13. See Aaron Levenstein, *Labor, Today and Tomorrow* (New York: A. A. Knopf, 1946), 102.

14. Unions did broaden the scope of bargaining, however, despite the board's lack of support. The UMW secured a royalty for every ton of coal mined to be used to create a fund for medical service, hospitalization, rehabilitation, and general economic protection (ibid., 103–4). Other unions like the International Ladies Garment Workers Union required employers to contribute to union health and vacation funds.

15. General Motors Company, 22 WLR 484 (1945).

16. Arcade Malleable Iron Co., 1 WLR 153 (1942).

17. Banner Iron Works, 15 WLB 332, 335 (1944).

18. Levenstein, *Labor, Today and Tomorrow*, 109; *In re* Fulton County Glove Industry, 4 WLR 307 (1942); Teller, "War Labor Board," 322 n. 11.

19. Mead Corp., 8 WLR 471, 474 (1943); Towne Robertson Nut Co., 3 WLR 40 (1942)

20. See, e.g., Detroit Steel Products Co., 6 WLR 495 (1943).

21. Bethlehem Steel, 11 WLR 190, 196 (1943).

22. Riverside and Dan River Cotton Mills, Inc., 8 WLR 274 (1943); Western Union Telegraph Co., 6 WLR 133 (1943); Petroleum Specialties Co., 24 WLR 597 (1945). (The board refused the union request to remove a supervisor who had been convicted of assaulting employees.)

23. Tinius Olsen Testing Machine Co., 11 WLR 301 (1943); Bethlehem Steel Co., 6 WLR 513 (1943). Yet, in one case the board approved a clause restricting subcontracting until all employees were fully employed and the full capacity of the plant was utilized (Fulton County Glove Industry, 4 WLR 307 [1942]).

Nor were "management functions" to be subject to arbitration (Teller, "War Labor Board," 329). Thus, the board had occasion to expressly exclude from arbitration the transfer and promotion of employees, the adjustment of piece rates, the determination whether additional employees should be hired for certain operations, the retention of probationary employees and the determination of work schedules (ibid., 339). See also Bethlehem Steel Corp., 11 WLR 190 (1943). Similarly, the hazardous nature of the work was used to deny arbitral jurisdiction over transfer and promotion grievances, suggesting some lack of faith in both arbitrators and unions (Atlas Powder Co., 5 WLR 371 [1942]).

24. McQuay-Norris Mfg. Co., 9 WLR 538 (1943).

25. Fairchild Press Inc., 11 WLR 296 (1943).

26. Young Radiator Co., 12 WLR 291 (1943).

27. Ibid.

28. Brewster Aeronautical Corp., 12 WLR 40 (1943).

29. See also Mueller Brass Co., 15 WLR 612 (1944), where the board held the company had the right to transfer employees in order to provide for efficiency despite the contention that such transfers violated the collective bargaining agreement.

30. Teller, "War Labor Board," 348–49; Atleson, *Values and Assumptions*, chap. 9.

31. The turmoil in General Motors plants created a strong managerial determination to protect its control and the authority of its supervisors. General Motors won the inclusion in the 1940 agreement of a managerial prerogatives clause specifying that the "right to hire; promote; discharge; discipline for cause; and to maintain discipline and efficiency of employees, is the sole responsibility of the corporation. . . . In addition, the products to be maintained, location of plants, the schedules production, the methods, processes and means of manufacturing are solely and exclusively the responsibilities of the corporation" (Nelson Lichtenstein, *Walter Reuther: The Most Dangerous Man in Detroit* [Urbana: University of Illinois Press, 1997; originally published as *The Most Dangerous Man in Detroit: Walter Reuther and the Fate of American Labor* [New York: Basic Books, 1995], 142).

32. Teller, "War Labor Board," 349.

33. United Aircraft Corp., 18 WLR 9 (1944).

34. Relations between the NLRB and the NWLB are discussed in Note, "The National War Labor Board and the National Labor Relations Act," *University of Pennsylvania Law Review* 92 (1943): 196; Ethel Denny, "Handling War Time Strikes: National Labor Relations Board and War Labor Board Compared," *George Washington Law Review* 11 (1942–43): 366. See also Fred Witney, *Wartime Experiences of the National Labor Relations Board, 1941–1945* (Urbana: University of Illinois Press, 1949).

35. David Montgomery, *Workers' Control in America* (New York: Cambridge University Press, 1979), 19.

36. See Teller, "War Labor Board," 358–59. The National Labor Relations Board in 1945 held that a unilateral change in working conditions, in this case the institution of an incentive pay plan without the consent of the union, was not an unfair labor practice unless it was done to discourage union organization (Libby, McNeal and Libby, 65 NLRB No. 156 [1945]). This limitation on the scope of bargaining would later be rejected by the National Labor Relations Board, and approved by the Supreme Court (NLRB v. Katz, 369 U.S. 736 [1962]).

37. Gary Gerstle, *Working-Class Americanism: The Politics of Labor in a Textile City, 1914–1960* (New York: Cambridge University Press, 1989), 210–11.

38. Ibid., 212.

39. Ibid., 210.

40. Ibid., 213–14.

41. Ibid., 314.

42. Ibid., 315. The 1941 French Spinning contract, for instance, stated that "any

change in the prevailing work load and working conditions throughout the mill shall be mutually agreed upon by the Employer and the Union" (ibid.).

43. Ibid., 316. Gerstle notes that between 1947 and 1949 "employer security" clauses found their way into thirteen of the fourteen ITU contracts either requiring union officials to order unauthorized strikers back to work or allowing employers to fire those who refuse to return or who struck in the first place. Thus, the ability of employees to circumvent the contractual bars and exercise independent power outside the union were eliminated (ibid., 317 n. 15).

44. Fibreboard Paper Products Corp. v. NLRB, 379 U.S. 203 (1964).

45. "We are thus not expanding the scope of mandatory bargaining to hold, as we do now, that the type of 'contracting' involved in this case—the replacement of employees in the existing bargaining unit with those of an independent contractor to do the same work under similar conditions of employment—is a statutory subject of collective bargaining under 8(d)" (ibid., 223).

46. Fibreboard Paper Products Corp. v. NLRB, 379 U.S. at 223 (Stewart, J., concurring).

47. First National Maintenance Corp. v. NLRB, 452 U.S. 666 (1981).

48. Ibid., 676 (1981). See, generally, Atleson, *Values and Assumptions*. The notion that some managerial rights are "inherent," and thus outside the mandatory scope of bargaining, parallels similar conclusions in thousands of decisions by private labor arbitrators. The failure of unions, for example, to secure explicit clauses restricting such changes as subcontracting or plant moves is often read as an implied permission for management to act. Similar positions have been taken by Canadian arbitrators despite the fact that the American mandatory-permissive distinction has basically been rejected in favor of a comprehensive duty to bargain collectively. See Brian Langille, "'Partnerships' in Labour Law," *Osgoode Hall Law Journal* 21 (1983): 497, 532–36. The War Labor Board went further, giving content to the notion of management prerogatives and stressing the procedures necessary for the fulfillment of management rights.

49. Joel Seidman, *American Labor from Defense to Reconversion* (Chicago: University of Chicago Press, 1953), 135–42; David Ziskind, "The Impact of the War on Labor Law," *Law and Contemporary Problems* 9 (1942): 385.

50. James Atleson, "Management Prerogatives, Plant Closings, and the NLRA," *New York University Review of Law and Social Change* 11 (1982–83): 89.

51. Alan Fox, *Beyond Contract: Work, Power and Trust Relations* (London: Faber & Faber, 1974), 279–80.

52. Katherine Van Wezel Stone, "The Post-War Paradigm in American Labor Law," *Yale Law Journal* 90 (1981): 1544–58; Atleson, *Values and Assumptions*, chap. 9.

53. William Murphy, "The Presidential Address: The Academy at Forty," in *Arbitration 1987: The Academy at Forty*, ed. Gladys Gruenberg (Proceedings of the 40th Annual Meeting of the NAA, BNA, 1987), 9.

54. See, for instance, John Dunlop, "Have the 1980's Changed U.S. Industrial Relations?" *Monthly Labor Review* 111 (May 1988): 29.

6

The Institutional Security of Unions

No issue presented to the War Labor Board precipitated more furious debate than union security.
—"Industrial Disputes and Wage Stabilization in Wartime," National War Labor Board, *Termination Report*, 1:81

The responsible character of the union's leadership is conceded by the company. There has been no stoppage of work since February 1941, shortly before the NLRB election. If there is any value to this responsible leadership, effort should be made to protect the union from disintegration. Out of fairness to the company, it must be said that it has not threatened the status of the union either by affirmative act or by implication. Realistically, however, it will be appreciated that the denial of any wage increase is bound to have a disturbing effect on the union membership. This, coupled with the company's policy of scrupulous adherence to legal obligation rather than active cooperation with the union, constitutes grave danger that work at the plant will suffer as the result of unrest among employees. Assurance that production of materials will not be interrupted can best come from a strong labor organization led by responsible individuals. There is warrant for a maintenance of membership clause.
—Towne Robinson Nut Co., 3 WLR 40 (1942)

Unions are dependent institutions and, as such, can rarely feel completely secure. To some degree, a sense of security might arise from both a supportive membership and nonhostile employers. Yet the rank and file are often restive, and American employers are among the most openly hostile in the world. In the labor relations field, however, "union security" has a special meaning, most commonly referring to contractual arrangements which either guarantee that all employees hired will be union members (the "closed shop") or, after hire, will be contractually required to join or at least financially support the union within a specified period (the "union shop").[1] Closely connected are contractual arrangements (the checkoff) by which employers withhold from employees' paychecks an amount equivalent to union dues.

After Pearl Harbor, one of the most significant public conflicts between unions and employers was over the role of the government in dealing with union security. Not surprisingly, the most discussed and analyzed decision of the WLB was its policy in relation to this contentious issue.[2] The board's determinations in this area created lasting changes in labor-management relations, some perhaps unanticipated.

Outside of certain craft unions with closed shops, union security provisions were not commonly found in prewar collective agreements, a legacy both of employers' anti-union "open-shop" philosophy of the 1920s and the relative weakness of unions. The newly invigorated unions of the 1940s, especially those facing an influx of workers with limited or no prior trade union experience, passionately desired some form of "union security." Union security had, of course, long been the goal of unions, especially fledgling unions, to protect institutional stability from the vagaries of employer opposition and economic fluctuations.

It is hardly surprising that union security should be a pressing concern. Since the fragility of the new unions had been made apparent by the depression in the late 1930s and by some significant organizing defeats, for instance in Little Steel, unions could be expected to seek some means to bind their members and develop a safe and regular source of funds, thus avoiding the time-consuming and troublesome method of collecting dues personally every month.[3] Labor might also have remembered that it enjoyed a period of growth during World War I, when union membership went from just under three million in 1917 to four million in 1919 and five million in 1920. Unionism had also advanced in some industries where virulent anti-unionism had existed. Most of the World War I gains, however, were lost in the postwar period, primarily due to the employers' open-shop campaign.[4]

The incidence of strikes over union security in 1941 suggests that it carried significance for the rank and file as well as for union officers. By the time of Pearl Harbor, the issue had halted construction of ships at a shipbuilding center, caused a seventy-six-day strike at Allis-Chalmers, led 150,000 coal miners to strike, and forced governmental seizure of several defense plants. The issue, as already noted, would eventually end the life of the National Defense Mediation Board (NDMB).

The proposed benefits to unions of union security provisions matched the effects which, it would be later said, were caused by the strictures of law. Thus, Golden and Ruttenberg, advisors to the United Steel Workers Union, argued that union security permitted a more cooperative union-employer relationship. The existence of a contractual union security clause meant, they asserted, that the employer explicitly recognized the permanent status and presence of the union and, most significantly, would alter the nature and types of local union leadership, for now locals would need officials "capable of administering contracts on a relatively peaceful basis."[5] The union administrators would be free from challenges from employers as well as unrest by their members.

Similar sentiments are found in early WLB decisions, as reflected in the introductory quotation from a 1942 decision. In another 1942 decision, the board granted the UE a "maintenance of membership" clause, a weak form of union security clause which only binds workers *already* members of the union to remain members normally for a specified period of time. The union leadership, said the board, should be freed from organizational efforts so it could direct its attention to improving production.[6]

There are two important aspects of these asserted benefits of union security, benefits that would seem to stem initially from union recognition, collective bargaining, and a resulting collective agreement. First, the Golden-Ruttenberg argument suggests that the militant union leader, who like Moses led the workers to the promised land of bargaining status, would now be replaced by a more managerial type, because the skills possessed by the militant were no longer relevant to the new administrative world created by the collective agreement. As Ruttenberg asserted in 1939, for instance, "the type of leader who has the courage to fight the company's anti-union activities has a difficult time making this adjustment," and the goal was to make union officials contract administrators. The task of top union leaders of organized locals was to "show the way toward industrial peace and fruitful labor-management relations."[7] Those union leaders who could not restrict their militant tendencies would be disciplined, that is, replaced by the union's membership. In short, militant "leadership was essential to the establishment of the union against bitter resistance, but after it had been fully accepted by management, such leadership was a handicap to the development of cooperative, union-management relations."[8]

Second, as the prior chapter dealing with arbitration suggests, workers' rights after recognition would be based upon the contract rather than on economic confrontation, and these rights would be administered through the cooler confines of the grievance process. It is important to note that the views of Clinton Golden and Harold Ruttenberg, influential at least on the Steelworkers' union, were penned between 1939 and 1942. These views concerning bureaucratization and contractualism thus preceded WLB rulings, the ultimately restrictive interpretations of the NLRA, and, indeed, the postwar pluralists. Indeed, these ideas can perhaps be related to the Wisconsin school and, certainly, can be seen reflected in

Sidney Hillman's vision of the garment industry as early as the 1920s.[9] These ideas of unionists and union sympathizers are perhaps based on a vision of both the modern factory and labor dispute resolution as a set of integrated technological operations; the goal of labor relations, as well as of engineers, was to make the situation as efficient as possible while reflecting human concerns.

Employers' statements in the 1940s highlighted the white-hot issue, calling union security "the most highly controversial and emotional question in industrial relations today."[10] They tended to oppose both the closed and the union shop because such arrangements concentrated power in the hands of union leaders and compromised the principles of the open shop movement begun in the 1920s. Employers obviously recognized that the union shop would increase union strength and affect relative bargaining power after the war, precisely one of the reasons the unions felt so strongly about the issue. Although arguments about individual freedom were commonplace, it should not be surprising that many of the employers who fought union organization most vigorously tended to develop strong, often passionate, concerns for the rights of individual workers.[11]

For unions, the rivalry between the AFL and CIO provided a new reason for union security clauses, which now offered a type of protection from the raids of rivals. Primarily, however, such arrangements made the unions "secure" in relation to new employees or those existing members who might become dissatisfied. During the war, protection from employees was felt to be an especially serious need since thousands of new workers had entered the plants and unions could not strike or secure wages in excess of government-set levels. Moreover, like the employers, unions were also concerned about the postwar effects of wartime policies. Continued employer opposition to union security suggested to union leaders that employers would move against unions, as they did after World War I, once the imposed truce of the wartime period ended.[12]

The president's labor-management conference, held ten days after Pearl Harbor, attempted to reach agreement on principles of labor-management relations.[13] The parties agreed to avoid all strikes and lockouts for the duration and to submit disputes to a war labor board for binding decision.[14] The conference deadlocked, however, on the contentious issue of union security. Despite the proffered benefits of union security arrangements, employers were adamantly opposed. FDR, warmly praising the conferees for the agreements reached, accepted the principles agreed upon and announced that he would set up a new board to handle disputes which would establish its own jurisdiction. The president shrewdly did not exclude the issue of union security, in effect passing the problem on to the new wartime labor agency.[15]

The ultimate compromise adopted by the WLB was the maintenance of membership clause, a position which derived both from War Labor Board policies as well as from prior actions of the NDMB.[16] The NDMB had recommended maintenance of membership in a variety of cases in 1941 but with some reluctance and a noticeable lack of consistency. Indeed, in July 1941 the NDMB voted *not* to adopt a uniform policy on union security.[17] Like the WLB, the NDMB in each case considered the attitude of management toward the union, the importance of the company in the defense effort, and the possibility of rival unionism.[18] The NDMB apparently believed that some form of union security was a justifiable benefit for a union which refrained from strikes, a benefit which did not impinge on any federal policy. Thus, the NDMB in *Federal Shipbuilding and Drydock Company* recommended a maintenance of membership clause on the ground that the company had been anti-union and the union's morale had thereby been undermined.[19] Union security of some type, therefore, was deemed important in protecting unions operating in a hostile environment. On the other hand, the NDMB opposed maintenance of membership where the union was obviously secure, as in the UMW/captive mines dispute.

Nevertheless, there was no consistent NDMB policy. In one case the NDMB recommended a closed shop[20] but all forty-five requests for a union shop were turned down.[21] During 1941, however, the NDMB granted the weaker maintenance of membership clauses in seven of the eleven cases in which the issue explicitly arose.[22] It granted the clause only where it felt it necessary to insure continued defense production or, as in *North American Aviation*, where "there was an urgent need for reviving the union in order to assure stable labor relations and the quarrel between local and national leadership made it doubtful whether the national leadership could restore it without the assistance of the maintenance of membership clause."[23]

On September 15, 1941, the mine workers in the captive mine fields went on strike to obtain the union shop. Although the mines were overwhelmingly organized and union security was accepted by 90 percent of the bituminous coal industry, the NDMB refused to recommend the union shop because these facts demonstrated to it that union security was not necessary. The president induced the parties to resubmit the issue, and the miners returned to work, but the NDMB again refused to recommend the union shop. Again, the miners struck. The next day (November 11, 1941), the two CIO members of the NDMB resigned. The CIO members may have been especially outraged because the two AFL board members voted against the union shop with William Green's prior approval.[24] Roosevelt bluntly warned Lewis and Murray that "the government of the United States will not order, nor will Congress pass legislation ordering, a so-called closed shop."[25] Nevertheless, the captive mines dispute was turned over to a three-man arbitration board which, not surprisingly perhaps, granted the union shop on December 7, 1941.[26]

Despite the NDMB's policies, employer members of the War Labor Board initially opposed any union security arrangement. And as Andrew Workman notes, the public members were placed in a difficult position because of the opposition of employer members and conservative criticism of the board as overly sympathetic to labor. On the other hand, public members may well have harbored the voluntaristic views propounded by employers.[27] Eventually, after the board's majority made clear its preference for maintenance of membership clauses, public members argued that in order to receive the clause unions must meet certain standards of democratic government, a position which related to the often stated view of employers that such clauses violated the liberty of individual workers. The unions replied that the clauses actually reflected principles of majority rule. The NDMB itself had eventually decided to grant the clause only when the union was "responsible" and "democratic."[28]

In short, then, the WLB routinely granted unions maintenance of membership clauses, a mild but still valuable form of union security.[29] This clause required employees who *were* members of the union to *remain* members for the term of the contract and to pay dues, often via a checkoff provision, although a brief fifteen-day window of escape was eventually provided. A typical version of the clause read as follows: "All employees who, fifteen days after the date of the Directive Order of the National War Labor Board in this case, are members of the union in good standing in accordance with the constitution and bylaws of the Union, and those employees who may thereafter become members shall, during the life of the agreement, as a condition of employment, remain members of the union in good standing."[30]

Like other policies of the WLB (or the earlier NDMB), some maintenance of membership clauses pre-existed the war, most often in street railways and in the clothing industry. Yet, similar clauses were found in only nine cases in a study of four hundred contracts between 1937 and 1939. By the end of the war, however, examples could be found in almost one-third of all collective agreements.[31]

In addition, despite FDR's earlier warning to the miners, the WLB decreed that existing prewar closed shop contracts would be protected from challenge for the duration of the war.[32] Such a policy, said the board, would eliminate union membership raiding and unwarranted organizational activities and in general promote war production by stabilizing labor relations.

In May 1942, George Taylor, then vice-chairman of the WLB, gave an address in Scranton in which he reviewed recent decisions which, he believed, had "disposed of the [union security problem] as a major issue in order that people may be free to bend their every effort to the winning of the war."

> In three successive major disputes, Walker-Turner, International Harvester and Federal Shipbuilding, the Board granted maintenance of membership clauses. Though the Board votes on these three cases were 8 to 4, with the employer members dissenting each time, the actual difference between the majority and minority was so narrow as to be almost invisible. In my opinion, the disposition of these three cases indicates that when a union claim for security has merit, a "maintenance of membership" clause may frequently be looked to as a solution and be developed in such a way as to insure that such a clause is acceptable. . . .
>
> In the International Harvester case, for example, a maintenance of membership clause becomes effective when it is approved by a majority of the union members in each plant. Both the Walker-Turner and the Federal Shipbuilding cases were significant in indicating that while failure of an employee to maintain union membership need not result in the loss of employment, [it carries with it] the imposition of some obligation such as continuing to assume certain financial costs to insure the proper carrying out of the agreement. A maintenance of membership clause requires simply that every person who has voluntarily joined the union is required to remain a member of the union for the duration of the contract. All those who joined later . . . [were] likewise bound to maintain their membership in good standing for the same period of time. This clause, as applied by the Board, protects the union's existence and protects the individual's freedom of choice. I believe that American management is coming to recognize the inherent soundness of such union security provisions. They do not require an employee to join the union. They do recognize the need for stabilizing industrial relations.[33]

The WLB's grant of a form of union security has often been viewed either as an inducement to encourage union control over a rambunctious rank and file or as compensation to unions for the relatively ungenerous wage allowances under the "Little Steel" formula, rewarding unions whose "responsibility" was demonstrated by failing to vigorously press the demands of membership. This may seem an odd form of reward for not seeking more adequate wage increases, but the WLB's decisions support both interpretations. Indeed, the WLB expressly stated that its policy was fair given both the unions' no-strike pledge and the fact that wages were tightly regulated by the board.[34] In such an environment union members, especially the thousands of inexperienced workers flowing into wartime factories, might well begin to question the value of union representation. Moreover, as the board often stated, stable unions could be more "responsible" in guaranteeing continued production. That is, unions were explicitly viewed as valuable controllers of the rank and file, a public role quite different than that stressed by Senator Wagner between 1933 and 1935.

The labor members of the WLB continually stressed that since labor had surrendered its strike weapon, compensation was required in the form of protection against membership losses resulting from either hostile employers or rival unions. They wanted, in Chairman Davis's words, protection "against a war in the rear while they're trying to fight in the front."[35] Unions, however, desired a stronger form of security than maintenance of membership.

Views of dissenters on the WLB are often difficult to discern. Often, dissents or concurrences are cited without opinion. Even opinions are inadequate when facts are stated tersely or references are made to regional board opinions. By far, most dissents were filed by employer members, and most of these were in union security cases. Employer dissenters objected to maintenance of membership clauses which forced employers to fire employees who failed to maintain membership and lacked an escape clause.[36] In late 1942, when the general thrust of governmental protection was no doubt clear, employer representatives began to suggest internal regulation of unions such as the mandatory filing of the union's constitution and bylaws and financial statements.[37]

The board's first grant of maintenance of membership did not involve a thorough explanation of the underlying theory or policy involved.[38] Subsequent cases began to develop reasons for *not* granting the security clause—if, for instance, the union had already gained sufficient strength as revealed by membership growth;[39] there was an absence of competing unions, suggesting that the possibility of raiding was not a relevant factor;[40] or the union was not threatened.[41] Thus, the early cases focused upon the strength and security of the union rather than its "responsibility."

Clearly, the grant of maintenance of membership was initially related to the perceived strength of the union. Firmly entrenched unions with no rivals would be denied the clause.[42] On the other hand, the board would grant the clause to avoid disintegration of the local.[43] Such actions illustrate the tradeoff between union democracy and union security. Perhaps the best known example is the grant to the Steelworkers, who had felt compelled to establish picket lines in many locations to prevent nonpaying members from entering the plant. Because of the immense amount of time spent in collecting dues and the hostility generated, the board added for the first time an automatic dues checkoff for all those covered by the maintenance of membership clause.[44]

It is reasonable, therefore, to see the board's grant of maintenance of membership as a compromise designed to avoid perceived industrial disruption should the board accept either the open or the closed shop option. The board's own statements indicated the compromise nature of its position:

> The two positions [open and closed shop] honestly and stubbornly held, if unreconciled, would result in industrial disruption and the monthly loss of many millions of man hours of production. . . . National necessity could not allow production to stop while this bitter issue was being long fought out on the picket lines. Some advised that the issue should be ignored. Others argued for the maintenance of the status quo. A fair and stable answer had to be found. The answer was found in the provision for the maintenance of the voluntarily established union membership.[45]

Scholars viewed the board's action as a brilliant compromise between two irreconcilable positions. In 1942 Louis Jaffe, then a professor of law at the University of Buffalo, described the maintenance of membership clause as "a brilliantly inspired device to reconcile an insoluble conflict, a positive preservation of the status quo. On the one hand, it did not force upon the employer the closed shop; it left him free to hire whom he chose, since a new employee may neither be in or join the union if for any reason he did not wish to do so. On the other hand, by requiring those employees who were members of the union to remain members it protected the union from disintegration." As Jaffe noted, the clause was often granted to protect a union from employer hostility, rival unions, or unfavorable employment conditions which might bring the union into discredit.[46]

A second factor was the desire not to weaken unions after they had made a voluntary no-strike pledge. Thus the board argued that unions who had waived their right to strike "need some security against disintegration under the impact of war. It is in the interest of equity that the union, which might win by a strike the more complete security of the union shop or even the closed shop, be assured the maintenance of membership which it already has or may voluntarily acquire."[47]

A subsequent explanation by Frank Graham was that since the unions had surrendered the use of economic power, the nation should, in equity, provide the unions with fair protection against disintegration both from the impacts and controls of war, and from the impacts of the reconversion, confusions and all the transitions of the peace. Responsible union leadership which patriotically cooperates with the national policy for winning the war and peace should not be endangered by demagogic and disruptive leadership. The responsible and cooperative union should not be crippled by refusals and failures of irresponsible members to pay union dues because the union does not have the disciplinary power of the union shop and does not use its striking power for increased wages.[48]

Graham's statement suggests that, first, the maintenance of membership clause was equitable given the no-strike pledge, again implicitly employing the notion that the clause was a trade-off for the right to strike. In addition, Graham stressed that the clause was also a payoff to responsible union leadership.[49] He noted, however, that there were limits to the board's willingness to grant the clause. As the board said in the *Little Steel* case, "the union asking for security in this case is worthy of the freedom and responsibility of the voluntary and binding maintenance of union membership and check-off. The United Steelworkers of America, on the record, is one of the most democratic, responsible and efficient unions in America. Elections are held periodically and by secret ballot. . . . It is the express policy of the union to cooperate with management in the keeping of agreements, and maintaining discipline, and improving production."[50] Note the characterization of the United Steelworkers as a democratic union and, especially, the reference to the union's cooperation with management in maintaining agreements and *discipline*. Graham stated that there was a "clear consensus of opinion in the Board that the maintenance of membership, with all its values, will not be granted to an irresponsible union which disregards the no-strike policy of the nation, or to a union which refuses to have reasonably frequent elections, or to a union which refuses to make reasonably regular financial reports to the members of the union."[51]

As the board stressed in its *United States Rubber Company* decision, its union security policy was based on a notion of fairness for unions, which had "weakened their bargaining power by voluntarily forfeiting their right to strike."[52] Yet, although a relationship was commonly drawn between the grant of maintenance of membership and strikes, it was normally directed to a quite different concern. Union security clauses were explicitly granted in exchange for union promises to control rank-and-file militancy.[53]

Thus, the WLB granted the standard maintenance of membership provision in *Mack Manufacturing* because it would make union members conscious of responsibilities under contract and enable the local of a responsible national union to discipline its members and engage wholeheartedly in the war effort without fear of self-destruction due to limitation of opportunity for improvements in wages and working conditions.[54]

Unions which were involved in strikes were often denied the clause or lost previously granted union security provisions.[55] A union would not be eligible unless it was "responsible," with no strikes in its wartime record. Election of officers had to be regular and open to all members, and the union was required to make audited financial reports to its members.[56]

As Joshua Freeman has noted, "By tying union security to the question of strikes, the WLB shrewdly used the unions themselves as the chief instrument of wartime labor discipline."[57] The union's obligation was to "absolve itself from all responsibility" so as to leave no doubt as to its relationship to the strike. Clearly, unions were expected to control union members so that they did not engage in unauthorized strikes. The language in one case is particularly strong:

> Indeed, it is unthinkable that there should be any deliberate interruption by those engaged in the war effort, however strongly provoked they may feel. A strike against an employer, no matter how intolerable working conditions may seem, is in reality a strike against the millions of American soldiers and sailors in foreign lands, completely dependent upon those at home, who have the duty of keeping them supplied with materials essential to their success and survival. Let there be no misunderstanding as to the fact that this Board will do everything within its power, consistent with its grave responsibility of furthering the war effort, to cope with those whose patriotism seems to be so frail that they cannot be trusted to subordinate their own self-interests to the interests of the nation.[58]

The WLB did not hesitate to deny maintenance of membership when it felt a union was not vigorously acting to suppress strikes, but there were other penalties as well. Thus, the board on occasion withdrew seniority rights, shift premiums, vacation pay, and the right of the union to handle grievances. As the incidence of short and wildcat strikes became even more frequent as the war progressed, the board pressured international union officers to exercise tight control over locals that failed to eradicate strikes. Thus, the board approved the union's fining of strikers in *Yellow Truck and Coach Mfg. Co.* because the action demonstrated the union's responsibility and, moreover, the fines reflected the individual responsibility of each employee. Because of manpower shortages, fines were believed to be more appropriate than layoffs or discharge: "work stoppages are the result of a lapse of good judgment for a time, flowing from the ill-considered suggestions of a few hotheads. The discharging of a large number of employees involved in such spontaneous stoppages would be ill-advised unless the workers demonstrate that they do not intend to live up to their obligations as employees."[59]

The board's actions thus encouraged union centralization and bureaucratization. "Leadership became more distant from the rank and file, while subtle Board intercessions in internal union politics set dangerous precedents for future government action."[60] The notion that unions would have to conform to some standards of "responsible unionism" in order to receive the maintenance of membership provision began early.[61] In the 1942 *Woods Machine Company* decision, for instance, the public members agreed that the clause should not issue until "the Board was satisfied that the union was responsible and was operating according to certain well-established democratic principles under its constitution and bylaws."[62] One aspect of "responsibility" was clear—the union's request for maintenance of membership would be denied where it had authorized a strike.[63] The board sometimes stressed that the union had violated its no-strike promise but at other times argued that the strike demonstrated irresponsibility and, thus, the union could not claim the maintenance of membership clause as an aid to production.

The existence of a strike, however, would not automatically result in the denial of the clause. "A work stoppage is not an automatic bar to union security but is only a bar if the facts show that the union is not sufficiently interested in maintaining sufficient production and, therefore, is unworthy of security."[64] Since the board viewed the clause as beneficial to stable, responsible leadership, it often granted the clause despite strikes. When rank-and-file union membership struck *despite* the opposition of the local and international, as in *Worcester Press Steel Co.*, the board stressed that the leaders had shown responsibility and needed additional power to discipline the irresponsible elements.[65] It also found that the company had not negotiated in a spirit of cooperation. In other words, the board felt that to some extent the company had goaded the union into a strike.[66] On the other hand, a strike in *compliance* with the 1943 War Labor Disputes Act, that is, where a union struck after the thirty-day cooling-off period and after a formal strike vote, could nevertheless result in a denial of the clause. Even though the statute had been complied with, the board held the union had broken the no-strike pledge.[67]

An exception was sometimes made for employer provocation: "The principle that no employer can be allowed to antagonize and provoke the union to such an extent as to bring about a strike and then expect to have the Board refuse any form of security to the union because of the strike . . . would not be fair."[68] Later cases, however, reveal a quite different attitude toward strikes alleged to be the result of employer provocation: "It is precisely when provocation exists that the pledge to restrain from work stoppage is tested. It is only then that the pledge not to strike has any real significance."[69] Thus, even if management provoked strikes, only labor would be punished for the use of economic weapons because strikes were evidence of irresponsibility. As the board stated: "Irresponsible unions are a detriment to the national war effort."[70]

The board also denied the clause in *Chrysler Corp.* because of strikes, despite evidence that management had provoked the strikes: "the local union cannot mitigate the seriousness of their past record of stoppages by a general reference to 'provocative acts' on the part of management. . . . The National War Labor Board cannot possibly acquiesce in the implied suggestion of the union that labor's no-strike pledge is to be suspended whenever a union claims, with or without merit, that management is provocative."[71]

The provocation cases made clear that, as far as governmental action was concerned, the union would be held responsible for disruptive actions. In one case employees sought pay for time lost during a work stoppage or, alternatively, work was lost when the power was shut off by the plant manager following certain actions by employees. The board determined that it would not order reimbursement for time lost during strikes or lockouts, and it noted that it was not in a position to judge whether the manager's action was warranted or not. Even if the activity was a lockout, with its resultant disruption of production, the board held that it would not order reimbursement for employees.[72]

Moreover, a strike might lead to the denial of the clause despite the fact that it "occurred at a time when the union was engaged in a struggle for its very existence." Despite this finding, the panel decided that the strike was evidence of immaturity and that the clause could only be awarded "in those instances where the union's responsibility is unquestioned."[73] It should be noted that the union panel members sometimes *agreed* in the denial of maintenance of membership on the ground that the union failed to demonstrate responsibility.[74] Such actions reveal the considerable pressures on union leadership during the period.

Given the strong union desire for security, the WLB's policies induced many unions to exercise a policing role over their membership, affecting the social relationship between unions and the rank and file.[75] The union now had an additional inducement to act as an enforcer of contractual obligations and as an obstacle to, and moderator of, independent rank-and-file action. This proved especially poignant in those CIO unions which had grown because of often decentralized, rank-and-file militance.

The connection between union security and union control over militancy should not, however, be overstressed. The WLB granted maintenance of membership clauses early in the war when strikes, wildcat or authorized, were merely a possibility and not yet a reality. Indeed, the WLB often granted the clause *prior* to the wildcat strike wave which began in 1943. Concededly, the clause, like arbitration provisions, was expressly granted *because* of the union's surrender of the right to strike, especially for union or closed shop clauses.[76] Although in midwar the grant of maintenance of membership clauses might be based, at least in part, upon the desire to support union efforts to police their rank and file, the provision instead was initially seen as fair because of the union's surrender of the right to strike.

In decisions involving Bethlehem and Republic Steel in July 1942, Graham expressed a slightly different concern:

> The maintenance of a stable union membership makes for the maintenance of responsible union leadership and responsible union discipline, makes for keeping faithfully the terms of the contract, and provides a stable basis for union-management cooperation for more efficient production. If union leadership is responsible and cooperative, then irresponsible and uncooperative members cannot escape discipline by getting out of the union and thus disrupt relations and hamper production. If the union leadership should prove unworthy, demagogic, and irresponsible, then worthy and responsible members of the union still remain inside the union to correct abuses, select better leaders, and improve production.[77]

Stability was the key goal, and it was believed that stability led to responsible union leaders. The argument that members would remain in the union and subject to its discipline could well be a rationalization, what lawyers refer to as a "make-weight" argument, but it does appeal to anti-radical sympathies.

Art Preis has argued that the maintenance of membership was granted, at least in part, to secure labor's acquiescence in the wage restrictions of the "Little Steel" formula.[78] Preis quotes WLB chairman Davis in an April 29 news interview as directly connecting the question of union security with the enforcement of a general wage freeze: "We're going to have to call on the leaders of labor to put this [wage stabilization] over," said Davis. "That being so, this is another reason for upholding the hands of leaders of organized labor."[79] Thus, Preis argues that maintenance of membership was to be the union leaders' reward for policing the rank and file, enforcing the no-strike pledge, the wage freeze, speedups, and other onerous conditions.

The connection of the board's union security policies to wage stabilization may be more subtle. Timothy Willard, for instance, argues that as the policy of wage stabilization tightened, the board increased the level of union security. Thus, by fall 1942, the checkoff was routinely granted with maintenance of membership clauses, and after April 1943 the checkoff was granted in almost every case in which it was requested. The two clauses were denied "only in the most blatant cases of violations of the no-strike pledge by union leaders."[80] Willard views the board as providing union leaders with a tool both to control their membership in a period of regulated wages and to thwart raiding efforts from rival unions.[81]

Whether or not one characterizes the board's support for this form of security as "brilliant," even this weak form of union security represented a substantial advance to most industrial unions, and craft unions were permitted to keep the union or closed shops that they had previously achieved through collective bargaining. The public members, who could not obtain a unanimous decision in a typical case, combined with the labor members to grant a maintenance of membership clause where no stronger form of union security had previously existed. Employer representatives, on the other hand, generally opposed it except in special circumstances.[82]

Perhaps because of the opposition of employer members, the WLB by the summer of 1942 included in the grant of its standard clause a requirement that neither the union nor its officers or members would intimidate or coerce employees into membership, and in the fall of 1943 the board resolved unanimously that workers were free to leave during an escape period without regard to the union's regulations or constitutional provisions related to withdrawal.[83] Thus, as Marcus Manoff stated in 1943, maintenance of membership came with a "price," the loss of full autonomy.[84] The relationship between the union and its members was no longer a private matter. The board felt it necessary to scrutinize union constitutions and bylaws and ordered all unions receiving the clause to amend their constitutions to permit withdrawal within the fifteen-day escape period.[85]

In *Ryan Aeronautical Company*,[86] Roger Lapham, an employer member of the WLB, quoting from an article in the *Saturday Evening Post*[87] argued that if the relation between the worker and an employer was to be controlled by a majority of the union, "the inevitable consequence is that the government must step in to make it certain that the manner in which the union leaders use its new power is in accord with justice, reason, and public interest." That is, if federal law supported the power of the majority over individual employees, that same law should necessarily protect individuals from abuse of that power.

In December 1944, the Supreme Court decided three cases which seemingly responded to this concern. The Court declared that the unions, as the beneficiaries of government action, must now submit to government regulation over the quality of their treatment and representation of employees. The Court, interpreting the Railway Labor Act and subsequently the NLRA, found that implicit in those statutes was an obligation on unions' part to treat all represented workers fairly, creating "duty of fair representation" for both members and nonmembers of unions.[88] These early cases, decided in wartime, primarily involved racial discrimination reflected in collective agreements between unions and employers. Ironically, no law prohibited employers from discriminating upon racial grounds on their own, say in hiring, and, despite their state charters and life-giving tax advantages, corporations were not required to treat their employees fairly. Representatives of workers were required to act fairly in relation to those they represented while nonorganized employers could continue to treat their employees and prospective employees arbitrarily. The justified concern for individuals in an organized workplace should not obscure the one-sided nature of the employment relation.

The legal literature on the War Labor Board and union security is vast.[89] What is interesting in these articles is the matter-of-fact description of the conditions under which the clause was granted.[90] Generally, the creation of maintenance of membership is seen as a compromise, often a brilliant one, necessary to reduce industrial strife and, secondarily, as compensation to unions for having abandoned the right to strike during the war. The discussion of the refusal to grant the clause or its removal for "irresponsible" action is typically expressed as if nothing was lost. Few commentators expressed any concern about or interest in the meaning of the trade of increased bureaucracy and control of the rank and file for secure membership and dues. Perhaps in wartime, or in the immediate postwar period, the cost of the trade-off was not seen as particularly serious or unwarranted. The absence of such discussion may reflect the general opposition to wartime strikes, a matter which perhaps needed little discussion at the time these articles were written. This also suggests the limited range of possible union options.

There is no doubt the board's policy increased the size and financial stability of wartime industrial unions.[91] The Steelworkers' union could terminate their dues picket lines, and the union's net worth grew sevenfold between May 1942 and November 1943 despite a falling-off in total steel employment. As new workers joined unions, not actually required by the clause, the wealth of the unions dramatically increased. Although union leaders might be aware of the costs of wartime regulation, the gains of union security were too obvious. "It is easy to forget how new and shaky the CIO was on the eve of the war."[92] Many important employers had yet to become organized. Especially after the devastating downturn of 1938, many unions did not establish new or stabilize old local unions. With restrictions on strikes beginning as early as the defense period, the increasingly conservative atmosphere, and the influx of thousands of new industrial workers into war industries, unions rationally feared for their stability. It must have seemed as if unions had little choice but to accept government regulation as well as government protection.

In September 1943, the *Monthly Labor Review* studied thirty-one cases in which maintenance of membership was introduced through the action of the War Labor Board.[93] In most cases, the study found that resignations during the escape period were negligible and that discharges of union members for failure to remain in good standing were not numerous. It also found that the maintenance of membership clause had "assisted the enforcement of the union's 'no-strike' pledge in several instances."[94] In most of the cases studied, employment had increased due to the military expenditures, but the turnover rate and losses in union membership in many of the plants were fairly high. The study noted, however, a "considerable degree of stability in union strength under the maintenance of membership provision." In only seven of the thirty-one cases studied had the union suffered a decrease in total membership during the period that maintenance of membership clauses had been in effect. This suggests that although maintenance of membership did not compel new employees to join, many new employees, although traditionally viewed as hostile or indifferent to unions, did in fact join unions even though not compelled do to so.

The study also found other beneficial effects. For instance, Bureau of Labor Statistics investigators were told by several union officials that "the additional power given to them by the maintenance of membership provision has enabled them to take strong measures to prevent stoppages from occurring. In one instance cited, the union prevented a group of workers from striking when a negro employee was brought into the department; many workers incensed at the union's attitude, tore up their union cards, but later rejoined when they realized that persistence in their action would mean loss of employment."[95]

It was significant that although employers generally became reconciled to maintenance of membership in three plants studied by the BLS, employers were strongly opposed and were trying, sometimes successfully, to prevent the union from making its "security" effective. A number of employers opposed maintenance of membership in principle, but were reconciled to accepting it only for the duration of the war. Unions, on the other hand, were generally satisfied but obviously recognized that the degree of security was much less than under a union or closed shop agreement.[96] As one union official said, "Maintenance of membership is not even a forty-second cousin to the closed shop. In fact, it is an open shop and encourages the company to continue its anti-union activity."[97]

Even with the maintenance of membership clause, and particularly in plants where labor turnover was high, unions were still required to spend a good deal of time organizing, collecting dues, and "tending fences" among the employees. Nevertheless, almost all unions stated that maintenance of membership had relieved the dues situation to some extent even where no checkoff clause was in existence. Enforcement of maintenance of membership was a problem in those cases where there was severe delinquency because "the unions felt that they could not place themselves in the position of asking for the discharge of large numbers of qualified workmen with the consequent disruption of production. In addition, the unions feared the effect on weaker union members should they be called before the company and be warned or disciplined for failure to pay dues."[98] Since new employees were not required to join, some unions would hesitate to force existing members to pay dues on pain of discharge.

At the beginning of 1944 approximately thirteen and three-fourths million workers, or almost 45 percent of all workers in private industry, were employed under the terms of union agreements. There was a net gain during 1943 of about three-fourths of a million workers under agreement. The increase may relate more to changes in employment in individual industries than to actual changes in the proportions of workers covered by agreements.[99] The significant change in 1943 was the increase in the proportion of manufacturing employees covered by agreements requiring maintenance of union membership during the life of the agreement. Generally overlooked in discussions of union security, however, is that in January 1944 closed shop agreements covered almost 30 percent of all workers under agreement, and union shop agreements covered almost 20 percent. Together, these far more effective forms of union security covered a total of about six and half million workers.[100] At the same time, 20 percent of all workers under agreement, or over three million workers, were covered by maintenance of membership clauses.[101] Thus the impact of maintenance of membership should, perhaps, not be overstressed.

Given the volume of writing on the WLB's policy favoring maintenance of membership clauses, it is astounding to find that at the beginning of 1944 approximately one-half of workers working under collective agreements were covered by more significant union and closed shop arrangements.[102] Such provisions had to have been privately negotiated, although the War Labor Board would approve the continuation of such clauses if they previously existed in collective bargaining agreements. Nevertheless at the beginning of 1943, two million workers or more than 15 percent of all workers under agreement were covered by maintenance of membership provisions.[103] Thus, there was a considerable increase in the incidence of maintenance of membership clauses during 1943. This was, not coincidentally, a year of considerable rank-and-file discontent and a high incidence of wildcat strikes. As noted in the *Monthly Labor Review,* such clauses "have become much more common during the recent months, largely as a result of orders of the National War Labor Board."[104]

Despite the board's alleged brilliant compromise on union security, its substantive policies did not survive the war. Maintenance of membership clauses virtually disappeared in the postwar era, and the closed shop was explicitly prohibited by the Taft-Hartley Act of 1947. The union shop was permitted, allowing contractual provisions requiring employees, not to join an existing union, but only to pay the equivalent of union dues "uniformly required as a condition of acquiring or retaining membership."[105] The "membership" required under a statutorily approved clause is, as expressed by the Supreme Court, "whittled down to its financial core"[106] and union security clauses may not be employed as a method of union discipline.[107]

Nevertheless, the policy of the War Labor Board probably increased bureaucratic tendencies already existing in unions and, given the considerations for the grant of maintenance of membership, involved the government in the regulation of intra-union affairs.[108] The union's desire for maintenance of membership, however, and the concurrent need to police the rank and file should not be seen simply as a trade of rank-and-file rights for institutional security. Indeed, the need to restrict workplace militancy should be seen as related to the union's grant of the no-strike pledge. Unions clearly supported defense mobilization and the war effort. Although union leaders were pragmatic, the importance of patriotism should not be overlooked. Certainly union officials believed, as the 1940 labor-management conference revealed, that some kind of governmentally set labor and wage policy was inevitable and even necessary in order to win the war.

Given the pressures upon unions, many believed that the CIO could not realistically have followed a radically different course. The passage of the Smith-Connally War Labor Disputes Act in 1943, over administration objections, and the introduction or one-house passage of many restrictive labor bills, to be subsequently discussed, provided vivid testimony of the likelihood of congressional approval for repressive labor legislation.[109] Throughout the war, the threat of restrictive legislative action was always real. The military and others had also pushed for national service legislation from the start of the war.

Moreover, wartime strikes were exceedingly unpopular. As UAW president R. J. Thomas said, "Our union cannot survive if the nation and our soldiers believe that we are obstructing the war effort."[110]

It is difficult, moreover, to see union bureaucratization solely as a response to the board's union security policy. Unions as large and often diverse institutions might well have tended in this direction anyway, acting no differently than other large organizations. Sociological concepts would suggest that, as unions grew, the distance between leaders and the rank and file would also grow. The distance would become vast when union leaders would spend substantial time consulting or advising politicians and administration officials or serving as members of governmental bodies. Size also encourages the creation of well-defined rules and the development of a rationalized organization, creating specific spheres of competence, following the principles of hierarchy to be found in union constitutions and bylaws.[111]

In addition, collective bargaining itself, along with grievance arbitration, is strongly directed to the development of dispute-resolution expertise and the creation of union hierarchy. Moreover, although the next two chapters will raise some doubts about this argument, unions were concerned about the entry of thousands of inexperienced workers into the war industries just as union veterans left for the armed services. As Nelson Lichtenstein has noted, this made for a "volatile but not particularly union-conscious proletariat," resembling the pre-depression, nonunion era.[112] The following two chapters discuss the causes and incidence of wartime strikes and the role of the "new" workers.

Notes

1. The closed shop clause was prohibited by section 8(a)(3) of the Taft-Hartley Act of 1947, which permitted employment to be contractually conditioned upon "membership" in a union thirty days after hire, normally referred to as the "union shop." "Membership" is, by law, limited only to the obligation to pay an amount equivalent to union dues.

2. See Nelson Lichtenstein, "Ambiguous Legacy: The Union Security Problem during World War II," *Labor History* 18 (Spring 1977): 217–38.

3. Nelson Lichtenstein, *Labor's War at Home* (New York: Cambridge University Press, 1983), 21.

4. See Joel Seidman, *American Labor from Defense to Reconversion* (Chicago: University of Chicago Press, 1953), 271.

5. See Clinton Golden and Harold Ruttenberg, *The Dynamics of Industrial Democracy* (New York: Harper and Bros., 1942), 218–26.

6. Pioneer Gen-E-Motor Co., 3 WLR 8 (1942).

7. Harold Ruttenberg, "Strategy of Industrial Peace," *Harvard Business Review* 17 (1939): 172–73; see also Golden and Ruttenberg, *Dynamics of Industrial Democracy*, 67.

8. Golden and Ruttenberg, *Dynamics of Industrial Democracy*, 61.

9. See Steven Fraser, "Dress Rehearsal for the New Deal: Shop-Floor Insurgents, Political Elites, and Industrial Democracy in the Amalgamated Clothing Workers," in *Working-Class America: Essays on Labor, Community, and American Society*, ed. Michael Frisch and Daniel Walkowitz (Urbana: University of Illinois Press, 1983).

10. James MacGregor Burns, "Maintenance of Membership: A Study in Administrative Statesmanship," *Journal of Politics* 10 (1948): 101 n. 1.

11. See Seidman, *American Labor*, 92.

12. Lichtenstein, *Labor's War at Home*, 67.

13. See Andrew Workman, "Creating the Center: Liberal Intellectuals, the National War Labor Board, and the Stabilization of American Industrial Relations, 1941–1945" (Ph.D. diss., University of North Carolina, 1993), 90–96.

14. Art Preis argues that Philip Murray's support for the board was a surprise because just a week earlier the *CIO News* had published a report of Murray's memorandum to the National Defense Commission which raised a number of strong objections to any war labor board. Such a board, the memorandum stated, "will necessarily find its attention directed against labor in order to maintain the status quo as much as possible," and will strive to restrict "wage increases or improvement of working conditions for labor." It also noted that "compulsory arbitration will result from board activities, since it would enter situations where collective bargaining was in process" and would bring pressure to bear on labor to agree to arbitration in practically all situations. There also was concern that the board would limit and interfere with the operation of the National Labor Relations Board. See Art Preis, *Labor's Giant Step: Twenty Years of the CIO* (New York: Pathfinder Press, 1972), 125–26.

15. Lichtenstein, *Labor's War at Home*, 70–71.

16. See, generally, Robert Zieger, *The CIO, 1935–1955* (Chapel Hill: University of North Carolina Press, 1995), 145–47.

17. Burns, "Maintenance of Membership," 105; National War Labor Board, *The Termination Report of the National War Labor Board. Industrial Disputes and Wage Stabilization in Wartime. January 12, 1942–December 31, 1945*, 3 vols. (Washington, D.C.: Government Printing Office, 1947–48), 1:81–82.

18. Burns, "Maintenance of Membership," 103 n. 6.

19. Federal Shipbuilding and Drydock Co., NDMB 46, (1941). See T. T. Hammond, "The Closed Shop Issue in World War II," *North Carolina Law Review* 21 (1947): 127, 151.

20. Bethlehem Steel Co., Shipbuilding Division, Case No. 37, 9 Lab. Rel. Rep. 539 (1942).

21. Burns, "Maintenance of Membership," 104 n. 9.

22. National War Labor Board, *Termination Report*, 1:81; Lichtenstein, *Labor's War at Home*, 68.

23. Bureau of Labor Standards, *Report on the Work of the National Defense Mediation Board* (Washington, D.C.: Government Printing Office, 1942), 27.

24. Burns, "Maintenance of Membership," 106.

25. National War Labor Board, *Termination Report*, 1:82.

26. See Louis Jaffe, "Union Security: A Case Study of the Emergence of Law," *University of Pennsylvania Law Review* 91 (1942): 275, 288–92. Aaron Levenstein argues that union security was not actually a critical issue until Lewis catapulted it to prominence with the captive mines dispute (*Labor, Today and Tomorrow* [New York: A. A. Knopf, 1946], 64).

27. Workman, "Creating the Center," 127.

28. See Little Steel cases, NDMB No. 30, 31, 34, 35 (July 16, 1942).

29. Lee Pressman described the WLB's policy as a critical factor in the CIO's growth during the war. The USW's net worth grew sevenfold between May 1942 and November 1943 (Lichtenstein, "Ambiguous Legacy," 231–32). For an excellent discussion of the role of the WLB's public members in seeking a united position on union security, see Workman, "Creating the Center," 123–63.

30. Marcus Manoff, "The National War Labor Board and the Maintenance-of-Membership Clause," *Harvard Law Review* 57 (1943): 183 n. 2.

31. Timothy A. Willard, "Labor and the National War Labor Board, 1942–1945: An Experiment in Corporatist Wage Stabilization" (Ph.D. diss., University of Toledo, 1984), 338.

32. The "closed shop" clause barred the employer from hiring anyone not already a member of the union and was primarily found in craft and casual work areas.

33. George Taylor, "The Role of Organized Labor in Winning the War," Address at the Annual Convention of the Pennsylvania Federation of Labor, Town Hall, Scranton, May 5, 1942, 4 and 5; cited in Edward B. Shils, Walter J. Gershenfeld, Bernard Ingster, and W. Weinberg, *Industrial Peacemaker: George W. Taylor's Contribution to Collective Bargaining* (Philadelphia: University of Pennsylvania Press, 1979), 137–38. See Workman, "Creating the Center," 137–50.

34. See, e.g., Towne Robinson Nut Co., 3 WLR 40 (1942); Bethlehem Steel Co., Shipbuilding Div., 3 WLR 17 (1942).

35. Cited in Burns, "Maintenance of Membership," 109.

36. See, e.g., Walker Turner Co., 1 WLR 101 (1942); International Harvester, 1 WLR U2 (1942). The grant of escape clauses led some employer members to move from dissent to concurrence. See, e.g., Ryan Aeronautical Co., 1 WLR 305 (1942).

37. Caterpillar Tractor Co., 2 WLR 75 (1942); U.S. Steel Corp., 2 WLR 453 (1942).

38. Marshall Field & Co., 1 WLR 47 (1942).

39. Arcade Malleable Iron Co., 1 WLR 153 (1942).

40. Bower Roller Bearing Co, 1 WLR 61 (1942).

41. White Sewing Machine Corp., 1 WLR 164 (1942); see also American Brass Co., 1 WLR 265 (1942).

42. Arcade Malleable Iron Co., 1 WLR 153 (1942).

43. Walker Turner, 1 WLR 101 (1942).

44. Bethlehem Steel, 1 WLR 327 (1942). To employee members, such clauses seem to force employees to tax employees for the benefit of private organizations.

45. Humble Oil and Refining Co., 15 WLR 380 (1944).

46. Jaffe, "Union Security," 275, 284, 301–2; see, e.g., Bethlehem Steel Co., Shipbuilding Div., 3 WLR 17 (1942).

47. Ryan Aeronautical Co., 1 WLR 305 (1942). See Workman, "Creating the Center," 158.

48. Frank Graham, "The Union Maintenance Policy of the War Labor Board," in *Yearbook of American Labor*, vol. 1, *War Labor Policies*, ed. Colston E. Warne (New York: Philosophical Library, 1945), 154.

49. In some cases the board mentioned that collection of dues was disorderly and wasteful and, because of critical labor shortages in the area, the "patriotic" union would not request discharges for nonpayment of dues (Bell Aircraft Corp., 10 WLR 126 [1943]).

50. Cited in Graham, "Union Maintenance Policy," 155. See also Willard, "Labor and the NWLB," 340–52.

51. Graham, "Union Maintenance Policy," 156. The rights of members to have free elections and to obtain financial records were not actually established under the LMRDA until 1959.

52. U.S. Rubber Co., 8 WLR 537 (1943). Member Lapham responded by asserting that unions were owed nothing for forfeiting a right which, at least in wartime, it did not possess.

53. See Seidman, *American Labor*, 104; Lichtenstein, "Ambiguous Legacy," 217–38. See, generally, National War Labor Board, *Termination Report*, 1:81–103.

54. Mack Mfg. Co., 3 WLR 87 (1947).

55. Monsanto Chemical Co., 2 WLR 479 (1942). In addition, the WLB could withdraw seniority rights, shift premiums and other benefits, or even deny the union's status as representative (Joshua Freeman, "Delivering the Goods: Industrial Unionism during World War II," *Labor History* 19 [Fall 1978]: 575 n. 8).

56. See Humble Oil, 55 WLR 380 (1944).

57. Freeman, "Delivering the Goods," 575.

58. Yale & Towne Mfg. Co., 14 WLR 486 (1944) (Regional Board 3, Philadelphia). Although the board denied the maintenance of membership in *Yale & Towne* because of a strike, it granted a voluntary membership maintenance clause which engendered a strong dissent by the employer members.

59. Yellow Truck & Coach Mfg. Co., 10 WLR 141 (1943).

60. Freeman, "Delivering the Goods," 575.

61. In some cases the board granted the clause *conditionally*, promising to ob-

serve the union's future conduct. In other cases, it held out the future prospect of granting the clause (Yellow Truck and Coach Mfg. Co., 5 WLR 244 [1942]). The board revealed its intention to police internal union affairs in a case involving the American Newspaper Guild (Patriot Co., 14 WLR 355 [1944]). The board granted the clause on the condition that the guild abide by a section of its constitution which prohibited the disciplining of members because of their writings. Though there had been no evidence that the union was violating its own rules, the board required the appointment of an impartial arbitrator to review any case that might arise.

62. Woods Machine Company, 1 WLR 159, 162 (1942).

63. See Monsanto Chemical, 1 WLR 479 (1942); General Chemical Co., 3 WLR 387 (1942).

64. Campbell Soup Co., 10 WLR 283 (1943).

65. See, e.g., Ohio Steel Foundry, 6 WLR 24 (1943); Campbell Soup Co. (1943). See also Seidman, *American Labor*, p. 105.

66. See Borg Warner, 6 WLR 233, where the union was not penalized for striking because the employer was not complying with a WLB decision.

67. Anson and Gilkey Co., 19 WLR 498 (1944). See Manoff, "National War Labor Board," 209.

68. Worcester Press Steel Co., 3 WLR 504, 509 (1942).

69. Miles Laboratories, 6 WLR 22 (1942). See also Buckeye Steel Castings, 9 WLR 799 (Reg'l Bd., Cleveland, 1942); Chrysler Corporation, 3 WLR 447 (1942).

70. Edward G. Budd Manufacturing Co., 11 WLR 465 (1943).

71. Chrysler Corp., 10 WLR 551 (1943).

72. Nash-Kelvinator Propeller Division, 10 WLR 356 (1943) (Regional Board 11, Detroit).

73. Commercial Solvents Co., 12 WLR 323, 328 (1943).

74. Shacht Rubber Co. Inc., 9 WLR 752 (1943). In some cases where the clause was denied, the board referred to other factors. Thus, in Retail Associates Inc., 14 WLR 678 (1944), the clause was denied because the union had only a small minority of employees as members and there was no organization attempting to undermine the union. This suggests the belief that the clause was valuable, in part, as a protection against union raids rather than employer opposition.

75. Roger Horowitz argues that the packinghouse workers were an exception to this trend due to both the militancy of locals and the weakness of the international. Strong participation and action by workers at the point of production may have strengthened union support and correspondingly reduced the value of WLB benefits (*"Negro and White, Unite and Fight!" A Social History of Industrial Unionism in Meatpacking, 1930–90* [Urbana: University of Illinois Press, 1997]).

76. See, e.g., Caterpillar Tractor Co., 2 WLR 75 (1942).

77. Bethlehem Steel Co., et al., 1 WLR 387 (July 16, 1942).

78. Preis, *Labor's Giant Step*, 154.

79. Cited in ibid., 155.

80. Willard, "Labor and the NWLB," 331.

81. Ibid.

82. See, e.g., dissent in Phelps-Dodge, 2 WLR 52 (1942); Seidman, *American Labor,* 100.

83. Seidman, *American Labor,* 102; Willard, "Labor and the NWLB," 348–49. On Dec. 1, 1943, the War Labor Board revised its maintenance of membership policy in a variety of ways. Instead of a pledge by the union not to resort to coercion or intimidation of employees to become members, it substituted a mandatory requirement in the form of a notice to be provided by the company or the union, or both jointly, that coercion would not employed. In addition, disputes over union membership would be taken to an arbitrator who would be selected under the collective agreement or by special agreement of the parties. See *Monthly Labor Review* 58 (Jan. 1944): 67.

84. Manoff, "National War Labor Board," 215–19.

85. 11 Lab. Rel. Rep. 433 (Dec. 7, 1942); cited in ibid., 217.

86. Ryan Aeronautical Company, 1 WLR 305 (1942). See Workman, "Creating the Center," 158.

87. *Saturday Evening Post,* June 13, 1942.

88. Steele v. Louisville & Nashville Ry., 323 U.S. 192 (1944); Tunstall v. Brotherhood of Locomotive Fireman, 323 U.S. 210 (1944); Wallace Corp. v. NLRB, 323 U.S. 248 (1944).

89. Some interesting examples are Jaffe, "Union Security," 275; Wayne L. Morse, "The National War Labor Board Puts Labor Law Theory into Action," *Iowa Law Review* 19 (1944): 175; Lester B. Orfield, "Union Security and Wartime," *University of Chicago Law Review* 11 (1943–44): 349; Manoff, "National War Labor Board," 183; Burns, "Maintenance of Membership," 101; Hammond, "Closed Shop Issue," 127; and Reynolds C. Seitz, "Validity of War Labor Board Orders of Union Security and Compulsory Arbitration under the War Labor Disputes Act," *Kentucky Law Journal* 32 (1943–44): 262.

90. See, e.g., Lucille Lomen, "Union Security in Wartime," *Washington Law Review* 19 (1944): 132.

91. See Lichtenstein, *Labor's War at Home,* 80.

92. Joshua B. Freeman, *In Transit: The Transport Workers Union in New York City, 1933–1966* (New York: Oxford University Press, 1989), 576.

93. *Monthly Labor Review* 57 (Sept. 1943): 524.

94. Ibid.

95. Ibid., 528.

96. The Taft-Hartley Act permitted the negotiation of a union shop arrangement in section 8(a)(3) but barred the closed shop (29 U.S.C. section 158[a][3] [1947]). In addition, states were permitted in section 14(b) to bar any union security provision. These state statutes are whimsically named "right to work" laws (29 U.S.C. section 164[b] [1947]). Studies indicate that these state statutes negatively affect the level of unionization as well as wage levels (Steven Abraham, "How the Taft-Hartley Act Hindered Unions," *Hofstra Labor Law Journal* 12 [1994]: 30–31).

97. *Monthly Labor Review* 57 (Sept. 1943): 531.

98. Ibid., 532.

99. *Monthly Labor Review* 58 (Apr. 1944): 697.

100. Ibid., 700.

101. Ibid., 704. In 291 cases involving maintenance of union membership decided between January 1941 and February 1944, the WLB granted maintenance of membership clauses in 271 cases involving almost one and a half million workers (Seidman, *American Labor,* 104). The clause was denied in eighteen cases (Graham, "Union Maintenance Policy," 145). At the beginning of 1944, over 20 percent of all employees covered by a collective agreement, or over three million workers, were covered by maintenance of membership clauses (Constance Williams, "Developments in Union Agreements," in *Yearbook of American Labor,* vol. 1, *War Labor Policies,* ed. Colston E. Warne [New York: Philosophical Library, 1945], 116). In some cases, employers granted the clause believing that the board would ultimately order it (ibid., 114). By the end of 1945 maintenance of membership covered 29 percent of all workers under union agreements (Burns, "Maintenance of Membership," 114).

In 1945, there were about thirty-one million employees in industries with unions actively involved in bargaining. More than fourteen million of these, or about 47 percent, were working under written union contracts. Of these, almost 28 percent were in closed shops; 18 percent in union shops—totaling six and a half million under closed or union shops. More than three million, 27 percent of those governed by collective bargaining agreements, were under maintenance of membership. In most cases, less than 1 percent of the members had attempted to withdraw during the escape period required by the WLB. Congress implicitly sustained the board's policy in June 1943, when it rejected by a vote of 204 to 73 an amendment to the antistrike bill which would have specifically prohibited the board from requiring that an individual become or remain a member of a labor organization as a condition of employment. See Burns, "Maintenance of Membership," 115. About six million, more than 40 percent, were paying dues to the unions through the checkoff system (*Monthly Labor Review* 60 [Apr. 1945]: 816).

102. The percentage of workers covered by agreements containing union or closed shop provisions seemed to have remained fairly constant. Thus over 45 percent of those under agreements at the beginning of 1943 were covered by closed or union shop provisions (*Monthly Labor Review* 56 [Feb. 1943]: 284).

103. Ibid., 286.

104. Ibid.

105. National Labor Relations Act, section 8(a)(3).

106. NLRB v. General Motors, 373 U.S. 734 (1963).

107. See, generally, Charles J. Morris, ed., *The Developing Labor Law,* vol. 2 (Washington, D.C.: Bureau of National Affairs, 1983), 359–95.

108. Levenstein, *Labor, Today and Tomorrow,* 69.

109. Freeman, *In Transit,* 577–78.

110. Ibid., 578. Ironically, throughout the war the AFL unions were often more

aggressive in defending their members' economic interests. They were often more organizationally secure and their ideology was generally more opposed to government intervention (ibid., 581).

111. Peter Blau, *Bureaucracy in Modern Societies* (New York: Random House, 1956), 37; Amatai Etzioni, *Modern Organizations* (Englewood Cliffs, N.J.: Prentice Hall, 1964), 53–54.

112. Nelson Lichtenstein, "Conflict over Workers' Control: The Automobile Industry in World War II," in *Working-Class America: Essays on Labor, Community and American Society*, ed. Michael Frisch and Daniel Walkowitz (Urbana: University of Illinois Press, 1983), 291.

7

The No-Strike Pledge in Principle and Practice

THE CAUSES OF WORKER UNREST

After a six-month tour of America's war production centers in 1943, Mary Heaton Vorse believed that the turmoil in the workplace, especially on the Pacific coast, was caused by promises which were not kept: "[Labor] had renounced its right to strike with the understanding that prices were to be stabilized or that wages would be revised to meet the cost of living. Instead, wages and jobs were frozen, and the OPA had failed to check the rise of prices. This was *tap root of the unrest* which kept the Pacific coast in a turmoil throughout the winter, later brought about the coal strike, caused a constant churning among the automobile workers, and led to a restless heave in the war industries from the north to the south, from the east to the west."[1]

Vorse's views are only partly supported by the evidence. Weekly earnings for factory workers had increased markedly between 1939 and 1942, but the gain was "partly illusory for living costs had risen materially" and the spendable income of wage earners was "affected appreciably by income tax and war bond deductions."[2] Living costs in large cities rose a modest 3.3 percent in 1943, but the increase from January 1941 was 23.4 percent, exceeding the wage increases permissible under the WLB's "Little Steel" formula.[3] The increase in average earnings was due less to a rise in hourly wage rates than to an increase in the number of factory workers, especially in high-wage durable goods industries, and to the lengthening of the workweek.[4] The increase in the yearly income of workers was exceeded by that of small businesses, whose income had increased 50 percent, and by farmers, who had enjoyed a rise of 134 percent. Moreover, a hundred prime war contracts, after taxes had been deducted, resulted in increased profits of 66 percent for defense contractors. As CIO researchers stated, "We are tired of being the inflationary goat. We're in a moment of labor shortage when a strike threat would have brought us a wage increase overnight. Now we're held back from strikes by our own promise."[5] Other factors were also at work, including a system of taxation which the workers considered unfair, persistent sniping by employers at union standards, the anti-labor barrage in the newspapers, uncomfortable shop conditions, and fatigue from excess overtime leading to increased injuries in the workplace.[6]

Even strikes usually deemed official may well have actually been caused by worker frustrations. John L. Lewis, like all other labor leaders, supported the no-strike pledge, and Robert Zieger argues that the miners' strikes were really led from below: "Lewis in reality followed the lead of the working miners. He responded to, and did not manufacture, their militancy."[7]

The "Little Steel" wage formula especially rankled the miners, although the anger was widespread. Since miners had secured the union shop and a dues checkoff in the 1930s, the WLB's willingness to grant a form of union security could not ameliorate the sense of unfairness at a time when coal production and profits were booming. Moreover, the great increase in coal production from 500 million tons in 1940, to over 640 million in 1942, 653 million in 1943, and 684 million in 1944, led to an historically familiar story—a terrible increase in injury and death. Between 1942 and 1943, three thousand miners lost their lives and each week five hundred miners were injured. By May 1943, "US armed forces in World War II had tallied 27,172 killed and wounded. During the same seventeen months, mining accidents had claimed 34,000 injured and almost 2,000 dead."[8]

During the early years of the war, miners and other workers may have believed that promises of "equality of sacrifice" were being met. Jobs were plentiful and the outcome of the war was still uncertain.[9] Workers and unions made great sacrifices throughout the wartime period. As Joshua Freeman has noted, "most workers and union leaders rallied to the war effort, accepting the idea that sacrifices were necessary for victory."[10] Many unions, like the Transit Workers Union studied by Freeman, initiated war bond drives and sponsored prowar rallies. By 1943, however, support for the no-strike pledge began to erode as corporate profits, executive salaries, and the cost of living rose while wages were concurrently restricted by the "Little Steel" formula. In addition, workers perceived a rising cost of living and declining quality of life, and many also feared the problems of reconversion and an expected postwar depression.[11] In Detroit, for instance, the heart of wartime work stoppages, the cost of living rose higher than the average of the country's thirty-four largest cities, led by sharp rises in food costs. Moreover, workers who had flocked to cities like Detroit often lived in substandard and unhealthy dwellings. "Detroit's schools, hospitals and other public facilities were stretched far beyond their capacity."[12] These conditions no doubt aggravated worker irritation with long hours, no vacations, and other employer policies.

Workers also saw their employers reaping the benefits of wartime production, benefits they believed were not shared. The wartime expansion involved military contracts of over $175 billion to more than eighteen thousand firms, but two-thirds of these funds went to one hundred companies. Indeed, 30 percent went to ten defense contractors. In addition, the 250 largest corporations "operated 79 percent of all new, privately operated plant facilities built with federal funds during the war." Exceedingly generous amortization plans permitted tax deductions for new construction, allowing corporations to lower their taxable earnings. As George Lipsitz notes, "Taxpayers financed the costs of industrial expansion, but business kept all of the profits and all of the increased money-making opportunities from new plants, equipment, and research."[13]

Despite these sources of economic stress, most of the wartime strikes seem to have involved issues of control at the workplace rather than wages or benefits. UAW stewards filed an extraordinary number of grievances during the war, raising disputes over the meaning of the collective agreement. Nelson Lichtenstein reports, for instance, that more than one hundred thousand grievances were filed annually at GM, and approximately one thousand reached the umpire.[14] According to James R. Green, "The dam broke":

> Strikers simply ignored labor leaders who wanted to maintain the wartime no-strike, maintenance-of-membership pact with the government and industry. By the end of 1945, 3.5 million workers had engaged in 4,750 work stoppages, costing employers 38 million workdays. In January, 1946, 174,000 United Electrical Workers and 800,000 Steelworkers joined the 225,000 GM auto workers already on strike, creating the greatest work stoppage in United States history. More was to come. In total, four industries experienced general strikes and a total of 4.6 million people engaged in nearly 5,000 work stoppages, costing employers a staggering 116 million workdays.[15]

The traditional attention given to the "undisciplined" new industrial workers, discussed in the following chapter, tends to ignore the anxieties and problems faced by all workers. Moreover, the no-strike pledge was perceived by some as crippling to the UAW, which had always depended upon militancy and the strike. As one local UAW newspaper succinctly stated: "Labor was like a powerful prize fighter whose hands are tied behind his back and who was confronted by an inferior opponent. Since the prize fighter is bound and all but helpless, the opponent can take liberties he would not dream of taking under usual ring conditions."[16]

The automobile industry was especially troubled. The auto companies' attitude toward labor was extremely hostile, and they had not fully accepted industrial unionism. Moreover, as Robert Blauner noted, the autoworker's historical "job dissatisfaction is a reflection of his independence and dignity; he does not submit as easily as other manual workers to alienating work."[17] In addition, workers were aware that corporate profits doubled and executive salaries skyrocketed. At General Motors, for instance, net profit rose from $47 million during the first six months of 1942 to $69 million one year later.

As early as mid-1942 workers even found reasons to doubt their employers' commitment to the war effort. A number of Detroit area plants had begun to hoard labor, hiring more hands than they needed in expectation of future shortages. Consequently, many workers spent the workday with little or nothing to do, creating great frustration.[18] Labor hoarding was also a common practice of West Coast shipbuilders to "compensate for anticipated high turnover." The result, according to Marilyn Johnson, was "enforced idleness" and "periodic mass layoffs at Kaiser and other shipyards."[19] Workers also bridled at the military's often high-handed approach to shop floor issues.[20]

Indeed, Kevin Boyle has stated that "many autoworkers believed that their patriotism far surpassed that of their employers, who, in fact, seemed much more interested in exploiting the national emergency than in sharing the sacrifices of war time." "This perception obviously reinforced the autoworkers' pre-war view that they, rather than their employers, supported basic American values and, by so doing, made rank-and-filers even more sensitive than they had been to the defense of those values on the shop floor." In short, Boyle argues that "the patriotic fervor of the war actually heightened tensions at the point of production."[21]

In addition, some two-thirds of UAW members surveyed in February 1943 expressed fear that their employers were trying to roll back their gains while the no-strike pledge was in effect. Workers, for instance, complained that the no-strike pledge induced employers to refuse to process grievances.[22] Many autoworkers began to take the defense of their rights into their own hands, viewing wildcat strikes as the most effective response to perceived managerial abuses. "The strike is still the only real weapon labor has," an inspector at Packard told the UAW. "It still must be used when the manufacturors [*sic*] are not patriotic."[23]

The no-strike pledge was no doubt approved by most workers in principle. According to Rick Fantasia,

> Most workers would have probably endorsed the no-strike pledge in principle. In practice, however, a very different picture would have emerged, as it did in the United Auto Workers, one union that *did* poll its membership, albeit late in the war. In the UAW poll (taken in the winter and spring of 1944), 65 percent of those voting upheld the pledge, while *during the same period* a majority of auto workers were conducting wildcat strikes. This apparent contradiction between belief and action was actually an accurate response to a contradictory set of conditions: whereas their leadership stood firmly united with both industriotists and the government in the name of patriotism, conditions on the shop floor were anything but satisfactory. Workers were faced with a hostile management, which they saw reaping enormous profits, while they were being expected to sacrifice in the form of speedup (through harassment) and a wage freeze (while the cost of living skyrocketed), without any guarantee that they would even have a job when the war ended. (Many expected a postwar reconversion depression.) Under such conditions, and with their leadership now perceived to be much closer to management than to the shop floor, workers took action that circumvented a hostile bureaucratic apparatus.[24]

Unrest at auto plants took many forms. In addition to an upsurge in grievances, most major war plants had a high degree of employee turnover: "many firms had to seek several times the number of workers actually needed to maintain an adequate workforce and to replace those employees who quit for one reason or another."[25] The average absence rate in Detroit war plants was small but was nevertheless higher than the peacetime rate.[26] The combination of the "Little Steel" formula and WLB delays[27] frustrated both unions and the rank and file, leading eventually to job actions and wildcats in many industries. In meatpacking, the frustration with WLB rulings and delays, as well as employer resistance, led to strikes in "virtually every plant in the Big Four companies, as well as many independent firms."[28] Roger Horowitz characterizes these actions as a form of shop floor bargaining, short job actions, usually within a department, often led by stewards or even local officials. However one describes these stoppages, it seems clear that most were directed to particular job-related issues, carrying over tactics and aims from the prewar period.

Faced with often obstreperous employers, unions sought ways to create economic pressure short of calling a full-blown strike. When the California Metal Trades Association (CMTA) repudiated an agreement to reopen wages every thirty days and even to continue the expiring agreement in effect pending further negotiations, machinists voted in April 1944 to bar all overtime assignments in CMTA workplaces after forty-eight hours, the workweek mandated by the administration in war industries. The machinists denied they were on strike, stressing that the slackened war effort had resulted in the layoffs of over one thousand machinists.[29]

The San Francisco Regional War Labor Board, supported by the staunchly antistrike ILWU, was almost unanimously opposed to the machinists' action. ILWU vice president Louis Goldblatt, a member of the regional War Labor Board, attacked the machinists in terms that seem to transcend the ILWU's wartime decision to devote all efforts to the defeat of Nazi Germany. Goldblatt, for instance, told a June 1944 closed session of the NWLB in Washington that the machinists' overtime ban was clearly a strike that: "unless this board takes decisive action is going to spread . . . it is contagious; because you have many unions throughout the Region that are pretty expert at job action, quickie strikes, and where for many years prior to the war that was really the common form of economic action—not the major strikes . . . and there are a number of forces within the labor movement . . . who are not a bit adverse to going back to that type of guerrilla warfare."[30]

Goldblatt then made the following remarkable statement, indicating, I believe, that he was not simply following a pro-Communist line, but that he had developed—in a profound break with the traditions of 1934—a genuine conservatism like that of many other union leaders: "We on the labor side don't want to see any resumption in the San Francisco Bay area . . . of the type of collective bargaining that prevailed six or seven years ago when you had a constant economic contest [and] one of the best strike records that anybody ever had in the country. We think we have had enough of that . . . we don't want the resumption of guerrilla warfare which will inevitably result if this board fails to act, because these employers will begin to fold one by one, and then you have taken the lid off."[31]

Like Goldblatt, many viewed the overtime ban as the equivalent of or a subterfuge for an actual strike. Finally, after considerable delay in Washington, a strike in one plant induced the federal takeover in September 1944 of the "bulk of the machinery industry in San Francisco and the industry in San Francisco and the industrial suburbs south of the city."[32] The Navy attempted to jail local leaders and successfully terminated the machinists' collective agreement, including the grievance procedure and hiring hall. Sanctions were applied against workers who refused to work over eight hours a day, and, according to Richard Boyden, fifty-eight machinists who refused overtime were referred to their draft boards for induction, gas rations of some workers were canceled, eight were fired and were blacklisted by the War Manpower Commission for the war's duration.[33]

Wartime labor conflict cannot be isolated from off-the-job problems, especially the critical housing shortage which often faced defense workers.[34] Housing was not only in short supply but much of what was available was substandard, and the problem was compounded by difficulties in transportation.[35] Fatigue was increased by the often arduous travel between home and plant. As Vorse and others noted, housing problems compounded the worries, tensions, and anxieties of wartime life, with patience already frayed by the fatigue of war-prolonged workweeks. By November 1943, Detroit industry was operating an average of forty-seven and a half hours per week and many factories worked fifty-four- or even seventy-hour weeks. The War Manpower Commission imposed a mandatory forty-eight-hour week on industry in thirty-two critical war centers in February 1943.[36] By midwar, however, many war plants were already working forty-eight hours a week.

Thus, the problem was not limited to the Detroit area. Marc Scott Miller's study of wartime Lowell, Massachusetts, refers to workers who worked up to twenty hours of overtime per week.[37] Many worked two jobs, working sixty hour weeks, like my father who worked two jobs and on off-hours toured the neighborhood at night as a civil defense volunteer to make certain curtains and drapes were drawn so as to mask Akron, Ohio, from enemy bombers. Overcrowded dwellings and exorbitant rent exacerbated the situation in many areas. During the war, sixteen million Americans joined the armed forces, six million women became industrial workers, and fifteen million Americans traveled to new jobs. "Under these conditions, established forms of family and community life broke down, and workers experienced new gender and family roles."[38]

Manpower allocation was also a constant problem. In late 1942, for instance, representatives of government, labor, and business drew up voluntary manpower stabilization plans for Muskegan and Detroit which provided that workers in crucial war occupations could not quit to seek jobs elsewhere without receiving clearance or a certificate of availability from their previous employer.

Working conditions and long hours created tensions and resentment in the workforce, especially among new employees who may have been unfamiliar with specific tools and machines. Employers as well as unions criticized the "new" workers. In March 1945, speaking in reference to charges of slipshod work, George Christopher of Packard declared that "the majority of persons observed in our employment increase would have been labeled unemployable for skill or attitude during peacetime. So what can you expect?"[39]

Another irritant to workers was that army inspectors and procurement officials often ignored manpower considerations in placing war orders, and they sometimes disregarded or abrogated provisions in collective agreements that they believed were unsuitable to military requirements.[40] In addition, management often refused to process grievances and disputes over line speed, wage rates, and other matters remained unsettled. Factory executives seemed especially intent on restoring their pre-union right to fire without reference to seniority. Thus, the high number of strikes, especially in 1943, must also be viewed in the context of employer intransigence and opposition. For instance, on January 2, 1943, a War Production Board representative in Detroit wrote Washington and noted: "The evidence which is piling up seems to indicate rather clearly that a well-organized and determined effort is being made on the part of many manufacturers and industrialists to do everything in their power to create incidents which will 'needle' and provoke labor into unauthorized stoppage of work."[41] Another problem was delay in the operation of the War Labor Board or its regional boards.[42] Many employers, it was thought, deliberately postponed settling grievances by sending them to the board.

The cost of living, fatigue, the opposition of management to certain restrictive government policies, union rivalry, and worker suspicion of union leadership, all contributed to the mounting wave of wartime strikes. These strikes, varying from serious to "bizarre and seemingly trivial outbursts [,] . . . expressed an important rebellion against work, authority and hierarchy."[43]

Given the variety and multitude of pressures on workers, it may be difficult to assess the precise causes of particular strikes. As will be discussed in Chapter 12, the underlying sources of worker dissatisfaction may be hidden by focusing upon the problem which triggers a walkout. Nevertheless, studies indicate that many wildcats seemed immediately caused by disciplinary matters such as discharges and grievances over working conditions. Clive noted that a "hard core of union militance" was often ready to strike at Michigan plants. Simply, it was retribution time. As one Ford unionist stated in 1942, "A lot of these companies deserve to be treated pretty miserable. They treated us that way during the depression. Didn't even say, 'sorry, old man, we ain't got nothing for you today.' Just said, 'Get the hell out of here.' So now it ain't no wonder if some of the boys treat the company miserable."[44]

The evidence indicates that wartime wildcats, like those of the late 1960s and early 1970s, primarily involved immediate workplace issues.[45] Some notion of the nature of wartime wildcats can be gained from a report of 108 work stoppages in auto plants between December 1944 and February 1945, presented to the Senate by George Romney of the Automobile Manufacturers Association.[46] (See appendix 1.) A breakdown of the presumed causes of these often brief stoppages reveals reactions to various kinds of discipline (forty cases) and protests over working conditions, job assignments and orders, and hours of work (forty cases). The general category of working conditions could be expanded by adding seniority issues (four) and disputes over proper job classification (twelve) and the right of management to transfer employees (five). Disputes over wages and piecework were relatively minor (nine), although job classification and job content conflicts may have essentially been wage disputes. Excluding the stoppages dealing with the imposition of discipline, the predominant cause of most stoppages, assuming the accuracy of the report, dealt with working conditions and job content. These disputes, then, reflect the battle for control at the workplace. Thus, it is possible to view the stoppages as occurring *in spite* of the absence of many experienced unionists rather than *because* of their absence. Thus, as Martin Glaberman noted in 1980, most of the situations that led to wildcat strikes "involved, as they do today, the whole range of conditions at work including production standards, hours of work, health and safety, free time, promotions and transfers, grievance procedure, etc., all of which the spokesmen for management correctly, if stridently, denounced as interference with the functions of management."[47]

Other studies confirm the normalcy of the causes of the wildcats. Rosa Lee Swafford's study for the Automotive Council for War Production, for instance, recorded the causes of work stoppages in automotive plants in December 1944 and January 1945. Although any such accounts should be considered in light of the difficulty of attributing causation, Swafford concluded that "most of the strikes were protests against discipline, protests over certain company policies, or protests against the discharge of one or more employees."[48]

In addition, a study of Chrysler's 1944 strike record prepared for a Senate investigation of defense production in 1945 indicated that workers were most likely to engage in wildcats after management took disciplinary action. Kevin Boyle, however, believes that discipline was rarely the root cause of walkouts, and other causes were wage concerns, shop rules, and disputes over job assignments.[49] Many wildcats, Boyle notes, for instance at General Motors plants, were caused by the perceived challenges to the workers' ability to set their own pace of production. Yet, Boyle believes most wildcats were not caused by violations of shop floor traditions. Chrysler's 1944 strike record indicates that most wartime strikes were staged in response to the same contractual issues over which workers filed grievances. "Indeed, two-thirds of the 126 Chrysler wildcats staged in the latter half of 1944 began as conflicts over seemingly routine issues."[50]

Although there were shop floor activists who hoped that the workers' job actions could be transformed into a broader struggle against both management and union policies, the evidence indicates that most factory-level conflicts during World War II were "generally defensive moves designed not to push the boundaries of worker control, but rather to prevent erosion of traditional practices or newly-won union rights."[51]

Boyle's study primarily focused on the Chrysler Corporation's Jefferson Avenue facility in Detroit. From December 1, 1939, to December 1, 1940, wage issues were the single greatest cause of grievances, accounting for 30 percent of those filed, followed by questions of upgrading, seniority, and safety. These four issues accounted for three-fourths of all grievances filed. On the other hand, and perhaps surprisingly, workers rarely grieved questions of work pace. "Autoworkers thus saw the grievance process as a way of enforcing work rules and correcting abuses, not as an avenue through which they could challenge managerial control of the production process."[52]

During the war, however, Boyle found that wage, upgrading, seniority, and safety issues accounted for two-thirds of all grievances filed. Interestingly, the number of grievances filed over the pace of work actually declined during the war. Boyle's evidence leads him to conclude that this pattern was fairly representative in other autoworkers' plants.[53] This is not to suggest that workers were unconcerned about the pace of work, but that workers had some degree of control over the pace of work by either setting it themselves or engaging in more covert tactics.[54]

To workers, strikes could be viewed as a rational response despite their strong support for the war effort. As Martin Glaberman has noted, "there is no contradiction in the worker's mind. Workers don't cause strikes; bosses cause strikes. If you want to end strikes, get the bosses to behave. It's not simply self-justifying rationalization, it is the reality. Workers in general don't want to strike—they can't afford to lose time. Yet they find themselves compelled, in order to be human beings, to carry on actions on the shop floor."[55]

Job actions in the meatpacking companies seem, as in the UAW, inconsistent with the internationals' strong support for the wartime no-strike pledge. On the shop floor, however, even Communist officials were tolerant of stoppages when they felt workers had no other option. Workers, conscious of their wartime obligations, defended their actions by pointing to managerial violations of contractual understandings or by distinguishing between a strike involving an entire plant and a short, limited work stoppage. Local toleration was reflected by the international, which generally failed to take strong action even when packing companies approached the WLB to remove union security provisions.[56]

Wildcats also seemed to be influenced by critical military events, for instance, Michigan strikes dropped sharply in the invasion month of June 1944, and fell again in the wake of the near disaster at Bastogne in late 1944. However, as Clive notes, it was generally impossible to "to convince the few hundred employees of a single department within a mighty war plant that their three-hour work stoppage threatened production or endangered the lives of GI's. To the contrary, militants believed that they were fighting a war against management autocracy at home that was at least as important as the battle against fascism being waged abroad."[57]

Jerome F. Scott and George C. Homans also noted in their well-known study of work stoppages in automobile plants that most of the strikes were protests against discipline, against company policies, or against the discharge of one of more employees. Many involved all three matters.[58] Although it was commonly believed that strikes were caused by the large number of young and inexperienced workers, Scott and Homans were impressed by the fact that several of the most paralyzing strikes were caused by the discharge of long-service employees. Sometimes, the experienced workers were fired for trying to induce younger employees not to make a new, higher work standard. There is some evidence, therefore, that strikes were sometimes used as a method of bringing new workers into an older industrial tradition.

THE INCIDENCE OF WORK STOPPAGES

Hundreds of strikes and slowdowns occurred during the war, especially after 1943, but except for highly publicized strikes involving John L. Lewis's mineworkers, few were union authorized. Lewis, like other labor leaders, had agreed not to strike for the duration of the war. By late 1942, however, miners, like other workers, began to feel "aggrieved by unfair rationing standards, victimized by administrative chaos, and abused by preferential treatment for the rich and powerful."[59] Although the UMW strikes were the most visible during the war, over fourteen thousand strikes occurred involving over six and a half million workers. Most work stoppages were of short duration, without clear direction, although there were some large strikes which were led by local union officials.[60]

Despite organized labor's strong support of the war effort, therefore, unauthorized workplace stoppages occurred with impressive frequency. Nelson Lichtenstein has noted that the reorientation of work, especially in auto plants, strengthened the power of workers to set informal production quotas and to control the flow and speed of production.[61] Patriotism did not lessen the suspicion that management would try to use the wartime emergency to weaken unions and heightened concern over the exercise of managerial direction. Indeed, patriotism probably helped cause the overall increase in productivity while pay levels basically remained the same.

Demand for workers was high, and growing worker power was reflected in increasing absenteeism and turnover rates. Layoffs accounted for 71 percent of worker separations from jobs in 1939; in 1943, on the other hand, voluntary resignations accounted for 72 percent of labor turnover.[62] The exercise of worker power at the workplace, with the corresponding decline of the foreman's authority, led to a managerial response which could now be based upon patriotic grounds. In addition, managerial reaction, now freed from the threat of official strikes, could take the form of more vigorous assertion of employer control and disciplinary power as well as general indifference to grievance processes.[63]

Grievances could be handled via arbitration or, as a last resort, by the WLB, but the agency received ten to fifteen thousand new cases a month by late 1943, a number to which the board could not possibly respond in any prompt manner. Indeed, frustration with the progress of the WLB seems to have fueled some strikes. As one Buick worker put it: "When we found that there was no other solution except a wildcat strike, we found ourselves striking not only against the corporation but against practically the government, at least public opinion, and our own union and its pledge. . . . The corporations were showing no sense of patriotism or loyalty and were contributing nothing. All the sacrifices were on the part of the workers."[64]

The staggering number of unauthorized strikes concerned management as much as the erosion of control in the workplace. Bargaining and rank-and-file militance had elevated the shop steward to almost coequal status with shop floor supervisors, a situation made more threatening to employers by the union organization of foremen in 1944 and 1945.[65]

The incidence of short, mostly unauthorized strikes rose dramatically in 1943 and 1944. (See tables 1 and 2.) Most were short or "quickie" strikes, and in the auto industry they often involved the alteration of job assignments or the pace of production, worker objection, and subsequent employer discipline. It is these kinds of issues—production control and discipline—which are often sublimated under a regime of grievance arbitration.[66]

As described by Joshua Freeman, "The typical wartime strike . . . was initiated without union involvement, might include the use of picketing, would last at most a few days, and generally ended as a result of union mediation. . . . It was the blatant, almost arrogant refusal of the business corporate producers to make even a gesture toward equal sacrifice that set the psychological background for the stoppages that did occur."[67] The series of UMW strikes, involving over four hundred thousand miners, in the soft coal industry in 1943 distort scope, duration, and man-days lost figures.[68] Even so, strikes in 1943 averaged five calendar days compared with twelve in 1942, eighteen in 1941, twenty-one in 1940, and twenty-three in 1939.[69]

The year 1944 marked both the wartime peak and all-time national high water mark for labor unrest, with more than 2,115,000 workers idle and about 8,721,000 man-days lost. In 1944, Michigan alone accounted for more than one-tenth of all strikes, more than a quarter of the workers involved, and more than one-fifth of the total time lost through work stoppages.[70] According to Clive, "It is possible that as many as 65% of all Michigan UAW members may have walked out in 1944. But Michigan strikers had not been

Table 1. Duration of Strikes and Lockouts Ending in 1940–44

	1940	1941	1942	1943	1944
Percentage ending in					
< 1 week	39.7	40.0	60.6	80.0	77.3
1 week–½ month	22.3	24.8	20.3	13.6	15.3
½ month–1 month	16.9	18.0	11.1	4.7	5.2
1–2 months	12.5	11.5	5.1	1.6	1.7
2–3 months	4.3	2.8	1.1	0.1	0.5
3+ months	4.3	2.9	1.8	a	—
Total strikes and lockouts	2,493	4,314	3,036	3,734	4,958

Source: Adapted from Rosa Lee Swafford, "Wartime Record of Strikes and Lockouts, 1940–45," 79th Cong., 2d sess., 1946, S. Doc. 136, 8.
a. Less than 0.1 percent.

Table 2. Duration of Strikes Ending in 1944

	Strikes and Lockouts		Workers Involved		Man-Days Idle	
	No.	%	No.	%	No.	%
1 day	1,066	21.5	235,170	11.1	235,170	2.6
2-3 days	1,714	34.6	767,479	36.1	1,464,597	16.5
4 days–1 week	1,051	21.2	504,586	23.7	1,630,282	18.4
1 week–½ month	759	15.3	398,522	18.7	2,493,977	28.1
½–1 month	260	5.2	188,145	8.8	1,786,059	20.1
1–2 months	85	1.7	18,781	0.9	662,371	7.5
2–3 months	23	0.5	14,609	0.7	607,622	6.8
Total	4,985	100.0	2,127,352	100.0	8,880,078	100.0

Source: Adapted from BLS, "Strikes and Lockouts in 1944," *Monthly Labor Review* 60 (May 1945): 967.

inactive earlier in the war; the number of state walkouts marginally increased in 1942 over 1941, while the national total of strikes declined. Uncounted thousands of workers who did not down tools participated in various forms of production slowdowns. Strikes were concentrated in the Detroit metropolitan area; by contrast, Bay City, a community with several important war plants, did not experience a major strike until June of 1945."[71]

Work stoppages in 1944 exceeded the number recorded for any previous year by the Bureau of Labor Statistics. The time lost per worker involved, however, was less than in any year for which information was available. Most strikes, as already noted, were of short duration. Thus, although there were 4,956 strikes and lockouts involving over two million workers, idleness was less than .1 percent of the available working time. Robert Zieger notes that the 1944 strike wave involved 7 percent of the entire workforce, almost as high a portion as the classic strike years of 1937 and 1941. Yet, strikers stayed out for an average of only 5.6 days, less than half the 1941 average and barely more than a quarter of the 1937 figure. Thus, although workers participated in a record number of strikes, "workers in 1944 lost only a minuscule .09 percent of *working time*, the lowest proportion since the late 1920s."[72] Indeed, throughout the wartime period, as the incidence of strikes increased, their duration dramatically decreased. Rosa Lee Swafford, author of a comprehensive account of wartime strikes, attributed the declining duration to the fact that most strikes were wildcats and public and governmental opinion strongly disapproved of interruptions in production.[73] Wage disputes accounted for about half of all work stoppages in 1944, but disputes over "intraplant working conditions and policies" and recognition and bargaining rights increased substantially.[74]

Both the incidence and the length of strikes increased in 1945. There were 4,750 work stoppages, greater than any year except 1944. The number of workers involved and the resulting idleness exceeded every year since 1919.[75] Approximately 60 percent of the strikes occurring in 1945 occurred prior to V-J day, and they generally followed the wartime pattern as disputes over wages and hours of work continued to account for approximately 50 percent of the cases studied. Disputes over fringe benefits were steadily more important and were more responsible for the total workers involved and the idleness in 1945 than wage demands.[76] Although wages again were involved in nearly half of the strikes, working conditions accounted for about 36 percent of the strikes and lockouts during the year.[77] Surprisingly, "AFL workers were involved in more strikes than CIO workers in every year except 1944," although strikes involving CIO workers were generally larger.[78]

The short duration of most wartime strikes is consistent with other evidence that most strikes were wildcats, that is, without union authorization.[79] Indeed, BLS statistics may understate the incidence of wildcats because the agency did not include stoppages involving fewer than six workers and lasting less than a full workday.[80] On the other hand, until 1944, the BLS recorded all strikes and lockouts as "strikes." The Automotive Council reported, for instance, that in the first eleven months of 1944 there were eight hundred strikes in the automotive industry which were not included in BLS statistics.[81]

Importantly, a high percentage of wildcat strikes occurred in Detroit area auto plants and in the Akron rubber industry.[82] American workers overwhelmingly supported the war, and the vast majority of workers did not strike. The behavior of automobile workers, therefore, was not necessarily typical of the wartime labor movement. No other industry saw a majority of its workers participate in wildcat strikes, and no other union experienced such a large and persistent rank-and-file revolt.[83] (See tables 3 and 4.)

Table 3. Labor Organizations Involved in Strikes, 1940–44

Organization	1940 No.	%	1941 No.	%	1942 No.	%	1943 No.	%	1944 No.	%
AFL	1541	61.9	2343	54.3	1620	53.3	1395	37.3	1696	34.2
CIO	689	27.6	1581	36.6	1034	34.1	1368	36.6	1946	39.2
Unaffiliated unions	138	5.5	68	1.6	112	3.7	586	15.7	5	0.1
Railway brotherhoods	3	0.1	3	0.1	4	0.1	7	0.2	995	20.1
2 rival unions	74	3.0	167	3.9	89	2.9	67	1.8	60	1.2
Company unions	3	0.1	22	0.5	33	1.1	43	1.2	47	0.9
No organization	45	1.8	130	3.0	142	4.7	268	7.2	206	4.2
Not reported	—	—	—	—	2	0.1	—	—	3	0.1
Total	2,493	100.0	4,314	100.0	3,036	100.0	3,734	100.0	4,958	100.0

Source: Adapted from Rosa Lee Swafford, "Wartime Record of Strikes and Lockouts, 1940–45," 79th Cong., 2d sess., 1946, S. Doc. 136, 34.

Table 4. Idleness in Strikes, 1940–44, Attributed to AFL and CIO

	1940	1941	1942	1943	1944
Workers who were members of:					
AFL	53.5%	24.7%	39.9%	19.6%	21.5%
CIO	38.9	69.5	45.1	44.3	52.2
Total idleness in strikes involving members of:					
AFL	54.5	30.3	46.5	10.7	27.6
CIO	39.9	64.8	38.9	16.0	38.5

Source: Adapted from Rosa Lee Swafford, "Wartime Record of Strikes and Lockouts, 1940–45," 79th Cong., 2d sess., 1946, S. Doc. 136, 34.

Highlighting wartime strikes, therefore, tends to stress the militance of auto and rubber workers and ignore other, more pacific, employees such as the steelworkers. Although steelworkers in the 1930s had engaged in long and widespread strikes, power was centralized in SWOC from the very beginning of the union.[84] Although CIO unions like the UAW began to restrict the freedom of locals to engage in independent economic activity by 1938,[85] steelworkers often had little local freedom to lose. Without denigrating the often spirited battles of steelworkers, no strike could be called without the approval of SWOC, the union's president appointed all staff, and the international controlled the top steps of the grievance process.[86] As Murray stated in 1940, SWOC "will insist on a centralized and responsible control of the organizing campaign . . . and will insist that local policies conform to the national plan of action upon which it decides. . . . Responsibility begins and ends with this Committee."[87]

The militance of wartime workers, especially those in the rubber and automobile industries, heightened management's fear that it was losing control of the work process. This concern, especially in auto, led to employer counterattacks before the end of the war and after its conclusion.[88] Management believed that "an insidious erosion of its authority was . . . taking place on the shop floor."[89] The loss of control was only partly the result of bargaining and arbitration, as many believed that more authority had been lost than had been formally surrendered in collective agreements.[90]

Managerial actions directed against worker production quotas and aimed at reversing perceived lax discipline helped generate the wave of wildcat strikes in late 1943 and 1944. "By 1944 one of every two workers in the auto industry took part in some sort of work stoppage, up from one in twelve in 1942 and one in four in 1943." Commonly, these strikes stemmed from attempts to alter job assignments or retime operations. Discipline might then be imposed, and short strikes would often follow. These strikes, then, were generally not wage related, despite BLS reports to the contrary. (See tables 5 and 6.)

There were only fifty strikes in the auto industry in 1942, averaging only one and a half days in duration. In 1943, however, there were 153 wildcat strikes in auto, often involving large numbers of workers. Although the median average strike involved 340 workers, forty-three involved over one thousand and two strikes involved more than ten thousand workers. In 1944, the number, size, and length of auto strikes grew. Two hundred twenty-four strikes occurred, which accounted for over 50 percent of available worktime lost due to strikes. The scope of the strikes is revealed in estimates that well over half of all automobile workers took part in strikes in 1944.[91] The strikes

Table 5. Major Issues Involved in Strikes Ending in 1943

	Strikes		Workers Involved		Man-Days Idle	
	No.	%	No.	%	No.	%
Wages and hours						
Wage increase	1,280	34.2	872,747	44.4	9,932,592	74.7
Wage decrease	85	2.3	21,116	1.1	57,390	0.4
Wage increase/hour decrease	18	0.5	2,311	0.1	8,209	0.1
Hour increase	10	0.3	3,967	0.2	6,861	0.1
Other	513	13.7	316,219	16.1	682,747	5.1
	1,906	51.0	1,216,360	61.9	10,687,799	80.4
Union organization, wages, and hours						
Recognition, wages, and/or hours	152	4.0	30,541	1.5	126,460	0.9
Strengthening bargaining position, wages, and/or hours	15	0.4	5,164	0.3	77,214	0.6
Closed or union shop, wages, and/or hours	47	1.3	12,066	0.6	42,899	0.3
Discrimination, wages, and/or hours	15	0.4	8,179	0.4	23,603	0.2
Other	3	0.1	1,374	0.1	2,173	a
	232	6.2	57,324	2.0	272,349	2.0
Union organization						
Recognition	92	2.5	14,440	0.7	71,168	0.5
Strengthening bargaining position	37	1.0	18,696	1.0	44,893	0.3
Closed or union shop	99	2.6	29,672	1.5	118,039	0.9
Discrimination	96	2.6	52,559	2.7	118,524	0.9
Other	29	0.8	53,200	2.7	118,220	0.9
	353	9.5	168,567	8.6	470,844	3.5
Other working conditions						
Job security	461	12.3	173,233	8.8	508,432	3.8
Shop conditions and policies	506	13.6	242,426	12.4	718,690	5.5
Workload	91	2.4	34,317	1.7	150,000	1.1
Other	36	1.0	11,832	0.6	27,512	0.2
	1,094	29.3	461,808	23.5	1,404,634	10.6
Interunion or intraunion matters						
Sympathy	5	0.1	510	a	952	a
Union rivalry or factionalism	77	2.2	27,916	1.4	159,059	1.2
Jurisdiction	53	1.4	9,362	0.5	40,544	0.3
Union regulations	13	0.3	23,135	1.2	262,304	2.0
Other	1	a	169	a	169	a
	149	4.0	61,092	3.1	463,028	3.5
All issues	3,734	100.0	1,965,151	100.0	13,298,654	100.0

Source: Adapted from BLS, "Strikes in 1943," *Monthly Labor Review* 58 (May 1944): 937.

a. Less than 0.1 percent.

Table 6. Major Issues Involved in Strikes and Lockouts Ending in 1944

	Strikes		Workers Involved		Man-Days Idle	
	No.	%	No.	%	No.	%
Wages and hours						
Wage increase	1,046	21.1	352,752	16.6	1,698,363	19.1
Wage decrease	66	1.3	30,933	1.5	206,895	2.3
Wage increase/hour decrease	10	0.2	1,093	0.1	4,675	0.1
Hour decrease	9	0.2	2,684	0.1	9,471	0.1
Hour increase	10	0.2	4,264	0.2	6,622	0.1
Other[a]	1,005	20.3	417,846	19.6	1,450,474	16.3
	2,146	43.3	809,572	38.1	8,880,078	38.0
Union organization, wages, and hours						
Recognition, wages, and/or hours	187	3.7	43,439	2.0	335,577	3.8
Strengthening bargaining position, wages, and/or hours	26	0.5	12,589	0.6	78,692	0.9
Closed or union shop, wages and/or hours	23	0.5	4,200	0.2	34,336	0.4
Discrimination, wages, and/or hours	8	0.2	5,638	0.3	45,288	0.5
Other	3	0.1	270	b	2,340	b
	247	5.0	66,136	3.1	496,233	5.6
Union organization						
Recognition	202	4.1	169,958	8.1	853,118	9.6
Strengthening bargaining position	56	1.1	22,054	1.0	92,787	1.0
Closed or union shop	131	2.6	32,395	1.5	193,599	2.2
Discrimination	128	2.6	76,758	3.6	279,774	3.2
Other	44	0.9	28,209	1.3	117,194	1.3
	561	11.3	329,374	15.5	1,536,472	17.3
Other working conditions						
Job security	792	16.0	412,862	19.3	1,212,709	13.7
Shop conditions and policies	801	16.1	311,746	14.7	1,036,228	11.7
Workload	168	3.4	72,508	3.4	305,226	3.4
Other	39	0.8	10,115	0.5	30,357	0.3
	1,800	36.3	807,231	37.9	2,584,520	29.1
Interunion or intraunion matters						
Sympathy	27	0.5	13,828	0.7	54,759	0.6
Union rivalry or factionalism	89	1.9	78,338	3.7	759,189	8.6
Jurisdiction	70	1.4	17,551	0.8	56,656	0.6
Union regulations	17	0.3	4,785	0.2	15,212	0.2
Other	1	b	537	b	537	b
	204	4.1	115,039	5.4	886,353	10.0
All issues	4,958	100.0	2,127,352	100.0	8,880,078	100.0

Source: Adapted from BLS, "Strikes and Lockouts in 1944," *Monthly Labor Review* 60 (May 1945): 968.
a. Includes stoppages involving adjustments of piece rates, incentive rates, wage classifications for new and changed operations, retroactive pay, holiday and vacation pay, payment for travel time, and so forth.
b. Less than 0.1 percent.

revealed the depth of worker dissatisfaction, but even in 1944 the average duration of strikes was three and a half days. Thus, few can be said to have posed any real threat to the war effort.

Lichtenstein attributes the auto walkouts not to newly hired industrial workers but, instead, to the "oppositional infra-structure and a preexisting tradition of struggle into which these new workers could be acculturated."[92] Secondary UAW leaders often channeled rank-and-file unrest into well-led, sometimes plantwide stoppages. Again, there seems considerable doubt about the customary thesis that strikes were caused by the new, undisciplined, or "pre-industrial" workers. Joshua Freeman, for instance, has characterized many of these strikes as "a throwback to an earlier and more primitive stage of historical development," and noted that as they "failed to produce an articulated social vision," these strikes were not significantly different than those which occurred in the 1930s.[93]

The incidence of strikes in the auto industry may be due not only to the heritage of militance from the 1930s but also to the nature of the work, especially the interdependence of the production processes.[94] The integration of production lines makes it relatively easy for a small number of workers to shut down an entire plant over a grievance that may only apply to their department. The electrical manufacturing industry, by contrast, had far fewer strikes—only 4.4 percent of these workers were involved in strikes in 1944 compared to 50.5 percent in auto plants. Although managerial policies in the two industries were similar, the electrical industry was less integrated than auto and also had a lower incidence of strikes before the war.[95]

THE UNION RESPONSE

Worker unrest posed serious problems for union officials.[96] Wildcat strikes were especially difficult in the UAW because they often had the support of local or workplace leaders and were consistent with the union's history of decentralization and workplace democracy. There were 256 wildcats alone at Ford's three Detroit plants in 1943, and the international feared that the lack of local control could be organizationally disastrous and that local leadership could not control the militants.

One of the pressures on union stewards, committee members, or other officials is the choice between supporting worker assertiveness, expected of officials, or arguing for the use of the grievance process, risking the charge of being in the company's "pocket." Increasing the dilemma is the early-developed arbitral rule that union officials have special responsibilities—as leaders—to avoid participating or encouraging unauthorized strikes. Indeed,

Harry Shulman in the first umpire case at Ford under the 1943 agreement held that committeemen could be disciplined unless they did "all in their power to restore order."[97]

In February 1944, the UAW adopted a new policy which significantly shifted control from locals to the international. Locals were to inform the international of any stoppages and the international would investigate. If union members were at fault, union officials would be told to withhold aid from employees who might be disciplined. In addition to the denial of the use of the grievance process, locals were told to try strikers pursuant to intra-union disciplinary procedures and to discipline or even expel them. Locals which refused to cooperate were subject to trusteeship, that is, they would be controlled by the international rather than by elected local officers. The policy, therefore, used the fear of the possible loss of official status as well as the loss of local freedom in the fight against wildcat activity.[98] Stewards and committeemen were now made directly responsible for the actions of the rank and file. Thus, the notion that employees should grieve rather than exercise self-help becomes institutionalized during the war, not after.[99] Indeed, although the pressures of war no doubt affected the UAW's policies, institutional protection seems to have served as an independent spur to centralized control.

Two weeks after the adoption of the UAW's new policy, union activists at the Ford's River Rouge discovered written evidence that management intended to provoke a strike and hundreds of workers rioted at a plant labor relations office. The company laid off or fired twenty workers, and UAW president R. J. Thomas supported the company's decision. Thomas asserted that the "UAW-CIO today faces the greatest crisis in its history. Public opinion has become inflamed against our union. There can be no such thing today as a legitimate picket line. Any person who sets up a picket line is acting like an anarchist, not like a disciplined union man."[100] The rank and file, however, continued to strike and continued to reelect local officials who had led wildcats.[101]

Once a policy like the UAW's is in place, enforcement often becomes more important than legal niceties. Nelson Lichtenstein's discussion of the noteworthy strike by Ford's Local 600 in March 1944 highlights this situation.[102] After the UAW investigated, 121 employees were fired or suspended. When some of the employees demanded a trial pursuant to the union constitution and the UAW's own policy, the UAW, fearing exoneration, "hurriedly 'abrogated' the section of the Los Angeles policy calling for a trial by a local trial committee. Instead, union disciplinary measures could rest entirely in the hands of the executive board itself."[103]

The feeling of some local leaders is clearly reflected in a statement to a UAW regional director by a local president in Cleveland who led a wildcat in defense of two fired employees. He allowed that his judgment could be affected by the number of aircraft engines lost by the walkout, but he said "I wasn't elected by those people to win the war. I was elected to lead those people and to represent them. I have tried my best to abide by the constitution, but at this time my conscience will not let me because of my duty to those people."[104]

The top leadership of the United Rubber Workers also took steps to regulate the behavior of rebellious locals. The URW expelled strikers from membership and then used the maintenance of membership clause to have them fired. Administrators were also imposed on some locals. One extraordinary case involved a strike at U.S. Rubber's Detroit plant. URW president Sheldon Dalrymple fined each of one thousand workers. Many workers refused to pay, and Dalrymple expelled 572, demanding that U.S. Rubber fire them under the contractual union security clause. U.S. Rubber, ironically, refused because of the likely disruption caused by such a mass discharge and because of the shortage of skilled labor.[105] Dalrymple appealed for help to the WLB, which responded by instructing U.S. Rubber to use the checkoff arrangement to force the payment of fines and reinstatement fees from those who refused to pay.

The unions acted largely out of a concern for self-defense, but their actions were to have long-term effects. As Lichtenstein has perceptively noted, unions were trying to "preserve their organizations to fight on more favorable terms in the post-war era. But the maintenance of labor peace in an era when grievances were rife required the permanent weakening of those elements in the union structure upon which trade union power ultimately rested. After the war the additional authority garnered by the international apparatus, by corporate management, and by government bureaucracy would not automatically return to the hands of the local union and the rank and file."[106]

Notes

1. Mary Heaton Vorse, "And the Workers Say," *Public Opinion Quarterly* 7 (1943): 443.

2. H. M. Douty, "Review of Basic American Labor Conditions," in *Yearbook of American Labor*, vol. 1, *War Labor Policies*, ed. Colston E. Warne (New York: Philosophical Library, 1945), 14. At the Lowell mills, and presumably elsewhere, employers began to pay wages via checks rather than in cash. Such a change "further rationalized labor-management interactions, making the exchange of money for labor

more impersonal and routine" (Marc Scott Miller, *The Irony of Victory: World War II and Lowell, Massachusetts* [Urbana: University of Illinois Press, 1988], 58). In addition, the Revenue Act of 1943 introduced withholding taxes, perhaps explaining the use of checks.

3. "Changes in the Cost of Living during 1943," in *Yearbook of American Labor*, vol. 1, *War Labor Policies*, ed. Colston E. Warne (New York: Philosophical Library, 1945), 53–56.

4. Ibid.

5. Vorse, "And the Workers Say," 444.

6. Increased production seems always to lead to a greater incidence of workplace injuries. It was common to blame these injuries on the number of "new" workers in the wartime plants (Miller, *Irony of Victory*, 27).

7. Robert Zieger, *John L. Lewis: Labor Leader* (Boston: G. K. Hall, 1988), 133.

8. Ibid., 135–36.

9. Although wage rates increased more slowly than the cost of living as a result of government controls, the average weekly earnings of manufacturing employees rose 70 percent between January 1941 and July 1945 because of steady war production and extensive overtime. See Joshua Freeman, "Delivering the Goods: Industrial Unionism during World War II," *Labor History* 19 (Fall 1978): 570–593.

10. Joshua B. Freeman, *In Transit: The Transport Workers Union in New York City, 1933–1966* (New York: Oxford University Press, 1989), 228–29.

11. Ed Jennings, "Wildcat! The Wartime Strike Wave in Auto," *Radical America* 9 (July–Aug. 1975), 104.

12. Roger Keeran, *The Communist Party and the Auto Workers Union* (Bloomington: Indiana University Press, 1980), 241–42.

13. George Lipsitz, *Rainbow at Midnight: Labor and Culture in the 1940s* (Urbana: University of Illinois Press, 1994), 57–58, 67 n. 48.

14. Nelson Lichtenstein, "Great Expectations: The Promise of Industrial Jurisprudence and Its Demise, 1930–1960," in *Industrial Democracy in America: The Ambiguous Promise*, ed. Nelson Lichtenstein and Howell John Harris (New York: Cambridge University Press, 1993), 135. Clyde Summers notes that the three umpires at GM produced 300 to 350 opinions a year during the period from 1943 to 1947. There were 250 opinions at Ford between June 3, 1943, and Nov. 7, 1947, although approximately 4,700 decisions were issued as "memoranda" (Foreword, Committeeman's Guide to Umpire Decisions [Ford-UAW-CIO] [1948]). Chrysler's arbitral process produced approximately fifty to sixty opinions a year during this period (Foreword, Digest of Umpire Decisions [Chrysler-UAW-CIO] [1949]). These numbers seem to indicate heightened grievance activity at GM compared to the two other main automobile companies (Clyde Summers to author, Mar. 15, 1995).

15. James R. Green, *The World of the Worker: Labor in Twentieth-Century America* (New York: Hill & Wang, 1980), 294.

16. Jennings, "Wildcat," 83. Although the number of strikes declined drastically during the first nine months of 1942, by year's end employees thought that fair

treatment was an illusion and that their union leaders would not fight for them. See ibid., 83–84, 88–89.

17. Robert Blauner, *Alienation and Freedom* (Chicago: University of Chicago Press, 1964), 115.

18. Kevin Boyle, "Autoworkers at War: Patriotism and Protest in the American Automobile Industry, 1939–1945," in *Autowork*, ed. Robert Asher and Ronald Edsforth (Albany: State University of New York Press, 1995), 116.

19. Marilyn Johnson, "Wartime Shipyards and the Transformation of Labor in San Francisco's East Bay," in *American Labor in the Era of World War II*, ed. Sally M. Miller and Daniel A. Cornford (Westport, Conn.: Praeger, 1995), 95.

20. Boyle, "Autoworkers at Work," 117. See also, Nancy Quam-Wickham, "Who Controls the Hiring Hall? The Struggle for Job Control in the ILWU during World War II," in *American Labor in the Era of World War II*, ed. Sally M. Miller and Daniel A. Cornford (Westport, Conn.: Praeger, 1995), 129–30. Quam-Wickham describes the perceived hostility to union organization in the West Coast shipyards. Military officials had reportedly been managers of steamship and stevedoring companies before the war. Rear Admiral Emory Land, the top official of the War Shipping Administration, stated that all union organizers during the war "ought to be shot at sunrise" (ibid., 130).

21. Boyle, "Autoworkers at War," 118–19.

22. Ibid., 120.

23. Ibid.

24. Rick Fantasia, *Cultures of Solidarity: Consciousness, Action, and Contemporary American Workers* (Berkeley: University of California Press, 1988), 50.

25. Alan Clive, *State of War: Michigan in World War II* (Ann Arbor: University of Michigan Press, 1979), 37.

26. Apparently, a small percentage of chronic absentees consistently counted for most of industrial nonattendance. Clive states that there were many causes of absenteeism, including disheartened workers when they could not see the necessity for their individual effort or when material shortages interrupted production. He also lists job shopping or work-connected illness or fatigue as well as housing and transportation difficulties (ibid., 39).

27. In the midwar years, the WLB received ten to fifteen thousand grievance cases a month and cases involving contract demands often sat for years.

28. Roger Horowitz, *"Negro and White, Unite and Fight!" A Social History of Industrial Unionism in Meatpacking, 1930–90* (Urbana: University of Illinois Press, 1997), 155.

29. These events are related in Richard Boyden, "The San Francisco Machinists and the National War Labor Board," in *American Labor in the Era of World War II*, ed. Sally Miller and Daniel Cornford (Westport, Conn.: Praeger, 1995), 105.

30. Exec. Sess., June 2, 1944, pp. 398, 401, quoted in ibid., 111.

31. Ibid., 411.

32. Ibid., 112.

33. Ibid. According to Boyden, continued militance by machinists and fears by employers of the cost of Navy heavy-handedness resulted in the softening of the employee disciplinary measures.

34. See Clive, *State of War*, 103–12. See also Lowell J. Carr and James E. Stermer, *Willow Run: The Study of Industrialization and Cultural Inadequacy* (New York: Harper Brothers, 1952).

35. See Clive, *State of War*, 112–15. For a discussion of the serious housing problem in many defense plant communities see Carr and Stermer, *Willow Run*, 62–86. Employees were often housed in makeshift or temporary housing and sometimes in cramped trailers (ibid., 87–120). For a sensitive account of housing problems in northern California's East Bay, see Delores Nason McBroome, "Catalyst for Change: Wartime Housing and African-Americans in California's East Bay," in *American Labor in the Era of World War II*, ed. Sally M. Miller and Daniel A. Cornford (Westport, Conn.: Praeger, 1995), 386.

36. Clive, *State of War*, 40.

37. Miller, *Irony of Victory*, 26–28.

38. Lipsitz, *Rainbow at Midnight*, 27.

39. Clive, *State of War*, 66.

40. Ibid., 67.

41. Ibid., 68.

42. A dispute at Boot Mills in Lowell was certified to the WLB in June 1944, and the board issued a decision in December. Appeals by both employer and union, however, kept the case alive until November 1945, when the parties finally reached agreement between themselves (Miller, *Irony of Victory*, 32–33).

43. Lipsitz, *Rainbow at Midnight*, 22. Triviality is often in the eyes of the beholder. Harry Shulman often believed the stoppages he dealt with were "trivial," as in Opinion A-70 where "allegedly a foreman had struck a worker."

44. Quoted in Clive, *State of War*, 76.

45. See, e.g., *Opinions of the Umpire, Ford Motor Co. and UAW-CIO, 1943–1946*, Case No. A-116. Opinion A-3, June 29, 1943; Opinion A-70, Mar. 1, 1944; Opinion A-84, Apr. 12, 1944; Opinion A-140, Sept. 20, 1944; Opinion A-156, Oct. 27, 1944.

46. Quoted in Martin Glaberman, *Wartime Strikes: The Struggle against the No-Strike Pledge in the UAW during World War II* (Detroit: Bewick Editions, 1980), 51–60.

47. Ibid., 42.

48. Rosa Lee Swafford, "Wartime Record of Strikes and Lockouts, 1940–45," 79th Cong., 2d sess., 1946, S. Doc. 136, 4.

49. Boyle, "Autoworkers at War," 120–22.

50. Ibid., 122–23.

51. Ibid., 100.

52. Ibid., 105.

53. Ibid., 107.

54. Ibid., 108–9. Boyle argues that "the unprecedented level of shop floor turmoil in the auto industry during World War II cannot be explained . . . as a consequence of the rank-and-filers' desire for greater control over their work lives" (ibid., 110). The wildcats, therefore, are seen by Boyle as merely attempts to maintain the patterns of labor-management relations worked out in the prewar years.

55. Martin Glaberman, "Shop Floor Struggles of American Workers," in *Within the Shell of the Old: Essays on Workers' Self-Organization*, ed. Don Fitz and David Roediger (Chicago: Charles Kerr, 1990), 49–50.

56. Horowitz, *"Negro and White, Unite and Fight!"* 150–59.

57. Clive, *State of War*, 76–77.

58. Jerome Scott and George C. Homans, "Reflections on the Wildcat Strikes," *American Sociological Review* 54 (June 1947): 278, 280.

59. Melvyn Dubofsky and Warren Van Tine, *John L. Lewis: A Biography* (Urbana: University of Illinois Press, 1986), 302.

60. Freeman, "Delivering the Goods," 579. Labor economist Flora Peterson noted that most strikes "were of short duration and a large portion of the time lost [almost 40 percent] was concentrated in the coal mining industry" (Joseph C. Goulden, *Meany* [New York: Atheneum, 1972], 93). According to the Bureau of Labor Statistics figures, only .05 percent of the available working time was lost to strikes in 1942, .15 percent in 1943, .09 percent in 1944, and .7 percent in 1945 (ibid., 94).

61. Nelson Lichtenstein, "Conflict over Workers' Control: The Automobile Industry in World War II," in *Working-Class America: Essays on Labor, Community, and American Society*, ed. Michael Frisch and Daniel Walkowitz (Urbana: University of Illinois Press, 1983), 288–89.

62. Douty, "Review of Basic American Labor Conditions"; Lichtenstein, "Conflict over Workers' Control," 111.

63. See Nelson Lichtenstein, *Labor's War at Home: The CIO in World War II* (New York: Cambridge University Press, 1982), 119–20.

64. Quoted in Glaberman, *Wartime Strikes*, 44.

65. Virginia Seitz, "Legal, Legislative and Managerial Responses to the Organization of Supervisory Employees in the 1940s," *American Journal of Legal History* 28 (Jan. 1984): 218–35.

66. Lichtenstein, *Labor's War at Home*, 121–22.

67. Freeman, "Delivering the Goods," 592.

68. Zieger, *John L. Lewis*, 132–49.

69. Bureau of Labor Statistics, "Strikes in 1943," *Monthly Labor Review* 58 (May 1944): 927, 936. The Bureau of Labor Statistics (BLS) concluded that 51 percent of the strikes in 1943 involving 62 percent of the workers on strike and 30 percent of mandays idleness involved wages, reflecting the increased cost of living (ibid., 937).

70. Those strikes were short and generally accounted for no more than 0.11 percent of all available working time. Ed Jennings has estimated that the average auto industry wildcat involved some 350–400 workers for a three-to-four-day period ("Wildcat," 90).

71. Clive, *State of War,* 75.

72. Robert Zieger, *The CIO, 1935–1955* (Chapel Hill: University of North Carolina Press, 1995), 150.

73. Swafford, "Wartime Record of Strikes," 8.

74. Bureau of Labor Statistics, "Strikes and Lockouts in 1944," *Monthly Labor Review* 60 (May 1945): 937. Excluding 1941, the number of strikes increased between 1942 and 1944 as did the number of workers involved. The man-days idle, however, were substantially larger in 1943 than either of the surrounding years (ibid., 958). The UMW strikes of 1943 substantially effect the statistics. It is interesting that more than one-fourth of the workers involved in labor stoppages were in the state of Michigan. The National War Labor Board was directly concerned with only 33 percent of the strikes which occurred in 1944.

75. See *Monthly Labor Review* 62 (May 1946): 718.

76. Ibid., 731.

77. Ibid., 968.

78. Ibid., 34.

79. As Joshua Freeman has stressed, care must be used in referring to strikes as wildcats. This study refers to strikes which occurred without union authorization, most of which were of short duration and involved a small number of workers. Some strikes were led, however, by local union officials, often responding to rank and file pressure. Freeman refers to a strike of fifty thousand rubber workers in Akron in May 1943, and another involving ten thousand Chrysler workers at six Michigan facilities in May 1944. Such strikes, even if led reluctantly by local leaders, were "essentially a continuation of pre-war activity and not fundamentally a new phase of working-class activity" (Freeman, "Delivering the Goods," 583–84). The nature of the pressure from below, however, may actually distinguish these strikes from those in the 1930s, however, and many of these were also "unauthorized" in the sense that international approval was not sought.

80. Ibid., 1.

81. Ibid., 2.

82. Some believe that the importance of these strikes has been overblown. The strikes were short term and particularly involved little social vision or goals (Howell John Harris, *The Right to Manage: Industrial Relations Policies of American Business in 1940s* [Madison: University of Wisconsin Press, 1982], 61).

83. In 1944, a majority of automobile workers participated in wildcat strikes.

84. Mark McColloch, "Consolidating Industrial Citizenship: The USWA at War and Peace, 1939–46," in *Forging a Union of Steel*, ed. Paul Clark, Peter Gottlieb, and Donald Kennedy (Ithaca, N.Y.: ILR Press, 1987), 47–49.

85. See James Atleson, *Values and Assumptions in American Labor Law* (Amherst: University of Massachusetts Press, 1983), 46–47; Edward Levinson, *Labor on the March* (New York: Harper, 1938; Ithaca, N.Y.: ILR Press, 1995), 169, 179–85.

86. See McColloch, "Consolidating Industrial Citizenship," 77; David Brody, "The Origins of Modern Steel Unionism: The SWOC Era," in *Forging a Union of*

Steel, ed. Paul Clark, Peter Gottlieb, and Donald Kennedy (Ithaca, N.Y.: ILR Press, 1987), 28; Lloyd Ulman, *The Government of the Steel Workers Union* (New York: John Wiley, 1962), 28.

87. Cited in Vincent D. Sweeney, *The United Steelworkers of America* (Pittsburgh: United Steelworkers of America, 1956), 12–13; Brody, "Origins of Modern Steel Unionism," 27.

88. See Harris, *Right to Manage*, 61–70.

89. David Brody, *Workers in Industrial America* (New York: Oxford University Press, 1980), 180; see, generally, Harris, *Right to Manage*.

90. Brody, *Workers in Industrial America*, 181; see James Atleson, "Wartime Labor Regulation, the Industrial Pluralists, and the Law of Collective Bargaining," in *Industrial Democracy in America: The Ambiguous Promise*, ed. Nelson Lichtenstein and Howell John Harris (New York: Cambridge University Press, 1993).

91. U.S. Dept. of Labor, Bureau of Labor Statistics, Impact of the War on the Detroit Area, Industrial Area Study No. 10 (July 1943). See also "Industrial Disputes," *Monthly Labor Review* 56 (May 1943): 694; Swafford, "Wartime Record of Strikes"; Keeran, *Communist Party and the Auto Workers Union*, 241–42.

92. Lichtenstein, *Labor's War at Home*, 296.

93. Freeman, "Delivering the Goods," 583–85.

94. James Atleson, "Work Group Behavior and Wildcat Strikes: The Causes and Functions of Industrial Civil Disobedience," *Ohio State Law Review* 34 (1973): 750, 770–72.

95. See "Memorandum to the Chief, Industrial Services Division, Subject: Industrial Conflict in Detroit," June 9, 1944, in *Records of the War Production Board*, cited in Ruth Milkman, *Gender at Work: The Dynamics of Job Segregation by Sex during World War II* (Urbana: University of Illinois Press, 1987), 179.

96. As early as mid-1937 the United Autoworkers sought to confine rank-and-file militancy when recurrent strikes led to demands by General Motors and others for greater stability. John L. Lewis, president of the CIO, feared that militance in the UAW would injure efforts to organize other industries. The union's attack on wildcat strikes continued in 1939, during a much less militant period. As Reuther noted, "we must demonstrate that we are a disciplined, responsible organization, that we not only have power, but that we have power under control." Similarly, Reuther noted that "the International Union and the National GM department is unalterably opposed to, and will not tolerate any unauthorized strikes or stoppages for work. . . . We who claim the right to strike must assume the responsibility of striking when it is right to strike" (Nelson Lichtenstein, *Walter Reuther: The Most Dangerous Man in Detroit* [Urbana: University of Illinois Press, 1997; originally published as *The Most Dangerous Man in Detroit: Walter Reuther and the Fate of American Labor* [New York: Basic Books, 1995], 110–11, 121–22, 133).

97. Opinion A-1, June 3, 1943. See also Opinion A-3, June 29, 1943; Opinion A-156, Oct. 27, 1944. The case involved a physical altercation at the plant gate between two security guards and a union official, said by the company to be drunk.

The guard struck the union official, who claimed that one of the guards had hit him first. Shulman, crediting the company's perception of the union official's condition and noting the size difference between the two men, felt it doubtful that the union official would "even have pushed . . . [the guard] were not his courage stimulated and his discretion dulled by intoxication." In any event, the guard knocked the union official down, and a tense and ugly moblike situation ensued, which resulted in multiple blows being directed at the guard.

This was not a wildcat situation, and no one defends the use of violence. What is especially noteworthy in Shulman's opinion is the recognition that behind the incident was a "hostility against plant protection men and a feeling that somehow their functions are inimical to the workers." This belief, he felt, was based not on the current situation but "on the recollection of real or fancied situations prior to the company's unionization." Moreover, guards were "not only necessary in this plant, but they are required by the government" and their numbers were increased "during the war for good reason." It was the union's responsibility "to discourage divisive hostility between these fellow workers." To many veterans of the 1930s, however, the thuggism of Harry Bennett's Service Department would not have seemed "fanciful," nor is it conceivable that Shulman would have believed this to be the case.

98. Lichtenstein, *Labor's War at Home*, 189–97.

99. Atleson, "Wartime Labor Regulation," 156.

100. Alan Clive, "Women Workers in World War II: Michigan as a Test Case," *Labor History* 20 (1979): 80.

101. Clive argues that centralized control over UAW locals was inevitable, even if they viewed their membership as what Lichtenstein calls a "radical and potentially majoritarian movement" which they did not (Nelson Lichtenstein, "Industrial Unionism under the No-Strike Pledge: A Study of the CIO during World War II" [Ph.D. diss., University of California, Berkeley, 1974], 721). As Clive notes, not all democratic actions by union locals, especially Briggs Local 212, were peaceful or consistent with democratic procedures (ibid., 88). As Marc Scott Miller's study of the war in Lowell indicates, "unions also played a role in weeding out dissident and 'poor' workers" (Miller, *Irony of Victory*, 37–38).

102. Lichtenstein, *Labor's War at Home*, 191–93.

103. Ibid., 192.

104. Quoted in ibid., at 193.

105. Ibid., 199–200.

106. Ibid., 202.

8

The "New" Industrial Workers

Analyses of the hundreds of wartime wildcat strikes often conclude that a major factor was the thousands of seemingly inexperienced workers who entered the war industries just as union veterans were being drawn into the armed services. The Detroit area, for instance, lost 30 percent of its predominantly male workforce, and half of the new workers were engaged in factory work for the first time. Many of these new workers, it has often been argued, had hostile or at least ambivalent attitudes toward unions and, thus, they often acted independently of the institutional norms, procedures, and goals of their unions.[1]

The war situation obviously caused the departure of experienced union cadres from the workplace. As Howard Kimmeldorf explained:

> The membership turnover was greatest in the mass-production unions, especially those based in the defense sector. Consider the case of the U.E. During the war more than two hundred thousand of its members, including many local officers, union organizers, and even an international official, left for the armed forces. At the same time, tens of thousands of incoming workers filled job vacancies as fast as they were being created by the mass exodus of military conscripts, on the one hand, and the war-stimulated demand for labor in electrical and machine-working plants, on the other. . . . The turnover in leadership was so high that at the union's biennial convention in 1944 more than half of all voting delegates were attending for the first time.[2]

This made for a "volatile but not particularly union-conscious proletariat," resembling the pre-depression, nonunion era.[3]

It is also commonly believed that as unions expanded with large numbers of workers who were indifferent or hostile to unionism, the more active and experienced unionists began increasingly to structure or "bureaucratize the union to prevent its disintegration or drift to the right."[4] Thus, "bureaucratization is not just the result of bureaucrats and opportunism . . . , but is also a natural outgrowth of the very success of unions in organizing new, less politically advanced sections of the working class."[5] The new workers, therefore, are often seen as the *cause* of union centralization and bureaucratization.

Legitimate union concerns were often clouded by hostility to the new workers, many of whom were migrants, women, African Americans, or, primarily in the West, Latinos. Racism and sexism were surely present in large doses, although older workers often spoke of the need to maintain control of crafts by workers who had organized unions in the 1930s. West Coast shipyard unions, for instance, created auxiliary unions for newcomers. The Boilermakers directly controlled local affiliates, especially the new locals created by wartime production. As described by Marilyn Johnson, the "international suspended all elections, meetings, and regular publications for the duration of the war" for its Richmond, California, local. As the international explained, "The vast majority of people seeking clearance to work in Richmond were complete strangers to this area, knew little or nothing about Unions or Union procedure, and unfortunately didn't want to learn. . . . Nothing but internal strife would have prevailed had this great mass of new members, uninitiated in the trade union movement, exercised control."[6]

Employers, as well as unions, responded to the demands of wartime production and the influx of new workers in two primary ways. First, employers attempted to de-skill and reorganize work.[7] At Kaiser's East Bay yards, for instance, work was reorganized and prefabrication introduced, with the result that skills were reduced and more traditional craft skills lessened.[8] Second, workers were placed in jobs thought appropriate, based on stereotypes of women, blacks, Asians, and other workers.[9]

The "new" industrial workers have often been described as unruly or undisciplined, comparable to nineteenth-century workers who are often said to have possessed "pre-industrial" ideas about work. Kimmeldorf, for instance, states that "In the wake of these departing CIO militants came a flood of less union-conscious workers. Recruited largely from among the urban unemployed, the surplus agricultural labor force, and other non-unionized sectors of the economy, most lacked even a rudimentary understanding of basic trade union principles."[10]

The implication is that these new workers had to be socialized into *both* the industrial work rhythms and the dispute resolution systems of the modern, organized factory. The "new" workers replace the rural or foreign-born immigrants of the nineteenth century as the focus of concern for "the adjustment and adaptation of immigrant workers to the social and cultural norms of an industrialized America."[11]

From the earliest days of American industry the "pre-industrial" norms of workers were seen as problems for efficiency and work discipline.[12] The argument in the 1940s was that the new workers had to be socialized to *union* as well as employer structures and procedures. Both employer and union discipline would be necessary to maintain production, resolve disputes through the grievance process rather than by employing self-help, and instill pro-union attitudes. This group of workers, therefore, is often seen as the source of rank-and-file militance and strikes during the war and, at the same time, the justification for union bureaucratization, intra-union discipline, and union security clauses.

The new members of CIO unions were often perceived to be apathetic, if not negative, about the labor movement.[13] Presumably, women and black workers, for example, were expected to be unaffected by the sexism and racism they often faced from fellow workers and, at times, from their unions. The argument assumes little difference of opinion between union officials and their membership in general. Robert Zieger, however, has noted that general public opinion polls sometimes revealed that significant divisions did indeed exist between union leaders and union members. In 1942, for instance, two-thirds of union members polled opposed dues checkoffs, and in July 1945, union members opposed the closed shop by a margin of three to two. Moreover, throughout the war, union members overwhelmingly supported the proposition that the government should regulate union affairs and finances. In addition, workers generally, and union members more specifically, favored repression of strike activity. As Zieger notes, union members throughout the war expressed support for strike regulation by a margin of two to one. In May 1943, an even greater proportion agreed that advocacy of a strike in a war plant should be made a crime.[14] Of course, UAW members, the source of most wildcat strikes during the war, also voted to sustain the UAW's no-strike pledge in 1944.

This conflicting data has sometimes been explained by the presence of thousands of new workers in organized plants and the absence of some of the organizational leaders of the 1930s. At the same time, however, more militant workers often viewed their union as insufficiently aggressive. Even veterans of the sit-down era "could neither understand nor readily accept the rapid change in labor tactics from the wielding of the strike weapon to the calling of tripartite conferences. Throughout the war, annual UAW local elections resulted in defeat for numerous incumbent officers found wanting in militancy by aroused and suspicious elements of the rank and file."[15]

The new workers were, in large part, women, blacks, and, often, workers from rural backgrounds. It is commonly assumed that these workers possessed no union histories or came from non-union or even anti-union backgrounds. Moreover, union officials feared that the high pay in wartime industries made unions seem irrelevant, a concern compounded by the inability of unions to strike or to raise wages substantially, even in lower wage industries like textiles or retail. The new entrants, therefore, would be viewed with suspicion by union officials who had organized in the heat of the 1930s.

Yet, why would these new workers, previously exploited because of race or sex or, at least, previously not well paid, behave in an unruly fashion in defense plants during a popularly supported war? The very statement of the question suggests that the answer may be quite complex. After all, wages were relatively high and many employees believed that their employers controlled their military deferments.[16] Sociologist Kate Archibald's comments on shipyard workers were no doubt applicable to all industrial workers of the time. "For the majority . . . the war was an experience of opportunity rather than limitation. Their wartime income was larger than ever before, and they ate more abundantly and lived more agreeably. The men of draft age were also aware that every day in the shipyard was a day not spent in a barracks or a foxhole."[17]

Despite the various pressures upon workers discussed in the previous chapter, wartime conditions clearly increased many workers' sense of power. As David Montgomery has noted, high levels of employment during World War II "gave millions of workers the confidence to quit jobs and search for better ones and to go on strike on a scale that dwarfed all previously recorded turnover and strike activity."[18] Given the militance of the wartime rank and file, as many have argued, secondary union leaders began in the midwar period to seek ways to harness worker restlessness by leading strikes. But this only suggests that the causes of these strikes were of concern to many workers, not just the new industrial workers, and, indeed, that many strikes were deemed justifiable by local leaders.

Initially, it is not at all clear that the new workers actually behaved differently than the veterans of the union-building drives of the 1930s, although they clearly would not have the same emotional attachment to the union or to its demands for formalized dispute resolution procedures. In fact, these new workers seem to have acted like those who joined the union movement between 1916 and 1920, when employment was at high levels.

Moreover, it is clear that many of the "new" workers were not new to the workplace. The entry of women workers into wartime industries largely involved a transfer of positions rather than a shift from home to factory, and this is especially true in regard to black women. Although Martin Glaberman found that women in the automobile industry sometimes initiated strikes, he argued that there was "no evidence available that women were more prone to strike action than auto workers generally." Indeed, women did not seem to "alter the level of militancy of the auto workers, either positively or negatively."[19]

Additionally, and perhaps counterintuitively, Glaberman concluded that southern whites tended to be among the most militant workers in the auto industry.[20] He attributed such behavior to "the individualistic mythology of the South," the availability of other jobs, and the lack of union experience which led to greater militancy. This may be especially ironic given the popular perception of the super-patriotism of southern whites. On the other hand, Glaberman argues that black workers could not find jobs as easily and, thus, they were less likely to initiate wildcat strikes.[21]

The common argument that the hundreds of wartime strikes were due to new, "pre-industrial" workers needs more support than it has received. Glaberman, for example, concludes that "too many of the names that appeared during the organizing days . . . reappeared in the wartime wildcats" to assume that military service removed unions activists from the workplace, thus creating an undisciplined workforce necessitating the bureaucratization of unions.[22]

In addition, as various studies noted in the previous chapter indicated, many of the wartime strikes involved immediate workplace conflicts over, for instance, disciplinary actions.[23] These are the same kinds of conflicts which had led to similar forms of collective action in the latter half of the previous decade. Such concerns are also reflected in the fact that the UAW filed over one hundred thousand grievances annually through 1943. Nelson Lichtenstein, for instance, described the militant wartime action of UAW Local 600 at Ford's Rouge plant. A militant cadre of shop stewards dramatically altered the power structure on the shop floor, and he lists a total of 773 strikes at the Rouge during the war, primarily over discipline, supervision, and working conditions, the cause of most wartime strikes. Importantly, these actions "were not counterposed to the union infrastructure, nor were they simply due to the wave of industrially-undisciplined workers who surged into war time factories. Rather, they represented an extra-contractual dimension of union influence and power. In Local 600's early years, most of the serious wildcat strikes were either led or condoned by union committeemen or veteran union activists."[24] The new workers, in other words, seem to have responded to the same concerns and in similar ways as the veterans of the 1930s.

There is, therefore, reason to question the argument that union bureaucratization was necessary to control a workforce composed of large numbers of inexperienced factory operatives. Moreover, there is also substantial doubt that the workers were as undisciplined or unsophisticated as they are often portrayed. As Steve Jeffreys has noted: "While their inexperience may have aided the centralization of the CIO unions, it should not be assumed that the new unionists were necessarily *less* conscious of their rights and interests against management. The presence of a core of pre-war militants ensured that union traditions were passed on in the older industrial centers, and, once introduced to a tradition that denied management the right to act arbitrarily, the new wartime labor force took over the pre-war frontier of control as if it were its own creation."[25]

Indeed, the record reveals little evidence that "new" workers, inexperienced in the requirements of the workplace, were the primary cause of strikes. Many women who flocked to defense installations, for instance, were not ex-housewives but, instead, women who already had work experience, albeit often in lower-paying jobs. It is perhaps not surprising that workers, old or new, would respond in a militant fashion in a period of labor shortage and the perception of growing worker power. The fact that many of these new industrial workers were women should not alter such a conclusion.[26] After all, many women proved to be effective and resourceful organizers in the 1930s,[27] and they performed in similar roles during the war.[28]

Male union organizers often seemed genuinely surprised at the organizability and militance of women workers. The willingness of women workers to join unions and to take part in collective action in the 1930s suggests that similar behavior in the 1940s should not have been viewed as novel. Yet, increased wages and upward mobility for women, it was said, were "clearly due to economic mobilization rather than to union efforts, so that women were often indifferent towards unionization."[29] Nevertheless, a substantial women's movement emerged within the CIO during the 1940s despite the obstacles created by predominantly male-centered unions. This group tended to consist of older women, especially those who had prior union or industry experience, younger women from union families, and those with leftist views.[30] What is different about the work stoppages in the 1940s is that they often occurred outside of formal collective bargaining structures and without union sponsorship.[31]

Southern men and women often came from Appalachia, possessing strong pro-union feelings. Ruth Meyerowitz's study of the GM Ternstedt plant in the 1930s, for instance, revealed that a southern background often involved contact or actual working experience with the United Mine Workers Union. Both men and women from mining regions tended to become "the backbone of the campaign and were among the first to join."[32] Moreover, UAW militants at Ternstedt in the 1930s were often black southerners who had worked with Communists in organizing tenant farmers or Poles who were influenced by Pilsudsky's socialism.[33]

During the war, union membership and female participation in the workplace grew rapidly. Between 1940 and 1944, the number of workers in unions grew from 7.2 million to 12.6 million, raising the percent unionized from 12.7 to 22.2 percent.[34] The number of unionized women grew even more dramatically: from 800,000 (or 9.4 percent) in 1940 to 3,000,000 (or 21.8 percent) in 1944.[35] During the war, the total number of working women increased from 14,600,000 in 1941 to 19,370,000 in 1944. In Michigan, female employment rose from 24 percent in March 1940 to over 34 percent in November 1943.[36] By 1945, women constituted 28 percent of the UAW membership and 40 percent of the membership of the UE.[37] The number of black women working in industry also rose. Prior to the war, 60 percent of employed black women worked as domestics while approximately 6 percent worked in factories. By war's end, the number of black women working as domestics declined to 48 percent while 18.6 percent worked in factories.[38]

The nature of the female workforce also changed: "Once dominated by single women under 30 years of age, the female labor force now contained substantially larger proportions of older and married women." The Women's Bureau, for instance, found Detroit's female workers were evenly divided, 45 percent to 45 percent, between single and married women, with the remaining 10 percent being widowed or divorced.[39] By 1944, another study determined that almost half of the female workforce were married, and the vast majority were either self-supporting or working because of financial necessity rather than purely patriotic fervor.[40]

Industrial employment for many women was obviously not something new but, rather, part of a continuing work experience.[41] On the average, about 75 percent of the women employed during the war in the ten areas studied expected to be part of the postwar labor force, and this proportion was even higher in four of the areas studied.[42] Thus, the war brought about great increases not only in the number of women employed but also the number of women who planned to remain in the labor force.[43] Even if many of the women workers, therefore, were new to paid work, they did not necessarily see their participation in the workforce as temporary.

Despite the need for additional labor, many employers, especially in the steel and automobile industries, were reluctant to hire women during the war, despite their lower rate of pay, until the male pool of workers was depleted by wartime conscription. In steel, many employers believed women could simply not perform the demanding work required.[44] The reluctance of automobile manufactures was seemingly more subtle. The employment system in auto had been built on the basis of high wage rates, and there was "relatively little incentive to substitute female labor for its more expensive male equivalent" because the "organization of production around the moving assembly line laid the basis for auto's development as a high-wage, capital-intensive industry."[45] Automobile employers insisted that women were not the equal of men in factory work and complained of the added cost of adjusting equipment and providing facilities for women, the insidious "bathroom" problem which was to re-arise in the 1970s. Yet, observers often noted that women's absenteeism rate was usually lower and their motivation was generally higher than that of men.[46] Eventually, the combination of governmental pressure and the relative absence of available men induced the auto industry to hire women in large numbers.[47] By 1943 the proportion of women in the industry grew to 25 percent from 5 percent just before Pearl Harbor.[48] The resistance to black workers was greater, perhaps because women were seen as temporary during the war period.[49]

Women faced a variety of discriminatory practices in wartime industry. Ruth Milkman found that women in the automobile industry were typically hired into specific job classifications which management deemed suitable and, thus, they were not evenly distributed throughout the job classifications available in wartime factories. Throughout the period distinctions were generally made between male and female jobs, primarily based on the belief that women were less strong than men.[50] From the beginning, it was assumed by both employers and male unionists that the women's place in the factories was only temporary, only for the duration of the war. Indeed, some firms made strenuous efforts to recruit wives and daughters of male employees who they had employed before the war on the assumption that there would be less difficulty in replacing them with males after the war.

Katherine Archibald's study of women shipyard workers at Moore Dry Dock in Oakland, California, in 1942, found that male workers viewed women as rivals of "men in a man's world."[51] Pressure also came from wives of workers who feared the temptation caused by single women workers would lead their husbands astray. One result was strict dress codes, rules not applied to women in white collar positions.

The response of male workers to the presence of women co-workers varied as the war proceeded, and the defensiveness of male workers was reflected in strikes even before the war. For instance, during the mobilization period a strike occurred in October 1941 at Kelsey-Hayes Wheel Company in Plymouth, Michigan, in which one of the demands was "the removal of all girl employees from machine work which, [the union] contends, is a man's job."[52] Despite the relatively low number of women in auto plants at this time, men apparently feared the substitution of women workers for men, presumably to reduce labor costs. During the war such fears would lead to wildcat strikes opposing the hiring of women.

When it became clear, however, that resistance to the hiring of women would be unproductive, unions often switched to a new set of tactics. One tactic attempted to make certain that women's employment in "men's jobs" would be limited to the duration of the war, and separate seniority lists or separate agreements were developed to accomplish this end.[53] A second tactic, which seems not to have vigorously survived the war, was the demand for "equal pay for equal work."[54]

Union support for the principle of equal pay for equal work often increased the pay of women workers while simultaneously maintaining the sexual division of labor. Thus, unions often protested the use of lower-paid women on jobs for which men received higher wages, but often argued that women should only perform "male" work when men were not available.[55] A variation occurred in the United Electrical Workers Union (UE) which had sought "equal pay for equal work" before the war, and, by the end of the war, 68 percent of UE members were covered by equal pay clauses. As Fillipelli and McCulloch note, however, the long-standing industrial practice of classifying jobs by sex seriously undercut the effort because, as would be learned over twenty years later when the requirement would become part of federal law, the policy had no effect on women's wages in traditional "women's" jobs.[56] Like other unions the UE feared management would make minor alterations in what had been male jobs, reclassify them as women's work, and pay the new women workers at a lower rate.

Although job classification would be a divisive issue throughout the war, perhaps the greatest controversy involved the issue of equal wages.[57] A Michigan state law guaranteed women equal pay for "similar" work, but the statue was apparently not enforceable due to its vagueness.[58] In September 1942, however, the War Labor Board ruled against GM in an equal pay case brought jointly by the UAW and the United Electrical Workers,[59] and the decision was soon followed by War Labor Board General Order 16, issued in November 24, 1942, which permitted companies to equalize male and female pay on a voluntary basis without reference to Washington.[60]

Few decisions involving the equal pay principle actually came to the board. In those cases that did, the board routinely directed that the collective agreement include an article incorporating the principle of equal pay for equal work. In the key *General Motors* case, for instance, the board stated: "The National War Labor Board has accepted the general principle that wages should be paid to female employees on the principle of equal pay for equal work. It believes that there should be no discrimination between employees whose production is substantially the same on comparable jobs."[61]

The board's policy, however, primarily applied to cases of women who were working in the same jobs as men or women who took men's jobs which were not changed in content. Where jobs were "diluted in content," wages for women could be reduced proportionately. Moreover, the board's equal pay policy did not apply to wage rates for jobs "employing women exclusively,"[62] and, thus, had little effect on departments segregated on gender grounds. The board might, however, suggest or order a job evaluation "to establish the worth of the job on the basis of content irrespective of the sex of any incumbent" or it might simply remand to the parties for further negotiations. A third stated alternative was that the board might simply presume "that rates for jobs traditionally performed by women were correctly rated in relation to the general wage schedule of the plant." The entire struggle, therefore, was

> explicitly confined to determining whether women within a relatively small spectrum of occupational categories were indeed engaged in "men's work," or work similar enough to "men's work" to merit similar compensation. Although the ensuing debate revealed the arbitrary aspect of the sex labeling of jobs, at the same time it reinforced the legitimacy of the sexual division of labor as a whole. Indeed, the previously established pattern of job segregation was elevated into the reference point for determining the legitimacy of particular claims for equal pay, at the margin between "women's" and "men's" jobs.[63]

In its last pronouncement on the issue, the WLB responded to arguments by the UE which approached what many years later would be called "comparable worth." The target involved women's wage rates in fifty General Electric and Westinghouse plants where, the board found, women "were paid less on a comparative job content basis, than jobs customarily performed by men."[64] An interim order required the parties to "negotiate a formula for narrowing . . . unreasonable wage rate differentials now existing between men's and women's jobs as such." The WLB approved a principle of a "single evaluation line for all jobs in a plant" regardless of the sex of the workers. The board asserted that women should generally receive the same wage rate as men on jobs "which differ only inconsequentially, and not in measurable job content, from jobs performed by men." Subsequently, after futile bargaining, the board on December 12, 1945, ordered that all women's wage rates in the plants should be increased four cents per hour, and it recommended the establishment of a fund for the elimination of "unusually large" differentials. The order, however, was issued after the war ended, and it was generally ignored by the companies.[65]

During the war, the "voluntary clauses of the WLB's order, together with qualifications later placed on the original General Motors decision, vitiated the Board's general initiative."[66] Moreover, organized labor failed to mount a sustained campaign on the equal pay issue, an issue they obviously adopted, at least in part, to protect against the dilution of male wages.[67] Employers continued to maintain sexual pay differential by such means as giving different titles to jobs or by changing job classifications from skilled to semiskilled.

The principle of equal pay for equal work arose long before the wartime period, and a similar conflict emerged. Early in the century male unionists viewed the growing workforce participation of women as a threat to both male jobs and wages. Unionists took two contradictory approaches. First, they argued that women's value as homemakers and mothers meant they should not work at all. At the same time, however, the AFL sought to organize women workers and secure equal pay for them. The former effort led, with the assistance of middle-class reform groups, to restrictive legislation. As Alice Kessler-Harris has argued, the AFL's equal pay demand had a double-edged quality: "While it presumably protected all workers from cheap labor, in the context of the early 1900s labor market it often functioned to deprive women of jobs."[68] Equal pay, then, would not only protect wage levels but restrict the value of hiring lower-paid women workers in the first place. The wartime period presented a different situation, but a similar ambiguity pervaded union attempts to secure wage equality.

The UAW, for instance, sometimes acted boldly, sometimes only haltingly, to protect the interests of its female members during the war.[69] UAW officials often expressed exasperation at the wage concerns of women workers, complaints officials believed were due to the women workers' presumed lack of prior union experience. As one union official stated, "They [women] only come when we tell them we will discuss *their* wages, or *their* up-grading."[70] In October 1943, UAW president R. J. Thomas, speaking to the New York Women's Trade Union League in New York City, criticized women for their "ingratitude" in refusing to support the unions.[71] At other times, union officials seemed downright hostile.

In addition, women were often informed that their work in defense plants might not survive the end of the war. Thomas, expressing no doubt on the issue, stated that barring significant change there would be no women in industry after the war. He acknowledged that management did not want women in industry after the war, but he also criticized women for not tackling or thinking through their own problems and for depending too much on men for solutions. Although he noted that the United Auto Workers had fought the issue of equal pay for equal work through the War Labor Board, of which he was a member, he noted that "not one woman has ever appeared before the War Labor Board to argue on that question. . . . It was done by men. And that is a women's problem." Women, he complained, did not seem to understand that the benefits they received were due to union efforts.[72] As will be discussed in Chapter 12, this "parental" complaint of lack of appreciation would again be sounded by union officials in relation to the militants of the late 1960s and early 1970s.

The union record in relation to black workers was also mixed, but there were cases in which unions acted with great determination and courage. Black workers first began to be employed in the automobile industry during the accelerated labor demand of World War I, and their entrance coincided with the northern migration of southern white workers. The number was small, however, and by 1930 only 4 percent of autoworkers were black. Ten years later it was still 4 percent. Employment increased during World War II but certainly not to extraordinarily high levels.[73] For instance, a UAW-CIO survey conducted in April 1943 of 389 individual establishments, mostly within the automobile industry, found that only 8 percent of workers were black. The forty-one General Motors plants had a workforce which was only 4.9 percent black. Ford's workforce, traditionally the highest in black employment, had 12.7 percent black workers and Chrysler's percentage was 10.3 percent.[74]

Significantly, black workers were both occupationally and geographically highly centralized. It is estimated that 70 percent of all black workers in the automobile industry in 1943 were employed in the Detroit metropolitan area.[75] Moreover, the bulk of black employment was limited to particular firms, predominantly the "big three," and even to particular plants. For instance, "fully 99 percent of all Ford negro employees were found in the Rouge plant in Dearborn in 1937."[76] Black employees at Chrysler and GM were similarly limited to certain plants. Moreover, black employees were primarily found at the bottom of the occupational ladder, in jobs which were not only unskilled but often hazardous.

According to the Detroit 1940 census, over 47 percent of all out-of-state newcomers came from the South. Nevertheless, the same census reported that less than 20 percent of the area's migrants said they resided on a farm; even among southerners, the proportion rose to no more than 25 percent.

Yet, as Alan Clive notes, no popular belief about the southern migrant, black or white, was so prevalent or incorrect as the notion that most had come directly from the farm.[77] Urbanites, it was commonly believed, possessed wider access to information and more of the skills necessary for industrial work.

The shift that did occur from small southern hamlets to crowded bustling Detroit or other northern cities was obviously traumatic. White and black songs lamented the pressures of big city life, although only white southerners sang nostalgically of the "old home place." A song, "Detroit City," although copyrighted in 1962, reflects a common sentiment of white southerners in the wartime north:

> Last night I went to sleep in Detroit City,
> I dreamed about those cotton fields back home.
> I dreamed about my mother, dear old papa, sister and brother,
> I dreamed about the girl who's been waiting for so long.
>
> CHORUS
> I want to go home,
> I want to go home
> Lord, how I want to go home.[78]

Natives often described the difficulties experienced by southern blacks and whites from Appalachia as caused by the inherent laziness of the migrants. Nevertheless, many of the same residents concurrently complained about the ability of southerners to work rapidly and efficiently for hours. Stamina, combined with the desire to make the maximum in wages, apparently either inspired or embittered fellow workers.

The most serious accusation against white southerners was that they played a key role in exacerbating racial tension. Generally, racial problems arose when black workers were moved out of racially segregated departments, like the foundry, to use one example, and into white areas. Yet, negative responses to the presence of black workers by white workers also occurred before the war began.[79] Concededly, serious racial tension occurred during the war, leading to a number of strikes, as well as to the horrifying Detroit race riot in June 1943.[80] As an official of the Detroit Urban League said, however, "these conflicts existed long before the latest influx of southern labor arrived."[81]

Katherine Archibald's study of the Oakland shipyards indicates that blacks and southwesterners (deemed "Oakies") received significant criticism from the existing workforce. Besides questions regarding their intelligence, there was fear that Oakies would "abuse their union privileges to the detriment of the organizations."[82] They were, apparently, deemed "pre-industrial" workers who did not comprehend the obligations of a unionized workforce.

The deepest antagonism, however, was toward African Americans. Archibald describes a world where racial antagonism was sharp, constant, and impervious to reason. Blacks were seen, like women, as rivals for white, male jobs, a fear which merged with non-job-related concerns dealing with sex-rivalry and contention for social status and prestige. Indeed, one of Archibald's primary conclusions was that economic rivalry in the shipyards could not be separated from competition for social privilege. Although the CIO Machinists' Union and the AFL's Laborers' Union at Moore welcomed black workers as members, other unions offered various degrees of resistance. The concern of prewar union members was heightened by the sheer number of newcomers. For instance, the prewar Bay Area local of the Plumbers and Steamfitters numbered three to four hundred members, but that number rose astoundingly to seventeen thousand in 1943.[83]

Most new workers, Archibald states, were unacquainted with unions, and, indeed, "distrustful of them." Moreover, new workers saw no connection between their good wages and benefits and union dues. Many expressed to Archibald, then a union steward, the belief that union officers were greedy and corrupt and not really interested in the membership. Unions, therefore, were seen as part of the "exploitive world" around the workers, not part of the solution. If a clear dispute arose between workers and management, however, "with amazing rapidity a sprawling, disunited cluster became almost an integrated group."[84] Archibald's workers highlight the complex relationship between worker distrust of unions and the concurrent willingness to engage in collective action.

Archibald's workers were patriotic, although they talked little of the war, assuming the inevitability of the U.S. victory. Few enlisted, and most "confessed . . . that they had never worked less proficiently." Indeed, and quite distinct from the midwestern defense plants, "an atmosphere of lassitude floated like a heavy vapor over the yards, and everywhere was evidence of an incredible waste of time." A good deal of this was due, Archibald believed, to poor managerial planning and direction, leading to cynicism that neither speed nor quality was central to management.[85]

Black workers encountered all of the frustrations of industrial work, compounded by racism. The resultant pressures on black workers are nowhere better described than in Chester Himes's novels describing work in Los Angeles's war plants.[86] Like Himes's barely functional heroes, black workers sometimes found white support but usually encountered indifference or outright hostility. "And how you could take two guys from the same place—one would carry his whitener like loaded stick, ready to loof everyone else in the head with it; and the other would just simply be white as if he didn't have anything to do with it and let it go at that."[87]

Indeed, racial militancy by black steelworkers led to numerous and rarely commented upon work stoppages and wildcat strikes.[88] Many of these strikes were reactions to racial discrimination and to black perceptions of indifference on the part of the union.[89] In the auto industry, the location of most wartime strikes, black workers engaged in a number of walkouts protesting racial segregation or discrimination in employment, sometimes seeking to increase opportunities for black women.[90] Company practices of promoting only white workers led to wildcats by black workers at many sites, including Dodge, Chrysler, and Packard in Detroit.[91] These strikes, like strikes by women protesting unequal treatment, can obviously be said to be caused by the "new" industrial workers, but their focus was on discriminatory practices that, because of greater numbers, could now be challenged.

These strikes must be contrasted to the more widely known racial disputes involving protests by white workers against the presence of black workers in previously all-white departments.[92] Lichtenstein argues that there may have been as many strikes led by black workers in Detroit as there were racially inspired hate strikes.[93] Nevertheless, more attention has been given to "hate strikes" by white workers than to resistance to discrimination by black workers. Clive states that with a few exceptions, hate strikes "characteristically involved a negligible number of man hours lost. Hate strikes were depressing to war time morale, but since many workers felt little compunction about shutting down a plant over the discharge of a steward, it was not surprising that they were prepared to strike over the more visceral issues of race."[94]

Interracial conflict and its complexities were highlighted by a series of disputes at the Packard Airplane Motor plant. Racial hostility flared in late May 1943, when three black workers were upgraded to the final motor assembly line. The strike ended when the black workers were withdrawn pending a conference on the issue. This action, however, was immediately followed by a strike of approximately fifteen hundred of the twenty-five hundred black workers. They returned to work due to the urging of union, company, and army officials. Following a meeting on May 30, the three black workers were reinstated on the final assembly line. Three days later, however, the white labor force, a large portion of which consisted of southern whites and workers of Polish descent, struck in response, and at least 90 percent of the white workers cooperated. Some strikers denounced their union officers for failing to represent the will of the majority. Although shop stewards had voted to urge the strikers to return to work, observers on the scene noted that some stewards counseled members to stay away from the job until the strikers' demands were met. The strikers eventually returned to work when their efforts failed, due in large part to a united front of union, government, and company officials.[95]

Despite the often forthright action of UAW officials, Kevin Boyle argues that the UAW's commitment to local autonomy restricted the international's ability to mount challenges to the racism of certain locals. Given the centralization of power in the UAW, the constraints may have owed more to internal electoral politics than to concern for local autonomy. A small number of locals, for instance, barred blacks from the bargaining unit, maintained separate seniority lists, or restricted job mobility within the plant. Although the more blatant forms of racism were abandoned during the war, over one-third of all black wartime workers in UAW plants were laid off by the end of 1945. Moreover, "many UAW locals returned to their pre-war discriminatory practices as soon as the war emergency ended."[96] Nevertheless, the growing and wartime-induced centralization of power in the UAW, used to constrain rank-and-file activism, was also used to confront local violations of the union's racial policies.

To their credit, officers of the United Auto Workers, including Walter Reuther and R. J. Thomas, repeatedly spoke out forcefully against racial discrimination. Their statements and actions were based upon principles of racial equality but, no doubt, also on sound institutional concerns.[97] UAW leaders felt that the acceptance of discrimination would divide and weaken the ranks of labor and, based upon prior experience with Ford, the exclusion of blacks would create a dangerous strike-breaking force. Thus, speaking to delegates of the National UAW-Ford Council in June 1942, Thomas referred to a strike of white workers at a Packard facility in Detroit protesting against the upgrading of black workers. Thomas's strong views against racial discrimination should be contrasted with his criticism of women workers noted earlier.

> Negroes pay a dollar a month dues the same as any other member. Negroes have fought for this organization the same as others. Negroes will fight for it in the future. And still some people ask why Negroes should be upgraded.
>
> At a Packard local meeting there were large groups of women workers protesting the upgrading of negroes. These women forgot that a few months ago women were discriminated against in our industry. We still have to fight in some plants for equal pay for women. If any group should support our fight against discrimination more than any body else, it is our women workers. . . .

I have given an ultimatum to the Packard workers that they must go back to work. I am going to make that ultimatum stronger and if it means that large numbers of white workers are going to be fired, then that's exactly what's going to happen.

The international union is not going to retreat from that position.[98]

At the CIO convention in 1942 Walter Reuther, then a vice president of the UAW, also emphasized the need for racial equality. "It is the duty of every delegate here to go back to his respective organization and see that it takes up the fight against racial discrimination, not as a secondary consideration, not as something you think about after you get your closed shop and your wage increases and your seniority agreements; but this fight against racial discrimination must be put on the top of the list with union security and other major union demands."[99]

Union and governmental support of black workers led to concrete gains. Robert Weaver stated in 1946 that "the significant development was not the hundred or so conflicts, but the fact that century-old patterns had been modified in five years without more opposition and more frequent clashes."[100] For instance, black workers, Weaver noted, obtained skilled and semiskilled industrial jobs. At the same time, Weaver ruefully noted that in 1946 "over 98 percent of the clerical and sales force in the country remained white," and a similar percentage of the professional and managerial jobs were held by whites.[101]

Moreover, discrimination by employers and unions obviously did not end. Some unions like the International Association of Machinists barred blacks from membership, and employers in some industries, for instance aircraft, failed to employ blacks even prior to the onset of union bargaining.[102] Employer reluctance often combined with local union sentiments, and local resistance, like the hate strikes, suggests the need to carefully evaluate critiques of union bureaucratization and the value of local autonomy. Thus, despite federal arrangements to issue work permits to black workers at Boeing, even after the international officers of the Machinists were ready to cooperate, local union officials opposed any such action.[103] As late as the spring of 1942, "the officials of the Boeing machinists local was still objecting to negro employment on the ground that the use of negroes represented a change in the agreement between the union and company and would avoid effective enforcement."[104] The heritage of local autonomy, and the need for local political support, hampered the effective imposition of national policies of racial equality.

Moreover, many African American workers, in both the South and

North, sadly discovered that union representation did not automatically end racial discrimination. Workers like George Holloway and Clarence Coe, at extraordinary personal risk, battled southern white UAW members as well as employer racism at Harvester's and Firestone's Memphis plants. The UAW's assistance in the South was spotty, clearly less energetic than in the North. A few unions, however, like the left-wing Food, Tobacco, Agricultural, and Allied Workers' Union (FTA) Local 19 demonstrated that even in the South unions could break down segregated job designations and seniority systems.[105] The CIO's policy stressing equal employment was put to severe tests in the South, where unions were concerned with maintaining the loyalty of white workers. This problem became especially severe in industries where the CIO competed with AFL unions.

Bruce Nelson has recently analyzed the problems involving shipbuilding employees in Mobile, Alabama, during World War II.[106] Nelson reveals that "the vast majority of white shipyard workers were unwilling to make concessions to their black co-workers' demands for greater equality, but whites were not a monolith. Veteran shipyard craftsmen accepted black laborers and helpers as necessary—but subordinate—participants in the workplace regime, while newcomers from rural areas of the deep south were more likely to see the very presence of black workers as a threat to their social status and economic leverage."[107] For instance, on May 24, 1943, the Alabama Dry Dock and Shipbuilding Company upgraded twelve blacks to welding jobs, leading enraged white workers to violently assault black co-workers, a riot which ended only when the United States army troops from nearby Brookley Field arrived.[108]

The results are mixed, however, and Nelson stresses the CIO's "contradictory character—as both an institutional reflection of the larger patterns of racial domination and subordination in American society *and* egalitarian social movement that challenged the boundaries of those patterns." Although CIO unions in the South formally "adhered to the CIO's commitment to racial equality," they "would not allow these issues to jeopardize the institutional survival of their organizations, which depended on the allegiance of white workers and generally reflected their consciousness." While CIO representatives often spoke of a more egalitarian structure which included equal rights for black and white workers, their actual practice often "privileged the interest of the white majority."[109]

Although the AFL has earned a justifiable reputation for racial exclusion and segregation, it secured some positive advances in the South. On the docks of Gulf Coast ports, blacks, after many years of conflict and accommodation with whites, either dominated longshoring or had achieved an equitable share of the work. Black longshoreman controlled their separate organizations and often resisted the calls to merge black and white ILA locals.[110] In many locals, however, auxiliary locals were decidedly second class, especially in terms of the possibility of becoming an apprentice or being promoted to a higher classification.

Unions, especially in the South, faced real institutional problems. The Industrial Union of Marine and Shipbuilding Workers of America (IUMSWA), for instance, was concerned that, given the willingness of blacks to join, subsequent attempts to force the upgrading of blacks would push most of the white workers into the AFL. In addition, they were even more concerned about the potential for violent conflict. The concern became a reality in May 1943, when whites directed their anger at black workers in general. Nelson concludes that the primary blame must be directed to the recent immigrants from the rural areas of the Deep South. From the various reports on the riot, Nelson noted the emphasis on the youth of the participants and, even more surprising, on the significant role of women.[111]

Although the hostility of white males to expanded job opportunities for black men focused primarily on the issue of promotion, some strikes did occur even in response to the hiring of blacks.[112] Karen Anderson believes that the primary motivation for the reaction of white males was the maintenance of their economic position whereas the opposition of some white female workers to black female workers, which also led to some recorded strikes, was primarily to "maintain social distance, rather than a wish to safeguard economic prerogatives."[113] Employers engaged in racial discrimination as well, of course, and even when they broke with tradition and hired nonwhite workers, they were generally segregated and given more disagreeable work.[114]

Anderson notes that even in a time of a high level of labor shortage, the economic system

> could tolerate a high level of unemployment and underemployment . . . in order to minimize the amount of change generated by temporary and abhorrent conditions. By stressing the modification of traditional patterns fostered by rapid economic growth, scholars ignored the degree to which prejudices inhibited change and constrained the rate of economic expansion even in the face of strong patriotic, political, and economic incentives favoring expanded output at all costs. For black women, especially, what is significant about the war experience is the extent to which barriers remained intact.[115]

Yet, bright spots also existed. As Roger Horowitz has noted, "patterns of inter-racial unionism inherited from the organizing era shaped the UPWA's policies toward World War II–era black workers."[116] Black employment grew markedly, as "packinghouses were the only war-related factories to employ blacks at levels equal to or greater than their proportion in the area's labor market."[117] Black workers were fully accepted at Armour's Kansas City plant into skilled and semiskilled positions while blacks in area UAW- and IAM-organized factories were restricted to custodial or other menial positions.

Like the issue of equal pay for equal work, the government opposed both race and sex discrimination. In a rare action, the United States Employment Service discontinued referrals to some Detroit trucking firms involved in interstate transportation of war material because they refused to hire black workers. However, in an all-too-common parallel to other wartime advances, "the vital nature of their work soon necessitated restoration of services."[118] More significant was the creation of the Fair Employment Practices Committee (FEPC), an agency created in 1941 by Executive Order 8802 in response to Philip Randolph's threatened march on Washington protesting discriminatory policies by war contractors.[119] All United States contracting agencies were to include in every defense contract a provision "obligating the contractor not to discriminate against any worker." The order also stated that "there shall be no discrimination in the employment of workers in defense industries or government because of race, creed, color or national origin and . . . it is the duty of employers and of labor organizations . . . to provide for the full and equitable participation of all workers in defense industries without discrimination because of race, color, creed, or national origin."[120]

Like most committees during the war, however, the FEPC lacked sufficient staff and enforcement capabilities and was, moreover, constantly harassed, especially by southern congressmen. Through the creative use of public hearings, however, the FEPC publicized the state or racial discrimination in employment.[121] In May 1943, the president set up a new committee with greater authority and an increased budget. Whereas the first FEPC declared that "full participation of all workers, without discrimination" was required in defense industries, Executive Order 9346 stated that unions had the duty to eliminate discrimination in membership based on race, creed, color, or national origin.[122]

Joel Seidman and others credit the FEPC with making "substantial progress toward reducing discrimination," but he also notes that some employers and unions simply defied the committee.[123] As Anderson has noted, "although effective in some cases, such tools proved ineffectual against recalcitrant violators, whose ranks included some major war industries. The large volume of complaints and the bureaucratic delays inherent in the situation facilitated evasion, even on the part of blatant violators officially ordered to cease restrictive hiring practices. Moreover, the reliance on individual, documented complaints, rather than on employer hiring patterns as the basis for action hampered effective enforcement."[124] Moreover, the committee's jurisdiction never extended beyond defense production. The government's antidiscrimination effort, therefore, was limited in scope as well as in time.

The FEPC, like the federal support for equal pay for equal work, would not survive the war.[125] Congress ended the committee in 1946, and no federal legislation involving employment would be enacted until the Civil Rights Act of 1964,[126] even though both political parties pledged their support for a permanent fair employment practices commission in 1944.[127] Thus, some of the more progressive policies and ideas of the wartime era would not survive the war except, perhaps, as an ideal that would much later be enshrined in federal and state legislation.

Notes

1. See Joshua Freeman, "Delivering the Goods: Industrial Unionism during World War II," *Labor History* 19 (Fall 1978), 587. Freeman relates the presence of these workers to the high incidence of militant and often violent wartime strikes, strikes which he argues were uncoordinated, primitive, and based upon no social vision (ibid., 585–88).

2. Howard Kimmeldorf, *Reds or Rackets* (Berkeley: University of California Press, 1988), 140.

3. Nelson Lichtenstein, "Conflict over Workers' Control: The Automobile Industry in World War II," in *Working-Class America: Essays on Labor, Community and American Society*, ed. Michael Frisch and Daniel Walkowitz (Urbana: University of Illinois Press, 1983), 291.

4. Freeman, "Delivering the Goods," 588.

5. Peter Friedlander, *Emergence of a UAW Local* (Pittsburgh: University of Pittsburgh Press, 1975), 93–97.

6. International Brotherhood of Boilermakers, Iron Shipbuilders and Helpers of America, *Arsenal of Democracy* (Berkeley, Calif.: Tam, Gibbs Co., n.d.), 33, 83, cited in Marilyn S. Johnson, "Wartime Shipyards: The Transformation of Labor in San Francisco's East Bay," in *American Labor in the Era of World War II*, ed. Sally M. Miller and Daniel A. Cornford (Westport, Conn.: Praeger, 1995), 97. The difficulty of distinguishing job consciousness and racism in the ILWU is explored by Nancy L. Quam-Wickham in "Who Controls the Hiring Hall? The Struggle for Job Control in the ILWU during World War II," in *American Labor in the Era of World War II*, ed. Sally M. Miller and Daniel A. Cornford (Westport, Conn.: Praeger, 1995), 134–39.

7. Lichtenstein, *Labor's War at Home*; Ruth Milkman, *Gender at Work: The Dynamics of Job Segregation by Sex during World War II* (Urbana: University of Illinois Press, 1987); Marilyn S. Johnson, "Wartime Shipyards."

8. Johnson, "Wartime Shipyards," 90–93.

9. Ibid., 92. Government regulation during the war is given substantial credit for bureaucratizing employment policies and practices. For instance, job analysis and evaluation grew because stabilization plans required employers to classify jobs by skill and wage categories. In short, government mandates provided incentives to management to expand personnel departments and bureaucratic controls (James Baron, Frank Dobbins, and P. Devereaux Jennings, "War and Peace: The Evolution of Modern Personnel Administration in U.S. Industry," *American Journal of Sociology* 92 [1986]: 350).

10. Kimmeldorf, *Reds or Rackets*, 139–40.

11. Stephen Meyers, *The Five Dollar Day* (Albany: State University of New York Press, 1981), 68.

12. See Alan Dawley and Paul Faler, "Workingclass Culture and Politics in the American Revolution: Sources of Loyalism and Rebellion," in *American Workingclass Culture: Explorations in American Labor and Social History*, ed. Milton Cantor (Westport, Conn.: Greenwood Press, 1979), 61–75.

13. Alan Clive, *State of War: Michigan in World War II* (Ann Arbor: University of Michigan Press, 1979), 74–75. On the other hand, Everett Harris, a union steward in Lowell, found that organization was easy because many workers had previously worked in organized plants. "There were people asking for organization. . . . It was an easy time to organize." Quoted in Marc Scott Miller, *The Irony of Victory: World War II and Lowell, Massachusetts* (Urbana: University of Illinois Press, 1988), 36.

14. Robert H. Zieger, *The CIO, 1935–1955* (Chapel Hill: University of North Carolina Press, 1995), 162–63.

15. Clive, *State of War*, 74.

16. Miller, *Irony of Victory*, 28–29.

17. Freeman, "Delivering the Goods," 589–90.

18. David Montgomery, *The Fall of the House of Labor* (New York: Cambridge University Press, 1987), 332.

19. Martin Glaberman, *Wartime Strikes: The Struggle against the No-Strike Pledge in the UAW during World War II* (Detroit: Bewick Editions, 1980), 17–24.

20. Ibid., 27.

21. Ibid., 32.

22. Ibid., 34.

23. Ibid., 51–60. In discussing a strike at the new steel and aluminum foundries built for war production at Ford's Rouge plant, Frank Winn stressed that black employees were new to factory routine and new to union privileges and responsibilities. Yet, without apparent awareness of the contradiction, he noted that "the immediate cause of the strike was failure of the company to settle routine grievances promptly, just as that is the cause of most unauthorized strikes in any other unit

or plant, regardless of the race of the employees." Nevertheless, the company issued a statement to newspapers that the strike instigators were "negro youths of draft age" whom it characterized as the "jitterbug element" (Frank Winn, "Labor Tackles the Race Question," *Antioch Review* 13 [1943]).

24. Nelson Lichtenstein, "Life at the Rouge: A Cycle of Workers' Control," in *Life and Labor: Dimensions of Working-Class History*, ed. Charles Stephenson and Robert Asher (Albany: State University of New York Press, 1986).

25. Steve Jeffreys, *Management and Managed: Fifty Years of Crisis at Chrysler* (New York: Cambridge University Press, 1986), 26–27.

26. A strike by about one hundred women workers, apparently in violation of a no-strike clause, occurred at the Bendix Aviation Corporation in April 1943. The strike began when women employees protested the transfer to the day shift of a male foreman they described as a "slave driver," one who "spied" on them and practiced favoritism. The walkout apparently involved 98 percent of the workers in the department.

27. See Ronald Schatz, "Union Pioneers: The Founders of Local Unions at General Electric and Westinghouse, 1933–37," *Journal of American History* 66 (Dec. 1979): 559–602.

28. Ruth Meyerowitz, Organizing the UAW: Women at the Ternstedt General Motors Parts Plant, 1935–1950 (forthcoming). Ruth Meyerowitz, for instance, has noted that women organizers often came from union families or from the ranks of left-wing groups, and they provided the leadership to organize other women.

29. Milkman, *Gender at Work*, 95.

30. Ibid., 95–96.

31. Nancy Gabin, *Feminism in the Labor Movement* (Ithaca, N.Y.: Cornell University Press, 1990), 8–46; Meyerowitz, *Organizing the UAW*. Women workers often engaged in wildcat strikes, accounting for 19 percent of the strikers in 1944 alone (Milkman, *Gender at Work*, 87; George Lipsitz, *Rainbow at Midnight: Labor and Culture in the 1940s* [Urbana: University of Illinois Press, 1994], 51).

32. Rural southern whites, however, without former contact with mining, "usually became passive members" (Meyerowitz, *Organizing the UAW*, 12–13).

33. Meyerowitz notes that many women at General Motors' Ternstedt plant in Detroit were second-generation Poles, a group she believes were more likely to support the UAW than other ethnic groups (*Organizing the UAW*, 329). See also Ruth Meyerowitz, "Organizing the United Automobile Workers: Women Workers at the Ternstedt General Motors Parts Plant," in *Women, Work, and Protest: A Century of U.S. Women's Labor History*, ed. Ruth Milkman (Boston: Routledge & Kegan Paul, 1985), 239. See also J. D. Hall, J. Leloudis, R. Korstad, M. Murphy, L. A. Jones, and C. B. Daly, *Like a Family: The Making of a Southern Cotton Mill World* (Chapel Hill: University of North Carolina Press, 1987). See also John G. Kruchko, *The Birth of a Union Local: The History of UAW Local 674, Norwood, Ohio, 1933–1940* (Ithaca: New York State School of Industrial and Labor Relations, 1972), 14; Friedlander, *Emergence of a UAW Local*, 7–8.

34. Milkman, *Gender at Work*, 85; Leo Troy, *Trade Union Membership, 1897–1962*, Occ. Paper 92 (New York: National Bureau of Economic Research, 1965), 1–2.

35. Ibid. In eight of the ten areas studied by the Women's Bureau of the U.S. Department of Labor, the employment of women doubled from 1940 to the time of the survey in 1944 and 1945. See U.S. Department of Labor, "Women Workers in Ten Production Areas and Their Post-War Employment Plans," Women's Bureau pub. no. 209 (Washington, D.C.: Government Printing Office, 1946).

36. Investigators for the UAW found that women comprised more than a quarter of the workforce at Briggs, Bendix's Wayne Division in Willow Run (Clive, *State of War*, 186).

37. For a history of women workers in the automobile and electrical industries during World War II, see Milkman, *Gender at Work*. Milkman argues that job segregation was not eliminated by the war; instead, the lines between male and female jobs merely shifted during the period.

38. Anna Long, "Women Workers after the War," *Political Affairs* (Mar. 1945), 258, cited in Lipsitz, *Rainbow at Midnight*, 66 n. 9.

39. Clive, *State of War*, 186.

40. Women's Work Project, *Separated and Unequal: Discrimination against Women Workers after World War II (The UAW 1944–1954)* (Silver Springs, Md., 1976), 2, 9, 11. Clive argues that some women took jobs "out of patriotism or as a way of escape from the tedium of separation from husband or fiance. They sought to enlarge their economic opportunities, but in many instances, women worked simply to maintain a standard of living equivalent to or even lower than that to which they had become accustomed before the war." The majority of women, he finds, "worked to live" (*State of War*, 51). See also Miller, *Irony of Victory*, 49–79.

41. The Labor Department's Women's Bureau survey disclosed that 51 percent of the 387,000 women that worked in Detroit during late 1944 and early 1945 had been employed before Pearl Harbor. Indeed, almost half of the women employed during the war had had five years of experience at the time of the survey and almost 30 percent had ten years experience. The experience of women workers was not unique to Michigan. At the Houston Ordinance Plant in 1945, for instance, one-quarter of the workforce was composed of female workers, and over half of the women were married. Thirty-eight percent of the women were family heads, and 40 percent had worked prior to the war ("Wartime Labor Force of Houston Ordinance Plant," *Monthly Labor Review* 62 [Mar. 1946]: 458). See also "Wartime Labor Force of St. Paul Propeller Plant," *Monthly Labor Review* 62 (Jan. 1946): 93.

42. Women's Work Project, *Separated and Unequal*, 4. See also Clive, *State of War*, 68; Lipsitz, *Rainbow at Midnight*, 49–50.

43. It is not difficult to understand women's attachment to industrial work. For example, "68 percent of the women employed at the Ford Willow Run Bomber plant earned at least three times as much in their war jobs than in their prewar jobs, while this was true for less than 15 percent of the men" (Milkman, *Gender at Work*, 357).

44. Kevin Boyle, "There Are No Union Sorrows That the Union Can't Heal:

The Struggle for Racial Equality in the United Automobile Workers, 1940–1960," *Labor History* 36 (Winter 1995): 5.

45. Ruth Milkman, "Redefining 'Women's Work': The Sexual Division of Labor in the Auto Industry during World War II," *Feminist Studies* 8 (Summer 1982): 341–42, 337–72.

46. Clive, *State of War*, 188.

47. Ibid., 348.

48. Ruth Milkman, "Rosie the Riveter Revisited: Management's Postwar Purge of Women Automobile Workers," in *On the Line: Essays in the History of Auto Work*, ed. Nelson Lichtenstein and Stephen Meyer (Urbana: University of Illinois Press, 1989), 135.

49. Ibid., 145. On the response of workers to blacks and the UAW's commitment to equal employment, see August Meier and Elliott Rudwick, *Black Detroit and the Rise of the UAW* (New York: Oxford University Press, 1979); and Robert C. Weaver, *Negro Labor: A National Problem* (New York: Harcourt, Brace and World, 1946). See also Karen Anderson, "Last Hired, First Fired: Black Women Workers during World War II," *Journal of American History* 69 (June 1982): 86–87.

50. Women in general, according to Milkman, tended not to object to such sex stereotyping because, first, such efforts might protect them from overly strenuous jobs and, second, they did not want to risk employment at relatively high rates of pay (*Gender at Work*, 70–72).

51. Katherine Archibald, *Wartime Shipyard* (Berkeley: University of California Press, 1947), 17.

52. Gabin, *Feminism in the Labor Movement*, 50–51. As Nelson Lichtenstein has noted, the introduction of many women workers was initially seen by Walter Reuther and others in the UAW as a "low-wage threat to the wage standards enjoyed by higher-paid men." The 1941 union convention adopted a resolution opposing any attempt to place women on skilled jobs "until such time as the unemployed men have been put back to work" (*Walter Reuther: The Most Dangerous Man in Detroit* [Urbana: University of Illinois Press, 1997]; originally published as *The Most Dangerous Man in Detroit: Walter Reuther and the Fate of American Labor* [New York: Basic Books, 1995], 200).

53. Gabin, *Feminism in the Labor Movement*, 53. An undeveloped area of research is arbitration decisions involving women workers. Laura Cooper has studied wartime cases decided by Harry Shulman under the Ford-UAW collective agreement. As Cooper discovered, women workers were involved not only with normal arbitral issues but also with questions of sexual harassment, discrimination, and equal pay. Thus, a number of cases dealt with the UAW's presentation of issues focusing on women's status. Significantly, Shulman held on various occasions that classifying workers based on gender was improper, sometimes based on implicit contractual obligations of good faith. Cooper argues, however, that Shulman's recognition of women workers' interests cooled after the war ended (Laura Cooper, "Harry Shulman: Deciding Women's Grievances in Wartime," in *Arbitration 1964: Controversy and Continuity*, ed. Gladys Gruenberg [Proceedings of the 47th Annual Meeting of

the National Academy of Arbitrators] [Washington, D.C.: Bureau of National Affairs, 1994], 153–68).

54. Jim Rose, "The Problem Every Supervisor Dreads: Women Workers at the U.S. Steel Duquesne Works during World War II," *Labor History* 36 (Winter 1995): 24. Some companies easily agreed to such a policy because they assumed that women workers were temporary and because the costs could be passed on to the government. See General Motors, 3 WLB 355 (1942); National War Labor Board, *The Termination Report of the National War Labor Board. Industrial Disputes and Wage Stabilization in Wartime. January 12, 1942–December 31, 1945*, 3 vols. (Washington, D.C.: Government Printing Office, 1947–48), 1:290–97. By the fall of 1942, the proportion of women in the auto workforce doubled from the previous year, and the percentage doubled again in the succeeding year. To counteract fear that women workers would dilute the wage standards of an overwhelmingly male workforce, the UAW demanded "equal pay for equal work," the principle eventually supported by the War Labor Board in General Motors decision in September 1942 (Lichtenstein, *Walter Reuther*, 200).

55. Roger Horowitz, *"Negro and White, Unite and Fight!" A Social History of Industrial Unionism in Meatpacking, 1930–90* (Urbana: University of Illinois Press, 1997), 163–66.

56. Ronald L. Fillipelli and Mark D. McCulloch, *Cold War in the Working Class* (Albany: State University of New York Press, 1995), 80–81.

57. Another modern issue which was widely discussed during the war was day care. The federal government "eventually spent nearly $53 million for hundreds of day care centers, established primarily in major production areas" (Clive, *State of War*, 60). Clive notes, however, that "most women rejected day care center services because they preferred to have their children cared for by relatives, neighbors or friends—or not at all—rather than by strangers in a nursery or canteen" (ibid., 65).

In April 1944, Mary Anderson, head of the U.S. Women's Bureau, urged unions to include in their national agreements clauses which barred discrimination based upon sex or marital status and stipulated that wage rates should be set by the job rather than by sex of the worker. In addition, Anderson proposed clauses which would prohibit pregnancy from being a ground for a dismissal. She proposed maternity leave of not less than six weeks before delivery and two months after (*New York Times*, Apr. 8, 1944, 18). These issues would not resurface until long after the war.

58. A similar Massachusetts statute also seems to have had little effect (Miller, *Irony of Victory*, 55–58).

59. General Motors, 3 WLR 355 (1942).

60. The War Labor Board's order no. 16 dealt with "Adjustments which equalized the wage or salary rates paid to females with the rates paid to males for a comparable quality and quantity of work on the same or similar operations" (National War Labor Board, *Termination Report*, 1:290).

61. General Motors, 3 WLR 355 (1942) (the board asserted that its policy was not new but paralleled that created by the National War Labor Baord in World War I); Gabin, *Feminism in the Labor Movement*, 63–65.

62. National War Labor Board, *Termination Report*, 1:293–96.

63. Milkman, *Gender at Work*, 77.

64. National War Labor Board, *Termination Report*, 1:295.

65. Fillipelli and McCulloch, *Cold War*, 80–81.

66. Clive, *State of War*, 189.

67. Nevertheless, women's average weekly wages tended to rise during the war faster than male wages. By August 1944, women in Michigan's engine turbine industry earned 94.3 percent as much as men, and females in the automobile industry had closed to within 89 percent of the male wage average (ibid., 189–90). Despite the increase in female employment and some reduction in the gender wage differential, there was considerable debate about whether the status of women had indeed improved. For a discussion of the various views and the situation of women workers in Michigan, see Alan Clive, "Women Workers in World War II: Michigan as a Test Case," *Labor History* 20 (1979): 44.

68. Alice Kessler-Harris, "The Labor Movement's Failure to Organize Women Workers," in *Major Problems in the History of American Workers*, ed. Eileen Boris and Nelson Lichtenstein (Lexington, Mass.: D. C. Heath, 1991), 258.

69. The union had established a women's bureau within its policy division in 1944 to offer counseling and other forms of aid. The UAW's first women's conference, in December 1944, voted against special seniority rights for women, but attempted to encourage the UAW executive board to act more vigorously on equal pay (Clive, *State of War*, 55). See also Gabin, *Feminism in the Labor Movement*, 91–94.

70. Theresa Wolfson, "Aprons and Overalls in War," *Annals* 229 (Sept. 1943): 46, 54.

71. *New York Times*, Oct. 23, 1943. Theresa Wolfson, a member of the War Labor Board Public Panel, Region 2, while expressing sympathy for the multiple burdens faced by many women workers, seemed to support the criticism of union leaders: "the job of educating the new woman worker to the responsibilities and advantages of unionism must be carried on with greater intensity and imagination by union officials. It is not easy for women workers who wear both aprons and overalls to find time for union meetings, to study the history of unionism, and to be able to see that all unions are not 'Peglerian rackets'!" (ibid., 54). The reference is to Westbrook Pegler, a notorious conservative and anti-union columnist.

72. *New York Times*, Oct. 24, 1943, 19.

73. Local groups demonstrated early in the war when blacks perceived that whites would be hired first. Drake and Cayton note that picket signs began to appear at factories near the "Black Belt" in Chicago with signs that read: "HITLER MUST OWN THIS PLANT: NEGROES CAN'T WORK HERE. IF WE MUST FIGHT, WHY CAN'T WE WORK? BULLETS KNOW NO COLOR LINE; WHY SHOULD FACTORIES?" (St. Clair Drake and Horace R. Cayton, *Black Metropolis: A Study of Negro Life in a Northern City*, rev. ed. [New York: Harper & Row, 1962], 90).

74. Lloyd H. Bailer, "The Negro Automobile Worker," *Journal of Political Economy* 5 (1943): 415–28. See, generally, Zieger, *CIO, 1935–1955*, 152–61.

75. Bailer, "Negro Automobile Worker," 416. Detroit city officials estimated in 1946 that some sixty thousand blacks had moved to the area since 1940. The level of black migration remained constant after 1943 while white migration actually declined. The black workforce in the Detroit area almost doubled during the course of the war, increasing during this period at a rate about three times faster than the entire labor force (Clive, *State of War*, 133). Black migration to other northern industrial cities was also substantial. Between Pearl Harbor and D-day, for instance, about sixty thousand blacks moved to Chicago (Drake and Cayton, *Black Metropolis*, 9). By 1944 Chicago "faced a labor shortage, and a new wave of migration from the South began" (ibid., 90).

76. Bailer, "Negro Automobile Worker," 417.

77. Southern migration was affected by renewed agricultural prosperity during the war, and the government granted draft deferments to farm workers.

78. "Detroit City," copyright 1962, Cedarwood Publishing Co., Inc.

79. Clive, "Women Workers in World War II," 44.

80. Bailer, "Negro Automobile Worker," 415–28. Robert Weaver discusses various hate strikes in "Negro Employment in the Aircraft Industry," *Quarterly Journal of Economics* 59 (1944–45): 597.

81. Clive, *State of War*, 180. Drake and Cayton write that few disturbances occurred in Chicago over the promotion of black workers into formerly white departments, because the rate of upgrading was slow and most blacks were hired into new industries and new plants without a tradition of discrimination. Moreover, they argue that Chicago had no substantial migration of white southerners with strong racial views (Drake and Cayton, *Black Metropolis*, 92–93).

82. Archibald, *Wartime Shipyard*, 47.

83. Ibid., 81, 116–17, 130.

84. Ibid., 131–35, 142.

85. Ibid., 193–95.

86. Chester Himes, *Lonely Crusade* (New York: Thunder's Mouth, 1986); Chester Himes, *If He Hollers Let Him Go* (New York: Thunder's Mouth, 1986). See Lipsitz, *Rainbow at Midnight*, 35–39.

87. Himes, *If He Hollers Let Him Go*, 41, quoted in Lipsitz *Rainbow at Midnight*, 36.

88. Outside of Detroit, the shortage of labor in western Pennsylvania steel mills encouraged the influx of over ten thousand black southerners, 14 percent of the total workforce. They moved into overcrowded, poor quality housing, and, in addition, they faced discrimination both in and out of the mills. Dennis Dickerson has referred to a "general mood of defiance" which characterized black workers during the war ("Fighting on the Domestic Front: Black Steelworkers during World War II" in *Life and Labor: Dimensions of American Working Class History*, ed. C. Stephenson and R. Asher [Albany: State University of New York Press, 1986], 224).

89. Ibid. A fictional account of racial hostility at a World War II shipyard is given in Himes, *If He Hollers Let Him Go*. See also Himes, *Lonely Crusade*, for a vivid portrayal of a union organizational campaign and the role of the Communist Party.

90. Lipsitz, *Rainbow at Midnight*, 50.

91. Ibid., 74–75.

92. See Christopher H. Johnson, *Maurice Sugar: Law, Labor and the Left in Detroit, 1912–1950* (Detroit: Wayne State University Press, 1988), 274–78; Meier and Rudwick, *Black Detroit and the Rise of the UAW*, 175–206; Freeman, "Delivering the Goods," 585. As Nelson Lichtenstein has noted, there was a dark side to the wildcat strikes during the war. Not only did violence occur but "such shop-floor syndicalism easily coincided with the determination by some workers to retain elements of an older work regime, which had been structured by race, skill and gender. Certainly this was the level of consciousness of many in Detroit's white male workforce who feared that factory managers would use the influx of black workers to erode work standards and dilute job security." The hate strikes, states Lichtenstein, "were a manifestation of the wartime recomposition of an ethnically heterogeneous, episodically employed proletariat into the self-confident, white working class of the postwar era" (Lichtenstein, *Walter Reuther*, 202–8).

93. Lichtenstein, *Walter Reuther*, 207.

94. Clive, *State of War*, 142.

95. See Louis Bails, "The Automobile Unions and Negro Labor," *Political Science Quarterly* 59 (1944): 548. Bails urged black workers to fully participate in union affairs because "experience has shown that full participation is the most successful means of dispelling resentment among white workers." See also Freeman, "Delivering the Goods," 572.

96. Boyle, "There Are No Union Sorrows That the Union Can't Heal," 5.

97. For praise of the UAW's role, see Irving Howe and B. J. Widdick, *The UAW and Walter Reuther* (New York: Random House, 1949), 219; and B. J. Widdick, *Detroit: City of Race and Class Violence* (Chicago: Quadrangle Books, 1972), 126. Lichtenstein, *Walter Reuther*, 207.

98. Quoted in Winn, "Labor Tackles the Race Question," 342.

99. Ibid.

100. Quoted in Clive, *State of War*, 142.

101. Weaver, *Negro Labor*, 79–81.

102. Weaver, "Negro Employment," 597, 605. See also Herbert Northrup, "Organized Labor and Negro Workers," *Journal of Political Economy* 51 (June 1943): 206–21.

103. Weaver, "Negro Employment," 607.

104. Anderson, "Last Hired, First Fired," 92. See books on FEPC cited at 92 n. 5.

105. The FTA was one of the unions expelled by the CIO in 1950, and the virtual destruction of Local 19 was completed by Senator James Eastland's Senate Internal Security Subcommittee in 1951 (Michael Honey, "Fighting on Two Fronts," *Labor's Heritage* 4, no. 1 [Silver Spring, Md.: Geo. Meany Memorial Archives, 1988]: 49). For a discussion of both racial militancy and interracial violence in and out of the workplace, see Harvard Sitkoff, "Racial Militancy and Interracial Violence in the Second World War," *Journal of American History* 58 (1971): 661–81.

106. Bruce Nelson, "Organized Labor and the Struggle for Black Equality in Mobile during World War II," *Journal of American History* 80 (Dec. 1993): 952.

107. Ibid., 954.

108. See Lipsitz, *Rainbow at Midnight*, 26. Joshua Freeman has noted that shipyards were often the site of the most serious incidents: "At the Sun Shipbuilding Yard in Chester, PA, black and white workers battled violently, while in Mobile, AL, 20,000 white shipyard workers struck and rioted, successfully forcing the FEPC to abandon its attempt to provide non-discriminatory advancement for blacks" (Freeman, "Delivering the Goods," 585).

109. Nelson, "Organized Labor," 955. Despite a strong policy against racism, Nancy Quam-Wickham asserts that the ILWU made only limited efforts to enforce its policy of equality. Its commitment was weakened by an even greater belief in the principle of local autonomy (Quam-Wickham, "Who Controls the Hiring Hall?").

110. Ibid., 970.

111. White women workers were first hired in Mobile's shipyards in July 1942, and nearly one hundred were working as welders by September. White women were later employed in other skilled occupations, occupations which excluded black workers. White women "could be rationalized as a temporary phenomenon that would not undermine the system's social relations in the Jim Crowe south" (ibid., 962, 979).

112. Anderson, "Last Hired, First Fired," 82, 86.

113. Ibid.

114. Ibid., 89.

115. Ibid., 97.

116. Horowitz, *"Negro and White, Unite and Fight!"* 162.

117. Ibid.

118. Clive, *State of War*, 143.

119. Joel Seidman, *American Labor from Defense to Reconversion* (Chicago: University of Chicago Press, 1953), 166–71.

120. See Lester Granger, "Barriers to Negro War Employment," *Annals* 223 (1942): 72.

121. Anderson, "Last Hired, First Fired," 92.

122. See Seidman, *American Labor*, 168–70.

123. Ibid., 170.

124. Anderson, "Last Hired, First Fired," 92. Robert Weaver, discussing affirmative civil rights actions in unions in 1944, noted that blacks had made more progress through the courts than through direct union action (Weaver, "Recent Events in Negro Union Relationships," *Journal of Political Economy* 52 [1944]: 249 n. 46).

125. Clive, *State of War*, 135.

126. 78 Stat. 241, 253–66.

127. Arnold Rose, *The Negro in America* (Boston: Beacon Press, 1948), 136–37.

9

The Threat of Restrictive Legislation

In the Seventy-seventh Congress alone, twenty-one bills were introduced to regulate wartime strikes. Following the pattern set during the period of defense mobilization, three bills sought to make strikes in defense plants treasonous and punishable by death.[1] Legislators were spurred on by employer groups, notably the National Association of Manufacturers, who charged that strikes were damaging war production even though the lost time figures were very low.[2] The successive miners' strikes of 1943, which were primarily responsible for making that year so exceptional, led to the passage of the War Labor Disputes Act and helped inflame public opinion against strikes.[3]

The WLB strongly criticized strikes as early as mid-1942, and public member Wayne L. Morse, especially upset over union jurisdictional disputes, warned that the laws against treason would be applied to strikers in such disputes.[4] For instance, San Francisco machinists strongly rebelled in fall 1942 against the creation of a new, lower-paid job classification at the Joshua Hindy Iron Works, which produced one-third of all American Liberty Ship engines. While the WLB attempted to arbitrate the issue, Morse characterized the machinists as "exhibit[ing] a callousness with respect to our national crisis which borders on lack of patriotism and indifference to our war effort."[5] Morse's statements during this period often seem to be excessively bellicose, but his rancor reflects the views held by many in wartime Washington.

The fact that the incidence of strikes rose dramatically in 1943 and increased even more in 1944 is relevant to any balanced assessment of the War Labor Board. By 1943, the board's view of arbitration was already set, and, therefore, its policy encouraging the arbitration of contractual disputes cannot be said to have been causally related to the wildcat activity.[6] Similarly, although the board punished strikers and withheld union security clauses from striking locals, its union security policy was also clearly established by 1943. Both arbitration and union security clauses were designed to strengthen unions, in part so that "responsible" union action could be encouraged. Nevertheless, these policies also stemmed from other goals which had been established prior to the great strike wave of 1943 and 1944. Indeed, Workman argues that the decisions of the WLB were "a bulwark against wartime reaction."[7]

One of the WLB's possible responses to strikes or other actions violating its orders was to certify the cases of recalcitrant unions or employers to the president, who could order the seizure of the company.[8] After June 1943, in addition, in the case of firms under government control, criminal penalties for striking could be assessed under the War Labor Disputes Act.

Short of presidential seizure, the WLB took a variety of actions against unions who were perceived to be troublesome. When a union struck against working more than eight hours a day, or forty-eight hours a week, the board directed its regional office not to approve any agreement reached by the local as long as the local's overtime restriction was in effect. In another case the board in 1945 suspended the shift premium and vacation privileges included in a prior board order because of a strike. In response to a strike of newspaper deliverers in New York City, the WLB suspended various benefits such as the closed shop and a provision for retroactive wage increases until the strike ended.[9]

The administration also expressed serious concern over the mounting number of strikes, and it was especially disturbed by the UMW strikes of 1943.[10] Wildcat strikes had occurred in the coalfields as early as 1942, but the four separate bituminous strikes in 1943 led to the most notorious labor controversy of the war. These strikes were union-authorized, although "all were short, ranging from forty-eight hours to six days in duration. In all, the coal industry lost about twelve days production."[11] Nevertheless, referring to yet another form of labor regulation, FDR stated that he would ask Congress to raise the age limit for noncombatant military service from forty-five to sixty-five years in order to be able to deal promptly with strikes at establishments operated by the government. If Congress acted on such proposals, strikers might be drafted into the army and then assigned to their customary civilian duties. As early as 1942, FDR had considered reviving Woodrow Wilson's 1917 plan to withdraw draft deferments from strikers in industries deemed essential. The plan was shelved, but variations were proposed throughout the war.[12]

The UMW strikes also induced the president to strengthen the War Labor Board. Executive Order 9370, issued on August 16, 1943, provided for direct penalties against workers who refused to comply with board orders as well as for sanctions against noncomplying unions and employers.[13] (See appendix 2.) Strikers might be punished by the cancellation of their draft deferments, unions could be deprived of contractual benefits, with checked-off union dues to be held in escrow, and employers could be subject to seizure or the withdrawal of "priorities, benefits or privileges" under government contracts.[14]

In a number of instances draft boards ended the deferment of eligible strikers and reclassified them 1–A, making them subject to immediate induction. Al Nash, discussing labor relations at Brewster Aeronautical Corporation during the war, noted the case of a local president who either supported or tolerated thirteen strikes, slowdowns, or walkouts. In 1945, because of alleged public and political pressure, the local president was drafted even though he was thirty-seven years old, married, and the father of three children.[15] In other cases, as in the coalfields, strikers were indicted under the criminal provisions of the Smith-Connally Act (War Labor Disputes Act).[16]

The coal controversy revealed another form of government involvement in labor regulation. As part of the campaign against John L. Lewis, Attorney General Francis Biddle apparently investigated the possibility of a tax evasion prosecution, and other officials sought AFL support against Lewis's tactics and against acceptance of the UMW request to reaffiliate.[17] Other unions also felt the heat. R. J. Thomas, president of the UAW, said that "public opinion has become inflamed against our union. Word of these strikes is going to our millions of men in uniform. Our union cannot survive if the nation and our soldiers believe that we have obstructed the war effort."[18]

Soldiers might well form the impression from both regular and service newspapers that there were numerous strikes led by irresponsible civilian workers. The last coal stoppage in 1943 coincided with a labor dispute on the railroads and a walkout of steelworkers.[19] General George C. Marshall, army chief of staff, declared that the combined rail and steel crisis might prolong the war against Germany by six months at the cost of hundreds of thousands of needless casualties.[20] Secretary of War Henry L. Stimson used the occasion to argue for a national service law. These strikes, he believed, violated employees' obligations to their country and to military forces. The pressure became so serious that the army, hardly a labor supporter, stated that no strike had been authorized by the national leadership of either federation, that less than one-tenth of 1 percent of total labor time available had been lost by strikes, and that wages had risen by little more than the cost of living.[21]

As early as 1940 and 1941 the War Department under Stimson expanded its labor subdivision by hiring corporate lawyers to deal with labor-management disputes. The department consistently pressured Roosevelt to support stronger legislation to control labor, and incited Congress and the public against strikes. Admiral Ben Morrell, chief of U.S. Bureau of Yards and Docks, speaking in October 1942 at a Toronto meeting of the AFL building and construction trades department, stated: "I will admit that no one can live without labor, but they certainly can live without labor unions. They are living without them in Germany, and in Italy, and in Japan and they seem to be doing right well—at least for the moment—and, in my opinion, they will damn well live without them here if all of us don't get in there and pitch."[22]

The army and navy departments repeatedly argued that strikes were jeopardizing the war effort and interfering with production, and that without national service legislation troops would be demoralized and the enemy's will to resist would be strengthened.[23] Stimson told the Senate Military Affairs Committee in 1944 that legislation was needed because of a "situation of anarchy" on the labor front: "The purpose of a national service law is to get at this basic evil which produces the irresponsibility out of which stems strikes, threat of strikes, excessive turnover, absenteeism, and other manifestations of irresponsibility with which we are now plagued."[24] Many of the CIO's targets during the war had defense contracts, and strikes at such firms necessarily involved not only employers but the government as well. The War Department viewed strikes as "an unpredictable drain on defense production."[25]

Molding public opinion to view strikes as "unpatriotic" was a relatively simple task in such feverish times, and the AFL joined in by denouncing strikes, particularly those that could be deemed "Communist-led."[26] Daniel Tobin of the Teamsters, always the source of pithy quotes, stated: "Tell the rat who advocates strikes that the blood of these young men across the seas fighting a fight for our freedom will not be on your hands or on your conscience."[27]

The wartime role of the state in relation to production was often crystal clear to workers in defense plants. Representatives of the armed forces spent considerable time in defense plants, and the presence of uniformed military personnel would seem to continually highlight the military function of production. Indeed, some enterprises were taken over by one of the branches of the armed services. For example, in September 1944, the U.S. Navy pursuant to executive orders "took possession of the bulk of the machinery industry in San Francisco and the industrial suburbs south of the city. The existing multi-employer contract was suspended, as were collective bargaining rights, union recognition, dues payment, the hiring hall, and the right of union representation."[28]

"The strike waves of 1943 and 1944," relates Zieger, "sent union representatives scurrying about, coaxing or forcing the local unionists back to work
and placating federal authorities who threatened to revoke maintenance-of-
membership clauses if they failed." Philip Murray noted in early 1944 that
the typical CIO union had become "a fire department." Indeed, "a very substantial portion . . . of the monies collected by each of the international organizations [in dues payments] is now being used to enforce the directives
of the National War Labor Board . . . which we do not believe in."[29]

No assessment of possible union options should overlook the very real
threat of hostile legislation throughout the war. The period of the unions'
great rise in numbers and strength was ironically also one of strenuous opposition. As already noted, the needs of, first, the mobilization period and,
second, a wartime economy provided a congenial atmosphere for calls for
legislation aimed at restricting strikes. Vociferous attempts to punish or draft
strikers, or, indeed, to draft all defense workers, were a real threat to unions
throughout the period. In addition, bills were routinely introduced after 1937
to either weaken or repeal the National Labor Relations Act or to otherwise place restrictions upon unions, even though only the War Disputes Act
was actually enacted. Nevertheless, many bills got far enough to make the
threat real. For instance, the Hobbs Bill making unions subject to anti-rack-
eteering legislation passed the House in 1943.[30]

Moreover, the threat of judicial reaction was apparent even before the
war began.[31] For instance, the 1937 *Jones & Laughlin* decision, upholding the
NLRA, is generally cited as a major landmark in constitutional law in expanding congressional power under the Constitution's commerce clause.[32]
At the same time, however, the Court spent a significant amount of time
stressing the *limitations* of the statute in relation to collective bargaining, and
it especially noted the modest inroads made by the statute into areas of
"managerial prerogatives." The scope of protection under the act was also
drastically limited by *Mackay Telegraph*,[33] another prewar Supreme Court
decision which permitted the permanent replacement of strikers, and by
Sands Manufacturing Company[34] during the war which restricted the scope
of allowable concerted action.

Court decisions during the war supplemented these prewar opinions
which limited the types of collective action that would be "protected" under the NLRA. Although section 7 of the NLRA explicitly protected the
right to strike, courts began to delimit the range of "lawful" strikes, and an
early casualty was wildcat strikes. Without the protection of section 7, strikers
could be fired because such retaliation did not "interfere" with the "right to
strike" or discriminate against statutorily protected rights. Although the

NLRB has never opted for a total ban on wildcat strikes, courts have generally held that such work stoppages interfere with collective bargaining or inherently interfere with the union's status. It is, however, no coincidence that the court's denunciation of wildcats, which began in 1939, was fleshed out during the war.[35]

Thus, judicial concern with the application of the NLRA to wildcat or unauthorized strikes was first expressed in wartime. Wildcatters, said the Third Circuit Court of Appeals in 1942 and the Fourth Circuit in 1944, were not protected despite the Wagner Act's explicit, and unrestricted, right to strike.[36] Moreover, the Fourth Circuit held that strikers were unprotected by the statute even though their action did not violate their collective agreement.[37] Instead, wildcat strikers violated the *purposes* of the statute: "[T]here can be no effective bargaining if small groups of employees are at liberty to ignore the bargaining agency thus set up, take particular matters into their own hands and deal independently with the employer." The court believed its decision was consistent with the purposes of the statute and the imperatives of collective bargaining which otherwise would be brought into "general disrepute."[38]

These decisions equated the employer's statutory obligation to bargain in good faith with the employees' obligation to channel their concerns through their collective representative.[39] According to these courts, reflecting most courts that have subsequently dealt with the issue, a statute encouraging collective bargaining meant that union bargaining and economic power had to be centralized within the union's structure. Harm to the bargaining institution, and to the union, was assumed without the need for factual inquiry. The NLRB, however, has generally viewed unauthorized strikes more leniently, aware that the statute provides no clear prohibition of unauthorized strikes. Thus, the board has tended to protect walkouts which do not "derogate" from the union's position or actually prejudice the collective bargaining relationship.[40]

Typically, both the courts and the NLRB relate the consequences of wildcat activity to collective bargaining and union status. Nearly all courts, however, have simply assumed that unauthorized strikes are harmful, without any significant inquiry into the aims of the strikers or the congruence of union and striker goals.[41] Yet, fact-finding would reveal that strikers are rarely seeking to "bargain" or to displace the union. In short, legal and nonlegal disapprobation of wildcats is not affected by the underlying causes of worker frustration, the size of the walkout, or the actual harm caused to union or employer.

One threat, supported in the early months of the war, was national service legislation.[42] As already noted, such legislation was repeatedly urged by the military services. This proposal would basically have empowered the government to conscript workers and then to assign them to particular defense-related jobs, compelling them to remain. National service was urged because it would prevent strikes, although some supporters based their arguments on the more neutral-sounding concern for the manpower needs of essential war industries. A bill was eventually introduced in July 1942 which would have created a general obligation for males between eighteen and sixty-five and for females between eighteen and fifty to serve as civilian draftees. The bill also permitted the president to assign workers to particular jobs in war industries, but no seniority protection was granted nor were reemployment rights mentioned. The bill subsequently died in committee, but constant pressure existed for such legislation throughout the war.

Although Roosevelt initially resisted pressure for a national service law, he ultimately joined the advocates in January 1944, after the long series of coal strikes and the steel and rail crises in 1943. He urged some form of national service legislation in his 1944 State of the Union message because it would "prevent strikes, and, with certain appropriate exceptions, will make available for war production or for any other essential services every able-bodied adult in the nation."[43] FDR's proposal was not expressly based on the need to restrict strikes but, rather, upon the need to increase production and to demonstrate to soldiers and the enemy that the nation fully supported the war effort.

Labor angrily denounced the proposal as "quack medicine" and a form of "slave labor."[44] It believed that such an enactment would weaken union security provisions and seniority systems. Just as seriously, such a statute could subject individual employees to criminal penalties for either quitting certain kinds of work, engaging in a collective strike action, or refusing to work where assigned. Unions also feared that such a statute might survive the war in some form, a concern directed to all wartime legislative proposals.

Although national service legislation was not enacted, executive orders and regulations limited worker mobility.[45] For instance, the executive order of April 8, 1943, prohibited the offer or acceptance of new employment except under regulations issued by the chairman of the War Manpower Commission with the approval of the economic stabilization director. The order also forbade changes in employment in order to secure higher wages or salaries unless the war effort was thereby promoted.[46] The agency also issued sweeping regulations designed to freeze some twenty-seven million essential employees in their jobs. Workers in essential employment could receive no pay increases if they changed their job, unless such change was consistent with local wage stabilization plans. Moreover, public opinion polls suggested great support for the drafting of civilians should shortages of labor occur in war industries.[47] From 1943 on, Congress each year considered the passage of national service legislation similar to Britain's manpower draft, and such a measure actually cleared the House in early 1945.[48]

Unions seemed more fearful of legislation directed specifically at strikes, statutes that might well survive the war. When coal miners struck in 1943 for a two-dollar-a-day increase, Representative Howard Smith and Senator Tom Connally introduced a bill which gave statutory sanction to the War Labor Board to handle all disputes that "may lead to substantial interference with the war effort."[49] The bill extended the power of seizure to any workplace involved in the war effort. Should a strike occur after the president ordered the seizure of a firm, criminal penalties would apply to those who encouraged or instigated the strike, although the act of striking itself was not outlawed. In nonseizure situations, the bill provided for a thirty-day cooling-off period during which production would continue. Although this was ostensibly a wartime measure, the bill ominously included measures aimed at peacetime and the union's ties to the Democratic Party. Thus, in a section obviously more concerned with political realities than wartime exigencies, the bill included a provision prohibiting union contributions to political campaign funds.[50]

In his veto message, FDR noted that the strike record was good: "For the entire year 1942, the time lost by strikes averaged only five one-hundredths of 1 percent of the total man-hours worked. The American people should realize that fact—that 99.95 percent of the work went forward without strikes, and that twenty-five one-hundredths of the work was delayed by strikes. That record has never before been equaled in this country. It is as good or better than the record of any of our allies in wartime."[51]

Although FDR stated he might accept the legislation if it only included the first seven sections dealing with certain illegal strikes, he objected to the thirty-day cooling-off period and the machinery for conduct of strike votes. He also, not surprisingly, objected to the ban on contributions to political campaigns. The alternative suggested by the president was, perhaps, just as unpalatable to the unions: "I recommend that the Selective Service Act be amended so that persons can be inducted into non-combat military service up to the age of 65 years. This will enable us to induct into military service persons who engage in strikes or stoppages or other interruptions of work in plants in the possession of the United States."[52] On June 25, 1943, Congress easily overrode FDR's veto. The ultimate passage of Smith-Connally no doubt confirmed the fears of many union leaders that legislative restriction would be the price of militance.

The new statute required a union local in a war plant to give formal notice of intent to strike, to wait through a thirty-day cooling-off period, and then submit the strike question to its membership in a secret ballot election supervised by the NLRB. (See appendix 3.) The government could seize a defense plant threatened by a strike or lockout and could impose criminal penalties for the instigation of an illegal work stoppage.

The passage of the War Labor Disputes Act, however, had none of the drastic effects anticipated by its opponents or its advocates. The thirty-day cooling-off period for workers in war industries tended to create a period in which emotions could actually become more heated, although the period allowed pressure to be generated against the threatened strike. Moreover, filing a notice of an intention to strike became a new tactic in labor relations as union leaders found it useful to obtain membership endorsement of a strike in a government-conducted vote. Such votes were valuable even if the membership had no intention to strike, for it strengthened the position of union bargainers.[53] Pre-strike votes would become a normal tactic in the postwar period.

An ironic effect of the new statute was that it placed the authority for calling now "legitimated" wartime strikes in the hands of often militant local leaders. In addition, the War Labor Disputes Act put the government's NLRB in the odd position of conducting strike votes despite its opposition to *any* work stoppages.[54] Moreover, strikes continued to erupt outside the procedures of the War Labor Disputes Act. During the last half of 1943, for instance, 1,119 strikes occurred. Only thirty-four occurred after the statutory strike vote, and most were spontaneous or wildcats.[55]

Congress also failed to appreciate the statutory burden placed on the National Labor Relations Board. The NLRB simply could not handle the volume of work created by the statutorily mandated notices of disputes and strike votes under section 8 of the statute.[56] Testifying for reworking the section, Daniel W. Tracy, assistant secretary of labor, stated in October 1945 that a recent notice involved over three thousand separate employers and many notices involved entire industries. Tracy also argued that the department felt that section 8 served "to increase friction between management and labor."[57]

Given the unanticipated weakness of the War Labor Disputes Act, government pressure upon unions remained intense. Nevertheless, FDR refused to formally adopt the policy, urged by the army and navy among others, under which strikers acting in defiance of WLB orders would lose their deferment and be blacklisted from further defense employment. The government fell back on plant seizures, although they often involved situations in which employer obstructionism was the problem.[58]

As far as unions were concerned, the threatened loss of union security, fringe benefits, or representational rights by the actions of the War Labor Board could not be ignored. Moreover, strikes could affect possible benefits in other WLB rulings. Ultimately, as already noted, unions began to punish strikers themselves.[59]

The thirty-six million man-days lost during the war due to strikes is a sizable and serious number. Yet, William Green noted at the 1943 AFL convention that although the United States had suffered 105,000 casualties, including 20,000 dead, 80,000 American workers had been killed in workplace accidents and 7 million had been injured on and off the job. Public attention, however, centered more on strikes and less on the other causes of delay. More interestingly, the sense of national urgency was obviously greater in England, yet England and Northern Ireland had relatively more strikes in 1942 and 1943, and more man-days idle in 1942, than the United States.[60] Canada, though part of the British Commonwealth, experienced many authorized strikes during the war. In 1943, for instance, "there were more strikes than in any previous year in Canadian history. Indeed, the number of work stoppages and striking workers exceeded figures recorded in following years until 1965."[61]

The reality of limited production losses due to strikes in the United States was, apparently, less important than the emotional and political significance of the fact that any strikes actually occurred. Moreover, the unauthorized nature of most wartime strikes and their short duration did not ameliorate the pressure upon unions. When public concern was combined with the constant threat of restrictive legislation or other forms of government control, unions were induced to contain the militance of their members, encouraging the notion that workplace disputes were to be resolved via the grievance process rather than at the point of production. The political effects of these work stoppages would be seen in the postwar era when anti-NLRA forces succeeded in limiting the statute.

Notes

1. David Ziskind, "The Impact of the War on Labor Law," *Law and Contemporary Problems* 9 (1942): 373–402. See Andrew Workman, "Creating the Center: Liberal Intellectuals, the National War Labor Board, and the Stabilization of American Industrial Relations, 1941–1945" (Ph.D. diss., University of North Carolina, 1993), 47–48.

2. Joel Seidman, *American Labor from Defense to Reconversion* (Chicago: University of Chicago Press, 1953), 136.

3. Ibid., 137–42. Although the press vigorously criticized strikes, there were some exceptions. An editorial in *Common Sense*, for instance, argued that: "Labor should not give up the right to strike for the duration. A strike that helps to achieve the indivisible purposes for which the war is being fought is part of the war. It does not 'prolong' the war. It *is* the war. Organized labor's fight against the menace of fascism at home, even when it involves striking, hastens the only kind of victory worth fighting for" (Ed Jennings, "Wildcat! The Wartime Strike Wave in Auto," *Radical America* 9 (July–Aug. 1975): 77.

4. Seidman, *American Labor*, 135.

5. Related in Richard Boyden, "The San Francisco Machinists and the National War Labor Board," in *American Labor in the Era of World War II*, ed. Sally Miller and Daniel Cornford (Westport, Conn.: Praeger, 1995), 108–9.

6. James Atleson, "Wartime Labor Regulation, the Industrial Pluralists, and the Law of Collective Bargaining," in *Industrial Democracy in America: The Ambiguous Promise*, ed. Nelson Lichtenstein and Howell John Harris (New York: Cambridge University Press, 1993).

7. Workman, "Creating the Center," iii, 7–8.

8. Although only a few noteworthy cases made news, mostly involving defiance of the War Labor Board, the board closed 17,650 dispute cases involving over twelve million workers. For cases of refusal to comply with WLB orders, see Wayne Morse, "The National War Labor Board Puts Labor Law Theory into Practice," *Iowa Law Review* 29 (1944): 175, 198–201. In more than 95 percent of these cases the decisions of the board or its agents were accepted. Only forty-six cases required direct action by the president in order to obtain compliance. In six of these cases a direct request from the president was sufficient to avoid a conflict, and the other forty were dealt with by plant seizures. See National War Labor Board, *The Termination Report of the National War Labor Board. Industrial Disputes and Wage Stabilization in Wartime. January 12, 1942–December 31, 1945*, 3 vols. (Washington, D.C.: Government Printing Office, 1947–48), 1:420–21; Seidman, *American Labor*, 148–49. Interestingly, the forty-six cases of noncompliance that were referred to the president involved management and union responsibility in almost equal parts.

9. See National War Labor Board, *Termination Report*, 1:419.

10. See Workman, "Creating the Center," 246–69; Robert Zieger, *John L. Lewis: Labor Leader* (Boston: Twayne Publishers, 1988), 132–49; Melvyn Dubofsky and Warren Van Tyne, *John L. Lewis: A Biography* (Urbana: University of Illinois Press, 1986), 302–22.

11. Zieger, *John L. Lewis*, 140.

12. See Patrick Renshaw, "Organized Labour and the United States War Economy, 1939–1945," *Journal of Contemporary History* 21 (1986): 3, 12.

13. National War Labor Board, *Termination Report*, 2:84.

14. See Seidman, *American Labor*, 139. Despite the order, Roosevelt was forced to seize the mines again in October 1943. A settlement did in fact increase miners' pay but remained technically within the "Little Steel" formula by paying them for portal-to-portal travel time and by reducing the lunch period. But the strikes had

cost labor heavily in public support and poorly thought-out labor legislation was on the statute books (ibid., 140).

15. Al Nash, "A Unionist Remembers: Militant Unionism and Political Factions," *Dissent* 24 (1977): 181, 185.

16. See Seidman *American Labor*, 145. Defiance from employers was also taken seriously by the WLB. In one case, for example, the Federated Fishing Boats of New England refused to attend a board hearing unless the board promised that the then current collective agreement would be continued for the duration of the war. The board emphasized the "serious implications of this unpatriotic act," berated the employers for placing their "selfish welfare above the interests of the country," and declared that their defiance "must be repudiated by patriotic Americans and challenged by whatever forces of government may be necessary to obtain compliance" (ibid., 145–46).

17. Nelson Lichtenstein, *Labor's War at Home: The CIO in World War II* (New York: Cambridge University Press, 1982), 168–69.

18. Seidman, *American Labor*, 142.

19. The USWA notified hundreds of firms that it would reopen its agreements and ask for a 17-cent-an-hour increase despite the "Little Steel" formula (Mark McCulloch, "Consolidating Industrial Citizenship: The USWA at War and Peace, 1939–46," in *Forging a Union of Steel*, ed. Paul Clark, Peter Gottlieb, and Donald Kennedy [Ithaca, N.Y.: ILR Press, 1987], 53). Over 150,000 steelworkers struck. The WLB took the case but did not decide until December 1944 to grant a wage increase and other benefits. As McCulloch notes, the WLB decision applied to eighty-six companies, setting the stage for centralized postwar bargaining.

20. Seidman, *American Labor*, 141.

21. Ibid., 144–45.

22. Quoted in Art Preis, *Labor's Giant Step: Twenty Years of the CIO* (New York: Pathfinder Press, 1972), 149–50.

23. Paul Koistinen, "Mobilizing the World War II Economy: Labor and the Industrial-Military Alliance," *Pacific Historical Review* 42 (1973): 459–60; Lichtenstein, *Labor's War at Home*, 182–86.

24. Quoted in Lichtenstein, *Labor's War at Home*, 183–84.

25. Henry Stimson and Frank Knox to FDR, May 29, 1941, quoted in Lichtenstein, *Labor's War at Home*, 47.

26. Rick Fantasia, *Cultures of Solidarity: Consciousness, Action, and Contemporary American Workers* (Berkeley: University of California Press, 1988), 50. The problem in the postwar period, said Charles E. Wilson, G.E. president, was "Russia abroad, Labor at Home." As Rick Fantasia has noted, "The Cold War barrage of anticommunism was to provide a key to the solution of both problems" (ibid., 55).

27. Seidman, *American Labor*, 142.

28. Boyden, "San Francisco Machinists," 111–12.

29. Robert H. Zieger, *The CIO, 1935–1955* (Chapel Hill: University of North Carolina Press, 1995) 178.

30. Seidman, *American Labor*, 191.

31. See chap. 2, above.

32. Jones and Laughlin, 301 U.S. 1 (1937).

33. Mackay Telegraph, 304 U.S. 333 (1938).

34. Sands Manufacturing Co., 306 U.S. 332 (1939). See Karl Klare, "Judicial Deradicalization of the Wagner Act and the Origins of Modern Legal Consciousness, 1937–1947," *Minnesota Law Review* 62 (1978): 265, 303–4. In addition, although it is argued that the war and especially the operation of the National War Labor Board encouraged unions to centralize power at the highest levels, thereby reducing the perimeters of possible rank-and-file action, the seeds of these limitations had begun even earlier. The steelworkers and autoworkers, for instance, had limited the power of local unions to strike by the end of the 1930s. See also James Atleson, *Values and Assumptions in American Labor Law* (Amherst: University of Massachusetts Press, 1983), 46–47.

35. See, e.g., NLRB v. Draper Corp., 145 F.2d 199 (4th Cir. 1944). See also James Atleson, "Work Group Behavior and Wildcat Strikes: The Causes and Functions of Industrial Civil Disobedience," *Ohio State Law Journal* 34 (1973): 751, 772–76; Christopher Tomlins, *The State and the Unions* (New York: Cambridge University Press, 1985), 261–64.

36. NLRB v. Condenser Corp. of America, 128 F.2d 67 (3d Cir. 1942); NLRB v. Draper Corp, 145 F.2d 199 (4th Cir. 1944).

37. The vast majority of collective bargaining agreements in the United States contain no-strike clauses, often broadly worded. A strike occurring in violation of such a clause will be deemed unprotected whether authorized or not. See American Beef Packers, Inc., 196 NLRB 131 (1972).

38. NLRB v. Draper Corp., 145 F.2d 199 at 203.

39. Most appellate courts agree. See, e.g., Plasti-Line, Inc., 278 F.2d 482 (6th Cir. 1960). The Supreme Court has never explicitly ruled on the protected status of unauthorized strikes, but a 1975 decision suggests hostility to employees who "bypass the grievance procedure" (Emporium Capwell Co. v. Western Addition Community Organization, 420 U.S. 50 [1975]).

40. See NLRB v. Berger Polishing, Inc., 147 NLRB 21 (1964); NLRB v. San Juan Lumber Co., 154 NLRB 1153 (1969); Tanner Motor Livery Ltd., 148 NLRB 1402 (1964). The board's most notable victory in the courts is NLRB v. R. C. Can Co., 328 F.2d 974 (5th Cir. 1964). But see NLRB v. Shop Rite Foods, Inc., 430 F.2d 786 (5th Cir. 1970), where the court held that wildcat activity will no longer be tested in accordance with the congruency of union and striker aims. Instead, the activity will only be protected if it is *consistent* with a "previously articulated" union goal.

41. See Atleson, "Work Group Behavior," 751, 772–76. Moreover, courts often refer to these strikes as "minority strikes," although it is unlikely the result would be different if the wildcatters constituted a majority of the bargaining unit.

42. Seidman, *American Labor*, 162; Koistinen, "Mobilizing the World War II Economy," 443, 456–57; Lichtenstein, *Labor's War at Home*, 182–86.

43. Seidman, *American Labor*, 163; Koistinen, "Mobilizing the World War II Economy," 458.

44. Seidman, *American Labor,* 163–64.

45. Ibid., 159–60.

46. See, generally, George Q. Flynn, *The Mess in Washington: Manpower Mobilization in World War II* (Westport, Conn.: Greenwood Press, 1979), 71.

47. Ibid., 85. The problem of labor shortages was made more serious by the practice of "hoarding" workers. Before the United States entered the war, employers recognized that mobilization would mean a likely shortage of skilled labor and managers took steps to make sure that they would not suffer. Some employers allegedly pirated workers from other firms by offering higher pay. When a firm had sufficient labor, it would then seek to "hoard" workers in anticipation of expanded production. A 1943 federal study of shipbuilding in the state of Washington, for instance, determined that the shipyards could lose from fifteen to eighteen thousand men without hurting production. This surplus existed even though nearby Boeing Aircraft was desperate for labor. This has to be viewed in light of management's constant position that benefits to labor would hinder the war effort (ibid., 43–44).

48. See Alan Clive, *State of War: Michigan in World World II* (Ann Arbor: University of Michigan Press, 1979), 78–79.

49. U.S. Public Law 89, Ch. 144. 78th Cong., 1st sess.; National War Labor Board, *Termination Report*, 2:80.

50. Aaron Levenstein, *Labor, Today and Tomorrow* (New York: A. A. Knopf, 1946), 56.

51. Ibid., 57. See also Seidman, *American Labor,* 188–94, and Lichtenstein, *Labor's War at Home,* 167–68.

52. Levenstein, *Labor, Today and Tomorrow,* 57–58.

53. Seidman, *American Labor,* 188–91. In the first year of the law's operation, unions sent the secretary of labor more than a thousand strike notices, the AFL accounting for almost 75 percent of them. Yet, strike votes were actually taken by the NLRB in only 232 cases. In most instances, workers voted to strike, but only sixty-four stoppages actually followed from such votes (Levenstein, *Labor, Today and Tomorrow,* 58).

54. This fact was noted by *Business Week,* among other journals, which opposed the provision (*Yearbook of American Labor,* vol. 1, *War Labor Policies,* ed. Colston E. Warne [New York: Philosophical Library, 1945], 529 n. 14).

55. Throughout the life of the act, approximately 125 persons were convicted for fomenting illegal strikes; most received $25 to $50 fines, a few up to $250. Jail sentences were usually suspended (Koistinen, "Mobilizing the World War II Economy," 443, 300; Levenstein, *Labor, Today and Tomorrow,* 58).

56. John M. Houston, a member of the National Labor Relations Board, testified on Oct. 17, 1945, that between Sept. 30 and Oct. 15, 1945, the number of notices filed rose from six hundred to thirty-nine hundred. The board, therefore, was required by statute to conduct a secret ballot election at thirty-nine hundred locations in a two-week period after a thirty-day cooling-off period. Houston described the effect of the notice as being similar to the falling of "an atomic bomb." Basically,

Houston argued that it is "administratively impossible for the National Labor Relations Board, or any other agency, to continue to administer section 8 of the War Labor Disputes Act" (Repeal of War Labor Disputes Act, Hearings before the Committee on Military Affairs, House of Representatives, 79th Cong., 1st sess., Oct. 17 and 19, 1945, 9). Note that this testimony occurred at war's end. Thus, Houston argued that the act no longer served any function at a time when peacetime production was resuming.

57. See ibid., 21–22.

58. Koistinen, "Mobilizing the World War II Economy," 443, 301. There were only approximately fifty plant seizures during the war. Government plant seizures are discussed in Paul Koistinen, *The Hammer and the Sword* (New York: Arno Press, 1979), 304–24.

59. In early 1944, the UAW announced that wildcatters could not use the grievance procedure to challenge company discipline. Local leaders who defended strikers could be removed, and unions could be placed in trusteeship. During the remainder of the war, Lichtenstein reports that hundreds of UAW workers were disciplined or fired by the auto companies without union response (Nelson Lichtenstein, "Defending the No-Strike Pledge: CIO Politics during World War II," *Radical America* 9 [July–Aug. 1975]: 59). Art Preis states that the executive board of the Industrial Union of Marine and Shipbuilding Workers revoked the charters of four locals and placed five others in receivership between September 1942 and September 1943. See Preis, *Labor's Giant Step,* 224–28.

60. Seidman, *American Labor,* 150.

61. Jeffrey Sack and Tanya Lee, "The Role of the State in Canadian Labour Relations" (unpublished paper, in author's possession). Sack and Lee report that "in 1943 one out of three workers engaged in strike action" (citing Laurel Sefton MacDowell, "The Formation of the Canadian Industrial Relations System during World War Two," *Labour/Le Travailleur* 175 [1978]: 195).

10

The Transference of Wartime Visions to Peacetime

During the war, some saw strikes as "treason" and strikers as "traitors." Strikes, moreover, could rationally be viewed as interfering with the war effort, and, therefore, they could no longer be deemed "private" economic matters. The very presence of "public" members on wartime boards signified the presence of an interest separate from, and obviously more significant than, that of unions or management.[1] The "public interest" would be a focus of postwar writing, making it possible for the disdain for wartime strikes to survive the war as the need to prevent interruptions to the peacetime economy.

> Even without the pressures of a world war, it was argued that large-scale production increases the sensitivity of the economy to disturbances in the system. All sectors of the economy are interdependent. Unions cut across industrial lines. The size and power of unions widens the effect of strike action. The economy as a whole is vulnerable to any disturbance which breaks the close chain of interrelations. These conditions operate to change the entire character of strikes. Strikes no longer affect single groups of workers and one company. They spread quickly to many other workers and companies nowise at fault and not involved in a specific strike. Modern strikes of almost any kind affect the entire economy, and hence the general public interest. In these circumstances, companies and unions are charged with the new responsibility in the public interest, which neither fully recognizes.[2]

The widening impact of union economic pressure against large-scale, multilocation enterprises is now viewed as creating a "public" responsibility, which means that the assertion of private interests may have to be restricted in light of the public interest. This "responsibility" combines with the public role unions were seen to have in War Labor Board decisions, especially those dealing with union security and strikes. The wartime need for continuous production required unions, and all other parts of the economy, to act in the public interest. As will be noted, the asserted relationship of strikes and patriotism continued after the war, demonstrating the confining (or defining) aspects of wartime constraints. Many wartime concepts concerning the appropriate labor-management system would continue after the war, ultimately to be reflected in substantive law. Earlier sections have noted that the body of law dealing with the administration and enforcement of collective agreements, which the Supreme Court began to create in the 1960s, almost precisely mirrors the rulings of the War Labor Board, albeit without attribution. In addition, the War Labor Board created a zone of managerial exclusivity, adopted after the war by the NLRB and, especially, the Supreme Court.

But less clearly defined notions were also transferred, concepts stemming from the needs of wartime rather than simply reflecting governmental regulation during the war. One is the distaste for strikes, obviously a serious matter in wartime, although certainly possessing a long lineage in American labor history. Strikes after 1945, for instance, although no longer an interference with war production, were often characterized as interfering with the public interest in continued production and efficiency. Eventually, collective bargaining law would reflect the judiciary's desire to restrict the strike weapon to disputes over the terms of new agreements and to stress arbitration rather than strikes where issues arose over the meaning of existing collective agreements.

There is considerable evidence for a postwar transference of both ideas and language, although none of the postwar judicial opinions, discussed earlier, referred to the war or to War Labor Board decisions. Yet, postwar legal decisions nevertheless tracked those of the War Labor Board, and writers were often more attuned to the connection between wartime regulation and postwar labor relations. For example, Alexander Frey, an influential postwar writer and arbitrator who had been vice chair of the Philadelphia Regional War Labor Board, urged in 1944 that arbitration of contractual disputes (as opposed to limiting union power to strike for new agreements) "must not be permitted to remain merely a war-time phenomena" for the needs of the postwar period will call for considerable production. "It will be every bit as important as in war-time to banish the impediments to production resulting from strikes and lockouts. . . . In the second place, without permanent abandonment by the people of this and other nations of any form of force as a method of settling internal disputes, there cannot exist the spiritual climate out of which, alone, lasting world peace can emerge."[3]

Constraints on organized labor, therefore, no longer necessary after 1945 to win the war, would still be necessary to win the peace. Additionally, strikes were increasingly viewed as exercises of force, "jungle warfare" in Harry Shulman's terms, a phrase interestingly similar to Lenin's equally demeaning "primitive democracy," rather than the simple withdrawal of labor. Shulman's experience at Ford included raucous and even moblike actions, but he no doubt meant to include stoppages that could be settled through the grievance process. When combined with this widespread postwar desire to find substitutes for the use of force, the alteration of perception completes the move from the *rights* to the *responsibilities* of labor. The other view, of course, is that restraints on bargaining and strikes are a blow against "freedom and liberty," necessary "during the emergency . . . for the good of the nation . . . , but such sacrifices" must not be allowed to become permanent when the emergency has passed."[4]

This tension between economic responsibility to the public good and the free expression of economic interest remains long after the war's end. The strike is still the linchpin of collective bargaining, the critical right granted by the NLRA, and the view that the strike represents "freedom and liberty" is strongly held by working people. Despite the search for peaceful means to resolve labor conflicts, the pluralists did not advocate restrictions on union power to seek new collective agreements. Arbitration, on the other hand, was trumpeted as a necessary alternative to strikes over grievances, and the courts often restricted collective action.[5] Moreover, the support given to unions by the public, as earlier sections have indicated, began to fade by 1944, if not earlier, because of the attention given to wartime wildcat strikes and the authorized work stoppages of the miners. Thus, a double irony occurs. During the war unions grew and stabilized, but they could not use their most potent weapon despite its apparent effectiveness. After the war, unions were "free" of wartime constraints, yet strikes were viewed by many as irresponsible.

The language and symbols of the wartime period could, of course, be used by unions as well as by politicians and employers. For instance, Walter Reuther, then the director of the UAW's General Motors department, led the GM strike in November 1945. Reuther adroitly employed the wartime combination of militancy and patriotism. Reuther asserted that the "GM workers' fight is the fight of the American people," and he insisted upon a 30 percent wage increase while maintaining GM's existing price levels. Reuther stressed wartime symbols by placing uniformed veterans on picket lines and by having pickets carry signs reading "We whipped the Axis, now we fight GM."[6] Of course, labor language has often been spiced with words taken from the world of war, for example, strike, skirmish, conflict, weapons, pickets.

A clear connection between war policies and those that would subsequently be enacted in the Taft-Hartley Act can be seen in the report of the House Committee on Military Affairs submitted to the Seventy-ninth Congress, in October 1945.[7] After hearings, the committee decided to recommend the repeal of the 1943 War Labor Disputes Act, except for section 313 which made it unlawful for certain organizations, including labor organizations, to make contributions to candidates in federal election campaigns.

Representative after representative dutifully criticized the War Labor Disputes Act of 1943 as an act born in "hysteria," "emotionalism," "bitterness and passion," and, perhaps just as important, a statute which did not work. As described earlier, this act permitted the president to seize any struck facility, punished strikes at plants which had been seized by the government by fine or imprisonment, and, with unintended irony, required a thirty-day "cooling off" period after a strike notice at a war plant to be followed by a strike vote. Objections were raised, however, because the source of the bill was not the seemingly more appropriate House Labor Committee.[8] Such criticisms were more than signs of turf protection because of the inclusion of the new regulatory measure along with the repeal provisions.

Although primarily seeking to repeal the remainder of the War Labor Disputes Act, the committee did recommend the enactment of the following provision:

> Section 4. In the event of any strike or concerted failure or refusal to work during the life of a collective bargaining contract which includes a no-strike provision, the employer shall be relieved of any obligation under the contract, and the labor organization shall lose its status as a bargaining agency for a period of one year. Any such labor organization which is a party to the contract may be sued in its own name in any federal district court in which any of its officers may reside, or be found, and shall be responsible in damages to any party injured as a result of the breach.

This proposed amendment also reflected much of the substance of the Taft-Hartley Act's section 301, enacted two years later, which provided for contractual relief and damages in federal courts for breaches of collective bargaining agreements. The most interesting part of the proposed section, however, is the focus on a particular kind of breach, that is, strikes by unions in breach of no-strike clauses. Not all strikes were to be prohibited, only those which the union had contractually promised to forego. Although the proposed section reflects the wartime opposition to strikes. it is certainly noteworthy that no attempt was made, either in this measure or later in Taft-Hartley, to restrict the strike weapon generally.

Although the "loss of status" provision would not be part of section 301 of Taft-Hartley, neither the 1945 bill nor the successful amendments of 1947 referred specifically to arbitration provisions. The 1945 bill referred to breaches of *express* no-strike clauses; there was no suggestion that the presence of an arbitration clause alone would imply a promise not to strike over arbitrable grievances.[9] Indeed, the bill's opponents repeatedly stressed that passage would induce unions to "take the obvious step hereafter of not signing a contract with a no-strike clause in it."[10] Opponents argued, therefore, that the existence of an effective enforcement mechanism for no-strike clauses would make these provisions anathema to unions.

Essentially, the impetus for section 301 in the Taft-Hartley Act of 1947 is reflected in the concerns voiced in support of section 4 of the Repeal Act, that is, that a federal remedy for damages be provided for unions that violate contractual no-strike clauses. The Supreme Court would later use the interest in protecting the integrity of arbitration, a concern reflected in War Labor Board decisions, to imply a coextensive, albeit implied, no-strike clause, a position that Congress seemed unwilling to take.[11] Moreover, despite the absence of congressional support for the use of the injunction to bar strikes in violation of contract, and the continuing existence of the Norris-LaGuardia Act, the Supreme Court in 1970 would permit injunctions against breach of contract strikes.[12] Indeed, the Court would go further, permitting injunctions against strikes not in violation of express no-strike clauses but in violation of the judicially created, implied no-strike promise in arbitration clauses.[13]

The addition of section 4 to a bill to repeal the War Labor Disputes Act shows how the antistrike atmosphere of World War II carried immediately into peacetime within two months of V-J day. As Representative Bailey, an opponent of the bill, stated, "This legislation . . . drafted as it was behind the closed doors of the Military Affairs Committee, smacks too much of wartime controls in peacetime."[14] Yet, the measure did not restrict strikes to achieve a new collective agreement, the cause of virtually all of the postwar strikes. Curiously, however, it was these numerous strikes that Congress used to justify the proposed legislation. Thus, one of the most fervent supporters of the repeal bill, Representative Curtis, stressed the need to settle the numerous postwar strikes in 1945: "Never was there a greater demand in the history of our country for products of all kinds than there is now. The public is eager to buy automobiles, clothing, furniture, equipment, machinery, lumber, and every other commodity. Yet, industry is at a standstill, our economy is being seized by a creeping paralysis."[15] Curtis stressed the existence of pent-up consumer demand due to wartime scarcity to urge passage of an act which would provide a damage remedy for strikes in breach of contract.

Curtis did not mention, nor did others, that nearly all of the then current strikes were disputes over the terms of new or successor collective agreements and, thus, would not be covered or affected by the proposal. As Representative Starkey suggested, perhaps "less than one-half of one percent of members of labor organizations have ceased work in violation of no-strike clauses in their agreements."[16] The expressed concern over breach of contract strikes in the deliberations on the Repeal Act, therefore, did not reflect the then current situation, and it is perhaps noteworthy that no one seemed to believe that the right to strike in general could be prohibited.

This odd situation could be explained by the memory of the wildcat, unauthorized work stoppages of the wartime period. The emphasis on breach of contract strikes, both in the repeal measure and subsequently in Taft-Hartley, seemingly reflects the concern that no-strike clauses, if they could be effectively enforced, would induce unions to control their rank and file. Because of the Norris-LaGuardia Act, perhaps, there was little discussion in these debates or in the subsequent Taft-Hartley deliberations about the use of the injunction.[17] Instead, the emphasis in both situations was the availability of damages to employers. Unions, fearful of suffering economic loss given the possibility that they would be found to have authorized or ratified a strike in breach of contract, would presumably act more forcibly to restrain their members.

Another example of the transference of wartime notions and symbols to peacetime involves the threatened railroad strikes in the spring of 1946, after two railway unions rejected President Truman's proposals of settlement. The threatened strike, Truman said to a nationwide radio audience on May 18, 1946, one day after he had seized the railroads, "is no contest between labor and management. This is a contest between a small group of men and their government. The railroads are now being operated by your government, and the strike of these men is a strike against your government."[18]

Truman's concern, however, was broader than strikes against industries in the government's control, and he had already expressed great concern about the volume of strikes in 1945.[19] Labor unions, now free of their wartime pledges not to strike, called for pay hikes which resulted in strikes in nearly every industry.[20] Truman responded with actions and angry language.

In the fall of 1945, for instance, he had seized oil refineries and ordered strikers back to work. Such strikes were characterized as "foolishness," involving a "few selfish men."[21] Similarly, Truman characterized a walkout by District of Columbia transit workers in November 1945 as striking at "the very roots of orderly government."[22] Truman, as David McCullough has noted, "failed to comprehend how a people who had shown such dedication in will through the war could overnight become so rampantly selfish and disinterested in the common good." Thus, Truman passionately stated that "the Congress are balking, labor has gone crazy and management isn't far from insane in selfishness."[23] Thus, union attempts to exercise the freedom of collective bargaining, after wartime restraints on collective action, were now seen as wicked and, indeed, still unpatriotic.

Concededly, a record number of strikes occurred in 1946, including both the numbers of strikers involved and workdays lost. Major strikes broke out in the coal, steel, and auto industries and on the railroads.[24] The autoworkers' strike at General Motors was followed by strikes by steelworkers, electrical workers, and meatpackers. Though widespread, most strikes were peaceful. There were few acts of violence, and most employers made no effort to employ strikebreakers.[25] Nevertheless, as the labor situation worsened, Truman initially asked Congress to forbid strikes in large national industries for thirty days until the situation could be appraised by a fact-finding board.[26] In other words, the administration's concern shifted from strikes in plants controlled by the government to those which would have a nationwide economic effect. The shift was from strikes against the state to strikes which unduly affected the nation's economic health, leading to the notion that unions had "too much power."

Indeed, in January 1946, after eight hundred thousand steelworkers walked off the job in the biggest strike in history, Truman stated: "I personally think there is too much power on each side, and I think it is necessary that the government assert the fact that *it* is the power of the people."[27] The view that labor had "too much power" would be used by the Republican majorities in 1947 to amend the NLRA, and the press would repeatedly refer to labor as "Big Labor."

Although the steel strike had been settled, strikes were in progress in coal and at General Motors. As David McCullough has noted, "the immediate post war period had become the longest, most costly siege of labor trouble in the nation's history. At one point more than a million workers were out on strike, and though the most crippling shutdown thus far, in the steel industry, was by now settled, the solution had been to cramp not just higher wages but an increase in steel prices, all of which was certain to spur further inflation."[28]

Truman was especially concerned about the very real prospect of a nationwide rail strike. A railroad strike, noted David McCullough, "coming on top of the coal strike would mean almost unimaginable catastrophe, paralysis everywhere."[29] In order to deter a strike, Truman signed an executive order permitting the government to seize and operate the railroads, although the railroad leaders agreed to postpone the strike for another five days.[30]

In a speech to the graduating class at William Jewell, a small college near Kansas City, Missouri, Truman stated: "we have a society which is organized, and if one cog in the organization gives out the whole structure begins to shake loose. Now let me urge upon you: get in line, get on the team, do a little work; help make the United States what it must be from now on: the leader of the world in peace, as it was the leader of the world in war. I urge you to be good workers in the ranks."[31] This statement clearly demonstrates how the language of wartime was easily transferred to peacetime, and the notion of sacrifice for the common good continued despite the recognition and promotion of what was called "free" collective bargaining. "Good workers," like good soldiers, were "in the ranks."

The railroad strike began on May 23, 1946, and "almost at once the whole country was brought virtually to a standstill. Of 24,000 freight trains normally in operation, fewer than 300 ran; of 175,000 passenger trains, all of 100 moved." As telegrams flooded the White House from all parts of the country, Truman began to write the draft of the speech which, according to McCullough, he had no actual intention of presenting.[32] The draft reflected his anger of wartime strikes, especially those led by John L. Lewis, and his belief that union behavior was often dictated by communists. Truman wrote:

> At home those of us who had the country's welfare at heart worked day and night. But some people worked neither day nor night and some tried to sabotage the war effort entirely. No one knows that better than I. John Lewis called two strikes in the wartime to satisfy his ego. Two strikes which were worse than bullets in the back to our soldiers. He held a gun at the head of the Government. The rail unions did exactly the same thing. They were all receiving from four to forty times what the man who was facing the enemy fire on the front was receiving. The effete union leaders receive from five to ten times the net salary of your President.
>
> Now the same union leaders on VJ Day told your President that they would cooperate 100% with them to reconvert the peacetime production. They all lied to him.
>
> First came the threatened automobile strike. Your President asked for Legislation to cool off and consider the situation. A weak kneed Congress didn't have the internal fortitude to pass the bill.

Mr. Murray and his communist friends had a conniption fit and Congress had labor jitters. Nothing happened. Then came the electrical workers strike, the steel strike, the coal strike and now the rail tie-up. Every single one of the strikers and their demagogue leaders have been living in luxury, working when they pleased. . . .

I'm tired of the Government's being flaunted, vilified and misrepresented. Now I want you men who are my comrades in arms, you men who fought the battles to save the nation just as I did 25 years ago, to come along with me and eliminate the Lewises, the Whitneys, the Johnstons, the Communist Bridges and the Russian senators and representatives and really make this a Government of, by and for the people. I think no more of the Wall Street crowd than I do of Lewis and Whitney.

Let's give the country back to the people. Let's put transportation and production back to work, hang a few traitors, make our own country safe for democracy, tell the Russians where to get off and make the United Nations work. Come on boys, let's do the job.[33]

Although the statement was factually inaccurate in a number of respects, it is more important to note how Truman equated strikes or the threat of strikes in peacetime with traitorous activity during time of war. The right to strike in peacetime, the linchpin of the 1935 Wagner Act, is now treated as subversive activity.

On the morning of May 24, 1946, Truman told the cabinet that he would go before Congress on the following day, but he first would address the country by radio that night and propose drafting the striking rail workers into the army.[34] The drafting of strikers or of all critical workers had been proposed at various times during the war but was repeatedly resisted by FDR's administration. Attorney General Tom Clark questioned whether the president was overstepping his constitutional bounds, but Truman reportedly remarked that "we'll draft them and think about the law later."[35]

Truman's speech was rewritten and moderated by White House staffers, primarily by navy captain Clark Clifford, who has referred to the speech as "one of the most intemperate documents ever written by a President."[36] The revised speech was read to the country that evening and, again, Truman equated the peacetime crisis with that of wartime. "The crisis of Pearl Harbor was the result of action by a foreign enemy. The crisis tonight is caused by a group of men within our own country who place their private interest above the welfare of the nation. . . . I am a friend of labor . . . [but] it is inconceivable that in our democracy any two men should be placed in the position where they can completely stifle our economy and ultimately destroy our country."[37]

Truman called on the railroad workers to return to their jobs. Should a sufficient number not return by 4:00 P.M. the next day, Truman threatened to call out the army and do whatever else was necessary to break the strike. Although the speech as presented did not refer to the possible drafting of strikers, McCullough states that Truman was "saving" this for a speech to Congress on the following afternoon.[38]

The following day Truman began his speech to Congress by stating that "strikes against the Government must stop," and he called for temporary emergency legislation "to authorize the President to draft into the armed forces of the United States all workers who are on strike against their Government." The audience, reports McCullough, "roared its approval."[39] At that moment the secretary of the Senate hurried into the chamber and handed Truman a note from Clifford. Truman looked at it and stated "the railroad strike has been settled, on terms proposed by the President!"[40] According to McCullough, "the whole Congress rose to cheer and applaud, everyone on both sides of the aisle." Nevertheless, Truman delivered the remainder of his speech.

Truman proposed that the president be authorized to declare a "national emergency" when a strike occurred in an essential industry after governmental seizure. Truman also proposed that officers of a striking union could be enjoined and also face fines and imprisonment if they failed to act promptly to end the strike. Employment rights would be lost should a striker fail to return to work, and such workers would be subject to induction into the army, a penalty apparently seen as the ultimate sanction.

Truman's bold action was subsequently praised in the press and by leaders of both parties. The *Atlanta Constitution* stated that he had "grown in national stature," and the *Philadelphia Record* declared he had "met magnificently one of the greatest tests of courage ever to face an American President."[41] Thousands of letters reportedly poured into the White House in support of Truman's proposals. After years of rationing, shortages, and inability to purchase consumer goods, many citizens were unwilling to put up with further delays in production.[42]

A bill containing most of Truman's proposals was introduced in the House and passed in less than two hours that evening by a vote of 306 to 13, even though the rail strike had already been settled. On the other hand, the proposals were immediately attacked by labor leaders in strong terms, reminiscent of the language they used to oppose Smith-Connally in 1943. The CIO's Philip Murray wired his response to the Senate, denouncing the proposals as "imposing the equivalent of involuntary servitude." Murray stated that the "measures constitute a beachhead for those sinister forces in

American life which seek to use the military power as a means of crushing labor." William Green, the AFL's president, explicitly employed terms that, he no doubt hoped, would resonate in the postwar period: "To compel free workers to remain on the job against their will by drafting them into the armed forces and making them subject to court marshal if they refuse is slave labor under Fascism."[43] A. F. Whitney, president of the Brotherhood of Trainmen, used similar terms, calling Truman's proposals "of the warp and woof of fascism" and comparing them to the "slave-labor battalions" of Adolph Hitler.

The Senate removed the draft provisions and passed its version of the legislation on June 1 by a 61 to 20 vote. Senator Robert A. Taft, who would return to haunt labor one year later, insisted that the draft proposal went "farther toward Hitlerism, Stalinism, totalitarianism than I have ever seen proposed in any strike."[44] As opposition increased, the entire measure eventually was permitted to lapse. Nevertheless, so quickly had the political winds changed that provisions unacceptable during the war would be seen as worthy of consideration after that emergency passed.

Prominent liberals were dumbfounded, and Sidney Hillman, then on his deathbed, spoke out against Truman as he never had previously. Richard Strout in the *New Republic* stated, "draft men who strike in peacetime, into the armed services! Is this Russia or Germany?" Eleanor Roosevelt, recognizing the irony of such repressive legislation, tactfully wrote that "there must not be any slip, because of the difficulties of our peacetime situation, into a military way of thinking."[46]

During the war, as noted in an earlier chapter, many bills were introduced to restrict union power. Patriotism was the rallying cry, but the postwar strikes now provided a new basis for attack. Many of these measures, like Truman's own proposals, focused primarily on major strikes which would cause severe economic hardship. The notion that strikes cause "national emergencies" was not new, or even limited to the twentieth century, but the phrase certainly had a special resonance so soon after the war. Other proposals had a broader focus. Prior to Taft-Hartley, the most popular was the Case Bill, which created strong penalties for violent or extortionate interferences with interstate commerce and provided penalties for wildcat strikers. Like the War Labor Disputes Act, it also provided a notice period prior to a strike or lockout, and a thirty-day period before a labor action could occur. The bill also included a number of provisions which would ultimately be included in Taft-Hartley. Thus, it excluded supervisors from the scope of the NLRA, banned boycotts, and, like the Repeal Bill, permitted suits against unions for breach of contract.

The Case Bill easily passed the House on February 7, 1946, by a 258 to 155 vote. Similar provisions were eventually drafted in the Senate, and that bill passed by a vote of 49 to 29 a few hours after Truman's speech requesting the power to end strikes in vital industries under government control. Truman, now apparently calmer, vetoed the measure on the grounds, in part, that it would force employees to work for private employers in peacetime. Truman's own proposal only referred to industries under government control. The veto was sustained in the House by only five votes.[46] Nevertheless, even before the congressional elections of 1946, the legislative forces concerned with restraining labor were clearly gaining momentum.

By 1947, therefore, Congress had come close to limiting the scope of the NLRA and providing for special measures in regard to "national emergency" disputes. The attack on the NLRA that began as early as 1939 would come to fruition after the Republican victories in the House and Senate in 1946, permitting the passage of Taft-Hartley over Truman's veto. The wartime experience was not mentioned in the debates and congressional reports on Taft-Hartley which, instead, stressed the ability of unions to disrupt the economy and to oppress individual workers. The statute's preamble, like that of the Wagner Act to which it was technically an amendment, would refer to the need to prevent interruptions in interstate commerce. The emphasis, however, was no longer the concern that the denial of worker rights led to economic disruption. Although stated in terms that applied literally to all participants, the clear message was that labor could not "engage in acts or practices which jeopardize the public health, safety, or interest."[47] Indeed, an addition to Title 1 of the NLRA noted that "certain practices by some labor organizations" have the effect of obstructing commerce "through strikes and other forms of industrial unrest or through concerted activities which impair the interest of the public in the free flow of such commerce."

Again, the strike, the key weapon protected by the Wagner Act, was now seen to be so destructive that it had to be restricted in certain situations. Yet, Taft-Hartley contained a fairly mild provision providing for a cooling-off period for national emergency strikes and did not restrict strikes for new agreements. Most of the act dealt with provisions which seemingly were unrelated to the postwar strike wave. For instance, some secondary boycotts were prohibited, as well as strikes caused by jurisdictional disputes. In addition, the labor injunction was reintroduced for certain union activity, the closed shop was outlawed although the parties could negotiate union shop clauses, union decertification votes were permitted, supervisors were excluded from the protections of the NLRA, union coercion of employees was prohibited, suits for breach of contract were permitted in federal courts, and individuals were given the right, of doubtful practical importance, to present grievances to their employer and have them resolved so long as the resolution was consistent with the collective agreement. As Joel Seidman noted in 1953, the act would likely have little impact on strong unions but would create severe organizational and economic problems for weaker unions and unorganized workers.[48]

The Taft-Hartley Act of 1947 was no doubt a product of the postwar strike wave. Typical was this statement in the House Report: "During the last few years the effects of industrial strife have at times brought our country to the brink of general economic paralysis."[49] Clearly, the statute would probably not have been passed or approved over Truman's veto, had not the Republicans taken control over both houses of Congress in 1946.[50] Republican strength in the House rose from 190 to 245 and in the Senate from 38 to 51. Yet, some of these gains were affected by the growing concerns about "Big Labor," reflected by the postwar strikes and, perhaps, by the decline in the public approval of unions caused by wartime strikes. But even more significantly, some of the contents of Taft-Hartley were developed throughout the wartime period and, indeed, even before Pearl Harbor.[51]

Thus, the tendency to focus exclusively upon the postwar strikes as the preeminent cause of the statute overlooks, first, the Republican congressional victories as a necessary condition, and, second, the fact that employers begin to seek ways to restrain unions soon after the NLRA was held constitutional. Importantly, the Taft-Hartley Act also reflected the fact that public sympathy with unions, strong in the late 1930s, had ended, altered by the anti-union sentiments caused (and whipped up) by wartime strikes.[52] The constant barrage of criticism during the war from the administration, the military, and the press had taken its toll, and labor's lessened public support was reflected in public opinion polls. It is certainly possible, of course, that negative public reaction against the postwar strikes alone could have led to calls for labor restrictions. After World War I, for example, nationwide strikes led to public opposition. The response then was not restrictive legislation but repression by the employers' open-shop drive.

Throughout World War II unions (and employers) repeatedly spoke of an early return to "free collective bargaining."[53] For instance, the AFL executive council declared in October 1945 that continuation of the War Labor Board would "inevitably bring about an increase in strikes and particularly the threat of strikes. It will force labor and management to go to the government for the solution of their disputes instead of finding their own solutions to the orderly and democratic processes of collective bargaining."[54]

Why would unions yearn for the end of wartime regulation under which they had prospered and grown so impressively? Doesn't "free" suggest returning unions to the jungle of the marketplace in which large employers generally have the upper hand? What unions apparently sought was primarily an end to their no-strike pledge and to controls such as the "Little Steel" formula that limited wage increases, which effectively restricted union bargaining power and hindered attempts to deal with wartime inflation. Nevertheless, most workers improved their living standards even though some failed to keep pace with the cost of living, which rose by one-third between January 1941 and July 1945. Basic wage rates in manufacturing increased 24 percent, less than the cost of living, and urban wage rates rose by 32 percent, while the weekly earnings of manufacturing employees rose a substantial 70 percent. Seidman noted that "those who had abundant opportunities for overtime earnings did best," and a "large number of workers obtained wage increases under other rules after they had exhausted the gains possible under the 'Little Steel' formula."[55]

Summarizing the War Labor Board's record in the *American Federationist* in April 1946, George Meany wrote that "There is a moral in this story of 'wage stabilization' by government that should appeal equally to American business and to American labor—keep politicians out of the field of labor relations."[56] The "Little Steel" formula weakened one of the reasons for unions and, in addition, subjected most workers to raises which were insufficient given wartime profits and inflation. Ironically, the return to "free" bargaining led to the postwar strikes and, ultimately, to Taft-Hartley. It should be noted that the CIO, more closely reliant and dependent upon government support than the AFL, viewed Truman's termination of the War Labor Board with greater trepidation. Murray, for instance, feared that a "vacuum" existed, and he correctly observed that the CIO would face vigorous resistance by employers in the postwar era.[57]

The "social compact" generally deemed created in the immediate postwar era was quite different than that envisioned by many labor leaders.[58] CIO leaders hoped to continue the pattern of bargaining existing during the war via a 1945 "Charter" with the liberal wing of capitalism. Management would, hopefully, support the policies of the Wagner Act, recognize unions and bargain in good faith, and adopt a high wage and employment strategy while unions would respect the "inherent right and responsibility of management to direct the operations of an enterprise."[59] The CIO, however, found that the liberal capitalists with which it sought to work were a small and, ultimately, uninfluential minority. For most of the leaders of heavy industry, state-managed bi- or tripartite arrangements had little appeal. In short, unions, now stronger than before the war and freed of wartime regulation, found themselves facing the same hostility that had always been present, and federal policy would never again effectively assert the primacy and value of strong, stable unions.

Notes

1. As Wayne Morse noted, the public members could also be expected to possess significant power. "Obviously, the public members hold the balance of power, and in the vast majority of instances, it is their vote that controls each decision of the Board" ("The National War Labor Board Puts Labor Law Theory into Practice," *Iowa Law Journal* 29 [1944]: 180). Yet, the board achieved unanimity in about 85 percent of its cases (ibid., 181).

2. Rosa Lee Swafford, "Wartime Record of Strikes and Lockouts, 1940–45," 79th Cong., 2d sess., 1946, S. Doc. 136, vii.

3. Alexander Frey, "Arbitration and the War Labor Board," *Iowa Law Review* 29 (1944): 202, 219.

4. William P. Witherow, "Labor Arbitration in Wartime," *Arbitration Journal* 6 (1942): 11–20.

5. See, generally, James Atleson, *Values and Assumptions in American Labor Law* (Amherst: University of Massachusetts, 1983).

6. Kevin Boyle, "Autoworkers at War: Patriotism and Protest in the American Automobile Industry, 1939–1945," in *Autowork*, ed. Robert Asher and Ronald Edsforth (Albany: State University of New York Press, 1995), 125.

7. House Committee on Military Affairs, Report No. 1183, 79th Cong., Oct. 30, 1945.

8. H.R. 1138, 79th Cong., 1st sess., Oct. 30, 1945.

9. This concept would eventually be adopted by the Supreme Court. See Local 174, Teamsters v. Lucas Flour, 369 U.S. 95 (1962).

10. Rep. Lane, Congressional Record, Oct. 1945, 79th Cong., 1st sess., 11834. See, also, Rep. Dirkson, ibid., 11825; Rep. Holifield, 11837.

11. As in section 301 of the Taft-Hartley Act of 1947, no mention is made of injunctions, suggesting strongly that neither bill was aimed at modifying the Norris-LaGuardia's ban on federal court injunctions. See James Atleson, "The Circle of *Boys Market:* A Comment on Judicial Inventiveness," *Industrial Relations Law Journal* 7 (1988): 88. Such a modification would be made by the Supreme Court in 1970, although the Court would attribute the change to congressional intent in 1947 (Boys Market, Inc. v. Retail Clerks Unions, Local 770, 398 U.S. 235 [1970]).

12. Boys Market, Inc. v. Retail Clerks Unions, Local 770, 398 U.S. 235 (1970).

13. Gateway Coal Co. v. United Mine Workers, 414 U.S. 368 (1970).

14. House Congressional Record, 71st Cong., 1st sess., Dec. 11, 1945, 11831.

15. Ibid., 11826.

16. Ibid., 11836.

17. The Norris-LaGuardia Act restricted the use of the injunctive power of fed-

eral courts in labor disputes. The act provided a broad definition of "labor dispute," seemingly including strikes in breach of collective agreements (47 Stat. 70 [1932], 29 U.S.C. 101–15 [1988]).

18. Joel Seidman, *American Labor from Defense to Reconversion* (Chicago: University of Chicago Press, 1953), 236.

19. Melvyn Dubofsky, *The State and Labor in Modern America* (Chapel Hill: University of North Carolina Press, 1994), 193–95.

20. See George Lipsitz, *Rainbow at Midnight: Labor and Culture in the 1940s* (Urbana: University of Illinois Press, 1994), 99–152; and Irving Richter, *Labor's Struggles, 1945–1950* (New York: Cambridge University Press, 1994), 47–67. Richter reports that there were 4,750 stoppages in 1945 and 4,985 in 1946. A total of 4.6 million workers were involved in strikes in 1946 (ibid., 48); see U.S. Department of Labor, "Postwar Stoppages Caused by Labor-Management Disputes," *Monthly Labor Review* 63 (Dec. 1946): 872–92. See also Stephen Amberg, *The Union Inspiration in American Politics* (Philadelphia: Temple University Press, 1944), 126–32.

21. Lipsitz, *Rainbow at Midnight*, 114.

22. Ibid. Over twenty-eight million man-days were lost during the last quarter of 1945, more than doubling the losses due to work stoppages during the wartime high in 1943. In the first two months of 1946 more time was lost due to strikes than the total lost during the entire war (R. Alton Lee, *Truman and Taft-Hartley: A Question of Mandate* [Lexington: University of Kentucky Press, 1966], 16).

23. David McCullough, *Truman* (New York: Simon & Schuster, 1992), 470. On Dec. 3, 1945, Truman asked Congress to enact legislation providing for fact-finding boards to make recommendations in labor conflicts. Labor viewed the proposal as troublesome, and management opposed governmental intrusion (Steven K. Ashby, "Shattered Dreams: The American Working Class and the Origins of the Cold War, 1945–1949" [Ph.D diss., University of Chicago, 1993], 236–37).

24. James Gross, *Broken Promise: The Subversion of U.S. Labor Relations Policy, 1947–1994* (Philadelphia: Temple University Press, 1995), 5.

25. Robert Zieger, *The CIO, 1935–1955* (Chapel Hill: University of North Carolina, 1995), 214.

26. McCullough, *Truman*, 475. See also, Zieger, *CIO, 1935–1955*, 221–22.

27. McCullough, *Truman*, 481.

28. Ibid., 494. The effect of current inflation was, however, one of the leading causes of the postwar strikes. See Ashby, "Shattered Dreams," 232–33.

29. McCullough, *Truman*, 494. See Ashby, "Shattered Dreams," 226–69.

30. McCullough, *Truman*, 495. See also Lee, *Truman and Taft-Hartley*, 35.

31. McCullough, *Truman*, 496.

32. Ibid., 498–500.

33. Ibid., 500–501.

34. Ibid., 501. See also Clark Clifford, *Counsel to the President* (New York: Random House, 1991), 87–92.

35. McCullough, *Truman*, 501.

36. Clifford, *Counsel to the President*, 89. See Ashby, "Shattered Dreams," 247–49. Clifford was specially stunned by Truman's statement that it was time to "hang a few traitors."

37. McCullough, *Truman*, 503; Lee, *Truman and Taft-Hartley*, 35–44.

38. McCullough, *Truman*, 504. Clifford claims he took out but Truman reinserted the first two "harsh" statements (Clark Clifford, "Serving the President—The War Years," *New Yorker*, Mar. 25, 1991, 56).

39. McCullough, *Truman*, 505. See also Seidman, *American Labor*, 236.

40. In fact, the heads of the Engineers and Trainmen had signed an agreement with the president's labor advisor, John Steelman, three minutes before Truman appeared for the congressional presentation. Wayne Morse, who later apologized for misperceiving the actual timing of events, caustically stated that "Truman had engaged in 'one of the cheapest exhibitions of ham acting I have ever seen'" (Seidman, *American Labor*, 236). See also Lee, *Truman and Taft-Hartley*, 36.

41. Richter, *Labor's Struggles*, 59–60. See also Clifford, *Counsel to the President*, 19–92; Lee, *Truman and Taft-Hartley*, 36–37.

42. Ashby, "Shattered Dreams," 265.

43. See Seidman, *American Labor*, 236–37.

44. Lee, *Truman and Taft-Hartley*, 38.

45. McCullough, *Truman*, 506. See also Steven Fraser, *Labor Will Rule: Sidney Hillman and the Rise of American Labor* (New York: Free Press, 1991), 567.

46. Seidman, *American Labor*, 256–57: Zieger, *CIO, 1935–1955*, 245–46: Lee, *Truman and Taft-Hartley*, 32–45. See also Harry A. Millis and Emily Clark Brown, *From the Wagner Act to Taft-Hartley* (Chicago: University of Chicago Press, 1950), 360–62.

47. Labor Management Relations Act, June 23, 1947, 61 Stat. 136.

48. Seidman, *American Labor*, 269.

49. National Labor Relations Board, *Legislative History of the Labor Management Relations Act of 1947* (Washington, D.C.: Government Printing Office, 1948), 294. The report highlighted the strikes and man-days lost due to strikes in 1945 and 1946. Similar statements are found in the Senate Report (ibid., 408).

50. Zieger, *CIO, 1935–1955*, 245.

51. See, e.g., Lee, *Truman and Taft-Hartley*, 30–31.

52. For a discussion of Taft-Hartley, see Christopher Tomlins, *The State and the Union: Labor Relations, Law and the Organized Labor Movement in America, 1880–1960* (New York: Cambridge University Press, 1985), 247–316; Richter, *Labor's Struggles*, 68–95; Gross, *Broken Promise*, 4–14; Lee, *Truman and Taft-Hartley*, 49–105; Millis and Brown, *From the Wagner Act to Taft-Hartley*, 395–468; Zieger, *CIO, 1935–1955*, 246–52; Dubofsky, *State and Labor*, 261–68.

53. See David Brody, "The New Deal and World War II," in *The New Deal: The National Level*, ed. John Braeman, Robert H. Bremner, and David Brody (Columbus: Ohio State University Press, 1975), 280.

54. Quoted in Seidman, *American Labor*, 218. The War Labor Board was ended by Executive Order 9672 (11 F.R. 221) which transferred its remaining duties, pri-

marily involving wage stabilization, to a new agency, the National Wage Stabilization Board.

55. Seidman, *American Labor,* 128–29.

56. Joseph C. Goulden, *Meany* (New York: Atheneum, 1972), 115.

57. Richter, *Labor's Struggles,* 19–29; Amberg, *Union Inspiration,* 15–16.

58. Alan Brinkley argues that the "possibility for transforming the industrial world did not disappear altogether during the war, the prospects for such a transformation—never great in the best of times—declined substantially." Prospects declined in part because of the resistance to labor gains and because many of labor's important liberal allies, and many of labor's own leaders, "were already gravitating in the early 1940s toward a new vision of political economy in which the idea of 'industrial democracy' played no important role."

Like American liberalism as a whole, the union movement was "beginning to shed its commitment to structural economic reforms and to a redistribution of wealth and power," and instead it was slowly accepting "that the key to a successful society was economic growth through high levels of consumption." Labor's agenda was becoming similar to that of the remainder of the New Deal, "a belief in the capacity of American abundance to smooth over questions of class and power by creating a nation of consumers" (Alan Brinkley, *The End of Reform: New Deal Liberalism in Recession and War* [New York: Alfred A. Knopf, 1995], 225–29).

59. *New York Times,* Mar. 29, 1945; CIO News, Apr. 1, 1945, cited in Nelson Lichtenstein, in *The Rise and Fall of the New Deal Order, 1930–1980,* ed. Steve Fraser and Gary Gerstle (Princeton, N.J.: Princeton University Press, 1989), 128–31. Richter, *Labor's Struggles,* 19–29; Amberg, *Union Inspiration,* 119.

The Contractualism of Labor Relations and the Postwar Consensus

As preceding chapters indicate, the wartime period involved great pressure on unions to suppress rank-and-file militance, at the very time when the expression of worker power theoretically could be highly effective. Maintenance of membership clauses, highly prized by unions unable to acquire more effective forms of union security, were granted by the WLB so long as unions avoided strikes. In addition, a variety of other benefits could be threatened by strikes which drew the ire of the WLB. Even aside from WLB pressures, public opinion and the constant threat of antilabor legislation led unions to suppress strikes, expel strike leaders, and to permit employers to discharge leaders without the protection of arbitration clauses.[1]

In conjunction with the WLB's encouragement of arbitration, a double bureaucratization occurred, institutionalizing both a contractual mode of dispute resolution and internal union control of the rank and file. The "workplace rule of law" evolved into "a pervasive method for containing shop-floor activism."[2] Lichtenstein notes that the constitutionalization of industrial jurisprudence poses a problem for labor for the "orderliness so imposed shifted the balance of class power into management's hands. Like the law of gravity, the collective power of workers is evident only when the everyday structures collapse. Only in the midst of 'disorder'—sit-down strikes and demonstrations and even the self-destructive wildcat stoppages—do workers have the leverage to focus capital's attention on the concessions necessary to restore a sense of predictability to the labor of their human assets." Yet the very same kinds of disorder that might strengthen the union on the shop floor might also threaten the institutional stability of the union itself.[3] Indeed, unions and employers had a common interest in designing a contractual relationship that restricted or at least contained rank-and-file militancy.[4] In the postwar period strong employers, especially in the auto industry, fought to regain control over production they believed had been lost during the war, and they were aided by grievance procedures which removed workplace issues from the immediate shop floor environment to be resolved at a later time, albeit often by elected officials.

The WLB's policies which promoted arbitration would be continued and eventually given judicial sanction.[5] The postwar law of collective bargaining reflected the notion that employment rights had become "legalized," that is, based solely on contract.[6] Eventually, the line between contract negotiation and administration would become clearly defined. The result is a system which makes autonomous, shop floor negotiation or action illegitimate. American employers, especially after the war, and often aided by unions, were able to place severe constraints upon shop floor activity, restraints which were ultimately reflected in legal rules.[7] As the next chapter indicates, workplace conflict did not disappear after the war and wildcats continued to occur, but the contractual system placed severe limits on the use of worker economic pressure at the point of production.

The president's labor-management conference met in November 1945, and agreed that grievances under existing collective agreements should be settled by voluntary arbitration rather than by strikes or lockouts. Such an accord was no doubt easily reached, as it was consistent with wartime labor policy and by war's end most collective agreements contained both arbitration provisions and no-strike clauses. The conference, however, also agreed that during bargaining for new agreements, strikes should be postponed until all peaceful procedures had been exhausted.[8] Thus, almost effortlessly, wartime policies were carried over to peacetime, and "industrial peace" became the critical principle of labor relations. Bargaining for new contracts and administration of existing agreements become separate spheres, with arbitration the preferred method of resolving disputes over interpretation of agreements.

The president's conference encountered strong disagreement, however, over the scope of legitimate union concerns and exclusive managerial prerogatives.[9] Despite the WLB's deference to managerial interests, management's primary concern was to regain those initiatives and prerogatives it believed had been eroded during the war. Wartime militance and collective bargaining developments had left business executives with "anxiety . . . about the future; uncertainty as to where the process will end; a fear that it will eventually culminate in such stringent impairment of management's freedom that it will not be able to do its job satisfactorily."[10] At the conference, however, unions refused to specify any functions that were exclusively managerial. The industry members, raised in an era of virtually unlimited managerial power, could only "conclude, therefore, that the labor members are convinced that the field of collective bargaining will, in all probability, continue to expand into the field of management. The only possible end of such a philosophy would be joint management of enterprise."[11]

Managerial prerogatives, such as the exclusive control over prices and financial records, were the focus of many of the postwar strikes, especially at General Motors, which ultimately would set the pattern of postwar bargaining. As Howell Harris has noted, the postwar strike period did not "raise fundamental questions about the very existence and essential practices of the labour movement—as, for example, the post–First World War strike wave had."[12] The workplace issues which had caused the wildcat actions of the war, as well as visions of union invasions into managerial prerogatives, would be jettisoned in favor of wage and fringe benefit increases in a troubling economic environment combined with managerial intransigence and power.[13] The issue of management prerogatives would nevertheless continue to the present day, and the WLB's protection of managerial interests would eventually be reflected in Supreme Court decisions.

In addition, collective agreements would make clear that self-help would not be permitted. In addition to no-strike clauses, employers demanded contractual provisions which would penalize wildcatters, forcing the UAW, for instance, to accept its own wartime policy which denied wildcatters the use of grievance procedures unless local unions undertook their defense. At Ford, the continuation of the union security clause seemed to be explicitly traded for such restrictions. Again, union security was used as a lever to force unions to police their membership. In December 1945, for instance, the UAW agreed with Ford that "any employee or employees found guilty of instigating, fomenting, or giving leadership to an unauthorized stoppage of work shall be subject to discharge."[14]

As during the war, therefore, unions would be responsible for controlling the rank and file. In November 1946, for instance, a steelworkers' local agreed to a "mutual responsibility clause" by which "the local union, any of its members, or the company" might be financially liable for the reasonable costs of "strike, work stoppages, or lockouts of any nature or condition" that might occur. Since the international or local could not be held responsible if it or a majority of its members did not participate in the strike, individual actors, presumably, could be found to violate the obligation. C. Wright Mills stated that the union's motive for accepting these provisions, strongly desired by employers, was the desire to continue union security provisions.[15] Thus, again, there seems to be a clear relationship between union security and strikes or union efforts to discipline unauthorized strikers.

By the war's end, or surely soon after, the rights of workers are seen as primarily based on contract, enforceable only through contractual dispute resolution procedures.[16] The legalization or contractualization of rights has great significance, for rights not in the collective agreement are considered to have no legitimate source. Union stewards and committeemen were now expected to process, at least to the final arbitration step, only those grievances supported by the language of the contract.[17] Under some agreements any dispute may be characterized as a "grievance," but only those claiming a violation of the contract could be pursued to arbitration. The approach parallels the WLB's view of the arbitration process.

The moral obligation to respect the agreement and not strike or refuse work orders during its term, of course, depends upon the determination of what has been agreed to in the first place.[18] Moreover, the range of bargaining is affected by the relative weakness of labor, for collective agreements reflect the existing balance—or imbalance—of power. The perceived power of employers which originally led to the passage of the NLRA has been altered but, perhaps, not significantly changed.[19] In addition, again following the lead of the WLB, the law generally confines the scope of mandatory bargaining to issues which do not invade the murky, never defined, zone of managerial prerogatives.[20] The current interest in worker participation schemes reflects, in part, the inability of collective bargaining to deal adequately with issues of personal integrity and the need for involvement in workplace decisions.

In the United States, the desire for "order" has been reflected both in arbitral decisions as well as in Supreme Court decisions which have expansively read arbitration clauses. The workplace, however, is often viewed as a place of disorder by many unions and employees, and rebellious actions such as wildcat strikes are often attempts to return to what workers believe was the previously shared understanding. The prohibition of self-help activities "restricts the union's power to challenge the frontiers of managerial control in the interests of maximizing 'efficiency.'"[21] This view of order is used to penalize unauthorized strikes and refusals to follow work orders as well as strikes over matters which could be arbitrated.

A UAW shop steward manual prepared in 1941 delineated the role of the steward or committeeman in representing workers in the workplace. The manual stressed the importance of the solid backing of the workforce in order to make the steward effective: "Unless he speaks for solidly organized workers, he [the steward] is as futile and helpless as the individual auto worker back in the days of the open shop." Since the steward both conducts negotiations and represents employees, "he is at once a diplomat negotiating with a foreign power and a general preparing his troops for possible conflict."[22] The language employs the language of wartime, but the handbook precisely sets out notions which would become commonplace in the postwar period. Thus, sources of worker rights were clearly limited as the contract was viewed as a "constitution governing union-management relationships" and the settlement of grievances under the contract is deemed the equivalent of an "industrial supreme court." The use of "governmental" metaphors to describe contractual dispute resolution would become commonplace after the war, and this early use of such terms, especially from a union, is especially noteworthy.

The handbook also cautioned stewards that although threats and "fist banging" might have been sufficient in 1937, the steward was now to act more like a diplomat, albeit a creative one. When "justifiable complaints" arise which are not clearly covered by collective agreement, stewards are admonished to go through the "contract with a fine-tooth comb to find some provision which will cover this particular situation." "Legitimate" or "justifiable" complaints should be handled because it will usually "be possible to find some clause of the contract which, with a little pulling and hauling, can be made to cover the situation." The manual, therefore, implicitly recognized some noncontractual sources of "legitimacy" with the contract serving only as a post-determination means of raising the issue.

Although the steward is admonished not to "sit on his hands and allow the company to break down union conditions," the requisite action was clearly to use the existing grievance process. Indeed, the manual stressed that the UAW was opposed to unauthorized strikes, which were viewed as "undemocratic." A strike by a small group could idle thousands of employees—"to give a minority such power is very opposite of democracy." Moreover, wildcat strikes would mean that the UAW "could not exist as a stable organization—could not prepare itself for meeting the tremendous problems that loom in the future of the industry." Thus, every steward and officer was "duty-bound to fight for the observance of the Constitution and Rulings of the International Executive Board for the elimination of all unauthorized stoppages and strikes."[23]

Aside from sticky questions of intra-union democracy, a prohibition on midterm strikes or worker refusals to follow work orders even in peacetime might legitimately be justified by the interest in maintaining orderly labor relations, but "order" is not a value-free concept. As Hyman and Brough slyly note, "Order looks rather different, depending as it were on which end of it one happens to be."[24] Moreover, not everyone benefits equally from any system of social order. As Katherine Stone has noted, "It is in disorder that workers experience and exercise their power in the production process. The entire history of the labor movement is a history of workers creating 'disorder'—strikes, disruptions of production, picketing—in order to achieve unionization and to better their working conditions. Like the law of gravity, the collective power of workers is only evident when the everyday structures collapse. Only in the midst of 'disorder' do workers have leverage to press for their demands."[25]

Management's desire for "order" is easily explained. An employer is relieved of ongoing bargaining during the term of a collective agreement, and it can treat labor matters as a fixed variable for the duration of the agreement. The "peace obligation," however, merely "relieves the symptoms of conflict; it does not cure the disease."[26] Dissatisfaction with workplace conditions can surface in other damaging ways, the application of sanctions for improper collective action can further upset morale, and sour relations can continue into subsequent bargaining situations, creating lawful strikes of longer duration.

Nevertheless, contractualism undoubtedly has considerable value to unions and workers as well as to employers. In a period of congressional and administration hostility to forceful union pressure, Steven Tolliday and Jonathan Zeitlin argue that U.S. unions successfully placed significant restrictions on managerial freedom especially in regard to discipline, seniority, and job classifications. Although these "rigidities" may have been tolerable or even advantageous to management at first, "rapid shifts in markets and technology have transformed them into major obstacles to the introduction of more flexible systems of work assignments needed to meet international competition, and contractual job controls have accordingly become a major stimulus to management's quest for a union free environment."[27] Moreover, unionized employers recently have vigorously attempted to reduce the number of job classifications, even though many job ladders were initially introduced to advance morale and individual initiative by the appearance of upward mobility.[28]

Tolliday and Zeitlin, therefore, challenge the notion that the "workplace rule of law" was as severe a constraint on shop floor struggles for job control as some legal and historical scholars have recently claimed, and they highlight a variety of situations in which grievance procedures were used either substantively or procedurally to gain influence over discipline, crew size, production standards, and discipline.[29] Thus, they believe that the "contractual system of collective bargaining emerging from the Second World War substantially constrained management's freedom to deploy labor and impose arbitrary discipline in the enterprise through the elaboration of seniority systems, grievance procedures, and binding arbitration."[30] Tolliday and Zeitlin concede, however, that these systems did not play as great a role in the postwar period as one might have expected, and managerial strength and opposition cannot be seen as the full explanation. Their conclusion that part of the answer lies in the unions' bargaining strategy mirrors one of the conclusions reached here. Workplace or control issues tended to play a decidedly secondary role in the postwar period to company-specific or industry-wide concerns over "broader" issues such as pensions and wage protection. Indeed, local grievances "were a potential threat to effective central union control." Thus, the UAW "tended to press its locals to curtail their strikes over production standards to avoid interfering with national negotiations."[31]

The centralization of union authority was matched and perhaps motivated in part by that of employers, and some of the bureaucratization on each side was no doubt due to the actions of the perceived adversary. For employers, however, an effect of the combination of increasing union organization and labor shortages may have been the creation of specialized personnel or employment departments which, in turn, led to greater centralization and bureaucratization of hiring, firing, and disciplinary determinations. "Personnel practices that became more widely used during this time included job analysis and evaluation, seniority provisions, employment testing, and performance rating systems."[32] Unions actually encouraged such formalization by, first, intentionally forcing employers to clarify policies for the purposes of collective bargaining and arbitration and, second, unintentionally inducing management to hire and train specialists to deal with bargaining, contract application, and grievance administration.[33]

Yet, something is lost, as C. Wright Mills noted in 1948, when business and labor cooperate, because such cooperation means the partial integration of company and union bureaucracies.

> The integration of union with plant means that the union takes over much of the company's personnel work, becomes the disciplining agent of the rank and file within the rules set up by the joint committee.
> . . . The Union bureaucracy stands between the company bureaucracy and the rank and file of the workers, operating as a shock absorber for both. The more responsible the union is, the more this is so. Responsibility is held for the contract signed with the company; to uphold this contract the union must

often exert pressure upon the workers. Discipline must be brought to bear if unauthorized leaders call unauthorized strikes. The rank-and-file leaders of the union, the shop stewards, operating as whips within the plant, become rank and file bureaucrats of the labor leadership. As foremen are responsible to the company hierarchy, so shop stewards are primarily answerable to the labor union hierarchy, rather than to the rank and file who elect them.[34]

CIO unions experienced rapid growth in bureaucracy during the war partly due to union leaders' fears for the stability of their organizations. Union leaders depended more and more directly on governmental support for their organization, for example, through maintenance of membership clauses and other benefits ordered by the WLB. At the same time, the growing militancy of workers in defense industries, reflected in increasing incidents of strikes, often forced union leaders to turn to the government for assistance in either placating or disciplining their rank and file. Moreover, the government increasingly insisted that the unions discipline their own workforce in order to receive benefits from the government or to avoid restrictive legislation.

It must also be stressed that union leaders shared the government's view of the war, its aims, and, thus, the need for labor peace. In addition, it is easy to forget that patriotic attitudes could have been as highly influential as more cynical, instrumental goals. The earlier world war as well as the Korean war reveal, moreover, the extent to which groups, often first- and second-generation American, felt the need to demonstrate patriotism—even superpatriotism. It may be nevertheless legitimate to argue that unions became less the representatives of the workers than the conduit of government policy to their members, a top-down form of organization that characterized much of postwar unionism.

CIO leaders constantly reiterated their no-strike pledge and drew into a close alliance with Roosevelt and the Democratic Party. Unionists were also obliged to enforce the no-strike pledge, and they defended the authority of the WLB even when to do so meant siding with the government against their own discontented memberships. In the short run, this policy may have served to alienate many CIO members from their union. In the long run, the increasingly severe methods used by CIO leaders to end wildcat strikes or punish strikers and to discipline oppositional factions drove from the ranks of their organization many of their most militant and dedicated local elements, just the type of ardent unionists that were in conspicuously short supply when the labor movement was confronted in postwar years with a strong anti-union backlash.

It has become common to fault unions in the 1940s and 1950s for failing to understand the cost of clamping down on workplace militance, but this is an exceedingly complex issue.[35] All institutions desire to control the direction of their organizations, and CIO unions began to restrict local strikes, and especially sit-down strikes, as early as 1938.[36] Centralization and bureaucratization, therefore, began before the war and may have occurred in any event.[37]

Collective bargaining itself is a conservative, not revolutionary, process, and new kinds of leaders, as Golden and Ruttenberg suggested, often arose once bargaining relationships were established. After all, many union leaders believed as early as 1940 in a bureaucratized dispute-resolution process involving a controlled and disciplined workforce. It would be wrong to see these beliefs as simply foisted upon unions by a co-optive-minded government or by academic pluralists.

The new CIO unions, for instance, strongly desired some level of institutional security, a rational desire in the circumstances, especially given wartime limitations on the scope of union bargaining.[38] Unions believed that without the right to strike and with the confining "Little Steel" formula, it would be difficult to build or keep membership loyalty.[39] Indeed, the CIO may never have been in a position to consider how it might control events. It was continually reminded of its weak status and, thus, it is not surprising that it should become primarily a reactive movement. Indeed, unions have historically been reactive and dependent institutions, generally having little control over the conditions which make their growth or stability possible.

Unions realized that the war created great opportunities but also great dangers, and threats were clear as early as the mobilization period. Employers, the military, the press, and members of Congress complained that strikes were sabotaging national defense. Here was a golden opportunity for unions to organize, but if they continued to take advantage of the wartime situation, they risked provoking a government reaction that could destroy or at least lessen all they had accomplished. FDR's use of troops in June 1941 to break an unauthorized strike at the North American Aviation Plant in Los Angeles highlighted the risks. So, the argument often goes, an arrangement was made. For the duration of the war unions would accept government-imposed limits on wage increases and in exchange receive maintenance of membership clauses or the continuation of union or closed shops that they may have secured through collective bargaining. This would protect unions from fluctuating membership and from having to impose dues picket lines.[40]

Many argue that this was a Faustian bargain, whereby the CIO gave up its self-reliance and militance for resources and influence that only subverted the movement's original vision. Although wartime strikes should not be romanticized, there is an aspect we should not forget to stress. Whatever the overall judgment about these strikes, many focused upon the immediate details of the work process itself, concerns often neglected by collective bargaining, especially when done on a multiplant basis. In short, these strikes reflected a battle for control "at the point of production." This battle was not ignored by employers, who in many cases were fighting a two-front war as supervisors were joining unions in increasing numbers.[41]

The wartime controls and the loss of the right to strike necessarily forced most unions to lessen reliance upon collective bargaining to determine working conditions and, instead, to depend on decisions of federal agencies. This especially drew the CIO into its well-recognized close relationship with the federal government and an even tighter connection with the Democratic Party.[42] "[The] institutional growth and security had its price. The conditions of wartime unionism accelerated those bureaucratic tendencies that had been inherent in the new CIO unions from their moment of birth." Thus, with membership growing and with their eyes focused on Washington, "union leaders felt less keenly the pressures generated within their own organizations, the grievances and complaints that inevitably arose out of the changing wartime work environment."[43]

Despite, or perhaps because of, ties to the dominant political party of the era, the constant fear of hostile labor legislation induced unions to strongly oppose wildcat strikes. Without the use of the strike or its threat during the life of a collective agreement, workplace disputes could only be resolved by contractual grievance procedures or, failing that, by some sort of government aid or intervention. Language in collective agreements and union constitutions merged to make this point clear. This was, obviously, the view of proper labor legislation held by the WLB and many union officials, at least at the national level.

Union suppression of rank-and-file militance cannot be viewed simply as a reaction to the WLB's carrot and stick policies, the needs of political coalitions, the real fear of hostile legislation, or to the natural tendencies of organizational leaders to assert control, although these are clearly relevant. Leaders no doubt believed that control *was* important for patriotic as well as institutional reasons,[44] and union tendencies toward bureaucracy, order, and control merged with patriotic concerns in creating the motivation to control the rank and file.

In addition, it is possible that a tendency toward centralization of power (the "iron law of oligarchy," if you will) merged with union leaders' vision of an efficient, smooth running industrial relationship. Management pressured union leaders to be "responsible," surely encouraging prewar tendencies in many unions to dampen rank-and-file militance after recognition. The war period clearly pressured leaders, especially secondary ones, to choose between supporting workers during a propitious time for the exercise of labor power or, alternatively, complying with the desires of top union leadership for "responsibility" and protection of the new unions. CIO officials, after all, knew that it was the war which had made them grow and at least appear to be strong. The union security policies of the WLB had solidified the CIO and guaranteed a much-needed financial base. The War Labor Board also forced recalcitrant employers to recognize unions and awarded benefits that unions might not have been able to win on their own. In many cases, it is doubtful that such benefits could have been gained via bargaining, despite the enhanced power of scarce labor in the wartime period. Unions had, after all, surrendered their most significant weapon.

Yet, union bureaucratization cannot be said to have been caused by the new workers, governmental regulation, or the no-strike pledge, as some unions, primarily the United Packinghouse Workers, emerged "from the war with the authority and independence of local unions fully intact."[45] Unlike other international unions, Roger Horowitz has noted, UPWA's local unions remained powerful, giving them substantial influence over the international. Significantly, local power was strengthened by informal agreements with supervisors on workplace issues at a time when the international was having little success with the virulently anti-union packing companies.[46] In addition, Horowitz argues that the union's use, rather than suppression, of militant shop floor tactics "familiarized new packinghouse workers in the union's pre-war techniques of exercising power at the point of production, and equipped them to utilize similar methods after 1945."[47] Local union power remained intact, and the union did not significantly suppress expressions of workplace militancy. The UPWA's experience, therefore, contrasts markedly with most of the other unions previously studied during the war.

"Industrial democracy," as vague as the phrase may be, does not necessarily mean that semi-autonomous work groups can freely assert power at the point of production especially in opposition to negotiated terms. Instead, the dominant view, generally supported by union leaders, was that democracy meant that workplace conflict would be resolved in a representative fashion, with representatives primarily serving the interests, rather than the desires, of workers.[48] At the same time, the language of "industrial democracy" was used by the WLB and many labor scholars not to describe the extent of worker influence or role in enterprise but, instead, to describe the union measures to contain militance and encourage smooth production.[49]

The approach is reflected by the views of many of the postwar pluralists and, as already noted, in the substance of the legal rules.[50] Such a concern is natural in wartime, and the preeminent value of production becomes entrenched after the war in, for instance, NLRA decisions.[51]

Collective bargaining itself is an integrative, albeit formally adversarial, institution, a fact recognized long ago by some manufacturers. William Phaler, for instance, the president of the National Founders' Association, which had reached a national agreement with the Iron Molders in 1899, promoted bargaining and arbitration of wage disputes. In encouraging union recognition and bargaining, he noted that union officers were often more "responsible" than their members. More importantly, the scope of bargaining had to be rigidly controlled so that recognition of unions led only to the making of agreements—unions could not insist upon "the right to enforce rules and methods in the conduct of business without the consent or cooperation of the employer."[52] Employers should trade union recognition and bargaining, therefore, for union attempts to regulate production.

As set forth by members of the National Civic Federation and others, agreements would be scrupulously maintained and strikes in violation of agreement would not be permitted.[53] Bargaining, moreover, would be limited to particular, targeted employers, and unions would have to suppress sympathy strikes, an expression of class solidarity employers believed inconsistent with bargaining. Indeed, many union activists prior to World War I understood that "collective bargaining was not synonymous [with] workers' control."[54]

David Montgomery has expressed perhaps the strongest critique of collective bargaining. He argues that collective agreements "replaced unions' reliance on the courage and commitment of individual members to enforce their rules and standards with institutionalized authority."[55] Contracts shifted "the locus of decisionmaking within unions . . . toward the officers and away from membership meetings." Nevertheless, the periodic "coverage and commitment" of union members is necessary under a collective bargaining regime to formalize contractualized rights, rights which once inserted into contracts can be enforced without additional sacrifice. The reliance on forms of representative democracy does not create nondemocracy but constitutes a different form than worker control. The use of "institutionalized authority" would become the dominant postwar model, supported both by union officials and the legal structure. It is this system that, although only called into being by the perception of workers that adversarial relations exist, is often currently seen as overly "adversarial."

Arbitration is but a part, albeit a necessary part, of collective bargaining, and it is no more confining than bargaining itself. Bargaining is affected by relative economic power, and imbalances will be reflected in the resulting contracts which arbitrators are called upon to interpret. Perhaps the most important legacy of the WLB is its view that the scope of bargaining must exclude a vaguely defined zone of critical managerial decisions, especially capital mobility. After the war, such assumptions became part of the underlying basis of the NLRA, rendering unions impotent when faced with the torrent of plant removals and closures in the 1970s and 1980s.

Many of the foci of current labor criticism are institutions, practices, and concerns that actually originated in or were strongly supported by labor. Arbitration and collective bargaining were union goals—and successes— concurrent with a dampening of the power of the rank and file to directly influence their workplace. Similarly, even before the war some union leaders sought government involvement in labor-management relations and the bonding of unions to government.[56]

In addition, collective bargaining in its decentralized American form has left the labor movement particularly dependent upon the success and viability of certain mass production industries. Their decline weakens the institutional strength of unions, but the unions' history provided no way to question current institutional arrangements or to propose transformative ideas.[57]

Collective bargaining, as it comes to be viewed and practiced, involves a recognition of hierarchy and control even if arbitration were not present. Moreover, union structure tends to match that of the employers they must deal with—locally based bargaining would appear to make little sense in relation to a large, multiplant firm with, typically, centralized labor policymaking.

Despite the negative aspects of contractualism and legalization, there were also clear advantages for unions. Guarantees written into contracts cannot easily be taken away, and this became the basis for one of the unions' most powerful arguments for representative status.[58] Unions also gained recognitional rights, and provisions recognizing seniority and limiting disciplinary power to "just cause" became common elements of collective bargaining.

Finally, the institutionalization of routine collective bargaining, in light of labor's relative weakness, should not be slighted as a significant union victory.[59] Any analysis of labor's condition in the postwar period must take into account the vulnerable status of unions at war's end. Unions had grown from 10.5 million to 14.5 million, but wartime strikes, especially those of the UMW, had eroded public support.[60] The extent of that erosion would be reflected in the national elections of 1946 and the Taft-Hartley Act of 1947. Capital received enormous credit for the production miracle of the war years, but unions had been forced to restrict internally the militance upon which their growth and vitality had been based.

The choice of union structure, between the centralized and bureaucratized form most common to us and locally based or rank-and-file-empowered models, is more complex than simply a choice between local autonomy and centralization, because the American structure is in many ways more decentralized than systems elsewhere. A number of unions in the United States, like the autoworkers and steelworkers, began to allow local bargaining as an outgrowth of the rank-and-file militancy of the late 1960s and 1970s. Local bargaining, combined with local administration of collective agreements, distinguishes American unions from those in some European countries traditionally content to bargain at industrial levels. Another way to phrase the issue is to ask why local or workers' control models are not found in the industrial world.

Moreover, local or rank-and-file control is not problem free. When American locals decide to go their own way, many sympathetically view such independent action as heroic. The best example may be Local P-9, the Hormel local of the United Food and Commercial Workers in Austin, Minnesota, which refused to go along with the decision of the international (and other locals in the bargaining chain) to accept a particular degree of concessions.[61] Many observers were rightly moved by the courage and creativity of these workers. But how does one view the current competition among UAW locals, offering concessions in order to be the home of new technologies or product lines instead of having them locate at the home of a sister local? These situations raise difficult questions concerning what we mean by democracy in the labor movement, where it should be located, and surely remind us that local autonomy may not always be the most socially advantageous alternative.

During World War II, labor was put in the position of suppressing rank-and-file militancy and wildcat strikes. These workplace actions are often seen as an alternative to centralized unions with bureaucratic dispute resolution systems. Indeed, these kinds of disruptive tactics were instrumental in the formation of certain unions in the 1930s. Yet, the combination of wartime pressures and legal regulation helped induce unions to centralize and to restrict autonomous worker power. Even though I stress the costs as well as the gains of centralization and contractualization, the picture is not one-sided. To take one example from the same period, it was the consistent pressure from the UAW headquarters during the war that lessened, or even suppressed, locally based resistance to the introduction of black and, to a lesser degree, women workers.

Concededly, the centralized mode of union organization, at this historical vantage point, has serious problems both economically and politically. The Democratic Party, the longtime recipient of worker dues and political action, now treats labor as a "special interest," akin to toothpaste manufacturers and beer distributors. Although a considerable amount of worker protective legislation has been passed in recent years, it is unlikely that legislation supportive of collective worker efforts will be enacted, no matter how many centers of governmental power are controlled by the Democratic Party. Unions, therefore, are faced with the necessity of turning to their own resources, rather than the support of the federal government, a reliance for which they are out of practice.[62]

Moreover, the centralized model has not proved to be responsive to the internationalization of capital, often referred to currently as "globalization." More and more workers are employed in firms that are organized in the conglomerate or multinational form. The conglomerate form, which may or may not be transnational, is the result of corporate diversification in which the parent acquires firms that produce unrelated goods or services. Conglomerates can cross-subsidize funds between unrelated parts of the business and thus reduce the effect of a strike in any one part of the enterprise. Multinational or transnational firms, on the other hand, can easily move capital and facilities around the world, or what is often just as effective, threaten to do so.[63] Yet, the internationalization and greater mobility of capital leads to questions about the viability of any model of worker organization. There have been some noteworthy examples of worker-community efforts to avert plant shutdowns,[64] but local efforts, no matter how widespread, are insufficient if the need is to coordinate joint efforts in more than one country.

It is possible to conceive of unions that are centralized in order to better carry out the functions most suited to this type of organization and, at the same time, are organized so as to grant greater participatory rights to workers at the workplace. This concern is not new, but the debate over the related question of the proper scope of internal union democracy suggests that there would be great resistance to the notion. Most union officials and some industrial scholars are suspicious or skeptical about individual rights in unions or union democracy, and courts, not the usual suspect when it comes to rounding up union supporters, have often tended to choose institutional interests over the interests of individual or groups of workers, especially when union and employer interests merge. The action of these courts are consistent with the largest body of opinion in law and other academic circles who argue that union democracy and individual rights in, for instance, contract administration, are inconsistent with a union's representative role and institutionally damaging. In short, they see unions as do union officers, as dependent organizations, which they surely are, which require order, hierarchy, and bureaucracy. A more sympathetic way to put this would be to say that democracy resides in representative institutions.

The workers who challenge local policies or expenditures, engage in wildcat strikes, or start rank-and-file movements within their unions are not "trouble makers" or malcontents. Instead, they are often among the strongest supporters of the idea of collective organization and action. They simply see no inconsistency between, say, freedom of speech or association within unions and the strength and viability of those organizations. Indeed, when complaints about unions are voiced by union members, they are often focused upon the lack of participation allowed and compassion demonstrated by admittedly often harassed and overworked local union leaders.

In the two most recent periods of worker militancy, during World War II and the late 1960s and 1970s, workers were seen as almost "pre-industrial," needing to be socialized into the modern factory as well as union structures, and, in the latter case, as too young to understand the realities and requirements of industrial relations. Despite the existence of real grievances, the workers were expected only to exercise the more passive virtue of discipline. Instead of characterizing the workers' actions as a valid form of industrial democracy, union officials viewed the workers' militancy at most as only a form of "primitive democracy," or, in Harry Shulman's words, "jungle warfare."

There is no question that workers often desire more participation at work, a desire employers have recently been able to harness more effectively than unions, and they often wish more participatory opportunities within their unions. Unions in which members believe they have a significant degree of participation tend to receive the highest degree of loyalty and support. The task is to devise systems that would offer greater democratic participation within the union as well as at the workplace.

Notes

1. See, generally, Nelson Lichtenstein, *Labor's War at Home: The CIO in World War II* (New York: Cambridge University Press, 1982), 71–81, 194–201.

2. David Brody, *Workers in Industrial America* (New York: Oxford University Press, 1980), 201. Brody, however, has recently argued that workplace contractualism was both beneficial and inevitable. See David Brody, *In Labor's Cause* (New York: Oxford University Press, 1993), 221–50. Cheryl Cothran's study of carpenters and bus driv-

ers in Arizona indicates that the wartime period had significant effects, especially on collective bargaining structures and relationships. Cothran argues that rulings and directives of the War Labor Board, the office of defense transportation, and other wartime agencies strengthened the hand of management at corporations like Greyhound in relation to worker discipline. The War Labor Board supported employer disciplinary systems and efforts by management to strengthen control of the workforce by specifying workshop rules. The War Labor Board concluded that a company did not have to secure the union's consent to its discipline program (Cheryl C. Cothran, "Arizona Workers and World War II: Wartime Collective Bargaining and Post-War Problems for Carpenters and Bus Drivers, 1940–1960" [Ph.D. diss., University of California at Davis, 1992], 143).

Cothran argues that the issue of workplace authority "might have turned out differently had the war and the WLB not intervened at a critical juncture in the early development of union-management bargaining relations. Scarce workers had great power during the war and might have prospered without the intervention and industry of the War Labor Board and federal agencies that decided issues in favor of managerial control to get a peaceful workplace and high production" (ibid., 144). In construction, as well, the insistence of federal agencies on the peaceful resolution of disputes slowly led the carpenters' union to surrender its tradition of workplace action and eventually rely upon contractual procedures (Lichtenstein, *Labor's War at Home*, 306–8).

3. Nelson Lichtenstein, *Walter Reuther: The Most Dangerous Man in Detroit* (Urbana: University of Illinois Press, 1997; originally published as *The Most Dangerous Man in Detroit: Walter Reuther and the Fate of American Labor* [New York: Basic Books, 1995]), 153.

4. See David Brody, "The New Deal and World War II," in *The New Deal: The National Level*, ed. John Braeman, Robert H. Bremner and David Brody (Columbus: Ohio State University Press, 1975), 204–8.

5. James Atleson, "Wartime Labor Regulation, the Industrial Pluralists, and the Law of Collective Bargaining," in *Industrial Democracy: The Ambiguous Promise*, ed. Nelson Lichtenstein and Howell John Harris (New York: Cambridge University Press, 1993). Katherine Van Wezel Stone, "The Post-War Paradigm in American Labor Law," *Yale Law Journal* 90 (1981): 1509.

6. Lichtenstein argues that the transformation of the foreman in the postwar auto industry into a grievance "buck-passer" had the concurrent effect of lessening the independent role of the steward, helping to "accelerate the demise of a vigorous steward system and transform local union officials into virtual contract policemen" ("Conflict over Workers' Control: The Automobile Industry in World War II," in *Working-Class America: Essays on Labor, Community, and Industrial Society*, ed. Michael Frisch and Daniel Walkowitz [Urbana: University of Illinois Press, 1983], 302). This would seem to be more likely the result of the arbitration system than of management strategy. The situation might also have been different in other industries, especially in single plant situations.

7. James Atleson, *Values and Assumptions in American Labor Law* (Amherst: Uni-

versity of Massachusetts Press, 1983), chap. 4; Atleson, "Wartime Labor Regulation."
Tamara Lothian has argued that the "contractualist," as opposed to the "corporatist," form of legal structure encourages "a moderate, intermediate level of union
activism" which "discourages the escalation of economistic militancy into an all-out
struggle over the basic institutional arrangements of society and the state" ("The
Political Consequences of the Labor Law Regimes: The Contractualist and Corporatist Models Compared," *Cardozo Law Review* 7 [1986]: 1001, 1034).

8. See Joel Seidman, *American Labor from Defense to Reconversion* (Chicago: Uni-
versity of Chicago Press, 1953), 222–24; Lichtenstein, *Labor's War at Home*, 220–21;
Steven Fraser, *Labor Will Rule: Sidney Hillman and the Rise of American Labor* (New
York: Free Press, 1991), 564–65.

9. For an insider's account of the conference and then current divisions within
labor, see Irving Richter, *Labor's Struggles, 1945–1950* (New York: Cambridge University Press, 1994), 34–46.

10. E. Wight Bakke, *Mutual Survival: The Goal of Unions and Management* (New
York: Harper, 1946), 7.

11. National Labor Management Conference, Nov. 5–30, 1945, Division of Labor Standards, U.S. Dept. of Labor, Bull. 77, 1946, 53–56.

12. Howell John Harris, "The Snares of Liberalism? Politicians, Bureaucrats, and
the Shaping of Federal Labour Relations Policy in the United States, ca. 1915–47,"
in *Shop Bargaining and the State*, ed. Steven Tolliday and Jonathan Zeitlin (New York:
Cambridge University Press, 1987), 149.

13. Brody, *Workers in Industrial America*, chap. 5; Lichtenstein, *Labor's War at Home*,
226.

14. See C. Wright Mills, *The New Men of Power: America's Labor Leaders* (New York:
Harcourt, Brace and Company, 1948), 224–25.

15. Ibid., 225.

16. See Brody, "New Deal and World War II," 201–3.

17. Individual unionists who balked at this approach were in for trouble. Lichtenstein notes the case of Stanley Orlosky, a long-term union steelworker, who criticized SWOC leaders for not aggressively pursuing grievances. He was expelled from
the union. Golden and Ruttenberg dryly conclude: "Stanley's leadership was essential to the establishment of the union against bitter resistance, but after it had been
fully accepted by management, such leadership was a handicap to the development
of cooperative, union-management relations." See Lichtenstein, *Labor's War at Home*,
23; Clinton Golden and Harold Ruttenberg, *The Dynamics of Industrial Democracy*
(New York: Harper and Bros., 1942), 60–61; Richard Lester, *As Unions Mature*
(Princeton, N.J.: Princeton University Press, 1958).

18. A "peace obligation" is created by law in Canada which bars strikes during
the term of a collective agreement. Despite the legal obligation, it is common to refer
to the obligation as part of the contractual understanding reached by the parties
(Geoffrey England, "Some Thoughts on the Peace Obligations," *Ottawa Law Review*
12 [1980]: 521, 602–5).

19. Moreover, some hard-fought victories had unintended consequences. As Ronald Schatz has noted, one of the great achievements of the union movements in the 1930s and 1940s was the inclusion of seniority provisions in collective bargaining agreements which were designed to limit the discretion of foremen and personnel departments. Although the foremen's power had been reduced by the 1930s, they could still distribute overtime and make recommendations regarding selection of employees for promotion or layoffs. These powers were attacked by the union movement by demanding distribution of work opportunities on the basis of seniority. As Schatz notes, however, "it is important to recognize that the application of seniority rights tended to brake the movement towards solidarity among workers as well as accelerate it. This contradictory tendency is inherent in the nature of seniority provisions which, like the constitutional amendments which compose the bill of rights, are collective agreements which protect individual liberties" (*The Electrical Workers* [Urbana: University of Illinois Press, 1983], 117). See also Ronald Schatz, "Union Pioneers," *Journal of American History* 66 (Dec. 1979): 586–602. "Although seniority rights result from collective action, workers often looked upon their seniority as an individual right representing the investment of employment security which has been acquired by length of service." Indeed, seniority rights do not create jobs but merely allocate employment opportunities among employees. Thus, seniority is often viewed as a means to distinguish between and compete with other workers (Schatz, *Electrical Workers*, 117–18).

20. Atleson, *Values and Assumptions*, chaps. 7 and 9; Atleson, "Wartime Labor Regulation."

21. See England, "Some Thoughts on the Peace Obligations," 521, 594.

22. UAW Education Dept., "How to Win for the Union: A Discussion for UAW Stewards and Committeemen," 1941, partially reprinted in *Major Problems in the History of American Workers*, ed. Eileen Boris and Nelson Lichtenstein (Lexington, Mass.: D. C. Heath & Co., 1991), 369.

23. Monsanto Chemical Co., 2 WLR 479 (1942). In addition, the WLB could withdraw seniority rights, shift premiums, and other benefits or even deny the union's status as representative. Joshua Freeman, "Delivering the Goods: Industrial Unionism during World War II," *Labor History* 19 (Fall 1978). For a similar view of the changing nature of the union in the workplace see Golden and Ruttenberg, *Dynamics of Industrial Democracy*.

24. Richard Hyman and Ian Brough, *Social Values in Industrial Relations: A Study in Fairness and Inequity* (Oxford: Blackwell, 1975), 177.

25. Stone, "Post-War Paradigm," 1565.

26. England, "Some Thoughts on the Peace Obligation," 592.

27. Steven Tolliday and Jonathan Zeitlin, "Shop Floor Bargaining, Contract Unionism, and Job Control: An Anglo-American Comparison," in *On the Line: Essays in the History of Auto Work*, ed. Nelson Lichtenstein and Steven Meyer (Urbana: University of Illinois Press, 1989), 222–23, 229–36. See also Neil Chamberlain, *The Union Challenge to Management Control* (New York: Harper & Bros., 1948).

28. Katherine Van Wezel Stone, "The Origins of Job Structures in the Steel Industry," *Review of Radical Political Economics* 6 (Summer 1974): 113–73; Charles E. Heckscher, *The New Unionism: Employee Involvement in the Changing Corporation* (New York: Basic Books, 1988), 58–59.

29. Tolliday and Zeitlin, "Shop Floor Bargaining," 232–35.

30. Ibid., 235. Indeed, it is clear that management believed that unions had seriously eroded managerial power (Chamberlain, *Union Challenge to Management*, chap. 4; Bakke, *Mutual Survival*, chap. 1.

31. Tolliday and Zeitlin, "Shop Floor Bargaining," 235.

32. Thomas Kochan, Harry Katz, and Richard McKersie, *The Transformation of American Industrial Relations* (New York: Basic Books, 1986), 35.

33. Sanford Jacoby, *Employing Bureaucracy: Managers, Unions, and the Transformation of Work in American Industry* (New York: Columbia University Press, 1985), 269–74; John Dunlop and Charles A. Myers, "The Industrial Relations Function in Management: Some Views on its Organization Status," *Personnel* 31 (1955): 406–12.

34. Mills, *New Men of Power*, 224.

35. See Freeman, "Delivering the Goods," 572.

36. Atleson, *Values and Assumptions*, 46–47.

37. Lester, *As Unions Mature*. AFL unions from the beginning jealously guarded their autonomy from encroachment by either their international union or the national federation, yet by early in the twentieth century "growth of international control at the expense of local union independence was a marked trend." As Karen Anderson noted, "Because local control of the strike weapon often led to financial disaster and inhibited the strategic use of concerted efforts to attain union demands, the internationals were called upon for centralized strike funds, which in turn led to their control over strike activities. Such control, moreover, enabled the international to determine the terms of the local collective agreement" ("Trusteeship Imbroglio," *Yale Law Journal* 71 [1962]: 1460, 1462–63).

38. No-strike clauses begin to appear in agreements during the war, and their obvious application is against individuals or wildcatters. After the war, these provisions, if traded for anything, are exchanged for union security clauses (not arbitration clauses).

39. A local union leader at U.S. Steel's Kearney, N.J., shipyards complained to the WLB that members felt that "There is no further need to pay dues to the union or to remain in a union because everything was going to be provided . . . by the government anyhow." Quoted in Nelson Lichtenstein, "Ambiguous Legacy: The Union Security Problem during World War II," *Labor History* 18 (Spring 1977): 228.

40. Maurice Isserman in his *Nation* review of Lichtenstein's *Labor's War at Home* notes that the secondary leaders, who are the heroes for Lichtenstein, may not have survived if CIO leaders had not been so accommodating to the powers in Washington. Isserman reminds us that in World War I governmental repression and vigilante attacks demolished the Wobblies when they refused to get in step with the war effort. Would the CIO would have fared any better if it had repudiated the no-strike

pledge? He notes, however, that one can deplore the consequences of actions such as the no-strike pledge while still recognizing its necessity, although he also recognizes that "short-term expediency has a nasty habit of turning into long-term structural restraints" ("Holding the Fort," *Nation*, Apr. 30, 1983, 548).

41. See Virginia Seitz, "Legal, Legislative and Managerial Responses to the Organization of Supervisory Employees in the 1940s," *American Journal of Legal History* 28 (Jan. 1984). Because of both battles, management began after 1945 to carefully separate supervisors from the rank and file by, for instance, creating separate dress standards, parking lots, and eating places. These actions suggested that foremen and workers belong in separate classes. The rhetoric is clearly seen in the House Report in 1947 which, like the subsequently enacted Taft-Hartley, excluded supervisors from the protections of the NLRA: "It seems wrong, and it is wrong, to subject people of this kind, who have demonstrated their initiative, their ambition and their ability to get ahead, to the leveling processes of seniority, uniformity and standardization that the Supreme Court recognizes as being the fundamental principles of unions" (H.R. Rep. no. 245, 80th Cong., 1st sess. [1947], 15–17, cited in NLRB v. Bell Aerospace, 416 U.S. 267 n. 47 [1974]).

42. Freeman, "Delivering the Goods," 570.

43. Lichtenstein, *Labor's War at Home*, 81.

44. The policies of the WLB cannot, however, be dismissed. Lichtenstein, for instance, argues that CIO leaders did not relish using their contractual or institutional power to fine or fire wildcatters, but the discipline imposed was motivated by the threat of WLB sanction (Lichtenstein, "Ambiguous Legacy," 237). Union leaders often invoked the threat of discharge to get wildcatters to return to work. However, the volume of wildcat activity during the war, as well as after, suggests that union threats did not always have a deterrent effect and may not have been taken seriously by the rank and file. The arbitration records, at Ford, for instance, involve attempts by the UAW to reinstate fired wildcatters.

45. Roger Horowitz, *"Negro and White, Unite and Fight!" A Social History of Industrial Unionism in Meatpacking, 1930–90* (Urbana: University of Illinois Press, 1997), 151.

46. Ibid., 150.

47. Ibid., 151.

48. UAW Education Dept., "How to Win for the Union," 369.

49. Indeed, "democracy" to the WLB had little to do with a union's responsiveness to members or the degree of relative democracy within unions. Thus, the WLB could characterize the autocratic, top-down Steelworkers' union as one of the most "democratic responsible and efficient unions," as opposed to the "coercive" UMW, because of their different degrees of cooperation with the government (Lichtenstein, "Ambiguous Legacy," 235–36).

50. See chap. 4, above. See also Atleson, "Wartime Labor Regulation."

51. See Atleson, *Values and Assumptions*.

52. Quoted in David Montgomery, *The Fall of the House of Labor* (New York: Cambridge University Press, 1987), 262.

53. Ibid., 263.

54. David Montgomery, "Industrial Democracy or Democracy in Industry?: The Theory and Practice of the Labor Movement, 1870–1925," in *Industrial Democracy in America: The Ambiguous Promise*, ed. Nelson Lichtenstein and Howell John Harris (New York: Cambridge University Press, 1993), 20–42.

55. Ibid., 31.

56. The most common, and perhaps critical, examples were Sidney Hillman and Philip Murray. Ronald Schatz, "Battling over Government's Role," in *Forging a Union of Steel*, ed. Paul Clark, Peter Gottlieb, and Donald Kennedy (Ithaca, N.Y.: ILR Press, 1987), 87; Steven Fraser, "Dress Rehearsal for the New Deal: Shop-Floor Insurgents, Political Elites, Amalgamated Clothing Workers," in *Working-Class America: Essays in Labor, Community, and American Society*, ed. Michael Frisch and Daniel Walkowitz (Urbana: University of Illinois Press, 1983); David Montgomery, *Workers' Control in America* (New York: Cambridge University Press, 1979); Christopher Tomlins, *The State and the Unions, 1880–1960* (New York: Cambridge University Press, 1985), 71–77.

57. Lothian, "Political Consequences," 1057.

58. Indeed, the stress on securing contracts by AFL unions in the 1880s and 1890s may have been a response to the unilateral reduction in wages by employers that sparked many of the massive strikes of the post–Civil War period.

59. Harris, "Snares of Liberalism?" 172.

60. The public's concern with man-days lost due to strikes has historically overshadowed other causes of lost time, especially losses due to injuries. In 1943, 274 million man-days of work were lost because of industrial accidents, compared with the 13.5 million lost by strikes. As Edwin Witte noted about 1946, "which was by far the year of greatest strike losses, reaching the immense total of 116,000,000 man-days lost through strikes, the total of man-days directly lost because of industrial accidents was 260,000,000 days—and this was a normal year for industrial accidents" ("The Future of Labor Arbitration—A Challenge," in *The Profession of Labor Arbitration, Selected Papers from the First Seven Annual Meetings of the National Academy of Arbitrators, 1948–1954* [Washington, D.C.: Bureau of National Affairs, 1957], 2).

61. See Peter Rachleff, "Supporting the Hormel Strikes," in *Building Bridges: The Emerging Grassroots Coalition of Labor and Community*, ed. Jeremy Brecher and Tim Costello (New York: Monthly Review Press, 1990), 57–69.

62. James Atleson, "The Prospects for Labor Law Reform," *Policy Studies Journal* 18 (Winter 1989–90): 364.

63. See generally James Atleson, "Reflections on Labor, Power, and Society," *Maryland Law Review* 44 (1985): 841.

64. See Eric Marin, "Labor-Community Coalitions as a Tactic for Labor Insurgency," in *Building Bridges: The Emerging Grassroots Coalition of Labor and Community*, ed. Jeremy Brecher and Tim Costello (New York: Monthly Review Press, 1990), 113–32.

The Limits of Mature Collective Bargaining

Sociological and industrial relations analyses of labor relations in the postwar period stressed the move from violent class conflict to "mature" industrial relations, which often referred now to the existence of "well developed institutions" and a "web of rules." It was thought that open warfare or wildcat strikes, as during the wartime period, had given way to a more regulated, governmental system with orderly procedures and binding precedents.[1] The pluralists defined the move from what Harry Shulman referred to as "jungle warfare" to bureaucratization and routinization as an advance and a significant move toward mature industrial relations.[2] In the midst of postwar prosperity, analysts found a new consensus, arguably missing the significance of the 1947 Taft-Hartley Act.[3] Problems would arise, but it was confidently believed that systems could be devised to contain and resolve them. These views fit neatly with views of pluralism after the war and the concurrent search for peaceful ways to resolve international conflicts.

Although there has been no sustained decline in the number of strikes during the century, until recently perhaps, Daniel Bell in 1960 assumed a decline in the incidence of strikes, and Arthur Ross and Paul Hartman wrote that strikes had withered away.[4] Presumably, they meant that the nature of strike had changed: strikes "settled down to a few standard formats, acquired their own jurisprudence, became objects of official statistics."[5] Regularity and process had won the battle, and the pluralists who had been schooled during their wartime governmental experience held unchallengeable sway over academic thought.

Below the surface, however, these generalizations made in the 1960s were more problematic. Indeed, the postwar 1940s and 1950s included many wildcats, again raising doubts about the "new" worker explanation often given for wartime strikes.[6] As during the war, wildcat strikes occurred in the auto industry in the late 1940s and 1950s. Thus, "workers in the auto industries staged constant wildcat strikes during the five-year life of the 1950 contract."[7] This phenomena was generally unstudied and little reported, only to become national news in the more restless militancy of the late 1960s and 1970s.

As during the war, militancy in this period seemed to be primarily centered in the auto industry, and the incidence of wildcat activity did not wane with the institution of bureaucratic grievance procedures or with the consolidation of power in the UAW.[8] Between 1960 and 1969 grievances more than doubled at General Motors while absenteeism markedly increased. Unauthorized or wildcat strikes at GM quadrupled during the period and, by the end of the 1960s, man-days of production lost due to stoppages increased to five times the level of the 1950s.[9] At the time of the Lordstown strike in 1972, twenty thousand grievances were awaiting resolution at the plant.[10] In the steel industry as well, written grievances doubled between 1963 and 1972, and in the mining industry a stalled or clogged grievance process led to hundreds of wildcat strikes between 1950 and 1975.[11]

After the relatively quiescent 1950s, electoral opposition to union leadership became the norm in the 1960s. Another manifestation of rank-and-file militancy was a number of refusals to ratify agreements, exceeding one thousand in 1967.[12] Analysts had great difficulty explaining the continuation of workplace dissent, especially wildcat strikes, in a period in which mature dispute resolution supposedly was the norm. It was, moreover, increasingly difficult in the postwar period to target new, "pre-industrial" workers as the cause of industrial civil disobedience.

The undercurrent of dissatisfaction would receive public notice after 1968, when for nine successive years the number of work stoppages would consistently top five thousand.[13] In 1970, for instance, there were fifty-seven hundred work stoppages, the highest number in over ten years. In addition, rank-and-file movements began among organized teamsters, autoworkers, and steelworkers.[14]

One example of the widespread militancy in the workplace was the rise of militant organizations of African American workers such as the Dodge Revolutionary Union Movement (DRUM), the League of Revolutionary Black Workers, and similar groups within the UAW. These organizations, stimulated by the Black Power movement, focused on racism within the union as well as on the part of their employers. Interestingly, however, these organizations also complained of the increase in the pace of work and the resulting rise in workplace accidents.[15]

As Heather Ann Thompson notes, the demographic profile of American autoworkers changed dramatically in urban centers like Detroit between 1950 and 1980. The "dramatic influx of northern blacks into industrial employment . . . recomposed the automotive working class" and "brought to the shop floor new traditions and expectations that were alien to the leaders of the autoworkers union." The militant response to perceived racism should not have been a surprise to UAW officials, especially given the union's role in seeking equal employment during the war. Yet, Thompson argues that the UAW was not well prepared "for the racial and ideological reconfiguration of its memberships. Conflict was almost assured when a growing number of black autoworkers found racism in the auto industry intolerable, while the union leaders saw the issue of racism as preeminently a moral and political issue, not a *labor* issue." Although the power and influence of the young black militants had waned by the early 1970s, the militant propensity of many shop floor workers did not. As during the war, immediate protests began to seem more rational and effective than awaiting resolution via the often slow union grievance procedures.[16]

Thompson's analysis of the situation at Chrysler in the 1960s is especially valuable. Although the demand for automobiles was rising, Chrysler refused to hire additional workers, relying upon mandatory overtime, which soon became the norm rather than the exception. Chrysler workers in Detroit were put on six- and seven-day work schedules with little opportunity for relief, and even twelve-hour shifts were not uncommon. Moreover, Chrysler's old plants created health and safety hazards for workers, a problem which grew as production quotas were raised. Thus, "A combination of Chrysler's inadequate internal investment, managerial aggressiveness and inhuman work hours contributed to dangerous working conditions, which in turn made the company a tinder box waiting to explode by the late 1960s."[17]

Young black workers at Chrysler had the least seniority and generally had the undesirable, low paying, and dangerous jobs. As plant working conditions deteriorated, confrontations arose, especially between black workers and their white foremen. As a result, the grievance machinery during the 1960s became clogged with complaints about overtime, safety violations, and alleged racist practices within the plant. Black workers believed the union to be ineffective in responding to the shop floor problems. As a response, in the late 1960s a number of dissident caucuses sprang up in the UAW.[18] These movements reflected more widespread dissension for, in addition to the black groups, white skilled workers began the United National Caucus (UNC) and multiracial groups were also organized.

These groups advocated reform of the union in order to make it "more democratic and responsive to the needs of the membership."[19] Organizations like DRUM rejected the grievance procedure as too slow to deal with critical workplace concerns and also too narrow to include their growing concern with in-plant racism. DRUM attempted to educate and mobilize workers in light of revolutionary black nationalist ideals. DRUM was eventually isolated, Thompson argues, partly due to their resistance to broadening their social base, but also through discharge.[20] By 1973, although DRUM was basically inactive, violence and wildcat strikes were still common in many of the big three plants, and most severe in Chrysler plants.

The tenor of the times is revealed in the August 14, 1973, wildcat at Chrysler's Mack Stamping Plant. The Mack plant, according to Thompson, was notorious for its dangerous working conditions, reflected by the high number of work-related accidents. The ostensible cause of the wildcat was a speedup and complaints about other working conditions, but UAW officials charged that the strike was the work of outsiders with various political aims. UAW vice president Douglas Fraser, for instance, informed reporters that "the agitators . . . represent only a very tiny fraction of the total Chrysler workers in the Detroit area and I advocate a policy of no surrender." Fraser later stated that "it was agreed that these people were not going to take our union and the plants where we represent workers."[21]

The multiracial United Justice Caucus, however, rejected the union leaders' charge and argued that the struggle was caused by "the anger of Mack workers and our unsafe and inhumane working conditions." The strike was not caused by a few troublemakers or outsiders, they claimed, but the workers' enemies were "trying to hide the fact that it was a genuine workers' protest against the unbearable conditions in the plant."[22] The conflict, therefore, was viewed either as a legitimate response to real grievances or, alternatively, the work of a small number of malcontents.

The UAW's leadership continued to deny that the wildcat was a genuine workers' protest. Police routed fourteen workers in the cafeteria, but the wildcat continued. Emil Mazey, no doubt reflecting the view of top UAW officials, stated that the workers were "a bunch of punks, [and] we are not going to let them destroy everything that we've built."[23] In an extraordinary move, union officials from the Detroit area marched to each of the four Mack gates in groups of 250, and within minutes of their arrival the Mack wildcat ended. As Thompson ruefully asserts, "the union had mobilized a thousand officials to keep its critics at bay. With this ominous display of force, the union had no trouble in crushing the Mack wildcat. None of the safety issues of the plant were resolved, and only 35 of the 75 UAW workers who had been fired were ever reinstated."[24]

It is unclear to what extent workers at Mack and elsewhere were influenced by the concurrent militancy of antiwar activists, although in many workplaces the average age of workers was quite low.[25] For instance, restlessness was clearly reflected by the young workforce, averaging twenty-five years of age, at GM's Lordstown plant.[26] As Staughton and Alice Lynd stated in *Rank and File:* "[workers] are beginning to question foremen and corporation executives whom they did not elect, and union officials who have lost touch with their membership. The group which took part in the cultural revolution of the 1960s are moving into the work place. Blacks have become a majority in many automobile plants and steel mills, students have graduated and taken jobs in white-color bureaucracies, veterans are returning from Vietnam, women have gone out to work in larger numbers than at any time since World War II. A new restlessness is evident."[27]

By extrapolating from a number of studies (while noting problems with BLS data), Rick Fantasia, in his rich sociological study of workplace conflict, found that wildcats in this period were a substantial phenomena and that "there have been more illegal, unplanned wildcat strikes than well-planned, routinized, union approved strikes."[28] Fantasia explains the significance of wildcats in this way:

> Instead of the rule-governance signaling an end to industrial conflict, as many sociologists had supposed, the contract itself has been used to delay, postpone, and nullify resolution of the issues. A contract signifies acceptance of its terms by management and union, but the workers themselves often demonstrate their dissatisfaction with bureaucratization by adopting forms of protest and struggle that circumvent and actually confront these established procedures. The failure of the union leadership to deal aggressively with grievances has been shown to be an important factor in precipitating wildcat strikes. Moreover, because the union leaders are bound to the terms of the agreement they have signed, they often become the disciplinarians of the rank-and-file membership. In response to this routinization, the wildcat strike has played a prominent role in postwar industrial relations, providing an important extra-institutional mechanism for the maintenance and pursuit of workers' rights. Essentially the wildcat strike has represented a critique by action of the postwar social contract, a sporadically employed, but nevertheless clearly stated, opposition by workers to the controlled contract unionism of their leaders and employers.[29]

In 1973, at the height of this new period of worker militance in the United States, I noted that "The common tendency to view social conflict as necessarily dysfunctional and to assume that basic conflicts of interests do not exist between employees and employers has caused many commentators to wax rhapsodically about collective bargaining and, more recently, arbitration. The stress on institutional structures and organizational interests tends to obfuscate their impact on individual employees—especially when an employee's interest conflicts with the joint interests of union and employer."[30]

The factory is a social system composed of the relations existing among the people making up the organization. As the subsequent discussion of conditions at GM's Lordstown plant will demonstrate, these parts are mutually dependent; a change in one part or set of relations can be expected to have repercussions in other parts of the organization. Changes in relative economic status or changes in the work flow tend to upset traditional relations and to cause disequilibrium. Workers often view institutional changes from a personal standpoint, and it is difficult to deflect an emotional response into the cooler confines of the rationalized grievance system. This is especially true if employees feel the need to immediately defend their dignity or status.

When systems experience disorganization, responses will be made which reduce the resultant tensions. Alvin Gouldner calls these responses to tension "defenses." In a sense, all reactions to disorganization can be considered "defensive," even though they may appear to be aggressive to an outsider.[31] Workers respond in a variety of ways, and the wildcat strike is only one response, although often the most dramatic. Unauthorized strikes clearly conflict with pluralist notions about mature collective bargaining. Thus, a number of objections have been raised, and these actions have often been mischaracterized. For instance, the wildcat's appearance of spontaneity, suggesting unplanned or thoughtless action, often stems from a failure to note the presence of other "defense" mechanisms such as an increased accident rate, work spoilage, labor turnover, psychosomatic illness, and a lower grade of productivity. Anxieties, grievances, and vague resentments regarding the type of work, supervision, or technical change seem to accumulate and reinforce one another. Even defensive action, however, can create tensions for others, and the workers' defensive wildcat strike is obviously a threat to management. A defense mechanism, then, is not merely a response to disorganization, since it may itself induce a disorganization pattern.[32]

Employees generally view management as the primary source of disorder in their working life.[33] From the workers' standpoint, many sources of instability in the work environment either are a consequence of managerial action or are perceived as originating with management.[34] After all, the clearest expression of "order" in an enterprise is the typical standardization of work routines, job description and progression, and wage determination. Technical change or changes in work schedules originate with management; less obvious changes like a shift in managerial attitude toward employees may have an equally disordering impact on workers. Workers, then, tend to view industrial disorder or change as having an immediate, personal impact upon them. Management, on the other hand, tends to view disorder as having an institutional impact.[35] This split in perception may explain management's inability to recognize, as well as to predict and avoid, wildcat strikes and other forms of disruptive behavior. Although arbitration and joint consultation may aid in the prevention of open labor conflict, structural devices will not entirely eliminate fundamental value conflicts between employers and workers.

Economic struggle between organized employees and employers is based on their particular roles and positions in an economic system. Employees will end their strike and reach an accommodation if they are persuaded it is wise to do so. Since the aim of workers is normally to achieve concrete results rather than to merely express diffuse hostility, such conflict is "realistic" in nature.[36] Significantly, conflict is less likely to occur when alternative means are available to reach the goal. This suggests that wildcats often occur whenever employees perceive that normal channels and procedures, whether contractual or informal, are inadequate. Their behavior cannot, therefore, be deemed irrational. Yet, industrial sociology often ignores the existence of realistic conflict or its function. Instead, conflictual behavior is almost exclusively considered to be nonrealistic, that is, behavior which is not occasioned by the conflicting ends of the antagonists but, rather, by the need for tension release of one of them.

It is important to note that workers who might be considered "troublemakers," or who (in the eyes of management) file "unjustified" grievances, may be very productive and efficient workers. High grievance activity and concerted activity may well be correlated with high productivity. Thus, a high grievance group which is most vocal in criticizing management may also be highly productive, comprised of active and loyal members of the union rather than malcontents or "pre-industrial" workers. Although work groups may perceive the need to pressure management or the union with possible short-run production blockages, over a long period of time these groups may tend to be above average in effort expended on managerial goals.[37]

The one element commonly believed to be characteristic of wildcat strikes is their unplanned or spontaneous nature.[38] There is, however, no uniformity on this question. Some union officials and most managers assert that wildcat strikes are planned, while some managers and a good many union officials believe that most wildcat strikes are spontaneous. In any event,

"it appears that in almost all instances a wildcat strike presupposes communication and a degree of informal group organization. The strike has some
kind of leadership, usually from within the group, and the leaders do some
kind of planning, if only but a few hours or minutes ahead."[39]

Concern over the spontaneity of wildcat strikes results in efforts to specify
the meaning of such strikes in terms of their attributes rather than their
causes. Participants tend to stress the way in which such strikes originate and
de-emphasize the things the strikes were about.[40] Labor unions are eager to
stress the spontaneity of wildcat strikes, in order to prevent any charge that
union officials participated in the instigation or planning of the strike. The
union is understandably concerned with maintaining its responsible image
and protecting its treasury from a damage action in cases where a contractual "no strike" clause is present. For management, designating wildcats as
spontaneous and irrational absolves them from the necessity of searching for
causes. The law often tends to reflect these views, assuming that wildcat
activity must be irrational, rejecting a detailed investigation into the conflict
situation.

The spontaneity claim, then, very often reflects the frame of reference
or the conceptual scheme of the speaker; the implicit assumption is that
spontaneous actions are irrational. Yet, whether planned or not, wildcat
strikes are neither irrational to the employees who are involved, nor are they
irrational to anyone doubting the efficiency or fairness of alternative channels of communication. Workers are no doubt aware of the serious risks of
such action, and they realize the potential costs to themselves even if they
are not discharged.

Nevertheless, many observers seem genuinely impressed by the seeming lack of correlation between the precipitating cause of an unauthorized
strike and the level of agitation necessary to precipitate such drastic action.[41]
However, the immediate cause of a militant outbreak often merely marks
the culminating point of a series of troubles, most of which in themselves
may appear to be of trifling importance, and the cumulative effect of these
concerns leads to overt conflict. Incentives to respond aggressively accumulate over time; one does not necessarily respond immediately by attacking
every barrier encountered.[42] The tension generated, however, does not dis-
sipate but is maintained and may intensify a later response, perhaps to an
entirely unrelated situation.[43]

The nature of industrial discipline is a common cause of dissatisfaction,
reflected in the studies of wartime and postwar work stoppages. Most workers are on the receiving end of a tightly drawn command system with little
opportunity to make decisions or to exercise responsibility. Social relations

in the workplace—whether or not workers can interact, form friendship groups on the job, provide support to each other under trying circumstances—may likewise prove an important source of frustration (as well as satisfaction). As noted in earlier chapters, many of these frustrations do not or, perhaps, cannot become formally translated into bargaining issues, and they remain sources of discontent.

Like unions, workers may engage in behavior which entails costs to themselves as well as to their employer. The costs are not always easily "economically" justified by the issues at stake. Although some worker frustrations may stem from the character of modern industrial society, many stem directly from the work environment. Mass production techniques, for example, with their fractionating, routinizing, and simplifying of work result in serious frustrations for large numbers of employees.[44] The employee is assigned a specific task and is generally not free to modify the job to better accommodate his or her abilities or style, for there is usually a job description to which the worker must conform. Neither the design of the machinery, even though it may present a danger of physical injury, nor the speed of the equipment is generally a matter of worker discretion, and the location of tools and work materials is generally rigidly proscribed. An overemphasis on the economic aspects of work life obscures the realization that rational protest may arise from these noneconomic causes.[45]

Of course, one of the primary purposes of regulating conflict through collective bargaining and arbitration procedures was to avoid sharper forms of social antagonism, and, indeed, mediation and arbitration might well reduce the incidence and violence of conflict. Arbitration, however, will not be more acceptable to potential strikers than the use of the strike weapon unless they initially accept certain normative prerequisites. In general, American workers do not always support the basic presupposition necessary for the creation of industrial peace—an acceptance in principle of the broad outlines of the existing industrial order and faith in collective bargaining.

To be totally acceptable, the arbitration system must appear to be fair, efficient, and reasonably representative. Fairness implies a reasonable allocation of gains and losses and is also affected by efficiency and responsible representation. Employees often do not believe it is fair to wait an undue length of time to learn the result of a grievance, and efficiency refers to the speed at which decisions are communicated to interested parties. Representativeness implies that the parties have someone to plead their case who understands the issues involved and is trustworthy.

A study of a large heavy-industry company, employing over ten thousand production and maintenance workers, found that the use of the grievance system and work stoppages were directly, rather than inversely, related.[46] Work stoppages seemed to be more of a problem in high grievance rate areas than in low grievance rate areas of the same firm. This suggests that even employees who are attuned to the grievance system tend to engage in work stoppages. Although grievances and work stoppages stemmed from dissatisfaction, and some work groups were obviously more unhappy than others, the key finding was that the grievance system was *not* necessarily used as an alternative to self-help. Moreover, employees who filed grievances tended to be active in the union as well. In the high grievance rate areas, stoppages tended to last longer, involved more employees, and resulted in a greater loss of production than stoppages in a low rate area, suggesting a higher level of cohesion in these groups.[47] Indeed, the majority of grievances in high grievance areas tended to be group grievances, whereas group grievances in low rate areas represented less than half of the total. Aggrieved workers tended to be younger than comparable nonaggrieved workers. Given the decreasing average age in many sectors of the workforce in the early 1970s, one might expect a heavier use of grievance systems, and perhaps greater use of wildcat strikes as well. Indeed, the two are related in another important way: as the number of grievances mount and time lag increases, frustration grows.

Indeed, as the subsequent discussion of GM's Lordstown facility will reveal, a commonly recognized cause of wildcat walkouts is the actual or perceived breakdown of regular grievance procedures. When complaints remain unanswered, grievances unsettled, and common problems unsolved, tension tends to build up.[48] Unadjusted grievances tend to be magnified in geometric proportion to the time elapsing from their initiation, and delay is usually given as one of the most potent precipitating causes of unofficial strikes. Although some delay is unavoidable and hasty decisions would not create confidence, delay does generate suspicion. As a foreman explained: "When the company acts slowly in handling grievances, the men get impatient and tired. They begin to talk about closing up the shop, and if they do not go that far you will still know about it."[49]

Concededly, delay in the grievance system may be partially the result of excessive or tactical use of the grievance mechanism. Supervisors may find it easiest to simply pass issues on, particularly if their decisions have been frequently reversed by the company's industrial relations department in the past. This adds to the flood of paperwork in the grievance channels. An industrial relations staff, ironically, does not always contribute to peaceful settlement: it may avoid its responsibility to decide against line supervisors and send troublesome cases to arbitration, thereby unduly delaying grievance settlement; it may interpret an agreement so strictly as to scare the line supervisors away from shop settlement and choke off the quick, informal negotiations that dispose of most shop problems; and it may simply be careless and let grievances pile up unattended.

Unions too may be at fault, either through indifference or inattention or through the employment of grievances for political ends. An ambitious steward may be tempted to demonstrate his militancy by pushing every problem to the point of arbitration. Weak union representatives may be unwilling to turn down weak or even worthless grievances, just as management may feel it must support its supervisors.[50]

If expectations are denied or frustrated or the workers feel that arbitrary methods have replaced the traditional system for maintaining their rights, they may feel they must publicize the neglect of their problems and protest the failure of the grievance system by invoking their only effective weapon—the disruption of work and production.[51] Peaceful processing of grievances makes sense to workers only as long as it assures them that they will be promptly compensated for any wrong incurred. If they file grievances and nothing occurs, they may conclude that management has unilaterally rejected the mutually agreed upon terms and conditions of employment.

Thus a walkout, slowdown, or other disruptive tactic may be used to protest a breakdown of judicial and administrative procedures. In fact, employees often argue that they resort to disruptive tactics only to support the grievance system and its full and efficient use. The argument is not necessarily disingenuous, for conflict may well lead to corrections in the grievance procedure. As James Kuhn has noted: "When a grievance is not being processed in good faith, it is sometimes necessary for the workers to take forceful action and assert their rights by work stoppages so that management will know that the existing conditions are intolerable."[52] Yet, delay in grievance processing may not be the prime cause of employee tension, which generally stems from the work environment itself.[53] That system, after all, is an objective, rational target, while the actual source of workplace frustration may be unknown or difficult to express.

An understanding of wildcat strikes does not, however, justify their existence. A significant and meaningful institutional objection is the one traditionally made—that wildcat strikes interfere with the administration of collective bargaining by the parties to the agreement. Thus, as the strike at Chrysler's Mack plant reveals, unions typically view the concerted activity of work groups as attempts to destroy the representative status of the union and perhaps the collective bargaining structure itself. This view, however, sometimes masks an attempt to turn political problems into problems of administration. Leaders of unofficial strikes tend to be described, and dismissed, as mere "agitators" or "troublemakers," thus eliminating the need to search for root causes of the conflict.

Concededly, wildcat strikes often cause serious problems for union administrations, and formal union leaders often have actually lost control.[54] "The network of informal relations which enable union officers to achieve advantageous settlements of grievances, even when these are not fully justified, by the contract, are based on the officers' ability to provide unimpeded production as a quid pro quo. If they cannot, their bargaining power is diminished."[55] Moreover management tends to characterize the membership's failure to conform to procedure legally established by their leaders and often ratified by the members themselves as "irresponsible."[56] An unauthorized walkout then may convince an industrial relations director not only that the union is unable to control its own members but also that the union membership lacks sufficient self-control to follow procedures which its own representative joined in establishing.[57]

The notion of union "responsibility," of course, reflects the view that employees and employers have congruent interests. The goals of union leaders and workers often seem to mirror those of the enterprise—they are, for instance, interested in production and labor peace. Support of these norms, however, may be based more on concerns that happen to coincide; seeming congruence of interests lacks the foundation of shared mores and social bonds. Informal leaders, on the other hand, often have goals which are clearly incongruent. Their goals are then more personal and often anti-organizational, and they tend to lead when their interests diverge from institutional concerns. Indeed, the worker's perception that the union and employer share mutual interests may lead to the type of frustration which can erupt in unauthorized strikes.

Mutual institutional interests of unions and employees are reflected in the tendency on the part of union and management to exploit the advantages of more centralized arrangements for bargaining and contract administration. This upward shift in the locus of decision making can make it more difficult for top officials to remain sufficiently aware of local or departmental problems and grievances. If grievances accumulate, a situation often found in wartime defense plants, the workplace can become explosive. Perhaps more importantly, the distance between people in the chain of authority may lead to differing views on the importance of a grievance, either because the officials take a "broader" or "more objective" view or simply because officials underestimate the critical nature of the dispute.

Disorder plays a definite role in industrial relations. Every enterprise has a structure and a pattern of expected behavior that governs the actions of each participant. Yet, disorder is not a stranger; indeed, disorder in industry is a device for resolving conflicts. Despite the urging of some sociologists and industrial relations writers, the conflicts of interest between employees and employers have not been eliminated nor are they likely to be.[58] Industrial order in the individual firm represents a delicate balance of numerous factors, many of which, like a change in the market for goods and services, availability of raw materials or parts, availability of credit, or special crises, are external to the firm. The typical response to unbalancing influences is internal accommodation and adjustment to these influences. Considering the relationship between management and its employees, however, management typically views its function as that of directing and controlling the workforce. This gives us a key to understanding the special significance that management attaches to disordering influences originating in the workforce.[59]

LORDSTOWN AND THE DISCOVERY
OF THE UNHAPPY WORKER

The more theoretical ideas discussed in the previous section help explain the militance of workers in the late 1960s and 1970s, a period which provides an interesting comparison and contrast to the wartime period. The best-known dispute of the period was the highly publicized three-week authorized strike in 1972 at General Motors new assembly plant in Lordstown, Ohio. GM's "super plant" was designed as a response to low-priced imports, and General Motors attempted to significantly alter both technology and product, and to increase its control of labor. The factory at Lordstown, opened in 1966, was intended to be the most modern and most automated assembly plant ever built. Although "there were automated welders in the body shop, computerized systems of determining options, assembly line adjustments of the height at which operations were performed, automated windshield installers and many other technical advances," David Moberg has noted that the plant was basically a "mechanized" rather than an automated operation, and the new technology actually represented a small part of the overall costs.[60] The critical fact, however, is that the facility was designed to produce Chevrolet Vegas at the then unheard of rate of one hundred cars per hour, almost double the speed at most plants. GM believed that the simplified Vega justified the reduction in the timing of most jobs from sixty seconds to thirty to forty seconds. Alvin Anderson, head of General Motors Assembly Division's (GMAD) new management team at Lordstown, acknowledged that the one-hundred-per-hour speed was a "miscalculation," but only because the machinery, not the workers, was "overtaxed."[61]

Problems grew when the initial excitement of a new project faded and work became extraordinarily intense. Workers objected to the new speed but seemed initially more concerned by the layoff of seven to eight hundred workers (GM claimed only 350), which, they believed, unfairly increased the workload of those who remained.[62] The response, according to GM, was increased sabotage, absenteeism, and turnover. GM conceded that since GMAD had taken over production management, "extensive disciplinary layoffs" had been issued for rule infractions.[63] The problems in the plant were subsequently viewed in 1972 by the *Wall Street Journal* by this revealing headline: "Paradise Lost: Utopian GM Plant in Ohio Falls from Grace under Strain of Baulky Machinery, Workers."[64] The *Journal* apparently recognized, as GM did not, that the workers as well as the machinery were "baulky."

Problems had intensified when the General Motors Assembly Division (referred to by workers as "Gotta Make Another Dollar" or "Go-Mad") took over the plant. B. J. Widdick described some of the resulting tensions:

> Leonard Woodcock, president of the UAW, remarked recently that GMAD is "probably the roughest, toughest division in GM. They admit they jerked 300 workers out of the system; our people say 700. The men are fighting back. That's all." For management, the issue soon became one of prestige as well as work output. GMAD's reputation was at stake, and that is one factor in the inability of the two parties to negotiate the grievances peacefully and satisfactorily. Before GMAD took over, there had been 300 grievances; under the new management there were more than 5,000 with hundreds of discipline cases to boot.
>
> GMAD's operational techniques are standard in the auto industry. Works standards engineers determine the number of seconds required for an operation and foremen are given the manpower to perform at that rate. Failure to meet the standard results in disciplinary action against the employee; being sent home, given days off, ultimately discharge. As men resist in one form or another, usually not meeting the workload, the cars go down the line incomplete. When repairs have piled up to a predetermined point, management sends the entire work force home. The key to understanding this performance conflict is that the assembly line determines the pace of the men, not the other way around. Hence workers feel manacled to the line.
>
> In management theory, when "send homes" have occurred a number of times, the men not working directly on the line and thus unaffected by the works standards dispute will begin to put pressure on the assembly workers. "We need the pay; write a grievance. Let's not lose all our power in small

fights." This attitude, plus disciplinary measures, is expected to break the resistance to the new work standards, which have been "scientifically" calculated and must therefore be "right." Frequently this process fails, and management faces and accepts a strike, which usually ends in compromise. Then management begins the whole process over again. (That is a thumbnail history of all auto assembly plants.)[65]

GMAD had been directed in November 1968 to combine and operate all Fisher and Chevrolet operations, in order to give "greater flexibility to assembly operations . . . and to cut costs and improve quality," according to GMAD vice president Andy O'Keefe.[66] GM's goal was to increase plant efficiency and respond to the threat of foreign, primarily Japanese, auto competition. GMAD took over a total of six auto plants, and by 1969, all six were on strike. One of these strikes, at Norwood, Ohio, lasted 174 days, making it difficult to understand why Lordstown, not Norwood, became so newsworthy.[67] In any event, workers perceived that GMAD wanted to "eradicate key contract language, and erode preexisting union rights in the plant as well."[68] For auto assemblers, "GMAD meant heavier work loads, tougher disciplinary penalties, closer supervision, more competitive pressure within the corporation, looser inspection, loss of jobs, more centralized decision-making, less settlement of disputes at low managerial levels and on the shop floor and an insistence on total managerial control."[69] Local union officers told Moberg that "working conditions deteriorated drastically under GMAD," and "wherever a GMAD had taken over, there had been a great increase in disputes over production standards and work loads."[70]

At Chevrolet-Fisher plants, such as Lordstown, management had initially assumed a work rate that would occupy workers 65 percent of the time, but GMAD wanted workloads that would keep workers busy with standard, defined operations 85–90 percent of the time or fifty to fifty-four minutes out of each hour. O'Keefe, sounding like Frederick Taylor, stated that "contractually we have the prerogative of working a man 60 minutes an hour. We known that that's not possible in this age. We want a fair day's work for a fair day's wage."[71]

GMAD installed more foremen and lower level supervisors, each covering a smaller group of workers, resulting in tighter and stricter supervision. Foremen also had less authority to settle grievances, especially any that might change policy. A union official from a Kansas City, Missouri, GMAD plant told Moberg that "The work pace is from 15 to 20 percent greater than it was. They're (GMAD) much harder to deal with, to bargain with. Their discipline is much harder, and much more frequent. They are more cold-hearted. Strictly business."[72]

When the Lordstown assembly plant was opened in 1966, its workforce was primarily composed of young, white males who predominantly had grown up in the unionized communities of Ohio's Mahoning valley. GM apparently did not expect trouble from Lordstown's workforce, whose average age was only twenty-five. Moreover, as the *Cincinnati Inquirer* reported, "GM thought that that [its] effort would be aided by locating the plant in the small northeastern Ohio community where the labor force would be unencumbered by prevailing Detroit antipathies."[73] General Motors apparently favored young workers when opening a new facility, but the prosperity of the 1960s also attracted younger workers, since there were fewer older, high seniority, unemployed autoworkers waiting to claim the new positions. These young workers came into the plant to make the Chevrolet Firebird and Camaro, and eventually the Vega, at an unprecedented line speed.

In addition to reducing the workforce, while maintaining the speed, GMAD also changed the work standard, reducing from three to two workers per job. Even more threatening to workers was its insistence that all prior agreements with Local 1112 be renegotiated. Disciplinary layoffs were issued in unprecedented numbers when workers often refused to do the work of two or sometimes three workers. By January of 1972 Thompson notes that fourteen hundred workers had been disciplined.[74] Unlike at Chrysler in Detroit, however, union leaders supported the rank and file and intended to support a strike. The Lordstown strike, one of the most commented upon in the 1960s, was settled within twenty-two days. The settlement provided for the return of almost all of the jobs lost after the GMAD takeover and resolved a number of the pending grievances and settled all of the disciplinary layoffs.[75]

David Moberg's thick description of the Lordstown situation indicates that the most significant events actually occurred before the 1972 strike. The plant was apparently a difficult place to work from the start, turnover was high, and firings were frequent. In addition, workers were frustrated with the normal inefficiencies in the beginning of a new plant. Many workers were fired during the ninety-day trial period and even more simply quit. "That's the only place I ever worked where people had to line up to quit," a long-time employee told Moberg.[76]

Lordstown went through five model changes in the first four years, and each change precipitated new conflicts. Constant breakdowns in mechanical equipment plagued the plant. "This unusually instability worsened the life on the job for workers, constantly challenged the union, and undercut the efficiency of the union and undercut the efficiency of the plant. This led to pressure on the local management and, therefore, the supervisors to get out production, by whatever means possible."[77] The result was a heightened level of disciplinary actions against workers. A local official told Moberg, "If you went from the marines to General Motors, you wouldn't notice any difference except the uniform."[78] From the early days of the plant there were running conflicts between the rank and file and the international, and many felt that the local and international officials' primary job was to "squelch their enthusiastic battles with red tape."[79]

Even prior to the famous 1972 strikes and starting even before the GMAD takeover, there were many wildcat strikes during the plant's early period. Some were small and short, but others involved nearly the entire plant. The issues in some of the major walkouts involved disciplinary suspensions given to workers involved in an earlier, smaller wildcat, protests over excessive overtime as well as grievances over seniority and transfer rights, work rules, safety, and production standards.

Some of these battles were offensive as well as defensive. An employee told Moberg that direct action was a way to "fight for something you are not entitled to but you know you should have and they can afford to give." Typical among employee comments was this one remarking on chaos in the plant: "You couldn't get anything done. Tools wouldn't get fixed. We were just sitting there talking and someone said, 'let's have a sitdown strike.' So we did. We sat down for 45 minutes. Management threatened discipline, then said they'd relieve each guy from the line to talk over problems. I got involved in the leadership thing. I was one of the first talked to. I said to Ed (a friend), 'they're not providing relief. What should we do?' Ed said, 'Let's go home at the next whistle.' So we did."[80]

Although some employees were discharged, fear of discipline seemed to be "a surmountable obstacle" as management was under great pressure just to get the production out and often had to concede to worker demands to keep the line moving. During the late 1960s there was also a general air of confidence that other jobs could be found if necessary, suggesting a parallel to the wartime period. Yet many employees were fired and a dismissal for wildcatting was thought to lead to an areawide blacklist among large manufacturing employers.[81] Indeed, there is some evidence that the incidence of wildcats was reduced starting in 1970 in part because there was a tightening of the area's employment opportunities, reflecting a concurrent downturn in the national business cycle. As union officers gained experience, there was also a greater reliance on the grievance procedure. Moberg suggests that the grievance procedure might have been strengthened by extra legal insurgency, "thereby diminishing the reliance on the very actions of rank and file and formal work groups which had finally made management more responsive to formal complaints."[82]

A number of employees were cynical about the role of the collective bargaining agreement, however, although they were certainly willing to use the grievance process to support their claims. Many viewed the contract as the minimum standard of acceptable relations with management. Moreover, workers assumed that the company would violate the agreement. Thus, a union loyalist told Moberg: "I'm a trouble maker. What I mean by 'trouble maker,' I read the book. It's like the Good Book. They'll sign the agreement just to get us back to work, but when we get back it's a different story. They violate it everywhere."[83]

After the resolution of the 1970 contract, Lordstown was on an extremely heavy overtime schedule, producing almost six days of production a week for two shifts that frequently ran ten to eleven hours. "For some workers in special departments, there was often 7 days of work or even longer shifts, but that was often although not always voluntary."[84] Complaints of overwork and supervisory harassment began to mount. Despite the success of the Vega, supervisors were told that they were expected to "cut manpower, increase the work load, enforce discipline, reduce waste, establish tight control and keep workers continually busy, sweeping up their areas even if the line broke down."[85] In the fall and early winter, a number of workers were laid off and major operations were dropped. With layoffs came massive reshuffling of employees, juggling of job descriptions, and additional layoffs of low seniority workers. In addition, disciplinary layoffs escalated sharply.[86] As discipline tightened, resistance spread. Resistance, therefore, was not simply the result of antiwar, anti-authoritarian hippies in the plant, although there were some, as even traditional or instrumental union members began to resist GMAD's pressure.

The work was boring, monotonous, and deadening, the traditional description of assembly line work, although issues of personal integrity may have been paramount. "When workers talked about dehumanization on the job," explained Moberg, "they were likely to be thinking even more of the way they were treated by management than the deadening effects of the assemblyline. People compared Lordstown to prison, boys industrial school (reform school), high school (with its petty, humiliating rules) and most of all, especially for veterans of the Viet Nam era military, the army. GMAD was known as the Gestapo."[87] As in many other disputes, the perception of arbitrary and dehumanizing supervisory treatment seemed to cause a good deal of the tension, and the perception that Lordstown's workers were primarily concerned with the need for humane and rewarding work may have been overstressed.

Gary Bryner, the twenty-nine-year-old president of UAW Local 1112, told Studs Terkel in 1972 that he was considered relatively old in the plant.[88] Many workers effected the "mod look," involving "long hair, big Afros, beads."[89] Bryner stated that the young worker, unlike their fathers, believed "he has something to say about what he does. He doesn't believe that when the foreman says it's right that it's right. Hell, he might be ten times more intelligent than the foreman."

Bryner described "working hard" as an attribute which the young workers characterized as belonging to their fathers: "The young guy now, he doesn't get a kick out of saying how hard he can work. I think his kick would be just the opposite. . . . It isn't manly to do more than you should. That's the difference between the son and his dad." Although their fathers may have defined "manliness" in working hard, Bryner noted that "there's some manliness in being able to stand up to the giant."[90] Tom Orlosky, however, whose son worked at Lordstown, observed that the new workers "think the plant owes them a living. When I was young, you put in a day's work. No question about it." The "younger generation," he believed, "just don't feel like working. . . . Gee, I wish I had 24 minutes off twice a day."[91]

Some workers in the plant were Viet Nam veterans, an experience which no doubt intensified a militant resistance to excessive work speed and a strong desire for dignity. Others were part-time students, perhaps influenced by student rebelliousness. The result, according to Bryner was to put "human before property value and profits." "The worker," Bryner stated, "wants a job he doesn't hate to come to. Make the jobs comfortable, make them purposeful. It will show results. The union guy has recognized the work place as a place he has to be, and we're going to make it a pleasant place to be."

Lordstown became a beacon, highlighting worker discontent with deadening, robotic work.[92] The three-week strike which began there in 1972 "drew national attention to the issue of alienation."[93] In Staughton Lynd's words, it was a rebellion against "arbitrary authority and the lack of respect for human rights in the capitalist workplace."[94]

Although the Lordstown workers were predominantly young, they were hardly more "pre-industrial" than their World War II predecessors. Although the press continually placed Lordstown in "middle-America," Lordstown is close to Warren and Youngstown, Ohio, both highly industrialized areas.[95] Moreover, workers commuted from Akron, Cleveland, and as far away as Pittsburgh. The region had been solidly industrial for most of this century, and there had been a history of militant labor struggles for many years, including organizing struggles in the steel industry in the 1930s and left-wing activity in the 1930s and 1940s. In addition, the dues protest movement within the United Steelworkers' union in 1956–60 began in Youngstown, as did an insurgent movement within the Teamsters Union.[96] Thus, the new Lordstown workers were not primarily recruited from rural backgrounds, but from families which often had long-standing industrial traditions.[97] Especially in light of Bryner's reference to their "fathers," it is likely that many of these workers came from families where at least one parent had union experience. Bryner himself had worked in factories since his high school graduation, beginning in a Republic Steel facility where his father worked.[98]

Nevertheless, the new generation of workers, although having absorbed some of their parents' values, were not as intimidated by fears of insecurity as the depression generation. As James Green noted, these workers were often more educated than their parents, and they shared some of the "anti-authoritarian values of their college-educated peers who were active in the radical student movement." The slowdowns and 1972 strike resulted from the traditional autoworker complaints about Taylorism and authoritarianism, but the workers also voiced concerns for fairness, dignity, and participation.

After the Lordstown strike, it was common to refer to the newly discovered problem of worker alienation or "blue collar blues."[99] The seemingly new problem was "the dehumanization of automation," which led to questions about the "individual's sense of worth in the robot-ruled workplace."[100] The *New York Times* editorialized that the Lordstown strikers resisted the "empty, repetitive nature of their duties" and noted that "the rigidities of standard work practices are breeding discontent that present challenges for employers and unions alike."[101] But the strike was also important because "a new generation of auto workers, with the UAW's blessing, taught the company that management could not always unilaterally change work rules and defy the union without resistance and cost."[102] Thompson argues that the workers' "experience with GMAD had politicized them, and . . . they recognized that GMAD's approach threatened the power of workers to defend even the status quo in working conditions."[103] In short, despite the long hair and hippie appearance of some workers, the strike fit "nicely into the established post-war labor agenda of the UAW, and therefore, caused no problems for the union."[104]

Although the "rebellion of young workers"[105] may have seemed new, the underlying concerns were not. A Lordstown worker, for instance, told Barbara Garson that his father worked in an auto plant for thirty-five years and never talked about his job. "What's there to say. A car comes, I weld it. A car comes, I weld it. A car comes, I weld it. One hundred and one times an hour."[106] As Andrew Levison noted in October 1972, the "jobs demand a mindless submission to the speed and rhythm of the line. There is not even a remote sense of mastery or craftsmanship." The nature of auto work had not changed substantially for over fifteen years, but what was new was the willingness of the young workers to reject the perceived submission of the older generation. Unburdened by the fears of the depression, skeptical of the American dream, and sharing the anti-authoritarianism of their generation, the workers tried to express the "shallowness and lack of fulfillment in American society."[107]

WORKER PARTICIPATION AND
MATURE COLLECTIVE BARGAINING

Lordstown was only the most well known sign of worker unrest in a period of significant industrial turmoil.[108] As P. K. Edwards notes, the revolt which began in the late 1960s, however, "remained an expression of protest and was not part of an articulated shop floor challenge to the 'formal system,'" and the potential for autonomous activity was "weaker and more constrained" by the New Deal than many realize.[109] Edwards relates the existence of autonomous workplace activity to the hostility of American employers to challenges to their authority, a hostility based upon their perceived need to control workers. The New Deal, he rationally concludes, reformed institutionalized workplace conflict without altering employer hostility.

The undercurrent of worker hostility which became newsworthy in the 1970s seemed surprising to many. It had generally been assumed that workers wanted greater wages in the postwar period, although both management and unionists "knew that wage demands ultimately held less importance for both workers and managers than did questions of control."[110] Social science studies and surveys repeatedly found that issues of control and integrity consistently ranked higher than wages.[111] Because wage increases via bargaining have often been granted as an incentive to higher productivity, however, "workers with qualitative non-wage demands recognize that their goals will appear illegitimate and unsuited to resolution in contracts. But money demands always seem legitimate."[112] Gouldner's 1954 study of a strike at a gypsum plant, for example, indicated that a strike seemingly over wages was actually precipitated by other issues which the workers felt were either illegitimate for them *as workers* to raise or which they were powerless to address.[113] Perhaps, as one worker told Gouldner, "Management feels the machines are none of our business and maybe it's not."[114] Moreover, unlike the clear-cut nature of a wage increase, nonwage grievances "might be experienced in widely different ways by different workers."[115] Thus, wage issues may often have masked anger and resentment over other issues.[116] Furthermore, contractual settlements involving wage gains can be treated as important victories by unions, and employers are generally more willing to grant wage increases than to countenance invasions of what they deem their managerial prerogatives. In a famous quote, a GM executive stated: "Give the union the money, the least possible, but give them what it takes. But don't let them take the business away from us."[117]

As noted earlier, the move from a system of workplace confrontation to higher-level bargaining alters the substance of bargaining, that is, the nature of the issues. Workplace conflict during the war, as well as at Lordstown and other locales, tended to deal with speed of production, discipline, or actions of foremen.[118] "Mature" collective bargaining, on the other hand, often tended to deal with other issues, for instance, wages rather than humanizing working conditions.[119] Thus, a change in focus of concern, in the definition of what is important, occurred, rather than simply a change in the location of and participants in workplace dispute resolution. It is true that during and after the war unions talk about invading hitherto exclusively management preserves, and employers clearly feel that such areas had been invaded.[120] The managerial prerogatives unions referred to, however, generally dealt with major capital decisions and not the types of workplace issues which often seem of greater immediacy to workers.

Obviously, unions are well aware of the need for dignity and meaning in one's work. Indeed, this is the reason why many workers join unions. As Golden and Ruttenberg recognized in 1942: "They join unions to become something more than a check number that is ordered around as a piece of material is forged. They crave to be recognized as human beings, to be treated with respect, to be given the opportunity to find satisfaction in their daily work through the free play of their inherent creativeness." As Golden and Ruttenberg also noted, however, "collective bargaining, as it is currently practiced in most productive enterprises, fails to satisfy this motive for union membership except in a limited sense." That is, "protecting a worker's job, getting him more money and better working conditions, and haggling over grievances largely satisfy the economic and social motives for union membership, and the extent to which workers have a voice in these matters partially satisfied their psychological motives for joining unions. But not until union-management relations become essentially constructive will workers find full satisfaction for their inherent creative desires."[121]

The move from rank-and-file action to grievance and arbitration procedures, from dealing with workplace issues of the moment to generalized collective bargaining patterns, seems to reflect an international problem. A number of European countries provide far greater participation and information sharing, via unions, worker representatives, or work councils, than Americans often find conceivable.[122] Nevertheless, studies have found that European workers often complain about their union's lack of interest in workplace concerns.[123] As Charles Heckscher has noted, the strikes in almost every European country after 1968 demonstrated degeneration of these systems. "The most visible point of criticism was that unions had become too *centralized;* that though they handled top-level strategic questions well, they had lost touch with their members."[124] Coexistence may exist in significant measure at the top, but workers tend to want "more on the floor." Indeed, American unions have often been more interested in high level coordination than in worker control at the workplace. Thus, even if unions after the war had been more successful in obtaining greater involvement in crucial capital decisions, the consistent concern of workers for greater involvement and respect at work would not have been satisfied. Even in Europe, and despite high level cooperation, "shop floor mechanisms of participation. . . . have not been well developed."[125]

The absence of effective union representation at the workplace in Europe has led to a variety of structural changes to accommodate the seemingly constant urging of workers for more involvement in workplace decisions. In Germany, for instance, various statutes have created and strengthened works councils. Not structurally related to unions, these councils are considered part of the plant's organic structure, dealing with a variety of matters which had traditionally been ignored by German unions. German unions were traditionally suspicious of such structures, which had existed prior to 1900 in some form, since they were often created to ward off unions. Nevertheless, German unions have found ways to coexist so long as the work of the councils does not impinge on bargaining matters.[126]

More important, perhaps, is England where, without statutory authorization, workers themselves set up structures to deal with workplace issues. In the United Kingdom workers at the plant level have created structures for dealing with specific issues not satisfactorily dealt with in industry-wide collective bargaining.[127] Although the English shop steward system began to develop in the 1950s, it received considerable assistance during the period of militant worker struggle in the early 1970s. Similarly, many statutes dealing with worker protection and participation were enacted on the Continent after the widespread disruptions in the late 1960s and 1970s.[128]

In the United States, job conscious local unions and more decentralized bargaining structures would initially seem to make structures such as works councils unnecessary. Yet, as in the United Kingdom and Europe, the late 1960s and early 1970s were a time of disruption and militance in American

unions. James Green noted that "the rank and file insurgencies that erupt-
ed in several major labor unions during the late sixties resulted essentially
from the degradation of work and from the unions' insistence on making
wages the central issue of collective bargaining."[129] Local grievances were
generally seen as secondary to company-wide problems, and the UAW, like
many other unions, often pressured its locals to curtail strikes over production standards to avoid interfering with national negotiations. Given these
rank-and-file pressures, however, the UAW was forced to grant approval for
strikes over local shop floor disputes "which soon dwarfed wildcat stoppages in terms of man hours lost in the industry as a whole."[130]

In this period dissatisfaction with "mature" bargaining and union bureaucracy was revealed by a propensity to turn out union officers and to refuse
to ratify contracts. In 1969, for instance, the FMCS noted that over one
thousand collective agreements were rejected in ratification votes, about 14
percent of cases in its file for that year.[131] Between July 1, 1965, and June
30, 1967, union members rejected 1,937 agreements negotiated by their
union officials. Mediators for the Federal Mediation and Conciliation Service believed that the problem was not due to the inadequacy of ratification
procedures. Although a variety of causes are listed, William E. Simkin, then
director of the FMCS, stated that

> The fact that the workforce at many plants is now composed of an increas-
> ing percentage of young, low-seniority employees creates sharp differences
> as to how a total economic package is to be divided between cash wages and
> such security fringes as pensions. When seniority is an issue, it is immeasur-
> ably complicated by new legal developments and new urgent pressures re-
> lated to race, sex, and age distribution of the workforce.
>   . . . [I]increasing disillusionment with arbitration as the terminal point
> of the grievance procedure is evident, due primarily to excessive delays and
> real or alleged excess of costs. In a very sizeable number of cases during this
> two-year period, membership rejections and strikes have been almost entirely
> noneconomic. This somewhat intangible generalized dissatisfaction with
> day-by-day relationships in the plant is the root cause.[132]

Paralleling many descriptions of the wildcats during World War II,
Simkin focused on the "new" members of the workforce: "Many younger
workers who have grown up in a period of relative affluence have never experienced either a real depression or the early history of union struggles.
Moreover, they are not very interested in attempts to acquaint them with
these hard facts of earlier years. Many have never experienced a strike of any
duration. When these facts are coupled with what may be loosely described

as the current disillusionment of youth in other areas of activity, negative ratification votes are not surprising."[133]

Simkin noted that the new, younger workers "had not yet been assimilated into the industrial community. We were in a war without the forms of control over the economy that existed in World War II and during the Korean conflict." Further, the "membership rejection problem, serious as it is, has been a type of psychological 'escape valve' that may have averted even more adverse manifestations."[134]

Simkin's statements reflect two perennial assumptions made about workplace conflict. First, the analysis tends to focus on worker dissatisfaction rather than the causes of that dissatisfaction, often leading to the attempt to explain conflict in terms of unacculturated workers. Second, the forms of conflict are often seen as "escape valves," suggesting that conflict is non-functional and unrealistic.

At roughly the same time in Europe, in France in 1968 and during the Italian "hot summer" of 1969, widespread rank-and-file militancy broke out. An ILO survey of fourteen European and North American countries revealed that between 1968 and 1972 industrial conflict had increased significantly in many countries along with increases in absenteeism and turnover.[135] Unofficial strikes became common, accounting for 95 percent of all strikes in the United Kingdom, over 85 percent in Sweden, and 83 percent in Germany. One result, as already noted, was a multitude of statutes protecting against arbitrary discharges, regulating plant closings and worker transfers, providing for severance pay and retraining, and creating innovative arrangements for worker participation in management, generally at the highest levels.[136] Despite increased worker militance in the United States, however, no legislative action occurred. Instead, a number of unions began to permit local bargaining as an outgrowth of the rank-and-file militancy of the time. These were seen as victories for workplace democracy, pulling at least some decisions down to the local level. Significantly, some companies instituted job enrichment and what would subsequently be called Quality of Work Life programs, patterned not after then unknown Japanese models but, instead, adapted from Scandinavian experiments.

The outbreaks of worker militance in the United States in the early 1970s also led to a remarkable book, prepared by a task force appointed by the secretary of health, education and welfare, titled *Work in America*. Elliot Richardson, secretary of HEW, noted in a foreword that "we cannot help but feel that however deeply we have cared in the past, we never really understood the importance, the meaning, and the *reach* of work." The HEW report concluded that by the late 1960s large numbers of workers were dissatisfied with "dull, repetitive, seemingly meaningless tasks, offering little challenge or autonomy." Reacting to the obvious signs of worker unrest, the report noted that "quality of work" had recently received considerable attention. Workers had also become disenchanted with the scope of collective bargaining and what they believed to be "unresponsive" or "irrelevant" union leadership.[137]

Thus, the HEW report expressed the belief that the needs of workers had not been satisfied by contractualizing the employment relationship or by the bureaucratization of dispute resolution. It acknowledged that the problem of dull, repetitive, and seemingly meaningless work was hardly new, but that "widescale changes in worker attitudes, aspirations, and values" along with an increase in "educational and economic status" had intensified worker demands for more interesting and varied work. Despite the report's primary focus on the quality of work rather than issues of control, a major and highly prescient conclusion was that Taylorism, with its stress on the detailed fragmentation of work, lack of autonomy, and rigid supervision, was no longer satisfactory for either productivity or worker happiness.[138] In other words, the social aspect of work had been ignored, and situations like Lordstown were seen as the result of such neglect. Citing Abraham Maslow, the report suggested that the very success of firms in satisfying the basic needs of workers had "unintentionally spurred demands for estimable and fulfilling jobs."[139] Those demands, the report concluded, should be met by placing greater emphasis on the redesign and enrichment of jobs. Startlingly current in tone, the report encouraged the creation of autonomous work groups and teams of workers operating with less or no supervision.[140] In short, workers were not so much "new" as possessing different aspirations, implicitly distinguishing them from workers in the 1930s and 1940s.

Thus, in the 1960s and 1970s, the unhappy American worker is discovered anew.[141] The "new" worker was now seen to desire involvement in workplace decisions and, importantly, a fulfilling and rewarding work life. Workers were not "troublemakers" or pre-industrial, but, instead, as the Maslow triangle suggested, now that they were well-off, well-educated, and well-nigh middle class, they were focusing on "self-actualization." It is this hunger for involvement which, at least in part, spurred the creation of Quality of Work Life (QWL) circles in some workplaces. Only in the 1980s, however, would "quality of work" and "involvement" arrangements be widely introduced.[142]

A letter of understanding added to the national UAW-GM collective agreement in 1973 eerily reflects Golden and Ruttenberg's statements over thirty years earlier about the need for worker involvement in workplace decision making: "General Motors Corporation and the UAW gave recognition to the desirability of mutual effort to improve the quality of work life for the employees. . . . Certain projects have been undertaken by management in the field of organizational development, involving the participation of represented employees. These and other projects and experiments improve the quality of work life, thereby advantaging the worker by making work a more satisfying experience."[143]

Wherever worker participation programs are established with the aid of unions, efforts are made to separate worker involvement groups or quality circles from collective bargaining structures as well as from the substance of collective agreements.[144] Such a separation may mirror the English steward system and the German works councils, but the line has proven difficult to maintain.[145] Moreover, these arrangements, therefore, actually recognize the failure of collective bargaining to deal with the full range of employee interests and to respond to employee concerns for integrity on the job.

In Europe "these revitalized shop floor representatives have been in many cases seeking direct control over areas previously considered management prerogatives."[146] The attempted separation in the United States, however, apparently reflects the belief that collective bargaining cannot deal with the total range of worker satisfaction and participation concerns. Such a belief is expressed in the Labor Management Cooperation Act of 1978; one of its goals is to assist "workers and employers in solving problems of mutual concern not susceptible to resolution within the collective bargaining process."[147]

Many argue that business unionism, defined as a narrowly economistic and bureaucratized contract-based system of collective bargaining, which systematically denied rank-and-file workers the right to participate directly in the organization and control of work, was a logical development from institutionalized collective bargaining based on contractual formalism.[148] Collective bargaining would win unions new members, but it would also leave many workers dissatisfied with existing avenues to redress individual concerns. During the war and after, the organizational imperative to maintain legitimacy and institutional clout lay in the ability of unions to remain viable as bargaining representatives. To accomplish this, union members had to be controlled. If unions were not to allow decentralized autonomy to the rank and file, they would have to guarantee monetary benefits.[149]

Collective bargaining, unions and most pluralists believe, can only be effective if the union is organized in as centralized a form as its adversaries. Bureaucratization and centralization also legitimized union leaders, but they became increasingly constrained in dealing with only those issues which could be easily accommodated into existing capitalist frameworks. "Thus, wages and benefits bargaining was reinforced, as distributional issues increasingly became the locus for bargaining. Consequently, the industry-wide bargaining that ensued predisposed organized labour to deal less with the relationship of men to work than with the tangible and incremental issues that did not threaten the assumptions and workings of a market economy."[150]

In addition, business unionism offered union leaders what they believed was an acceptable format for satisfying both their members' demands for economic benefits and the employers' demands for "reasonable" or realistic contractual terms. Business unionism, however, meant that certain issues were to be conspicuously absent from negotiations. A broadly based shop floor movement with extensive involvement of the rank and file would be opposed by management, and often by labor union leaders as well, because such a system would involve a devolution of institutional power and decision making which would be inconsistent with the structure of bargaining that has become the norm since wartime. If rank-and-file activity over productive relations occurred, it would have to be unauthorized.

Recent studies show that workers are frequently attracted to unions when they are dissatisfied over traditional economic terms of employment but, after they join the union, they invariably focus their dissatisfaction on their inability to exercise influence over job conditions.[151] These concerns led in the 1960s and the early 1970s to an increase in wildcat strikes, as well as other forms of protest, and there was a notable increase in the number of protests over job control. Much of this dissatisfaction became directed toward unions for apparently failing to deal with what were perceived to be substantive inadequacies in contract terms.[152] Unions may have been unfairly blamed for a situation they were realistically too weak to alter, but they also seemed to have no idea of possible alternatives.

The leaders of wildcats in the more modern period were "new" in the sense that they were not willing to sublimate workplace concerns to a system they felt was inadequate or uncaring. The generally young workers in the 1960s and 1970s were thought to be more politicized than their predecessors, in part because they were better educated and had higher expectations but also because of the general social and political activism of the period.[153] Yet, the intensity of worker opposition in the late 1960s and early 1970s was "a result of accumulated dissatisfaction with union leaders' reluctance to address salient job-control issues."[154] Like the "new" workers of the wartime period, they were often not willing to wait for a formalized dispute resolution system to process their grievances. Each group of workers operated in a confrontational context, or at least one in which the costs of militancy did not seem to outweigh the perceived advantages.

Unions in this period, like those in wartime, found themselves caught between the desire to satisfy workers while also maintaining their precarious position. Legal and contractual constraints restricted union action in support of rank-and-file militancy during the life of the contract and, just as crucial, restricted the content and scope of collective agreements. Unions could not authorize or ratify wildcat strikes since no-strike clauses, found in almost all collective agreements, could be enforced by injunction or an action for damages. The law often, but not always, proscribed wildcat strikes, but union treasuries were at risk if unions approved or ratified strikes in breach of collective agreements.[155] Moreover, organizational structures limited input concerning the organization of work. Concentration of power in the union leadership "discouraged decentralized or shop floor decision making, the articulation of ideas from below, and frowned upon militancy which it did not orchestrate."[156] The result, as in wartime, was a conflict between the desire for organizational stability and efficiency and the rank and file's interest in influencing policymaking and, especially, the nature of work itself.

Notes

1. Clark Kerr, John T. Dunlop, Frederick H. Harbison, and Charles A. Myers, *Industrialization and Industrial Man* (Cambridge, Mass.: Harvard University Press, 1960), 198–99.

2. See James Atleson, "Wartime Labor Regulation, the Industrial Pluralists, and the Law of Collective Bargaining," in *Industrial Democracy: The Ambiguous Promise*, ed. Nelson Lichtenstein and Howell John Harris (New York: Cambridge University Press, 1993), 156–59.

3. There is considerable debate over the effect of the Taft-Hartley Act. An excellent discussion of the causes, content, and effect of Taft-Hartley can be found in Christopher Tomlins, *The State and the Unions* (New York: Cambridge University Press, 1985), 242–316. See also George Lipsitz, *Rainbow at Midnight* (Urbana: University of Illinois, 1994), 157–79.

4. Daniel Bell, *The End of Ideology* (Glencoe, Ill.: Free Press, 1960), 217; Arthur Ross and Paul T. Hartman, *Changing Patterns of Industrial Conflict* (New York: John Wiley, 1960).

5. Charles Tilley, *From Mobilization to Revolution* (Reading, Mass.: Addison Wesley, 1978), 159; cited in Rick Fantasia, *Cultures of Solidarity: Consciousness, Action, and Contemporary American Workers* (Berkeley: University of California Press, 1988), 62.

6. See Lipsitz, *Rainbow at Midnight*, 99–117, 229–48. See also Ruth Milkman, *Farewell to the Factory* (Berkeley: University of California Press, 1997), 54–55. Roger Horowitz, "*Negro and White, Unite and Fight!" A Social History of Industrial Unionism in Meatpacking, 1930–90* (Urbana: University of Illinois, 1997), chap. 7. Horowitz

states that job actions in UPWA locals were less an irritant than an aid to the international.

7. Lipsitz, *Rainbow at Midnight*, 247.

8. James Zetka, Jr., *Militancy, Market Dynamics, and Workplace Authority: The Struggle over Labor Process Outcomes in the U.S. Automobile Industry, 1946–1973* (Albany: State University of New York Press, 1995), 77. Zetka argues there was more activity in the late 1950s than there was in the late 1940s, and there was no significant decrease in wildcats until 1959. Indeed, the peak wildcat years in auto were 1955 and 1958. Zetka's numbers may even underestimate the number of wildcat strikes. For instance, he lists thirty-one wildcat strikes for the entire auto industry between 1966 and 1970. David Moberg's study, on the other hand, suggests that there were many wildcat strikes at Lordstown alone ("Rattling the Golden Chains: Conflict and Consciousness of Autoworkers" [Ph.D. diss., University of Chicago, 1978] vols. 1 and 2). Zetka concedes that his data, taken primarily from the *Wall Street Journal* and the *New York Times* and supplemented by other publications, no doubt underestimates the incidence of wildcat strikes (ibid., 44–45).

9. Stephen Amberg, *The Union Inspiration in American Politics* (Philadelphia: Temple University Press, 1944), 257–58.

10. See Fantasia, *Cultures of Solidarity*, 62–63. See also Stanley Aronowitz, *False Promises* (New York: McGraw-Hill, 1973); Barbara Garson, *All the Livelong Day* (Harmondsworth, Eng.: Penguin, 1973). The number of pending grievances should always be viewed with some caution as filings are sometimes used as a union pressure tactic, especially just prior to bargaining.

11. Fantasia, *Cultures of Solidarity*, 62–63.

12. David Brody, "The New Deal and World War II," in *The New Deal: The National Level*, ed. John Braeman, Robert H. Bremner and David Brody (Columbus: Ohio State University Press, 1975), 209–10.

13. See chart in Fantasia, *Cultures of Solidarity*, 61. It might not be coincidental that the first break with the employment-at-will doctrine occurred in 1974 (Monge v. Beebe Rubber Co., 114 N.H. 130, 316 A.2d 549 [1974]). Throughout the 1960s unemployment levels in the United States remained higher than in virtually any other major industrial country, with black unemployment generally twice that of whites. During any period, "unemployment affected a much larger percentage of the population than the unemployment indexes suggest." In the various recessions following the war, and especially in the 1970 recession, unemployment persisted at high levels for a couple of years after other economic signs suggested that a recovery was underway (Moberg, "Rattling the Golden Chains," 7).

14. Peter Levy, *The New Left and Labor in the 1960s* (Urbana: University of Illinois Press, 1994), 166.

15. Ibid., 157–58

16. Heather Ann Thompson, "Autoworkers, Dissent, and the UAW: Detroit and Lordstown," *Autowork*, ed. Robert Asher and Ronald Edsforth (Albany: State University of New York Press, 1995), 181, 184.

17. Ibid., 185.

18. Ibid., 187.

19. Ibid.

20. Ibid., 189–90.

21. Ibid., 197–200; Fraser cited on 198.

22. Cited in ibid.

23. Mazy quoted in ibid., 199.

24. Ibid., 199–200.

25. During this period of rank-and-file ferment, labor unions were initially wary of the signs of solidarity coming from the New Left. There were well-known signs of opposition, such as the revolt of construction workers in New York's financial district on May 8, 1970, but there also examples of cooperation. According to Peter Levy, unionists "tended to accept and encourage it as time passed" (*New Left and Labor in the 1960s*, 165). During the GE strike of 1969, for instance, the IUE initially expressed its resentment of attempts "by outside groups to exploit the cause of the GE strikers for the advancement of their own political or ideological aims" (Levy, ibid., 150). As the GE strike progressed, however, the AFL-CIO News expressed some support of the student radicals, drawing connections between their struggle and that of the GE workers (ibid., 150). New Left support for unions varied considerably, perhaps based on the presence or absence of connections to the Old Left, yet even criticism of the conservatism of current union leaders mirrored complaints that arose from workers themselves.

26. Ibid., 157.

27. Alice Lynd and Staughton Lynd, *Rank and File* (Boston: Beacon Press, 1974), 2.

28. Fantasia, *Cultures of Solidarity*, 64. See also James Atleson, "Work Group Behavior and Wildcat Strikes: The Causes and Functions of Industrial Civil Disobedience," *Ohio State Law Review* 34 (1973): 750, 770–72.

29. Fantasia, *Cultures of Solidarity*, 63.

30. Atleson, "Work Group Behavior," 762. See also James Atleson, "Disciplinary Discharges, Arbitration and the NLRB Deference," *Buffalo Law Review* 20 (1971): 355.

31. Alvin Gouldner, *Wildcat Strike* (New York: Harper Torchbooks, 1954), 169–70.

32. Atleson, "Work Group Behavior," 797.

33. Robert Dubin, "Constructive Aspects of Conflict," in *Collective Bargaining: Selected Readings*, ed. Allan D. Flanders (Harmondsworth, Eng.: Penguin, 1969), 51.

34. Employers often tend to assume that the most legitimate expectations are those which have been given explicit consent. Yet, contractual relationships often include numerous expectations which have not been mutually agreed upon in advance. According to Emile Durkheim, "[E]verything in the contract is not contractual. . . . But what shows better than anything else that contracts give rise to obligations which have not been contracted for [explicitly agreed upon] is that they make obligatory not only what there is expressed in them, but also consequences which equity, usage, or the law im-

putes from the nature of the obligation" (*The Division of Labor in Society* [New York: Free Press, 1947], 211–12; quoted in Gouldner, *Wildcat Strike*, 161).

As a result, the importance of past practice and custom in the interpretation of collective agreements has traditionally been recognized (United Steelworkers of America v. Warrier & Gulf Navigation Co., 363 U.S. 574 [1960]).

35. This permits employers to take "therapeutic measures," for the source of conflict is assumed to be in "sentiments which distort relations rather than in the nature of these social relations themselves" (Lewis Coser, *The Functions of Social Conflict* [New York: Free Press, 1966], 52–53). Concern then can be directed at social control, i.e., devices to manipulate employees into contented producers.

36. Ibid.; see, e.g., Georg Simmel, *Conflict and the Web of Group Affiliations* (New York: Free Press, 1955).

37. Leonard Sayles, *Behavior of Industrial Work Groups: Prediction and Control* (New York: John Wiley, 1958), 112. See Nancy Morse, *Satisfactions in the White Collar Job* (Ann Arbor: Survey Research Center, Institute for Social Research, University of Michigan, 1953), 59–61. These paragraphs have been adopted from Atleson, "Work Group Behavior," 761–70, 793–809.

38. See Jerome F. Scott and George C. Homans, "Reflections on the Wildcat Strikes," *American Sociological Review* 12 (1947): 278–87.

39. Ibid., 283. A study found that informal organization of employees was involved in those wildcats investigated rather than genuine spontaneity (Carl Gersuny, *Punishment and Redress in a Modern Factory* [Lexington, Mass.: Lexington Books, 1973], 69).

40. Gouldner, *Wildcat Strike*, 91.

41. Similarly, the fervor with which jurisdictional disputes are fought often amazes observers, but an analysis of the economic and personal interests at stake can help explain such actions. See James Atleson, "The NLRB and Jurisdictional Disputes: The Aftermath of CBS," *Georgetown Law Journal* 53 (1964): 93–99.

42. Ross Stagner, *Psychology of Industrial Conflict* (New York: John Wiley, 1956).

43. See citations given in Frank Tannenbaum, "Unions," in *Handbook of Organization*, ed. J. March (Chicago: Rand McNally, 1965), 710, 724.

44. For a current and personal account, see Ben Hamper, *Rivethead* (New York: Warner, 1991).

45. Ross Stagner and Hjalmar Rosen, *Psychology of Union-Management Relations* (Belmont, Calif.: Wadsworth Publishing Co., 1965), 46. See also Robert H. Guest, "Men and Machines: An Assembly-Line Worker Looks at His Job," *Personnel* 31 (1955): 496.

46. See Philip Ash, "The Parties to the Grievance," *Personnel Psychology* 23 (1970): 13–37.

47. Ibid., 20–21.

48. James Kuhn, *Bargaining in Grievance Settlement* (New York: Columbia University Press, 1961), 40–41.

49. Ibid.

50. A traditional criticism of the grievance system, and one sometimes acknowledged by management, is that management representatives in the lower stages of the grievance procedure either lack authority or refuse to exercise authority in the disposition of grievances (Neil Chamberlain, *The Union Challenge to Management Control* [New York: Harper & Bros., 1948], 239). Typically, this reluctance or inability to act quickly increases the anxiety and frustration of employees.

51. Kuhn, *Bargaining in Grievance Settlement*, 47.

52. Ibid.

53. The importance of delay is considered serious enough, however, so that a number of employers and unions have created expedited arbitration systems with panels of arbitrators (Dennis Nolan and Roger Abrams, "Trends in Private Sector Grievance Arbitration," in *Labor Arbitration under Fire*, ed. James Stern and Joyce Najita [Ithaca, N.Y.: Cornell University Press, 1997], 56–57).

54. Gouldner, *Wildcat Strike*, 93.

55. Leonard Sayles and George Strauss, *The Local Union*, rev. ed. (New York: Harcourt, Brace, 1967), 37.

56. Chamberlain, *Union Challenge*, 206.

57. Refusals of workers to follow grievance procedures are often seen as a rejection of the union's organization and authority. Compliance with existing procedures of dispute resolution cannot be fostered by "control" from top officials of the organization, however, though it can be encouraged by them.

58. These conflicts have traditionally been explained by Marxian analyses, but reliance can also be placed on democratic theory. See Dubin, "Constructive Aspects of Conflict," 42–44. An illustration of an attempt to effectuate collective bargaining absent conflict is found in General Electric's practices, referred to as "Boulwareism." General Electric assumed that management could decide for itself what a "reasonable" contract would be, free of union interference. Its aim of doing "right" voluntarily sounded admirable, but it completely ignored the basic conflict of interest inherent in bargaining or the union's statutory role. See NLRB v. General Electric Co., 418 F.2d 736 (2d Cir. 1969). For a sympathetic view, see Herbert Northrup, *Boulwareism* (Ann Arbor, Mich.: Bureau of Industrial Relations, 1964).

59. Dubin, "Constructive Aspects of Conflict," 48–49.

60. Moberg, "Rattling the Golden Chains," 36–37.

61. *Wall Street Journal*, Jan. 31, 1972, 28.

62. Thompson, "Autoworkers," 201.

63. *Wall Street Journal*, Mar. 6, 1972, 4.

64. *Wall Street Journal*, Jan. 31, 1972, 28.

65. B. J. Widdick, "The Men Won't Toe the Vega Line," *Nation* 214 (Mar. 27, 1972), 403–74; B. J. Widdick, "Workers in Auto Plants: Then and Now," in *Auto Work and Its Discontents*, ed. B. J. Widdick (Baltimore, Md.: Johns Hopkins University Press, 1976), 12–13.

66. Moberg, "Rattling the Golden Chains," 42.

67. Although the Lordstown strike was the most famous of the auto conflicts in

the early 1970s, James Zetka argues that the most significant strike actually occurred at Norwood, Ohio. GMAD had reorganized production, installing its first line of robot welders, and workers were induced to produce within tighter production rates. In addition, GMAD eliminated 749 jobs but maintained the same line speeds, forcing the remaining workers to increase their work pace considerably. The grievance backlog soared to four thousand cases, and the UAW international authorized the local strike. The strike began in early April 1972, lasted 174 days, and was the longest authorized local strike in the industry's history. The local settled with slim concessions on seniority, overtime, and shift preferences. The problems with work loads on the assembly line were still unresolved when the workers went back to work (Zetka, *Militancy, Market Dynamics*, 234).

68. Thompson, "Autoworkers," 202.

69. Moberg, "Rattling the Golden Chains," 42.

70. Ibid.

71. Ibid., 43.

72. Ibid., 44.

73. Quoted in Thompson, "Autoworkers," 202.

74. Ibid., 203.

75. Moberg, "Rattling the Golden Chains," 342. Moberg states that militancy seemed reduced after the 1972 agreement, although there was considerable feeling that the union had sold the workers out. Nevertheless, some wildcat strikes occurred even after the settlement.

76. Ibid., 96–100.

77. Ibid., 105.

78. Ibid.

79. Ibid., 112–14.

80. Ibid., 115–16.

81. Another unfortunate parallel to the 1940s was the various expressions of sexism and racism in the plant, although no wildcats resulted from the introduction of women in the workforce. Nevertheless, the same type of stories involving promiscuity or family problems created by women working were rife throughout the plant (ibid., 141–43, 119).

82. Ibid., 124.

83. Ibid., 294.

84. Ibid., 146.

85. Ibid., 157.

86. Ibid., 162.

87. Ibid., 170.

88. Studs Terkel, *Working* (New York: Avon, 1972), 256–65.

89. The counterculture look of some workers was often stressed in press accounts of the strike. See, e.g., *Newsweek*, Feb. 7, 1972, 65; *Time*, Feb. 7, 1972, 76.

90. Terkel, *Working*, 259. Bryner's reference to "manliness" provides a nice parallel to David Montgomery's description of the tradition of nineteenth-century

machine workers requiring a "manly" bearing toward one's employer. The worker who possessed this virtue "refused to cower before the foreman's glare" (David Montgomery, *Workers' Control in America* [New York: Cambridge University Press, 1979], 13).

91. "Why One Worker Sticks with a Job He Finds Dull," *Life Magazine*, Sept. 1, 1972, 36.

92. *Work in America* noted that workers under thirty, then over one-fourth of the workforce, seemed to place more emphasis than their elders on the value of interesting work and were demanding a voice in workplace matters (*Work in America*, Report of Special Task Force to the Secretary of Health, Education, and Welfare [Cambridge, Mass.: MIT Press, 1973], 43–51).

93. James Green, *The World of the Worker* (New York: Hill & Wang, 1980), 219.

94. Staughton Lynd, quoted in ibid., 220. Others as well noted parallels between rank-and-file militance and the antiwar movement. Indeed, Vietnam veterans may have been leaders at Lordstown. See comments of strike leader Gary Bryner in Studs Terkel's *Working*.

95. Youngstown was the site of RAFT (Rank & File Team), a dissident group of steelworkers who objected to USW concessions on productivity (Green, *World of the Worker*, 214).

96. Moberg, "Rattling the Golden Chains," 84–85.

97. Ibid., 89–90.

98. Other workers, highlighted in press accounts, had similar histories. See *Life Magazine*, Sept. 1, 1972, 73.

99. Thompson, "Autoworkers," 205.

100. *New York Times*, Mar. 7, 1972, 7.

101. *New York Times*, Mar. 7, 1972, 38.

102. Thompson, "Autoworkers," 205.

103. Ibid., 205–6.

104. Ibid., 206.

105. Andrew Levison, "The Rebellion of Blue Collar Youth," *Progressive* (Oct. 1972), 38.

106. Barbara Garson, "Luddites in Lordstown," *Harpers Magazine*, June, 1972, 69.

107. Levison, "Rebellion," 41; Garson, "Luddites in Lordstown," 68.

108. For a discussion of sabotage by autoworkers at General Motors' Van Nuys, Calif., assembly plant, see Craig Zabala, "Sabotage in an Automobile Assembly Plant: Worker Voice on the Shop Floor," in *Autowork*, ed. Robert Asher and Ronald Edsforth (Albany: State University of New York Press, 1995), 209. Zabala argues that sabotage makes collective bargaining work and is an important dimension of worker voice. The paradox is that "orderly and predictable collective bargaining can be abetted by disorderly, unpredictable subterranean conflict" (ibid., 225).

109. P. K. Edwards, "The Exceptionalism of the American Labor Movement: The Neglected Role of Workplace Struggle," unpublished paper in author's possession, 14, 26.

110. Lipsitz, *Rainbow at Midnight*, 230.

111. Eugene Benge, "Non-Financial Incentives: A Management Motivation Analysis," *Advanced Management* 19, no. 6 (1954); Benjamin Selekman, "Resistance to Shop Changes," *Harvard Business Review* 123 (Autumn 1945): 24.

112. Lipsitz, *Rainbow at Midnight*, 231.

113. Gouldner, *Wildcat Strike*, 30–37. This might explain why the BLS's studies on wartime strikes, unlike others, tended to find wages the predominant cause, despite the rigid control over wages that existed throughout the war.

114. Ibid., 35.

115. Ibid.

116. Ross Stagner, "Psychological Aspects of Industrial Conflict," *Personnel Psychology* 3 (1950): 1, 3; for an excellent discussion of these studies see Lipsitz, *Rainbow at Midnight*, 230–33.

117. Quoted in David Brody, *Workers in Industrial America* (New York: Oxford University Press, 1980), 187–88.

118. See Martin Glaberman, *Wartime Strikes: The Struggle against the No-Strike Pledge in the UAW during World War II* (Detroit: Bewick Editions, 1980). In some cases, these matters are part of local bargaining and are commonly dealt with in grievance procedures.

119. Wage increases are obviously advantageous to workers, although the fact that they are often the main focus of bargaining may be related to the political needs of union officers and the concern that agreements be ratified. Wage increases, in other words, are an objective and tangible measure of bargaining success.

120. See, e.g., Howell John Harris, *The Right to Manage: Industrial Relations Policies of American Business in the 1940s* (Madison: University of Wisconsin Press, 1982). These issues were dropped during 1945–49 but there were economic reasons for such behavior. Although David Brody seems to criticize the union behavior, his own writing reflects the overpowering issues of job security, protection against raging inflation, and the vehemence with which management counterattacked in the immediate postwar period. See Brody, *Workers in Industrial America*, chap. 5.

121. Clinton Golden and Harold Ruttenberg, *The Dynamics of Industrial Democracy* (New York: Harper & Bros., 1942), 240.

122. See, e.g., Clyde Summers, "Worker Participation in the U.S. and Germany: A Comparative Study from an American Perspective," *American Journal of Comparative Law* 28 (1980): 367; Clyde Summers, "Worker Participation in Sweden and the United States: Some Comparisons from an American Perspective," *University of Pennsylvania Law Review* 133 (1984): 175; Charles Heckscher, "Democracy at Work: In Whose Interests, the Politics of Worker Participation" (Ph.D. diss., Harvard, 1981).

123. Heckscher, "Democracy at Work," 220 n. 34. Even in the United States, unions have been far more concerned with high-level cooperation

124. Charles Heckscher, *The New Unionism: Employee Involvement in the Changing Corporation* (New York: Basic Books, 1988), 123–24.

125. Heckscher, "Democracy at Work," 220.

126. Summers, "Worker Participation in the U.S.," 367, 375; Janice Bellace, "The Role of Law in Supporting Cooperative Employee Representation Systems," *Comparative Labor Law Journal* 15 (1994): 441.

127. John F. B. Goodman, "Great Britain: Toward the Social Contract," in *Worker Militancy and Its Consequences: 1965–75*, ed. Solomon Barkin (New York: Praeger, 1975), 52–54.

128. Heckscher, "Democracy at Work," 221–22.

129. Green, *World of the Worker*, 219.

130. Steven Tolliday and Jonathan Zeitlin, "Shop Floor Bargaining, Contract Unionism, and Job Control: An Anglo-American Comparison," in *On the Line: Essays in the History of Auto Work*, ed. Nelson Lichtenstein and Stephen Meyer (Urbana: University of Illinois Press, 1989), 235.

131. Brody, *Workers in Industrial America*, 209.

132. William E. Simkin, "Refusals to Ratify Contracts," *Industrial and Labor Relations Review* 21 (1967–68): 518, 529.

133. Ibid., 530.

134. Ibid., 538.

135. Solomon Barkin, "Redesigning Collective Bargaining and Capitalism," in *Worker Militancy and Its Consequences, 1965–75*, ed. Solomon Barkin (New York: Praeger 1975), 370–73. This volume contains articles on the state of labor relations in various countries.

136. Alan Hyde, "A Theory of Labor Legislation," *Buffalo Law Review* 38 (1990): 383.

137. *Work in America*, vii. See also Jerome Rosow, ed., *The Worker and the Job: Coping with Change* (Englewood Cliffs, N.J.: Prentice-Hall, 1974), one of many books of the period dealing with the new focus upon "better work performance and a better quality of life in the society."

138. For a trenchant criticism of Taylorism, see Harry Braverman, *Labor and Monopoly Capital* (New York: Monthly Review Press, 1974).

139. Ibid., 12. See Abraham Maslow, *Motivation and Personality* (New York: Harper, 1954).

140. *Work in America*, 96–105. See also Rosow, *Worker and the Job*, 93–120.

141. See Harvey Swados, "The Myth of the Happy Worker," in *A Radical's America* (Boston: Little, Brown, 1962).

142. Unions have recently been more willing to participate in "nonadversarial" participation schemes, such as quality circles and team arrangements, generally more favored by employees than union officials. These arrangements, hearkening back to employee representation structures in the early part of the century, will likely become the hallmark of unorganized employers as well. A 1982 survey found that at least a third of Fortune 500 companies, organized and unorganized, have some form of participative management or quality of work life program and that such programs have generally resulted in improved employee morale and increased productivity. See

generally Thomas Kochan, Harry C. Katz, and Robert B. McKersie, *The Transformation of American Industrial Relations* (New York: Basic Books, 1986); Harry C. Katz, *Shifting Gears: Changing Labor Relations in the U.S. Automobile Industry* (Cambridge, Mass.: MIT Press, 1985); John F. Witte, *Democracy, Authority, and Alienation in Work* (Chicago: University of Chicago Press, 1980).

143. Cited in Katz, *Shifting Gears,* 74.

144. See Kochan, Katz, and McKersie, *Transformation of American Industrial Relations,* 146–77.

145. See, e.g., Katz, *Shifting Gears,* 74–85.

146. Heckscher, "Democracy at Work," 222. See also Heckscher, *New Unionism.*

147. 92 Stat. 2020, 29 USC section 175a.

148. David Brody, "Worker Contractualism in Comparative Perspective," in *Industrial Democracy in America: The Ambiguous Promise,* ed. Nelson Lichtenstein and Howell John Harris (New York: Cambridge University Press, 1993), 176–205.

149. Taplin, "Contradictions of Business Unionism," 258.

150. Ibid., 259. "The institutional support for the type of bargaining unions have engaged in since the 1940s is being eroded by disinvestment, plant relocation, outsourcing, and productivity bonus schemes which are forms of piece rate work. These devices are now replacing earlier management forms of hostile resistance to unions. Each in its own way contributes to a further de-legitimization of union hierarchies and leadership and undermines a wider institutional support for unions as bargaining bodies" (Ian M. Taplin, "The Contradictions of Business Unionism and the Decline of Organized Labour," *Economic and Industrial Democracy,* 2 [May 1990]: 249–78, 251). One might suggest that these devices reinforce rather than replace employer resistance.

151. Ibid., 263.

152. Moreover, reactions by workers can be seen in a growing number of charges filed in the NLRB by workers against unions, from about five hundred per year in the early 1950s to almost eight thousand per year by the late 1970s. Between 1970 and 1980, charges filed by workers against unions exceeded the number filed by employers against unions. See Robert J. Flanigan, *Labor Relations and the Litigation Explosion* (Washington, D.C.: Brookings Institution, 1987).

153. See Sumner Rosen, "The U.S.: A Time for Reassessment," in *Worker Militancy and Its Consequences,* ed. Solomon Barkin (New York: Praeger, 1975), 364–404.

154. Taplin, "Contradictions of Business Unionism," 265.

155. James Atleson, "The Circle of *Boys Market:* A Comment on Judicial Inventiveness," *Industrial Relations Law Journal* 7 (1988): 88.

156. Taplin, "Contradictions of Business Unionism," 265.

AFTERWORD

In certain chapters the wartime regulation of labor relations, legal decisions, and legislation is highlighted. Underlying this discussion are difficult issues concerning the actual effect of law, that is, to what extent does law matter? And beneath this simply stated issue lie at least two other vexing questions—what do we mean by "law" and what do we mean by "matter"? A general answer to these questions has not been offered, and that is by design. The deep theoretical questions embedded in the question of the law's actual effects have taken up entire professional lives, and others are far more qualified to delve into this briar patch. Although many theories have been offered concerning when and how law affects society or culture, I have decided not to follow any of them but, instead, to offer empirical answers in support of a nontheoretical answer—law sometimes matters and sometimes it does not.

Let's begin first with the meaning of "matter." To the immediate parties law matters if, and this is far from guaranteed, a legal ruling actually affects their behavior. For instance, rulings of the War Labor Board and the Fair Employment Practices Committee on equal pay may have had some effect, but in certain cases the reluctance or opposition of both bargaining parties limited the actual impact of such decisions. Similarly, state equal pay statutes, perhaps because of their ambiguity or loopholes, seem to have had little effect. Other decisions, for instance, the War Labor Board's grant of union security, arbitration, and management prerogative clauses, permanently affected the relationship of the bargaining parties.

The "law" of the War Labor Board also mattered in the sense that some rulings and doctrines had immediate effects upon the behavior and relative strength of unions and employers who were not the immediate parties to the litigation. More importantly, some rulings had effects beyond the war. As earlier chapters demonstrate, postwar legal doctrines seem clearly to have been affected by War Labor Board decisions, although usually without attribution. For example, the notion that a zone of managerial supremacy and autonomy exists, free of union involvement, was initially recognized not by the National Labor Relations Board but in rulings of the War Labor Board. Concededly, it seems likely that the courts or NLRB would have deferred to managerial prerogatives even if no war had occurred. Interestingly, however, the wartime emergency was not the occasion for *broadly* defining the area of mutual concern so as to encourage cooperation and reduce the risk of disruption. Similarly, the contours of the postwar law dealing with the administration and enforcement of collective bargaining agreements closely mirrors decisions of the War Labor Board, and I do not believe this similarity is coincidental despite the Supreme Court's failure to refer to it.

To recognize the "effect" of law, however, is to focus only upon the impact of formal, written decisions and their included doctrines. The "does law matter" question includes within it another especially difficult question— what do we mean by "law"? For instance, are the contemporaneous speeches or writings of War Labor Board members, say those of Frank Graham or Wayne Morse, "law"? Speeches of government officials are carefully parsed by certain audiences who attempt to glean or predict future government action. It is certainly possible that such perceived messages affect behavior. The same is true for speeches or proposed bills by members of Congress. The often draconian legislation proposed during and just preceding the war clearly created fear among union officials, heading unions which were often just becoming stabilized, that serious constraints on union power would become part of federal law and, even worse, survive the war. The same can be said for military calls for civilian conscription of strikers at defense plants. If these legislative proposals and threats are "law," then they seem to have mattered to union officials, though they seem not to have affected the often militant rank and file who engaged in a staggering number of work stoppages in the midst of a popularly supported war. Yet, these strikes were often short, and workers often heeded the calls from union officials to return to work, again highlighting the ambiguity of finding legal "effect."

Specific policy proposals and pronouncements are, however, not the only products of decision makers that extend beyond "law," which is normally perceived as consisting of formal legal decisions and statutes. The language of decision makers, as many have argued, often affects the way people think about or conceptualize their worlds. Beyond informing people what they can and cannot do, the product of decision makers may help set boundaries to what is deemed possible. It is at this point that the question of what we mean by "matters" and "law" begin to merge. As indicated in chapter 10, the language of wartime, for instance, the need for uninterrupted production and sacrifice, was effortlessly carried over into the peacetime era. This language, including images of responsible unionism and the appropriate model of labor-management relations, does not arise simply from official government rulings. Instead, as I have attempted to demonstrate, it was the particular conditions of wartime that helped to create or cement certain views about the proper contours of labor-management relations and dispute resolution.

The war necessitated continuous defense production, unimpeded by strikes, a situation that would more likely occur, it was said, with stable, responsible unions. Such unions would develop because contractual union security and arbitration provisions would strengthen them, and a combination of positive and negative pressures would induce stable unions to pacify the often unruly rank and file. Disputes then could be resolved via contractual grievance procedures, not at the point of production. These wartime ideas came to be the foundation of the postwar conception of mature industrial relations, in large part because most of the influential scholars and arbitrators in the postwar period worked for the government during the war. Their experience during wartime, and not simply the official decisions they participated in or observed, affected their sense of what should be the appropriate policies of postwar labor relations. Their total experience, in other words, helped determine the postwar world of labor relations.

Once we recognize that it is difficult, perhaps impossible, to separate the rulings of governmental agencies from the felt needs of wartime, and the experiences of the wartime actors from their understanding of postwar possibilities, one must face another hidden mine in the field of "does law matter?" Once the notion of "law" is broadened beyond positive law to include more than legislation and governmental decisions, law begins to encompass everything. If so, then obviously, and trivially, law matters.

Rather than confront all these sticky issues, I have chosen to disaggregate them into more manageable units. I have concluded that many legal rulings do matter. As noted in chapters 4 and 5, the decisions of the War Labor Board significantly affected the shape of postwar bargaining. Supportive legal rulings, aided by the immense growth of defense production, greatly enhanced the strength of unions. But in a period when unions grew dramatically in size and stability, they ironically experienced severe restraints. Their greatest weapon, the strike, was denied just when its very threat would carry the most weight. Although unions voluntarily surrendered the right to strike for the duration of the war, they may have had little choice given doubts about their ability to withstand governmental pressure and the lure of the benefits provided by the War Labor Board, usually granted with the condition that "responsibility" be demonstrated. Beyond the effect of legal decisions, the wartime atmosphere encouraged unions to limit the ability of the rank and file to assert themselves at the workplace through the development of bureaucratized union structures. Admittedly, union bureaucratization may have occurred in any event, but the pressures from the government, the possible denial or withdrawal of contractual benefits, and the constant threat of hostile legislation surely strengthened the resolve of union officials. Thus, irrespective of how law is defined, the entire context of the war had long-term effects.

The latter chapters deal with some of these long-term effects, with the way that both rules and other ideas mattered. Moreover, the discussion attempts to delineate the gains as well as the costs of the contractualization of labor relations. The influence and predominant position of the postwar pluralists meant that critics of the existing paradigm were either ignored or shunted to the sidelines. Indeed, even modest questioning or proposals for reform were often met with the inevitable question—"what would you put in its place?" Few had the temerity to think about alternative labor relations structures, and certainly no one was encouraged to do so. As a result, the gains and losses inherent in the system that emerged from the war were institutionalized.

As union officers seemed to be located further from the workers they represented, as bargaining seemed unable to deal with some of the problems workers felt were important, the emotional tie between worker and union weakened. The pacification of labor relations and the decline of the strike noted by writers in the 1960s seemed to flow naturally from the pluralist vision of mature labor relations that followed from the wartime experience. Thus, it may not be surprising that this vision made it difficult for observers to explain the militant worker actions of the late 1960s and 1970s. These workers, unhappy with the accommodations accepted by their parents, expressed frustration with both their employers and their unions. Although these workers would be characterized as "new," though in fact they were only young, they sought greater involvement in workplace decisions and a higher degree of participation in their work lives. The response was a recognition by writers, and a handful of employers, that greater worker involvement was necessary, but this could only be accomplished by the creation of arrangements outside of existing collective bargaining structures. So clear were the limitations of the existing bargaining system to the participants, or, alternatively, so firmly were they wedded to the wisdom of the dominant paradigm, that little thought was given to reforms of those structures or of the background legal rules.

Reported Work Stoppages in Automotive Plants in December 1944 and January 1945

Company	Inclusive Dates	Workers Involved	Man-hours Lost	Dispute
Briggs	Dec. 1–2, 1944	5,649	89,531	Protesting company policy concerning seniority of demoted foreman.
Ford	"	282	1,122	Protest against demoted foreman replacing a No. 1 roller, despite this being his former classification.
General Motors	"	154	506	Sand-blast employees demanded 10 minutes to clean up at the end of the shift and walked out when this was not granted.
Ford	Dec. 2, 1944	66	297	Committeeman forbade bricklayers and helpers to hook stock pans, as had been the custom, claiming it was outside their classification.
Mack	"	33	132	When a number of employees did not show up for work the remainder decided to go home also.
Briggs	Dec. 2–3, 1944	459	1,693	Protest of warning notice given to employees.
Perfect Circle	Dec. 4, 1944	75	37	Result of misunderstanding in inspect-grind department concerning the grinding of certain rings.
Briggs	Dec. 5, 1944	100	105	Protest discharge of 2 employees.
Ford	"	29	44	Protest against possibility of disciplinary action against first helper who permitted furnace roof to burn.
Hudson	"	80	79	Protesting padlocking of entrance to toolroom to keep unauthorized persons from entering this area in order to eliminate theft of tools.
Chrysler	Dec. 5–6, 1944	349	1,200	7 employees stopped work in protest of discharge of employee for refusing to perform his operation; 5 of this 7 were discharged when they refused to return to work; 320 employees then stopped work and left plant.
L. A. Young	Dec. 5, 1944	101	62	Protest against chairman of plant committee having been sent home for refusing to do as instructed.

Company	Inclusive Dates	Workers Involved	Man-hours Lost	Dispute
Ford	Dec. 5–6, 1944	407	2,986	Protest against suspension of 2 committeemen for countermanding orders of supervision and reading newspapers on job.
"	Dec. 6, 1944	36	18	Employees protested removal of stools.
International Harvester	"	89	354	Demand for special piecework allowance.
Mack	"	20	20	Protesting the transfer of 1 employee.
Chrysler	"	155	219	Employees stopped work in protest when a conveyor loader was removed from an operation which could be handled by only 1 man.
"	"	163	163	Recurrence of above stoppage.
Briggs	Dec. 6–18, 1944	1,243	13,273	Protest step-down of employee, claiming that he should be transferred to another department instead.
General Motors	Dec. 7, 1944	37	13	Employee sent home for refusing to do job assigned to him; 37 other employees refused to go to work unless employee sent home was permitted to return.
Hudson	Dec. 7–8, 1944	87	348	Protesting dockage of 15 minutes for reporting late from lunch.
Chrysler	Dec. 8, 1944	8	6	Protesting 3-day disciplinary lay-off of an employee for refusing to perform his operation.
Ford	"	24	18	Protest against dockages for leaving job. Also, demand for the removal of foreman.
American Brake-Shoe Co.	Dec. 8–11, 1944	414	4,000	Small group in press department demanded discharge of 1 man disliked by the group. No grievance was filed. Company refused to dismiss, and workers walked out.
Chrysler	Dec. 9, 1944	8	40	Employees stopped work and left plant when 1 employee was denied pass to go home after he had refused to go to the first aid in order that they might determine extent of his alleged illness.
Briggs	Dec. 11–12, 1944	31	235	Questioning company application of seniority provisions.
"	Dec. 11–13, 1944	488	1,140	Crane operators refused to work more than 8 hours.
Ford	Dec. 14, 1944	47	71	2 men were reprimanded for smoking. Fellow employees accompanied them to labor relations office in sympathy.
General Motors	Dec. 14–15, 1944	1,126	9,813	Material-unloading men refused to work until 4 men suspended for refusing to do their jobs were put back to work.

Company	Inclusive Dates	Workers Involved	Man-hours Lost	Dispute
General Motors	Dec. 14–17, 1944	411	10,954	Mass smoking demonstration protesting shop smoking regulation.
"	Dec. 15–18, 1944	391	4,936	Lack of material due to work stoppage after mass smoking demonstration in Hull plant.
Chrysler	Dec. 15, 1944	21	7	Stopped work claiming that band-saw blades were not sharp.
"	"	9	3	Stopped work in protest when notified that they would not be paid for time not worked during above stoppage.
"	"	51	37	51 employees in transportation department refused to begin work in protest against disciplinary lay-off given 1 driver who had been drinking during working hours.
"	Dec. 18–19, 1944	1,081	11,892	Protesting discharge of employee for threatening foreman with bodily harm after being informed that he would not be paid for time he did not work before end of shift.
"	"	89	1,112	Employees left plant in protest of discharge of assistant chief steward for countermanding orders of supervision.
Ford	"	32	94	Employees demanded 5 cents increase in rate, claiming they were performing duties of a higher classification.
Chrysler	Dec. 19, 1944	68	34	Employees stopped work because females having more seniority than men on the same classification were laid off because of inability to perform heavy work.
Briggs	Dec. 20, 1944	3,744	22,948	Protest discharge of 2 employees.
"	Dec. 20–21, 1944	147	419	Protest company refusing to allow employee of another plant into this plant without credentials.
General Motors	Dec. 20, 1944	25	166	Employee transferred to automatic department from external grinding. Employees in automatic department requested transferred employee to be given lower-rated job and lower-classified employee in automatic department be promoted. Answer promised by next day. However, entire day shift did not report for work.
Briggs	Dec. 20–27, 1944	323	11,735	Claim job required more men.
Chrysler	Dec. 21–22, 1944	7	11	Protesting removal of chairs and stools from production machines.
"	Dec. 21–28, 1944	209	630	"
"	Dec. 21–22, 1944	2	8	Sympathy with stoppage caused by removal of chairs and stools from production machines.

Company	Inclusive Dates	Workers Involved	Man-hours Lost	Dispute
Chrysler	Dec. 22–26, 1944	116	880	Protesting removal of chairs and stools from production machines.
Ford	Dec. 23, 1944	13	10	Outside dock workers refused to work indoors as necessitated by excessive absenteeism.
Chrysler	Dec. 23–24, 1944	61	46	Employees stopped work for 45 minutes because of discharge of employee for spoiling work.
Ford	Dec. 26, 1944	9	40	Key employees failed to report to work causing job to shut down.
Packard	"	14	23	Chief steward claimed supervision would not recognize district steward.
Ford	Dec. 26–27, 1944	181	875	Protest against suspension of committeeman for being off job without pass.
Chrysler	Dec. 27–30, 1944	290	3,433	Left plant because of 3-day lay-off given 2 employees for refusing to assist in setting trimmer dies.
Packard	Dec. 28, 1944	759	3,894	Objected to being paid on Saturday instead of Friday.
Chrysler	Dec. 28–29, 1944	14	28	Left plant because they did not wish to perform some emergency work.
Ford	Dec. 29, 1944	14	4	Employees accompanied fellow worker being sent to labor relations for smoking.
Packard	Dec. 30, 1944	55	523	Protest against employees being docked for leaving plant early.
Ford	Dec. 30–31, 1944	1,295	5,699	Protest against temporary transfers to another job and suspension of worker for striking foreman.
Eaton	Dec. 31, 1944– Jan. 5, 1945	10	610	Rolling-mill operator refused job assignment and was suspended; 9 of his fellow workers in same department walked out in sympathy.
Chrysler	Jan. 1–2, 1945	387	522	Employees struck and left plant at midnight, 2 hours before end of shift, because they were only to receive straight time for hours after midnight following a holiday.
Muskegon Motor Specialties	Jan. 2, 1945	425	786	Attended union meeting not authorized by management.
Murray Corp.	Jan. 2–3, 1945	68	408	Would not work outside because of cold.
Ford	Jan. 4, 1945	18	5	Core makers stopped work in protest against disciplinary suspension of employee for slowing down production.
Chrysler	Jan. 4–5, 1945	68	776	Left plant because of disciplinary action on probationary employee who refused to perform duties assigned.
Ford	Jan. 5, 1945	45	70	Switchmen protested the sending of 2 men to the labor relations office for leaving job before quitting time.

Company	Inclusive Dates	Workers Involved	Man-hours Lost	Dispute
Chrysler	Jan. 5–6, 1945	23	179	Employees on second shift in department left plant because they alleged the first shift was putting more overtime work in than they were.
"	Jan. 6, 1945	433	323	6 inspectors refused to resume work after lunch, claiming there was a draft and no heat on; 427 employees on line assembly were affected.
General Motors	"	30	8	Protest by employees of the scheduled working hours. Employees disliked the late quitting hours (6:06 P.M.).
International Harvester	Jan. 8, 1945	576	3,440	Demand that foundry job rate be increased or placed on an incentive basis.
Packard	"	35	40	Refused to test 2 engines on test stand.
Briggs	Jan. 8–9, 1945	114	163	Protesting of wage rates.
Chrysler	Jan. 9, 1945	60	25	60 employees stopped work when general foreman brought employee discharged for striking foreman to tool crib to clear his tools.
Briggs	Jan. 9–10, 1945	37	168	Protesting lay-off.
"	"	23	151	Protest discipline for refusing to take orders from foreman.
"	"	34	126	Dispute over classification of 1 employee.
"	"	201	603	In sympathy with other strike called over classification of 1 employee.
Ford	Jan. 10, 1945	17	11	Protest against dockage for changing into work clothes on company time. Employees claimed they should be allowed to change after starting time.
Packard	"	4	12	Inspector taken off job by steward. Mechanics left job.
Ford	Jan. 11, 1945	48	36	Workers demanded that storm sheds be built on the receiving dock to prevent drafts when trucks enter or leave.
General Motors	Jan. 11–15, 1945	274	5,633	Protest because locker rooms were locked during working hours to prevent loafing.
Ford	Jan. 12, 1945	50	41	Protest against disciplinary penalty imposed upon a fellow employee for deliberately slowing down production.
Eaton	Jan. 12–13, 1945	56	266	Sent second-shift people home because of the threatened illumination company strike which was to have been called in the early evening hours of Jan. 12.
"	"	739	3,345	Threatened strike at Cleveland Electric Illuminating Co.
"	"	63	130	Work stoppage occurred during the second and third shifts due to shortage of electric power.

Company	Inclusive Dates	Workers Involved	Man-hours Lost	Dispute
Ford	Jan. 12–16, 1945	46	394	Employees requested to work out of their classification exercised their pre-rogative to go home. The resulting shortage of manpower created the stoppage.
Ferro Machine & Foundry	Jan. 13–15, 1945	13	52	Protesting refusal to pay for time not worked.
Chrysler	Jan. 15, 1945	282	282	14 employees stopped work because they claimed there was not enough manpower on their jobs; 268 others were affected.
Ford	"	31	31	Inspectors protested removal of desks.
Packard	"	96	197	3 employees refused to do work assigned.
"	"	270	68	Demand change in classification.
Chrysler	Jan. 15–16, 1945	225	460	95 employees stopped work and left plant because they did not want to work the scheduled 12-hour shift; 130 others had to be sent home.
General Motors	Jan. 16, 1945	6	1	1 of 6 female employees involved stated they had stopped working in protest of the transfer of a colored employee into their departmental group.
"	"	21	100	Protest of suspension of job setter in screw machine department who re-fused to do job assignment.
"	Jan. 18, 1945	8	1	In sympathy with 1 of their group who was in the office for disciplinary action.
"	Jan. 20, 1945	5	2	Spot welder was asked to move stock to his machine so he could continue working. He refused and was penal-ized; 5 other spot welders then stopped work.
Chrysler	"	14	10	Employees in material handling depart-ment stopped work in protest of a 3-day lay-off given an electric-truck driver for failure to report on accident and leaving scene of accident without giving aid to the injured.
"	Jan. 22, 1945	14	28	Same employees refused to work for 2 hours when employee failed to report for work after above lay-off.
Briggs	Jan. 20–22, 1945	686	4,349	Protest of time standards.
Motor Wheel	"	2,168	11,113	Dispute over inspection rates.
General Motors	Jan. 22, 1945	4	2	Employees in carburetor core job refused to make-up discount cores even though they had adequate time to do so.
Briggs	Jan. 22–23, 1945	164	853	Reported late. Attended union meeting.
Chrysler	Jan. 24, 1945	9	3	Employees stopped work because of dis-ciplinary action on employee for threatening foreman.

Company	Inclusive Dates	Workers Involved	Man-hours Lost	Dispute
Ford	Jan. 24, 1945	26	26	Protest against dockage of 3 men who lined up at the time clock before quitting time. Employees also demanded removal of foreman who imposed dockage.
"	"	205	835	Employees refused to carry out supervisor's orders to clean their working areas.
"	Jan. 24–30, 1945	170	3,001	Protest against sending 2 employees to the labor-relations office for failure to show and wear badge and for striking a plant-protection man, respectively.
"	Jan. 24, 1945	37	51	Employees refused to accept change in lunch-period starting time. This change was necessitated by a union-requested change in the starting time of the shift.
"	Jan. 25, 1945	51	78	3 employees refused to sweep their working areas as requested by supervision. Other employees joined them in a protest stoppage.
"	"	25	16	Employees stopped work in sympathy with workers of department 930 who were striking in protest against the disciplining of 2 men for refusing to show badges and hitting a plant-protection man.
"	"	36	72	Protest against alleged defective machine.
"	Jan. 25–26, 1945	57	228	9 employees were ordered to labor-relations office for refusing to sweep their working areas. They succeeded in getting others to join them in a protest stoppage.
"	Jan. 25–29, 1945	187	1,593	Protest against a 2-day disciplinary lay-off of committeeman for pushing a foreman during an argument.
General Motors	Jan. 26, 1945	55	408	Protesting failure of National War Labor Board to act favorably on a joint request for wage increase.
Chrysler	Jan. 26–27, 1945	6	23	Left plant because they were not paid for the time they did not work when they lined up at clock before quitting time.
"	Jan. 29–30, 1945	134	1,072	10 machine operators were sent home for refusal to operate 2 machines as instructed; 23 others walked out in sympathy, necessitating sending home 99 others.

Company	Inclusive Dates	Workers Involved	Man-hours Lost	Dispute
Chrysler	Jan. 29, 1945	9	5	Employees stopped work because management requested the men to produce 1 additional unit per hour.
Ferro Machine & Foundry	Jan. 29–30, 1945	4	59	Dispute concerning piecework rates of jobs to be run that day.
Ford	Jan. 30, 1945	55	24	Protest against disciplinary suspension of a committeeman for using foul and profane language and threatening a foreman.
International Harvester	"	19	30	Demand for continuation of average piecework earnings after productive interruption was corrected.
Chrysler	Jan. 31–Feb. 1, 1945	441	2,407	Protesting disciplinary action.

Source: Automotive Council statement by George Romney to the Senate Investigating Committee on Manpower Problems and Their Effect on War Production, Mar. 9, 1945, Automotive Council for War Production, exhibit 14.

APPENDIX 2

Executive Order 9370: Enforcement of Directives of the National War Labor Board
Issued August 16, 1943

By virtue of the authority vested in me by the Constitution and the Statutes of the United States, it is hereby ordered:

In order to effectuate compliance with directive orders of the National War Labor Board in cases in which the Board reports to the Director of Economic Stabilization that its orders have not been complied with, the Director is authorized and directed, in furtherance of the effective prosecution of the war, to issue such directives as he may deem necessary:

(a) To other departments or agencies of the Government directing the taking of appropriate action relating to withholding or withdrawing from a non-complying employer any priorities, benefits, or privileges extended, or contracts entered into, by executive action of the Government, until the National War Labor Board has reported that compliance has been effectuated;

(b) To any Government agency operating a plant, mine, or facility, possession of which has been taken by the President under Section 3 of the War Labor Disputes Act, directing such agency to apply to the National War Labor Board, under Section 5 of said Act, for an order withholding or withdrawing from a non-complying labor union any benefits, privileges, or rights accruing to it under the terms or conditions of employment in effect (whether by agreement between the parties or by order of the National War Labor Board, or both) when possession was taken, until such time as the non-complying labor union has demonstrated to the satisfaction of the National War Labor Board its willingness and capacity to comply; but, when the check-off is denied, dues received from the check-off shall be held in escrow for the benefit of the union to be delivered to it upon compliance by it.

(c) To the War Manpower Commission, in the case of non-complying individuals, directing the entry of appropriate orders relating to the modification or cancellation of draft deferments or employment privileges, or both.

Franklin D. Roosevelt

The White House
Aug. 16, 1943

LETTER FROM PRESIDENT TO WLB CHAIRMAN

Aug. 16, 1943

Dear Mr. Davis:

I am writing you regarding the question of compliance with Board orders under the War Labor Disputes Act which you and I have been considering. The Act empowers the Board to prescribe the "terms and conditions * * * governing the relations between the parties, which shall be in effect until further order of the Board."

Congress intentionally left the enforcement of these orders to executive action. I agree with you that it would be helpful, in the light of our combined experience in dealing with disputes under Executive Order 9017 and more recently under the Act, to define a program for bringing about compliance in the relatively few cases in which Executive action may become necessary.

1. When an employer refuses to comply, his plant may be seized and operated by the government in accordance with the terms and conditions of employment prescribed by the Board. Less drastic sanctions, however, including control of war contracts, of essential materials, and of transportation and fuel, should be applied if this can be done without impeding the war effort. I am accordingly requesting the Director of Economic Stabilization to direct the application of any or all available sanctions of this sort by the appropriate agencies of government, in cases of non-compliance reported to him by the Board.

2. When a local union refuses to comply, by directing or advising workers not to work under the terms and conditions prescribed by the Board, action by the responsible national or international officers has thus far, in all but one or two cases, sufficed to bring about compliance. If such action should prove ineffective, or if a national or international union should itself be the offender, the plant will be taken over under the War Labor Disputes Act and operated by the government, if this is necessary to prevent interference with production and to protect the workers who wish to work.

The Act provides that in such cases the terms and conditions of employment effective at the time of taking over shall continue, unless the Board modifies them upon request of either the union or the government agency operating the property. As a part of the compliance program the appropriate government agency at the time of taking over shall ask the Board to modify its order so as to withhold from the union (by escrow in the case of checked-off funds) the benefits, privileges, or rights accruing to it as such under the agreement or proposed agreement with the employer, until the union demonstrates its willingness and capacity to abide by the obligations thereof. All questions of fact in this connection, and the extent of any modification of the order, should be determined by the Board. I am authorizing the Director of Economic Stabilization to issue any necessary instructions to government agencies in carrying out this policy.

Government operation in these cases will be conducted with the least possible interference with existing management. Plants will be returned to their owners as speedily as conditions permit, and in any event, as provided in the Act, within 60 days after the restoration of productive efficiency. The Board may, of course, on its own motion, except during government operation, modify its orders in any way it deems appropriate to ensure compliance.

3. As to compliance by individuals, the Act contains penalties for certain types of interference with production which it is the province of the Attorney General to enforce. In addition, sanctions can be applied by the Selective Service and the War Manpower Commission, and I am requesting the Director of Economic Stabilization to direct the application of any or all of such sanctions in necessary cases upon report by the Board of non-compliance.

I am informed that during the past eighteen months the Board disposed of over a thousand disputes. Only seven had to be referred to me because of persistent non-compliance. This is a remarkable record, in the making of which the industry, labor and public members of the Board have each played an effective part. They could not have succeeded, however, without the patriotic support given to the national no-strike, no-lockout agreement by the great mass of American employers and workers and their leaders. I am confident that that agreement, which calls for final determination by the Board of all disputes not settled by collective bargaining or conciliation, will continue to be supported; and it is my earnest wish that the sanctions described above, which exist only as a matter of wartime necessity, may not have to be invoked.

Sincerely yours,
Franklin D. Roosevelt

APPENDIX 3

War Labor Disputes Act

AN ACT

Relating to the use and operation by the United States of certain plants, mines, and facilities in the prosecution of the war, and preventing strikes, lock-outs, and stoppages of production, and for other purposes.

Be it enacted by the Senate and House of Representatives of the United States of America in Congress assembled, That this Act may be cited as the "War Labor Disputes Act".

DEFINITIONS

SEC. 2. As used in this Act—

(a) The term "person" means an individual, partnership, association, corporation, business trust, or any organized group of persons.

(b) The term "war contract" means—

(1) a contract with the United States entered into on behalf of the United States by an officer or employee of the Department of War, the Department of the Navy, or the United States Maritime Commission;

(2) a contract with the United States entered into by the United States pursuant to an Act entitled "An Act to promote the defense of the United States";

(3) a contract, whether or not with the United States, for the production, manufacture, construction, reconstruction, installation, maintenance, storage, repair, mining, or transportation of—

(A) any weapon, munition, aircraft, vessel, or boat;

(B) any building, structure or facility;

(C) any machinery, tool, material, supply, article, or commodity; or

(D) any component material or part of or equipment for any article described in subparagraph (A), (B), or (C);

the production, manufacture, construction, reconstruction, installation, maintenance, storage, repair, mining, or transportation of which by the contractor in question is found by the President as being contracted for in the prosecution of the war.

(c) The term "war contractor" means the person producing, manufacturing, constructing, reconstructing, installing, maintaining, storing, repairing, mining, or transporting under a war contract or a person whose plant, mine, or facility is equipped for the manufacture, production, or mining of any articles or materials which may be required in the prosecution of the war or which may be useful in connection therewith; but such term shall not include a carrier, as defined in title I of the Railway Labor Act, or a carrier by air subject to title II of such Act.

(d) The terms "employer", "employee", "representative", "labor organization", and "labor dispute" shall have the same meaning as in section 2 of the National Labor Relations Act.

POWER OF PRESIDENT TO TAKE POSSESSION OF PLANTS

SEC. 3. Section 9 of the Selective Training and Service Act of 1940 is hereby amended by adding at the end thereof the following new paragraph:

"The power of the President under the foregoing provisions of this section to take immediate possession of any plant upon a failure to comply with any such provisions, and the authority granted by this section for the use and operation by the United States or in its interests of any plant of which possession is so taken, shall also apply as hereinafter provided to any plant, mine, or facility equipped for the manufacture, production, or mining of any articles or materials which may be required for the war effort or which may be useful in connection therewith. Such power and authority may be exercised by the President through such department or agency of the Government as he may designate, and may be exercised with respect to any such plant, mine, or facility whenever the President finds, after investigation, and proclaims that there is an interruption of the operation of such plant, mine, or facility as a result of a strike or other labor disturbance, that the war effort will be unduly impeded or delayed by such interruption, and that the exercise of such power and authority is necessary to insure the operation of such plant, mine, or facility in the interest of the war effort: *Provided,* That whenever any such plant, mine, or facility has been or is hereafter so taken by reason of a strike, lockout, threatened strike, threatened lock-out, work stoppage, or other cause, such plant, mine, or facility shall be returned to the owners thereof as soon as practicable, but in no event more than sixty days after the restoration of the productive efficiency thereof prevailing prior to the taking of possession thereof: *Provided further,* That possession of any plant, mine, or facility shall not be taken under authority of this section after the termination of hostilities in the present war, as proclaimed by the President, or after the termination of the War Labor Disputes Act; and the authority to operate any such plant, mine, or facility under the provisions of this section shall terminate at the end of six months after the termination of such hostilities as so proclaimed."

TERMS OF EMPLOYMENT AT GOVERNMENT-OPERATED PLANTS

SEC. 4. Except as provided in section 5 hereof, in any case in which possession of any plant, mine, or facility has been or shall be hereafter taken under the authority granted by section 9 of the Selective Training and Service Act of 1940, as amended, such plant, mine, or facility, while so possessed, shall be operated under the terms and conditions of employment which were in effect at the time possession of such plant, mine, or facility was so taken.

APPLICATION TO WAR LABOR BOARD FOR CHANGE IN TERMS OF EMPLOYMENT AT GOVERNMENT-OPERATED PLANTS

SEC. 5. When possession of any plant, mine, or facility has been or shall be hereafter taken under authority of section 9 of the Selective Training and Service Act of 1940, as amended, the Government agency operating such plant, mine, or facility, or a majority of the employees of such plant, mine, or facility or their representatives, may apply to the National War Labor Board for a change in wages or other terms or conditions of employment in such plant, mine, or facility. Upon receipt of any such application, and after such hearings and investigations as it deems necessary, such Board may order any changes in such wages, or other terms and conditions, which it deems to be fair and reasonable and not in conflict with any Act of Congress or any Executive order issued thereunder. Any such order of the Board shall, upon approval by the President, be complied with by the Government agency operating such plant, mine, or facility.

INTERFERENCE WITH GOVERNMENT OPERATION OF PLANTS

SEC. 6. (a) Whenever any plant, mine, or facility is in the possession of the United States, it shall be unlawful for any person (1) to coerce, instigate, induce, conspire with, or encourage any person, to interfere, by lock-out, strike, slow-down, or other interruption, with the operation of such plant, mine, or facility, or (2) to aid any such lock-out, strike, slow-down, or other interruption interfering with the operation of such plant, mine, or facility by giving direction or guidance in the conduct of such interruption, or by providing funds for the conduct or direction thereof or for the payment of strike, unemployment, or other benefits to those participating therein. No individual shall be deemed to have violated the provisions of this section by reason only of his having ceased work or having refused to continue to work or to accept employment.

(b) Any person who willfully violates any provision of this section shall be subject to a fine of not more than $5,000, or to imprisonment for not more than one year, or both.

FUNCTIONS AND DUTIES OF THE NATIONAL WAR LABOR BOARD

SEC. 7. (a) The National War Labor Board (hereinafter in this section called the "Board"), established by Executive Order Number 9017, dated January 12, 1942, in addition to all powers conferred on it by section 1 (a) of the Emergency Price Control Act of 1942, and by any Executive order or regulation issued under the provisions of the Act of October 2, 1942, entitled "An Act to amend the Emergency Price Control Act of 1942, to aid in preventing inflation, and for other purposes", and by any other statute, shall have the following powers and duties:

(1) Whenever the United States Conciliation Service (hereinafter called the "Conciliation Service") certifies that a labor dispute exists which may lead to substantial interference with the war effort, and cannot be settled by collective bargaining or conciliation, to summon both parties to such dispute before it and conduct a public hearing on the merits of the dispute. If in the opinion of the Board a labor dispute has become so serious that it may lead to substantial interference with the war effort, the Board may take such action on its own motion. At such hearing both parties shall be given full notice and opportunity to be heard, but the failure of either party to appear shall not deprive the Board of jurisdiction to proceed to a hearing and order.

(2) To decide the dispute, and provide by order the wages and hours and all other terms and conditions (customarily included in collective-bargaining agreements) governing the relations between the parties, which shall be in effect until further order of the Board. In making any such decision the Board shall conform to the provisions of the Fair Labor Standards Act of 1938, as amended; the National Labor Relations Act; the Emergency Price Control Act of 1942, as amended; and the Act of October 2, 1942, as amended, and all other applicable provisions of law; and where no other law is applicable the order of the Board shall provide for terms and conditions to govern relations between the parties which shall be fair and equitable to employer and employee under all the circumstances of the case.

(3) To require the attendance of witnesses and the production of such papers, documents, and records as may be material to its investigation of facts in any labor dispute, and to issue subpoenas requiring such attendance or production.

(4) To apply to any Federal district court for an order requiring any person within its jurisdiction to obey a subpoena issued by the Board: and jurisdiction is hereby conferred on any such court to issue such an order.

(b) The Board, by its Chairman, shall have power to issue subpoenas requiring the attendance and testimony of witnesses, and the production of any books, papers, records, or other documents, material to any inquiry or hearing before the Board or any designated member or agent thereof. Such subpoenas shall be enforceable in the same manner, and subject to the same penalties, as subpoenas issued by the President under title III of the Second War Powers Act, approved March 27, 1942.

(c) No member of the Board shall be permitted to participate in any decision in which such member has a direct interest as an officer, employee, or representative of either party to the dispute.

(d) Subsections (a) (1) and (2) shall not apply with respect to any plant, mine, or facility of which possession has been taken by the United States.

(e) The Board shall not have any powers under this section with respect to any matter within the purview of the Railway Labor Act, as amended.

NOTICE OF THREATENED INTERRUPTIONS IN WAR PRODUCTION, ETC.

SEC. 8. (a) In order that the President may be apprised of labor disputes which threaten seriously to interrupt war production, and in order that employees may have an opportunity to express themselves, free from restraint or coercion, as to whether they will permit such interruptions in wartime—

(1) The representative of the employees of a war contractor, shall give to the Secretary of Labor, the National War Labor Board, and the National Labor Relations Board, notice of any such labor dispute involving such contractor and employees, together with a statement of the issues giving rise thereto.

(2) For not less than thirty days after any notice under paragraph (1) is given, the contractor and his employees shall continue production under all the conditions which prevailed when such dispute arose, except as they may be modified by mutual agreement or by decision of the National War Labor Board.

(3) On the thirtieth day after notice under paragraph (1) is given by the representative of the employees, unless such dispute has been settled, the National Labor Relations Board shall forthwith take a secret ballot of the employees in the plant, plants, mine, mines, facility, facilities, bargaining unit, or bargaining units, as the case may be, with respect to which the dispute is applicable on the question whether they will permit any such interruption of war production. The National Labor Relations Board shall include on the ballot a concise statement of the major issues involved in the dispute and of the efforts being made and the facilities being utilized for the settlement of such dispute. The National Labor Relations Board shall by order forthwith certify the results of such balloting, and such results shall be open to public inspection. The National Labor Relations Board may provide for preparing such ballot and distributing it to the employees at any time after such notice has been given.

(b) Subsection (a) shall not apply with respect to any plant, mine, or facility of which possession has been taken by the United States.

(c) Any person who is under a duty to perform any act required under subsection (a) and who willfully fails or refuses to perform such act shall be liable for damages resulting from such failure or refusal to any person injured thereby and to the United States if so injured. The district courts of the United States shall have jurisdiction to hear and determine any proceedings instituted pursuant to this subsection in the same manner and to the same extent as in the case of proceedings instituted under section 24 (14) of the Judicial Code.

POLITICAL CONTRIBUTIONS BY LABOR ORGANIZATIONS

SEC. 9. Section 313 of the Federal Corrupt Practices Act, 1925 (U.S.C. 1940 edition, title 2, sec. 251), is amended to read as follows:

"SEC. 313. It is unlawful for any national bank, or any corporation organized by authority of any law of Congress, to make a contribution in connection with any election to any political officer, or for any corporation whatever, or any labor organization to make a contribution in connection with any election at which Presidential and Vice Presidential electors or a Senator or Representative in, or a Delegate or Resident Commissioner to Congress are to be voted for, or for any candidate, political committee, or other person to accept or receive any contribution prohibited by this section. Every corporation or labor organization which makes any contribution in violation of this section shall be fined not more than $5,000; and every officer or director of any corporation, or officer of any labor organization, who consents to any contribution by the corporation or labor organization, as the case may be, in violation of this section shall be fined not more than $1,000 or imprisoned for not more than one year, or both. For the purposes of this section 'labor organization' shall have the same meaning as under the National Labor Relations Act."

TERMINATION OF ACT

SEC. 10. Except as to offenses committed prior to such date, the provisions of this Act and the amendments made by this Act shall cease to be effective at the end of six months following the termination of hostilities in the present war, as proclaimed by the President, or upon the date (prior to the date of such proclamation) of the passage of a concurrent resolution of the Two Houses of Congress stating that such provisions and amendments shall cease to be effective.

SEPARABILITY

SEC. 11. If any provision of this Act or of any amendment made by this Act, or the application of such provision to any person of circumstance, is held invalid, the remainder of the Act and of such amendments, and the application of such provision to other persons or circumstances, shall not be affected thereby.

78th Congress. 1st sess. Chapter 144

INDEX

JAMES B. ATLESON is a law professor at the State University of New York's Faculty of Law in Buffalo, New York. He teaches courses dealing with labor law, collective bargaining history, and labor history, as well as legal issues in the visual arts. He has published widely in law reviews as well as in journals of history, political science, and law and society. His first book, *Values and Assumptions in American Labor Law*, was published by the University of Massachusetts Press in 1983. He is the father of two sons and lives with his wife, Carol, and Rollie, a bearded collie, in Amherst, New York.